Y0-EOT-039

REAL ESTATE CONSULTANT'S HANDBOOK

REAL ESTATE CONSULTANT'S HANDBOOK

Edwin M. Rams

Reston Publishing Company, Inc.
A Prentice-Hall Company
Reston, Virginia

Library of Congress Cataloging in Publication Data
Rams, Edwin M
Real estate consultant's handbook.

Bibliography: p.
Includes index.
1. Real estate business—United States. 2. Real estate business—United States—Miscellanea. I. Title.
HD1375.R27 333.3'3 77-16096
ISBN 0-87909-720-5

© 1978 by Reston Publishing Company, Inc.
A Prentice-Hall Company
Reston, Virginia 22090

All rights reserved. No part of this book may be reproduced in any way, or by any means, without permission in writing from the publisher.

10 9 8 7 6 5 4 3 2 1

Printed in the United States of America

To my
Mother
and
Mother-in-law

about the author

As a consultant to business, industry, and government, Edwin M. Rams has had extensive experience in many facets of the real estate industry. His activities and assignments have included feasibility studies, urban economic and market supply-demand analyses, and valuation of various kinds of property interests for many different clients.

Author of numerous articles and research papers published in American and foreign professional journals, he has written several books, the most recent being *Analysis and Valuation of Retail Locations* (1976), *Rams' Real Estate Appraising Handbook* (1975), and *Valuation for Eminent Domain* (1973).

Early in his career (1952–1953) as Lecturer in Real Estate, he was the youngest member of the faculty in the Department of Real Estate, School of Business, at Roosevelt University. A special and guest lecturer at conferences and seminars, his activities include presentation of research papers before annual meetings of the National Academy of Sciences.

Contents

List of Tables

Preface

A real estate consultant is a professional who provides objective expert investment advice to a broad segment of society on the proper use of land and related improvements. Such consulting activities involve providing assistance by identifying, defining, and solving problems pertaining to real estate and various kinds of real property interests. Formulating a valid and appropriate fresh point of view is a hallmark of a good counselor and investment advisor.

Real property is a resource that usually depends upon adjunct resources, like management, capital, and financing. The central function of a consultant is the understanding, application, and adaptation of resources and the factors of production to achieve maximum satisfaction of human wants and needs. Since resources are not limitless, skills, experience, and education in countless different situations represent the unusual talent requirements of an effective and knowledgeable consultant and investment advisor. The skills and talents outlined transcend functional specialties like financing, brokerage, or management. Foremost attributes are breadth and depth of "know-how" concerning the real estate industry and its function in the American economic system. The ability to relate, uncover, and outline the best course of action and synthesize new innovations applicable to a client's areas of interest is the foremost requisite of a competent counselor.

This book should have special appeal to three groups of people. The first segment represents the active professional real estate consultant and investment advisor. The material provides a means for a review of current topics, techniques, and practices, along with an updating concerning new concepts and approaches to many typical client situations. In some instances, new vantage points for analysis may be evolved for immediate and day-to-day adaptation.

Other real estate industry groups who will find the subject matter of interest include those aspiring to be real estate and investment counselors. They can develop skills, talents, and a degree of knowledge in fields outside their area of specialization. Within this group are real estate brokers and salespeople, and those engaged in financing, development, appraising, or management. The problem-oriented situations portrayed and discussed provide a basis for the development of analytical skills in a number of areas essential to many basic and elementary consulting and advisory assignments.

A third and rather important group of readers and users of this book may be the clients themselves. While the subject matter is only representative of knowledge, information, and techniques, it does reflect the necessary interdisciplinary talents and skills of knowledgeable and seasoned consultants and investment advisors. In addition, client expectations concerning potential utilization of real estate specialists may be expanded.

The book was organized, researched, developed, and written principally in question-and answer form. The method reduces the material to specifics, thus largely omitting the general and rather introductory subject matter that is common to many textbooks and handbooks. The assumption is that the majority of users are already well versed in the basics of the real estate industry. Thus, the entire content is highly condensed, providing the specifics "why" and "how" in a broad array of situations and problems. The book is presented in three parts, permitting a logical sequence of reading and study ranging from the general context of real estate problems to the specifics of problem solving.

The first part provides basic and general data and information valuable in many typical assignments. The information is representative of prevailing background and orientation material researched from numerous sources which a consultant and investment advisor should be prepared to draw upon as needed in given assignments.

Part two covers area analysis and urban dynamics. Included are various techniques of analysis in the broader context of contemporary urbanism. While not encyclopedic in content, the subject matter provides guidelines and appropriate techniques and methods directed toward an understanding of the dynamics of real estate and real estate development.

The third part of the book is distinctly oriented toward an analysis of specific property interests and is problem solving in content. Here the details of given problems along with suggested solutions provide a credible format for the solution of most real estate advisory assignments. Alternate strategies in a decision-making context are illustrated.

A common thread traversing all three parts is an awareness of the objective function of all human endeavor, that is, the production of value and benefits. In a real estate context, we are concerned with the present and/or future value of a house, lot, office building, and so forth. Alternatively, given the value and benefit flow today, we wish to discover how the value-benefit matrix can be increased through the use and application of differents kinds and levels of resources, while reducing or minimizing risk, and increasing the wealth factor of a client.

Collectively, the three parts may serve as a guide to the "basics of real estate consultant and investment advisor competency" for professional service to individual clients and to society as a whole. As readers and users of this handbook will probably discover, there is more to serving and performing in this capacity than merely adding the word "counselor" or "consultant" to a business card. Because this book is the first of its kind in this area of professional practice, only time and use will determine its contribution to the real estate industry.

ACKNOWLEDGEMENT

The agility and restlessness of the human spirit and mind are the mainsprings for advancing the frontiers of knowledge in all human endeavors. These attributes, coupled with a constant and unrelenting probing and resolving of issues, collectively contribute to the novelty and innovativeness needed for the solution of problems of society.

The tapping of other people's ideas gleaned from research studies, reports, and other writings is self-evident and acknowledged by all authors. It would be mind boggling to attempt to estimate the endless number of mind-hours of effort expended by countless associates, peers, and scholars whom I have drawn from here. Needless to say, the well has been tapped—but by no means exhausted. This reportorial effort is merely representative of the state of information and knowledge concerning one of the necessities of life, that is, land and shelter for the human race.

A note of thanks to all the editors and authors noted herein for their splendid cooperation and willingness in permitting the use of the material. A special note of acknowledgement to George S. Anderson, who provided computer assistance and dialogue on a number of interesting problems.

EDWIN M. RAMS

part one
BASIC CONCEPTS AND PRINCIPLES

The exploding state of knowledge and information in recent years has had a profound impact on the "know-how," techniques, and methods in virtually all disciplines. This growth resource, with an ever-expanding base, requires diligent monitoring by any learned profession if its membership is to remain current, effective, and competitive.

A number of basic concepts form the common thread that transcends individual undertakings or problem situations in the real estate industry. They represent the foundations and fabric upon which numerous variations and embellishments can be formulated to accomodate individual goals, objectives, and strategies.

An experienced real estate consultant relies upon information from a number of disciplines. Among these are land economics, investment analysis, the building and construction industry, finance and financial analysis, and real property law. Detailed knowledge at an optimum professional level in all these disciplines is virtually impossible. What is achievable is a working basis and framework of reference in the various disciplines, with sufficient depth in each area to provide a synthesized level of operational knowledge, which is brought to bear on various everyday assignments. A singular benefit is to be derived from an appreciation of the multi-discipline needs of a real estate consultant.

This appreciation affords better recognition of a problem in all its ramifications. A multi-discipline approach serves as a basis for astute counseling of clients, providing advice on central issues and solutions concerning their particular areas of interest.

A knowledge of the parameters of the current state of knowledge of a discipline can be either supportive in nature or operational for actual use and implementation. The first part of this book provides a reasonable sample of both. While not exhaustive, due to the inherent breadth and depth of subject matter, the material cuts across a number of areas that apply to real estate consulting activities. This informational profile then serves as a basis for a number of areas covered in the second part of the book. Accordingly, categorization has been avoided because of the interdependence of concepts, techniques, and principles in the broad field of real estate analysis.

Q. *What is the dominant factor governing investor motivation toward real estate investments of one kind or another?*

A. Expectations represent one of the leading determinants concerning the actual real estate investment process. Expectations are essentially subjective beliefs concerning the actual, planned, or potential use or benefits and/or income to be derived from a real estate investment. The investor's perceptions of factors concerning future economic conditions and developments represent the foundation of an expectation or a set of expectations. The futuristic nature of expectations makes them nebulous in nature and, consequently, not readily measurable. Therefore, uncertainty is a concept relevant to expectations and their relationship to a real estate investment decision.

Because expectations are a pervasive force in the dynamics of the economy, they are a causal factor of great significance in the economic process. For example, whether a potential purchaser of an apartment building perceives the short-term and/or long-term economic outlook as trending "upward" or "downward" can determine not only the subsequent decision to purchase or not to purchase, but may also determine the price to be paid for the property. Accordingly, entrepreneurial forecasts and expectations require close attention.

Q. *What are some marketplace myths in the real estate game?*

A. Webster defines a myth as an imaginary or unverifiable person or thing; a legendary narrative that presents part of the beliefs of a people or explains a practice or natural phenomenon.

The following are several illustrations of "myths" which, when cleverly disguised in fancy brochures and placed in the hands of superb pitchmen, literally create miracles (real estate sales) in the real estate marketplace:

1. *Land never depreciates*—the abandonment of hundreds of thousands of parcels of improved real estate in dozens of large cities proves this to be false. Where urban improved properties (which can be economically rehabilitated) sell for only the cost of the street, sewer, and water line costs, the land and structure is, in essence, free; this dramatizes the fact that real estate and its corresponding value is directly related to its environment.

2. *There is a shortage of land*—since 75 percent of all the people live and utilize only about 2 percent of all the land, this is, at best, a misleading statement. Good areas and excellent locations command a premium because of very strong demand

among a number of different potential urban land users (housing, shopping centers, etc). For example, should technology in water and sewage treatment and in transportation advance significantly, both the cost of utilizing land for urban use diminish and the time-distance and costs to centers of economic activity be reduced, then the availability and potential use of hundreds of thousands acres of land would be readily marketable for urban use.

3. *You can't go wrong by investing in real estate*—totally false; notice that one hears only of the select few success stories and not of the thousands of failures and related huge financial losses. Time, timing, and product are key elements of successful real estate investments.

4. *High leverage is the best*—an investor may enjoy the tax shelter for a year or two and then lose the property. High leverage assumes that the economic condition of the property (net cash flow) will remain the same or improve. Change in neighborhood, increased vacancies, and pre-emption by new competitive facilities are just a few items which contribute to a negative cash flow. This myth is similar to the mysticising of a certain tree without realizing that it is merely one part of a large forest.

5. *Buy now, prices always go up*—asking price may go up, but closing (sale) prices may be another thing. Further, even though land and construction costs may increase, the prices realized on the standing inventory of real estate depend on "effective demand" that is, consumer's wants and needs coupled with financial ability. How consumers perceive the future, their employment and other present and anticipated financial obligations may be more important than what a dozen sellers are asking for their property. There are two sides of a real estate market, sellers and buyers. The thinking, plans, and actions of the buyers is just as important as those of the sellers.

6. *If a large developer buys a large block of land, quickly step in and buy close to him and reap a fortune*—a foolish notion simply because: (1) this may be a speculative purchase on a very thin down payment—a tax shelter with no liability in event of default, and (2) unavailable information concerning what the developer plans to do with the property and when may be very relevant.

7. *If three executive-professionals bought recreational land over the weekend, this must be a good deal*—totally false. Competence in law, medicine, or industrial plant management is one thing, while astute investment in real estate is another. To mimic the action of other market participants may add an element of confidence but the foundation relied upon may turn out to be quicksand!

Q. *In understanding urban economic and real estate studies, the use of assumptions is employed. What are some of the reasons for this and what classes of assumptions generally prevail?*

A. Assumptions are important to (1) define the problem, (2) establish alternatives, (3) provide means for treating unknown or difficult matters to quantify, and (4) quantify findings.

There are two classes of assumptions: state-of-nature and mathematical. Mathematical assumptions relate to the underlying formula relationship of quantities, that is, $V = I/R$, the income divided by the capitalization rate is equal to value. Four examples of key elements of state-of-nature assumptions include:

1. Time—relating to cash flows, economic life, and so on.
2. Quantity—for example, the present dollar volume of retail trade at a shopping center.
3. Activity Level—for example, operating expenses of an apartment building at a given level of occupancy.
4. Degree of Support—equity requirements (assets) needed to undertake a proposed real estate investment or development.

Q. *In dealing with uncertainty concerning investment decisions, how can* a fortiori analysis *(with greater reason) be helpful?*

A. This kind of analysis deliberately attempts to formulate assumptions that tend to uniformly favor or disfavor a particular alternate investment. For example, three investments might be analyzed for selection of one for final purchase, having an initial rank of C, A, and B. A series of assumptions on certainty of net cash flow, operating expenses, locational stability, and so on, may enhance or reduce the relative ranking. Where the ranking does not change following these criteria tests, then the analysis further supports the initial ranking and thus reduces the extent of uncertainty concerning a final selection and decision.

Q. *In the general analysis and treatment of data, what is the difference between variable data and attribute data?*

A. Variable data involves measurement while attribute data involves classification. For example, in an analysis of household incomes a grouping is made based on division of households into those with incomes of less than $10,000 per year and those earning more than this base figure. These groupings are treated as attributes. However, if incomes are grouped, $3,000–4,999, $5,000–7,999, and so on, this categorization constitutes a variable. Attributes can also be viewed as a special case in which only two values are possible: (0) if the element does not possess the characteristic, and (1) if it does.

Q. *In analyzing data (from a universe), why is it important to distinguish between groups that are "heterogeneous" and those that are "homogeneous"?*

A. One must first specify a characteristic, for example, houses over forty years old, to establish whether a data group is either homogeneous or heterogeneous. Additionally, in terms of one characteristic, the group may be homogeneous while in terms of several other characteristics it may be heterogeneous. Likewise, where analysis is inductive rather than descriptive, differences may be statistically significant in the case of heterogeneity and not statistically significant in the case of homogeneity.

Q. *What is "Okun's Law" and how can it help me to understand current levels and forecasts for employment, unemployment, economic growth, and other trends indicating potentials for upside or downside economic conditions?*

A. Okun's Law provides a rule of thumb concerning the relationship of economic growth (Gross National Product, GNP) to unemployment. It is essentially a 3-to-1 rule, that is, for every 3 percent of real GNP increase (without inflation), unemployment will decrease 1 percent. A study of prior years has shown that a real increase of about 4 percent is needed to keep the unemployment rate steady. Therefore, annual growth must reach a level of 7 percent for unemployment to reduce by 1 percent.

In testimony before the Joint Economic Committee, United States Congress, January 12, 1977, Julius Shiskin, Commissioner of Labor Statistics, presented Tables A and B, which related unemployment, GNP, and growth in the labor force. For example, if the labor force grows by 2 million (Table A), there will have to be 1.8 million more jobs in the economy to keep the unemployment unchanged (7–8 percent in December, 1976); to reduce unemployment by 2 percent, a total of 3.8 million new jobs will have to be generated by the economy. If productivity is at 3 percent (assumption of Table B), real GNP growth must be 5.6 percent to reduce unemployment by 1 percent; GNP growth must be 6.7 percent to effect a 2 percent reduction of unemployment—this is predicated on the same level of increase in labor force as above—2 million.

The following tables and charts provide examples of the validity of Okun's Law.

Table A
Required increases in employment under various targets for decreases in the unemployment rate and assumed growth in the civilian labor force (numbers in millions)

Assumed Growth of the Civilian Labor Force	No change in Unemployment Rate	Target Percentage Point Reduction in Unemployment Rate				
		1%	1.5%	2%	3%	4%
0.0	0.0	0.9	1.4	1.9	2.8	3.8
0.5	0.5	1.4	1.9	2.4	3.3	4.3
1.0	0.9	1.9	2.4	2.8	3.8	4.8
1.5	1.4	2.3	2.8	3.3	4.3	5.2
2.0	1.8	2.8	3.3	3.8	4.8	5.7
2.5	2.3	3.3	3.8	4.3	5.2	6.2
3.0	2.8	3.7	4.2	4.7	5.7	6.7
3.5	3.2	4.2	4.7	5.2	6.2	7.2
4.0	3.7	4.8	5.2	5.7	6.7	7.6
5.0	4.6	5.6	6.1	6.6	7.6	8.6
6.0	5.5	6.5	7.1	7.6	8.6	9.6
7.0	6.5	7.5	8.0	8.5	9.5	10.5
8.0	7.4	8.4	8.9	9.4	10.5	11.5
9.0	8.3	9.3	9.9	10.4	11.4	12.5
10.0	9.2	10.3	10.8	11.3	12.4	13.4

NOTE: 1976 annual averages were used as the bases for these calculations.

Change in unemployment rate during recessions
(percentage points)

Peak Quarter	Trough Quarter	Actual Change	Predicted Change	Difference
1953–2	1954–2	3.2	2.3	0.9
1957–3	1958–2	3.1	2.2	0.9
1960–2	1961–1	1.6	1.5	0.1
1969–4	1970–4	2.3	1.6	0.7
1973–4	1975–2	4.1	4.9	−0.8

Table B

Implied increases in real GNP growth under various targets for decreases in the unemployment rate and assumed growth in the civilian labor force

Change in Civilian Labor Force (Millions)	Target Reduction in Unemployment Rate (Percentage Points) 0.0	1.0	1.5	2.0	3.0	4.0
	Change in Real GNP (1972 Dollars) (Average Annual Rate of Change)					
1.0	3.3	4.5	5.0	5.6	6.7	8.8
1.5	3.9	5.0	5.6	6.1	7.2	8.3
2.0	4.4	5.6	6.1	6.7	7.8	8.9
2.5	5.0	6.1	6.7	7.2	8.3	9.4
3.0	5.5	6.7	7.2	7.8	8.9	9.0
3.5	6.1	7.2	7.8	8.3	9.4	10.5

ASSUMPTIONS

- 0.7 million increase in civilian government jobs (0.6 in State and local government and 0.1 in Federal government). Assumptions about growth in government employment are necessary because of difference in public and private labor productivity.
- 0.1 million reduction in armed forces.
- 0.4 percent decline in the private economy's average weekly hours.
- 3.0 percent growth in the private economy's labor productivity. This growth assumes a cyclical recovery in private labor productivity as it returns to its long-term trend.

These derivations do not consider potential capacity constraints, nor the fiscal or monetary policies necessary to generate the projected real GNP changes, nor the inflationary impacts of the projected real GNP changes.

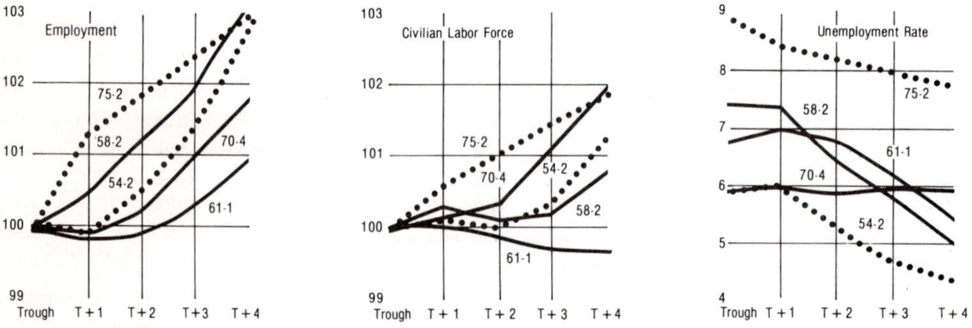

Change in unemployment rate during first year of recovery (percentage points)

Trough Quarter	Actual Change	Predicted Change	Difference
1954–2	−1.4	−1.6	0.2
1958–2	−2.3	−1.9	−0.4
1961–1	−1.2	−1.4	0.2
1970–4	0.1	−0.5	0.6

Q. *Recent discussions concerning growth have brought forward matters concerning the fiscal impact of development on a community. In several instances the courts have ruled in favor of controlled growth as determined by the local governing body. What are some parameters and elements involved in a fiscal impact study concerning urban development?*

A. Fiscal impact analysis is essentially a cost-revenue study to ascertain the significance of a new development on the quality, level, and related costs of community services; it is a look at the relationship between the benefits of development (revenues) versus the obligated services (costs) of a community to its residents.

Cost-revenue studies have been utilized by local government bodies for a number of reasons. The following is representative of purposes and objectives:

1. *Land Use Decisions.* Cost-revenue analysis of alternative land uses, from the scale of small developments to complex multi-use proposals for large areas has been used to ensure that important land use decisions are based on fiscal impacts as well as other considerations. These studies generally take a long range view (up to 20 years) in order to ascertain the continuing service costs and revenues anticipated to be generated by the development well beyond the initial construction years.

2. *Planning Alternatives.* Areawide planning alternatives involving different combinations of land uses or rates of development may have widely diverging fiscal consequences. Cost-revenue analysis has been used effectively to measure these impacts.

3. *Service Pricing.* Elements of cost-revenue analysis have been used traditionally by governments to establish service charges for various types of users that are intended to cover the costs of service to existing or future development.

4. *Annexation Studies.* Cost-revenue analysis has been used to project the anticipated costs and revenues associated with municipal annexations. The technique is especially useful where the area to be annexed includes substantial existing development that will require extension of city services.

5. *Fiscal Management.* Budgeting, capital programming, and long range fiscal planning require projections of both service costs and revenue capabilities. Projection techniques parallel those used in cost-revenue studies.

6. *Cost-Benefit Studies.* Cost-revenue analysis forms an important part of broader efforts to measure total benefits by assigning value to nonfiscal factors such as environmental enhancement, recreation potential, attainment of social goals, travel time reduction, and similar objectives.
7. *Growth Management.* Analysis of the fiscal impacts of alternative rates, directions, or other characteristics of urban growth has been used to set long range development objectives that are consistent with fiscal capabilities.

The following example involving a community with a population of approximately 70,000 people outlines the elements (Tables A and B) and their application (Table C) concerning proposals for several different kinds of developments:

Table A
Unit costs of services*

Urban Use	*Acres*	*%*	*Police*	*Human Resources*	*Public Services*	*Lighting*	*Parks*
Low Density Residential	550	15.3	$28.00	(0.30/capita)	$33.92	$22.27	$35.38
Medium Density Residential	253	70.4	21.89	(0.30/capita)	30.71	22.27	35.38
Multifamily Residential	55	1.5	13.25	(0.30/capita)	3.37	89.07	(a)
Mobile Homes	76	2.1	17.50	(0.30/capita)	6.49	89.07	21.26
Commercial	315.5	8.8	342.60	42.18	77.72	118.55	—
Industrial	70	1.9	160.33	42.18	107.42	54.02	—

*All residential costs are on per unit basis; commercial and industrial on per acre basis; other as noted.
(a) Scaled from $11.48 for studio apartments to $21.26 for four-bedroom apartments.

Table B
Per unit revenues

Urban Use	*General*[1]	*Sanitary District*	*Property Tax*	*Lighting Maintenance*	*Park Revenue*[2]
Low Density Residential	$51.18	$36	Tax Rate based on	(a) $17.23	$50.74
Med. Density Residential	51.18	36	costs/ revenues	(b) 17.23	50.74
Multi-family Residential	38.11	36	for each	(c) 13.99	41.18
Mobile Homes	28.73	36	year	0.96	2.83
Commercial	534.68	$186/A		144.57	405.88
Industrial	168.66	176/A		185.75	174.61

[1]Includes sales tax, business and franchise taxes, Federal grant revenues, and building permits.
[2]Scaled up for new construction.
(a) New, $27.98 (b) New, $23.78 (c) New, $16.79

Table C
Urban development—Fiscal impact
(15-year time frame)

Kind of Development	Cost/Revenue Ratio
A. Low Density Residential @ 3.3 units/acre total of 250 units, estimated market price of $45,000; 2.17 acres public area maintenance.	
City Operating Revenues	2.21 / 1
Sanitation District	0.66 / 1
Lighting Maintenance	0.86 / 1
Recreation-Park District	1.30 / 1
B. Multifamily Residential @ 20 units/gross acre total of 132 units on 6.59 acres; 896 square feet of public maintenance area	
City Operating Revenues	0.78 / 1
Sanitation District	0.60 / 1
Lighting Maintenance	0.29 / 1
Recreation-Park District	1.51 / 1
C. Commercial, 6.59 gross acres	
City Operating Revenues	0.55 / 1
Sanitation District	0.68 / 1
Lighting Maintenance	0.72 / 1

SOURCE: Cost Revenue Analysis Model, Feb. 1976, City of Simi Valley, Calif.

Q. *A great deal of discussion is under way in your city concerning the impact of land development. To resolve many pros and cons that are emerging, you have been appointed as chairperson of a committee. What is a good outline for guiding discussion and probable measures for land development impacts?*

A. The following is probably the most comprehensive outline on the subject:

Measures for evaluating the impacts of land developments

Impact Area[1]		*Measure*
I. *Local Economy*		
Public Fiscal Balance	1.	Net change in government fiscal flow (revenues less operating expenditures and annualized capital expenditures).
Employment	2.	Number of new long-term and short-term jobs provided.
	3.	Change in numbers and percent employed, unemployed, and underemployed.
Wealth	4.	Change in land values.
II. *Natural Environment*[2]		
Air	5.	Change in level of air pollutants and number of people at risk or bothered by air pollution.
Water	6.	Change in level of water pollutants, change in tolerable types of use, and number of persons affected, for each body of water.
Noise	7.	Change in noise and vibration levels, and number of people bothered by excessive noise and vibration.
Greenery and Open Space	8.	Amount and percent change in greenery and open space.
	15.	Percent of citizens who think the development improves or lessens the overall neighborhood attractive ness, pleasantness, and uniqueness.[4]
Landmarks	16.	Rarity and perceived importance of cultural, historic, or scientific landmarks to be lost or made inaccessible.
IV. *Public and Private Services*		
Drinking Water	17.	Change in rate of water shortage incidents.
	18.	Change in indexes of drinking water quality and safety.
Hospital Care	19.	Change in number of citizens who are beyond x minutes travel time from a hospital emergency room (using such time as the community considers reasonable).
	20.	Change in average number of days of waiting time for hospital admittance for elective surgery.

Wildlife and Vegetation	9.	Number and types of endangered or rare species that will be threatened.
	10.	Change in abundance and diversity of wildlife and vegetation in the development and community.
Scarce Resource Consumption	11.	Change in frequency, duration, and magnitude of shortages of critically scarce resources, and the number of persons affected.
Natural Disasters	12.	Change in number of people and value of property endangered by flooding, earthquakes, landslides, mudslides, and other natural disasters.
III. *Aesthetics and Cultural Values*[3]		
Views	13.	Number of people whose views are blocked, degraded, or improved.
Attractiveness	14.	Visual attractiveness of the development as rated by citizens and "experts."
Crime Control	21.	Change in rate of crimes in existing community or new development (or expert rating of change in hazard).
	22.	Change in percent of people feeling a lack of security from crime.
Fire Protection	23.	Change in fire incidence rates.
	24.	Change in rating of fire spread and rescue hazards.
Recreation[5]	25.	Change in the number of people within—or beyond—a reasonable distance (x miles or y minutes) from recreational facilities, by type of facility.
	26.	Change in usage as a percent of capacity; waiting times; number of people turned away; facility space per resident; and citizen perceptions of crowdedness at recreational facilities.
	27.	Change in perceived pleasantness of recreational experience.[8]

NOTES:
1. These impact areas correspond to community objectives for regulating land development.
2. In some situations, a measure of the change in the microclimate near a development should be added to the list.
3. Measures 5 through 10 also reflect aspects of aesthetics. See text for discussion of overlapping of objectives and interrelation of measures.
4. Some may find a new development physically attractive (Measure 14), but prefer the current appearance of the neighborhood for its "character," image, relation to personal identity, and so forth.
5. Changes in the use of informal recreational facilities such as streets, sidewalks, and open space should be included.

continued

Measures for evaluating the impacts of land development (cont.)

Impact Area[1]		*Measure*
Education[6]	28.	Change in number of students within x minutes walk or y minutes ride from school, by type of school.
	29.	Number and percent of students having to switch schools or busing status (from walking to busing or vice versa).
	30.	Change in crowdedness "breakpoints" (such as need for added shifts) or indicators (such as student-teacher ratios); student, teacher, and parent perceptions of crowdedness and pleasantness of schooling.
Local Transportation[7]	31.	Change in vehicular travel times between selected origins and distinations.
	32.	Change in duration and severity of congestion.
	33.	Change in likelihood of finding a satisfactory parking space within x distance from destination or resident.
V. *Housing and Social Conditions*		
Housing Adequacy	39.	Change in number and percent of housing units that are substandard, and change in number and percent of people living in such units.
	40.	Change in number and percent of housing units by type (price or rent range, zoning category, owner-occupied and rental, etc.) relative to demand or to number of families in various income classes in the community.
People Displaced	41.	Number of residents, or workers, displaced by development—and by whether they are satisfied with having to move.
Population Mix	42.	Change in the population distribution by age, income, religion, racial or ethnic group, occupational class, and household type.
Crowdedness	43.	Change in percent of people who perceive their neighborhood as too crowded.[8]

	34.	Change in numbers and percent of residents with access to public transit within x feet of their residences; and numbers and percent of employees who can get within x distance of work location by public transit.
	35.	Change in the rate of traffic accidents (or expert rating of change in hazard presented).
	36.	Number and percent of citizens perceiving a change in neighborhood traffic hazard; and change in pedestrian usage of streets, sidewalks, and other outdoor space.[8]
Shopping	37.	Change in number of stores and services, by type, available within x distance of y people.
	38.	Change in the percent of people generally satisfied with local shopping conditions (access, variety, crowdedness).[8]
Sociability-Friendliness	44.	Change in frequency of visits to friends among people in the existing neighborhood, and frequency of visits between people in the existing neighborhood and the new development.
	45.	Change in percent of people perceiving the neighborhood as friendly.[8]
Privacy	46.	Number and percent of people with change in "visual" or "auditory" privacy.
	47.	Number and percent of people perceiving a loss of privacy.[8]
Overall Contentment with Neighborhood	48.	Change in percent of people who perceive their community as a good place to live.[8]
Fairness to All Groups		The above measures should be considered with respect to specific clientele groups or population segments that are affected to reflect the quality of fairness in new developments.

6. No satisfactory measure of development impacts on the quality of education received has been found.
7. Impacts of land use changes on accessibility by foot are reflected in part in measures for recreation (25), schools (28), and shopping (37).
8. Measures dealing with citizen perceptions are much harder to estimate quantitatively for proposed developments than for past developments. However, bounds or ranges may be estimated in some situations, and in all they should be considered at least qualitatively.

SOURCE: "Measures for Evaluating the Impacts of Land Developments." Washington, D.C.: The Urban Institute, Nov. 1974.

Q. *In working with various real estate investors, what are some key points to consider in structuring the legal form of ownership in a venture?*

A. A number of important factors must be considered prior to final structuring of a real estate investment from a legal entity standpoint. These might be labeled as criteria for selection of the mode of ownership. Generally six elements make up the criteria. They include (1) the extent of liability that the parties are prepared to undertake, (2) the extent of investor participation in the management of the investment, (3) the desired flexibility of operation and potential transfer of interest, (4) ease of transfer of interest, (5) probable holding period of the investment, and (6) the tax impact under various forms of ownership.

The attributes and characteristics of various forms of ownership are outlined below:

I. *Land Trust*
- a. Management by trustee
- b. Undivided interest held by beneficiaries
- c. Ease of transfer of beneficial interest
- d. Death of any beneficiary does not terminate venture
- e. Risk of being treated as a corporation for tax purposes

II. *Tenancy In Common*
- a. Tax benefits shared by co-tenants
- b. Co-tenants have exposure to liability
- c. Undivided interest held by each co-tenant
- d. Investment venture has limited continuity
- e. Flexibility is limited in handling of property interests
- f. Interest passes by will on demise of co-tenant
- g. Some tax benefits

III. *General Partnership**
- a. Flow-through tax benefits
- b. Liability of partners is unlimited
- c. Permits participation in management
- d. Represents a separate legal entity
- e. Agency relationship governs operation of property
- f. Termination on withdrawal or death of partner
- g. Permits informal and flexible management
- h. Some limitations concerning transfer of interests

IV. *Limited Partnership**
- a. Flow-through tax benefits
- b. Liability of partners is limited

*Additional aspects include: guarantees of developer, tax elections, marketing fees as a developer, potential tax-free exchanges of interests, division of interests including losses and profits, general partners' indemnity, depreciation shares and distribution, broker's and other venture related fees, and so on.

c. Management is centralized
d. Transfer of interests is limited
e. Must comply with statutory conditions
f. Good continuity for venture in event of death, bankruptcy, etc.
g. Public disclosure requirements must be met
h. Some net worth considerations/requirements

V. *Corporation*

a. Provides means for continuity of venture and interests
b. Legal entity (creature of law) with means for holding of title
c. Control by and through directors and officers
d. Limited liability

Q. *What is meant by the term "housing gap" and how can it be measured?*

A. "Housing gap" refers to the existing disparity between the demand for residential property and the current housing inventory. The extent of a housing gap in any community is assessed by matching households by income and size with housing units by rent and number of rooms, thus identifying the types of units that might be required to adequately house the population. Criteria for matching involve (1) a rental-to-income ratio not to exceed 25 percent, and (2) a persons-per-room ratio not greater than one to one. A working base unit is usually the census tract.

Q. *What is the significance of the vacancy rate as a market indicator and what are its limitations in use?*

A. Generally, vacancy rates are an index of the extent of utilization of the standing inventory of one kind of facility or another. Recent studies have shown that vacancy rates are relative. Where population growth is significant, increases in vacancies of housing units may reflect the anticipated need for new facilities. Additionally, vacancy rates, to be meaningful, must reflect differences in the kind and quality of rental units involved, recognizing such product attributes as location, functional viability, and so on.

Some research has suggested that foreclosure rates are highly correlated, lagging one year, to increasing vacancy rates involving single family dwellings and rental housing. Time series analysis of vacancy rates in the same local market is the most plausible basis for an estimate of utilization. This coupled with the what, where, and why of vacancies furnishes a sound basis for accounting for the use and non-use of many urban facilities.

Q. *What three indexes serve as measures of inflation and deflation?*

A. The three most commonly observed and analyzed indexes are:

1. Gross National Product (GNP), which is issued quarterly. The extent of the GNP deflator indicates the increased level of inflation.
2. Wholesale Price Index, which is issued monthly and reports the list prices of over 2,700 items of farm and industrial commodities.
3. Consumer Price Index (CPI), which is issued monthly, covers the actual retail prices in 18,000 establishments of approximately 400 items.

Q. *What are some of the reasons for using a wrap-around mortgage (sometimes called an overlapping deed of trust or all-inclusive loan) and how does it work?*

A. Assuming a sale is taking place, the buyer executes a note to the seller that includes the basic existing financing plus an amount that would be, in essence, a second mortgage. A contract of sale is used (no deed passing) and is effective until purchaser assumes (or takes subject to) the existing mortgage(s). On refinancing, for example, an existing mortgage may be at 6 percent with a balance of $5 million; the property can carry $7 million. Two million is advanced as a loan, and the borrower pays 7 percent on the total, that is, 7 million dollars.

Some typical business reasons for employing this kind of financing include:

1. Avoiding paying a prepayment penalty on an existing mortgage.
2. Retaining lower interest rate on first mortgage.
3. First mortgage does not permit a contract for deed sale or a transfer of title to property.
4. Seller wants to derive a higher yield than that which would accrue from a conventional second mortgage.
5. Purchaser, in states which provide no deficiency judgments on purchase money debts, may want to avoid any personal liability.
6. Because of thin equity on part of buyer, the seller may not want to pass title until he receives more cash.
7. Because a number of loans exist on the property, a buyer may want an all-inclusive loan for one of many reasons.

To illustrate how a wraparound mortgage works, assume that the sale price of an existing apartment building that a group of investors desires to buy at the end of 1975 is $1,500,000, and that there is an existing 7 percent first mortgage on the property, the unpaid balance of which is $1 million.

Conventional Financing

Under conventional terms, the buyers might pay $100,000 cash down, take the property subject to the existing first mortgage, and agree to a $400,000 second mortgage at a 9 percent interest rate. The investors would agree to pay interest and principal on the existing first mortgage. However, without the permission of the lender of the first mortgage, the buyer/investors cannot prepay interest in 1975 on the first mortgage. They could, however, agree with the seller to prepay interest on the new financing extended by the seller under the second mortgage. The seller would then receive a total of $136,000 in the year of sale, as follows:

Conventional financing—Purchase price: $1,500,000

Seller	*Buyers (syndicate)* *Pay:*	
Existing 1st mortgage (7 percent), unpaid balance $1 million.	Cash down payment	$100,000
	1st mortgage (taken subject to)	1,000,000
	2d mortgage (9 percent)	400,000
	Total	1,500,000
Cash flow:	Total paid by buyers:	
$136,000 received from buyers and retained.	Down payment—1975	100,000
	Prepaid interest (1 year on 2d mortgage)—1975	36,000
	Total	136,000
	Interest paid by buyers on 1st mortgage—1976	70,000
	Total	$206,000

Under this type of conventional financing, the investors would probably claim prepaid interest deductions for 1975 in the amount of $36,000.

Wraparound Technique

Using the wraparound mortgage technique, the investors might make a down payment of $66,000 and execute to the seller a mortgage for $1.4 million at 7 percent. (The face amount of the new obligation executed by the investors includes, or "wraps around," the existing first mortgage on the property.) The buyers then prepay one year's interest on the face amount of the wraparound mortgage, or $98,000 (7 percent of $1.4 million). They might also pay the seller three points on the wraparound mortgage, or $42,000. The seller would agree to continue to be responsible for making payments on the first mortgage. (In the following year, the seller would therefore pay $70,000 to the lender on the first mortgage, and retain a net of $136,000.)

The wraparound mortgage can be described as follows:

Wraparound mortgage—Purchase price: $1,466,000

Seller		*Buyers (syndicate)* *Pay:*	
$1,000,000 mortgage (seller will continue to discharge out of payments he receives from the buyers).		Cash down payment	$66,000
Cash flow:		Purchase money mortgage (wraparound) 7 percent	1,400,000
Received from Buyers—1975	$206,000	Total	1,466,000
Less: Interest due on 1st mortgage 1976	70,000	Three points on new mortgage	$42,000
Retained by seller	$136,000	Total paid by Buyers—1975:	
		Down payment	66,000
		Prepaid interest—1 year on purchase money mortgage	98,000
		Three points on new mortgage	42,000
		Total	$206,000

By using this technique, the seller nets the same $136,000 as under conventional terms, but the wraparound technique enables the investors to claim $140,000 in interest deductions in 1975 (rather than $36,000).[1]

In this example the total purchase price of the property has been reduced from $1.5 million to $1,466,000. The seller nets the same amount ($136,000) under either financing method. However, the buyers/investors have increased their claim to deduct one year's prepaid interest from $36,000 to $98,000. They have also paid points on the face of the wraparound mortgage which gives the seller the same dollar amount ($136,000) which he would have received under conventional financing and also gives the investors an additional interest deduction. The investors have in effect prepaid interest on the first mortgage without obtaining the lender's permission to do so. They have also converted $34,000 of purchase price dollars (if conventional financing had been used) into deductible interest dollars.

Recently, the Service has taken an administrative position indicating that it will measure the permissible prepaid interest deduction (under the tests of Rev. Rul. 68–643) not by reference to the face amount of the wraparound note but only by reference to the new credit which the seller extends to the buyer.[2]

[1]Typically, in lieu of having the investors pay points to the seller, the interest rate on the wraparound is higher than the existing interest rate on the first mortgage. In this example, the interest rate on the $1,400,000 wraparound mortgage would likely be higher than the presumably lower interest rate on the first mortgage. In such cases, the seller would retain (and profit from) the increased interest amounts on the first mortgage which the investors will pay to him but which he will not have to pay over to the lender on the first mortgage.

[2]In Rev. Rul. 75–99, 1975–12 I.R.B. 14, a party owning real estate encumbered by a $300x first mortgage (7 percent) executed a note to a real estate investment trust in the amount of $400x at 8 percent per year. The trust advanced $100x to the borrower. The trust also agreed to make the periodic principal and interest payments on the first mortgage. The ruling holds that the indebtedness between the trust and the borrower giving rise to an obligation to pay interest to the trust is not the face amount of the wraparound note, but only the $100x "actually" loaned by the trust. Payments by the trust on the first mortgage were considered made on behalf of the borrower.

SOURCE: Committee on Ways and Means, *Tax Shelters: Prepaid Interest*, September 16, 1975

Q. *What is the difference between a sale-leaseback and a sale-condoback?*

A. A sale-leaseback is essentially a means for the total sale of a property. A sale-condoback involves the sale of only a portion of the property with the owner (seller) retaining the part not conveyed. For example, an owner of a group of retail stores may decide to sell several units under a condominium arrangement and retain the remaining units for his own use and/or for his investment portfolio. The seller can maintain control over the resale of the unit by retaining a right of first refusal to repurchase.

From a tax analysis standpoint the following points and differences are important:

1. For the leasehold tenant: Annual rental expense is deductable from taxable income.
2. For the condoback owner: An annual depreciation allowance is deductable from taxable income.

For further information on this subject see David Clurman, *The Business Condominium, A New Form of Business Property Ownership*, John Wiley & Sons, 1973.

Q. *What are some basic guidelines to keep in mind when advising an investor in the choice between sale-leaseback deals and mortgages?*

A. Generally, three broad categories should be kept in mind when formulating investment strategies for clients. They include the legal aspects, tax aspects, and economic aspects. Principal points are noted below.

LEGAL ASPECTS

1. In a mortgage the permitted interest rate under local usury statutes is important, whereas in a sale-leaseback (S-L) this is not a factor.
2. Under a S-L, title is held by the investor, whereas in a mortgage the mortgagee's claim is that of a security interest.
3. On repayment of a loan under a mortgage, clear title passes to the mortgagor, while a S-L title remains with the investor.
4. In a bankruptcy action, the mortgage continues as a lien with no limitations as to damages against real property, whereas under a S-L there are limits on damages plus a potential for tenant disaffirmance of the initial contractual arrangements.
5. Under a S-L the lease compliance can be strictly enforced as to covenants of maintenance, use, and various lessee violations, whereas under a mortgage a mortgagor might gain concessions in a court of equity on some of these matters.
6. In the absense of judicially recognized mitigating circumstances, a tenant is under total liability, whereas under a mortgage a mortgagee may have to resort to deficiency judgements to satisfy claims.
7. While a mortgagor has redemption rights, a S-L tenant generally waives these rights.

TAX ASPECTS

1. The mortgagor can deduct only interest, whereas rent is fully deductible.
2. Under a mortgage, only interest is treated as income; under S-L, the entire rental fee is treated as income.
3. Under a S-L, there is some flexibility in the treatment of depreciation, allowing for a division of depreciation between landlord and tenant; under a mortgage, only the mortgagor has the benefit of depreciation provisions.

ECONOMIC ASPECTS

1. Avoid arrangements that involve a low purchase (sale) price and high rentals.
2. The lease term in a S-L should be adequate to amortize investment as well as to justify any additional capital improvements undertaken by the lessee.
3. The controlling instrument of tenancy should contain all standard and typically utilized lease provisions.
4. The tenant (vendor) in a S-L arrangement is charged with a loss/gain treatment of sale proceeds.
5. The investor's (landlord) tax in a S-L is based upon the purchase price of the property.
6. The credit rating and track record of a S-L tenant are crucial to the integrity of this kind of investment.
7. Any potential imputation in a S-L agreement requiring repurchase can result in the S-L agreement being treated, as a matter of law, as a mortgage; avoid any attempt to disguise a mortgage by calling it a sale-leaseback.
8. Guarantee(s) of rent should not be taken at face value; in some states the law limits any corporate guarantee of rent.
9. When corporations are involved, the rental cash flow may be limited by statute in some states; this is particularly likely in cases involving bankruptcy of the tenant.

Q. *What special incentive legislation has been enacted to encourage investors to build low and moderate income housing and what have been the benefits and tax advantages to such investors?*

A. From time to time the Federal Government enacts legislation to encourage investment in low and moderate income housing. One such activity of Congress involved the passage of Section 167(K) of the Tax Reform Act of 1969; essentially a tax incentive measure. Generally, an investor could elect to compute depreciation under a straight line method using a five-year useful life and no salvage value for rehabilitation expenditures made after July 24, 1969 and before January 1, 1975 provided:

1. The taxpayer must expend at least $3,000 per unit over a period of two consecutive years.
2. The aggregate amount depreciated in a five-year period could not exceed $15,000.
3. Occupancy must be by low income families and individuals.

The benefits, on a comparative basis, are illustrated in the following table.

Annual per unit benefits derived by the owners from selected property types

	*All Section 167 (k) Projects in the Sample**		*New Low- and Moderate-Income Properties in the Sample*		*Existing Properties in the Sample*	
Total Project Income	$1,883		2,367		988	
Total Project Expense	3,463		3,274		1,022	
Taxable Income (Loss)	(1,594)		(844)		62	
	$ per unit	*% total benefits*	*$ per unit*	*% total benefits*	*$ per unit*	*% total benefits*
Tax Benefits (Cost)[1]	$956	97%	$506	82%	$(37)	(73%)
Cash Flow	29	3	114	18	88	173
Total benefits	$985	100%	$620	100%	$51	100%
Properties in sample:	153		52		45	

[1]Assumes all investors are in 60% tax bracket; ignores minimum tax on preference items.
[2]Because data are medians, details may not add to totals.
*Section 167(k) is part of Tax Reform Act of 1969.

SOURCE: *The Impact and Effects of Section 167(K) on the Rehabilitation of Multifamily Property.* Washington, D.C.: Touche Ross & Co. for HUD, 1974.

Q. *I represent commercial and industrial tenants in negotiating leases involving office and warehouse space. Is there any efficient checklist or format to be followed that would provide a means for evaluating a proposed lease?*

A. The following checklist provides an exhaustive tabulation of matters needing attention when considering a proposed lease for nonresidential facilities:

I. General Provisions
- A. *Kind of Lease*
  1. Is this a net lease or a conventional commercial lease?
- B. *Term*
  1. How many years is the lease to run?
  2. When can the lessee obtain possession?
  3. Options to renew:
     - a. Is there to be an option to renew?
     - b. How many options?
     - c. Term of each option in years?
     - d. Rent for each option term?
     - e. Does the rent go down on successive options to reflect the fact that the lessor has paid off the mortgage over the original term of the lease?
- C. *Holding Over*
  1. Will a holding over create a month-to-month tenancy?
  2. What will be the rental as a percent of the regular monthly rental?
- D. *Rentals*
  1. What is the gross rental per year?
  2. What is the gross rental per square foot of usable space?
- E. *Grace Period*
  1. Does the lessor agree to a grace period in the lease?
  2. If so, what is the number of days of grace allowed the lessee to cure a default:
     - a. in nonpayment of rent?
     - b. for other breaches of the lease?
  3. Is there to be a confession of judgment clause in the lease?
- F. *Measure of Damages*
  1. Is the measure of damages for breach of the lease by the lessee to be the deficiency in rental that the lessor realizes by renting the premises to a new lessee?
- G. *Attorney's Fees*
  1. Will the lessee be required to pay the lessor's attorney's fees incurred in enforcing the lease?

2. If so:
    a. Must the fees arise out of a court suit?
    b. Must the fees be reasonable?
    c. Must the fees be approved by the court?
    d. Must the lessor win the suit to collect such fees?
    e. Will the provision work both ways so that the loser pays the winner's fees?

H. *Assignment and Subletting*

1. Does the lessee have the right to assign and sublet the premises?
2. If the lessor's written consent is required, will the lessor agree not to withhold his consent unreasonably?
3. Does the lessee have the right to sublet without the lessor's consent to a responsible tenant with a specified credit rating?
4. Does the lessee have the right to assign to a subsidiary without lessor's consent?
5. What is the legal effect of a merger of lessor or lessee on the lease?

I. *Option To Purchase*

1. Will the lessee be given the option to purchase the land and building?
2. At what price?
3. When is the option to be exercised—by what date?

J. *Present Lease Commitment*

1. When will the lessee's present lease term expire?
2. Does the lessee have the right to sublet or assign?
3. Will the present lessor consent to a subletting?
4. Will the new lessor assume the lessee's liability under his present lease?
5. If so, from what date?

II. TAXES AND EXPENSES

A. *Real Estate Taxes*

1. Will lessor pay all the real estate taxes?
2. If lessee agrees to pay all the taxes:
    a. What were the real estate taxes on this property for the past five years?
    b. Were taxes on vacant land or improved property?
    c. What is the trend in real estate taxes in this area?
3. If the lessee agrees to pay any increase in the taxes over the base year:
    a. What is the base tax payable by lessor?
    b. Is there to be a maximum annual increase payable by the lessee?

c. If so, what is the annual increase payable by the lessee expressed as a percent of the base tax?

B. *Utility and Service Charges*
1. Who will pay utility charges—lessor or lessee?
2. Who will pay maintenance and services charges (snow removal, painting, cleaning refuse disposal, janitorial, etc.)?
3. If lessee agrees to pay for these items, he should have the right to contract for them directly, rather than to purchase them from the lessor.
4. Does the lessor agree to pay the normal utility service connection expenses?

C. *Ordinary Repairs and Maintenance*
1. Will the lessee be required to make all ordinary, necessary repairs to the building, roadways, and so forth?
2. Will the lessee be required to perform all usual maintenance of the premises?
3. Who will be responsible for extraordinary repairs?
4. Who will be responsible for structural repairs and alterations?

III. RESTRICTIONS ON LAND USE

A. *Zoning*
1. In what zone is the building located?
2. Is the use contemplated by the lessee permitted in that zone?
3. Will the lessor furnish the lessee a copy of the zoning ordinance and a plat of survey so that the lessee can satisfy himself that the zoning requirements are met?

B. *Title to the Land—Restrictions, Easements*
1. Does the lessor own the land in fee simple?
2. What is the legal description of the land?
3. The lessee should be furnished copies of all covenants and restrictions of record that regulate the use that the property may be put to.
4. Is it necessary to cross the land of other property owners or to use private roadways to gain access to the public streets or highways? If so, the lessee should be furnished copies of the recorded easements entitling him to use such land or roadway for ingress and egress.
5. Are there utility easements to serve the leased property? If so, the lessee should be furnished copies of the recorded easements.

IV. Building Requirements

A. *Compliance with Building Code*

1. If the building is to be constructed for the lessee, lessor should obtain and deliver to lessee a certificate of occupancy or a certificate of compliance evidencing that the building conforms to all laws, ordinances, building codes, and so forth.
2. If it is an existing building, lessor should agree to warrant in the lease that he has conformed to the laws, etc., and that he will reimburse the lessee for the full cost of any repairs or alterations required to be made after the lease commences to correct code violations that existed before the lessee took possession.
3. If the lessor is unwilling to extend to lessee the protection afforded in paragraphs *1* and *2* above, the lessee should retain the services of a local attorney to check these matters.

B. *New Building To Be Constructed for Lessee*

1. Is a building to be constructed on vacant land by lessor for the lessee?
2. Have plans and specifications been prepared for the building and site improvements?
3. What is the name and address of the architect retained by the lessor to prepare these plans and specifications?
4. Are the plans and specifications to be made a part of the lease as an exhibit?
5. Will the lessor pay the architect's fees?
6. If the final plans and specifications will not be ready when the lease is signed (but only preliminary plans and specifications will be attached to the lease), will the final plans and specifications be subject to review and approval by lessee (which approval will not be unreasonably withheld)?
7. By what date must a complete set of final plans and specifications be delivered to lessee?
8. When will construction work begin?
9. When will construction work be completed?
10. If completion is delayed beyond the completion date, and lessee is forced to give up his space in his former building, will the lessor pay liquidated damages during the period of delay?
11. If completion is delayed beyond the completion date through events beyond the lessor's control (strikes, acts of God, and so forth), is the lessee entitled to terminate

the lease after an agreed period of delay to seek other space?

C. *Existing Building To Be Leased*
   1. Has the lessee inspected the building? What is the condition of the building?
   2. Will the lessor grant the lessee the right to inspect the building prior to the execution of the lease and prior to taking actual possession?
   3. Will the lessor warrant that the building conforms to the building code?
   4. What is the size of the building—usable floor area?
   5. Can the building be enlarged?
      a. Can additional stories be added?
      b. Can a wing or addition be added? Is there adequate land available?
      c. Will the zoning ordinance permit such expansion or addition?
      d. Are there setback and side yard lines that would prevent additions?
   6. What is the location of the building?
   7. What is the type of construction?
   8. What is the age of the building?
   9. What is the condition of the equipment in the building (furnace, crane, elevator, and so forth)?
   10. Will the lessor warrant that the equipment will be in good operating condition at the beginning of the lease term?
   11. Will the lessor extend to the lessee the benefit of all equipment warranties?
   12. Does the lessor agree to make special alterations and improvements to the building to make it suitable for the lessee's use?
      a. What improvements will be made?
      b. At whose cost and expense?
      c. Who will prepare the plans and specifications? (Name of architect and address.)
      d. Are these plans subject to the lessee's prior approval?
      e. When will the work commence?
      f. When will the work be completed?

D. *Transportation Facilities*
   1. Are the dock and loading facilities available and accessible to large trucks?
   2. Is rail transportation service to the building available?
   3. Is truck transportation service to the building available and adequate?

4. Is there ample room to maneuver, load, and park trucks?
5. Is there ample parking for employees who will drive to work?
6. Is public transportation available for employees who do not drive to work?

V. LIABILITY COVERAGE AND RELEASE FROM LIABILITY

A. *Insurance*

1. Is the lessee to carry the public liability insurance for both parties?
2. If so, what are the policy limits to be carried?
   a. Personal injury:
   b. Property damage:
   c. Workmen's Compensation:
3. The lessor should agree to accept the liability insurance company that insures the lessee and the policy form it issues.
4. Is the lessee to carry fire and extended insurance for both parties?
5. If so, what is the amount of insurance to be carried?
6. The lessor should agree to accept the fire insurance company that insures the lessee's properties and the policy form it issues in the state where the building is located.

B. *Waiver of Subrogation*

1. Will each party agree to waive claims against the other party for damage to property?
2. Is the waiver to be only to the extent such property is covered by fire insurance policies?
3. Does each party agree to notify its fire insurance carrier of this provision?
4. Does each party agree to have the fire insurance policies endorsed, if necessary, to prevent invalidation of coverage by reason of such mutual waivers?

C. *Lessor's Non-Liability for Damages*

1. Does the lessor request a provision excusing him from all liability for injuries to persons or property arising out of the use of the property?
2. Does the lessee wish to excuse the lessor from injuries caused by his lessor's own negligence in making structural repairs, alterations, and so forth?
3. Does the lessee wish to excuse the lessor from injuries caused by latent defects in the building when it was turned over to the lessee?

VI. Destruction or Condemnation

A. *Total Destruction of Building*

1. Does the lessor agree that it is his responsibility to rebuild the building if it is a total loss by fire or other casualty?
2. All parties should agree that the fire insurance proceeds are to be made available for such rebuilding.
3. Is the lessor to have a reasonable period of time after the fire in which to decide whether to rebuild or not? (The lessor should have the right to elect not to rebuild only if a year or two is left to run on the lease term when the fire occurred.)
4. Will the lessor agree to notify the lessee of his decision on whether he elects to rebuild or not within that time?
5. Does the lessor agree that the rent is to abate from the date of the fire until the premises are rebuilt and again ready for occupancy?
6. What is the meaning of the term "total destruction"?
7. If the lessor is required or elects to rebuild:
   a. The lease should continue in effect during the rebuilding.
   b. Will rent abate during rebuilding?
   c. When is the rebuilding work to commence?
   d. Does the lessor agree to undertake the work promptly after being able to take possession of the premises and to prosecute the work diligently?
   e. When is the rebuilding work to be completed?
   f. Is the lessee to have the right to approve the architect selected by the lessor to supervise the rebuilding (which approval is not to be unreasonably withheld)?
   g. If the insurance proceeds are insufficient to cover the entire cost of rebuilding, does the lessor agree to put up the difference?
8. If the lessor has an election not to rebuild, and so elects:
   a. Is the lease to terminate as of the date of the fire or other casualty?
   b. Will the rent abate as of the date of the fire or other casualty?
   c. Is the lessee to have the right to then elect to rebuild, using the fire insurance proceeds to do so? If so, the lessee should give the lessor notice of his election within a specified time.

B. *Partial Destruction of Building*

1. Will the lessor or lessee agree that it is his responsibility to rebuild the building if it is partially destroyed or damaged by fire or other casualty?
2. All parties should agree that the fire insurance proceeds are to be made available for such rebuilding.
3. Does the lessor agree that a portion of the rent is to abate from the date of the fire until the premises are rebuilt and again ready for occupancy?
4. What is the formula or standard for measuring what portion of the rent is to abate?
5. What is the meaning of "partial destruction"?
6. When is the rebuilding work to commence?
7. Does the party responsible for rebuilding agree to undertake the work promptly after taking possession of the damaged portion and to prosecute the work diligently?
8. When is the rebuilding work to be completed?
9. If the lessor has the right to select the architect who is to supervise the rebuilding, does the lessee have a right to approve the choice?
10. What is the standard of quality of the rebuilding?
11. If the insurance proceeds are insufficient to cover the entire cost of the rebuilding, does the lessor or lessee agree to put up the difference? Is there any maximum limit on the amount to be put up?
12. If the insurance proceeds are diverted to the lessor's mortgage company to pay off a portion of the outstanding mortgage debt, does the lessor agree to replace the proceeds thus diverted?

C. *Condemnation*

1. Does the lessee agree to surrender his share of any condemnation award if all or a portion of the land and building are taken for public purposes?
2. Is condemnation in this vicinity probable or likely?
3. If only a portion of the property is taken, has the lessee the right to terminate the lease if the portion that remains is not sufficient for lessee's needs?
4. How do you measure that portion?
5. Is the rent abated from the date that the lessee must surrender possession and not the date title to the property passes to the public body?
6. How much is the rent to be abated in the case of a partial taking? What is the formula to determine this?

SOURCE: Copyright 1971 by The American Law Institute. Reprinted with the permission of *The Practical Lawyer*. Subscription rates $15 a year; $2 a single issue. "Negotiating the Lease of an Office-Warehouse Building" by Philip G. Meyers appeared in the March 1971 issue, Vol. 17, No. 3.

Q. *How does tax abatement work with regard to rehabilitation and other construction outlined in special legislation?*

A. The following rehab case in New York City provides a good example of how a tax abatement program works:

PROVISIONS OF THE NEW YORK CITY PROPERTY TAX INCENTIVE PROGRAM

New York City provides both an exemption from and an abatement of real estate taxes in order to stimulate residential rehabilitation. Any increase in assessed valuation resulting from certain types of qualifying expenditures is exempt from taxation for a period of 12 years. In addition to this exemption for rehabilitation expenditures, taxes on the property are abated for nine years under a formula that applies 8⅓ percent of the improvement cost (rehabilitation cost) against the taxable assessed value of the property. Because the 8⅓ percent abatement credit frequently exceeds the tax due, the property taxpayer is permitted to apply the cumulative unused abatement credit against taxes assessed for an additional 11 years. The total amount of the abatement cannot exceed 90 percent of the improvement cost (rehabilitation cost).

The effect of the New York City property tax relief program can be demonstrated through an analysis of the tax relief enjoyed by one rehabilitated unit. The unit chosen is a composite based on median data for low-income rehabilitation projects in New York City:

Median per unit development cost in New York City

Land cost	$ 400
Acquisition of existing structure	1,300
Rehab cost	18,900
Cost expended during construction	2,200
Total Development Cost	$22,800

Assumed Assessed Valuation

Median assessed value prior to rehab	$ 2,200
Assumed assessed value of rehab expenditures	12,500
Total Assessed Value	$14,700

Assuming that the entire assessed value of the unit were taxable at the 1973–1974 New York City tax rate ($6.90 per $100 of assessed value), the unit would ordinarily be subject to an annual property tax of $1,014 (14,700 × 0.069 = $1,014). Under the exemption provisions of the program, however, the $862 that would otherwise be due as tax on the assessed value of the improvements ($12,500 × 0.069 = $862) is exempt. In addition, $152 would ordinarily be due on the assessed value of the property prior to the improvements ($2,200 × 0.069 = $152). This tax is fully abated by the credit applied against it under the abatement provisions of the program.

ABATEMENT CREDIT

Annual Abatement Credit = 8⅓ percent of improvement cost (rehabilitation cost) for each of the first nine years.

Annual Abatement Credit = 0.083 × $18,900
Annual Abatement Credit = $1,570

The abatement credit exceeds the tax by $1,418 ($1,570 − 152 = $1,418). This amount can be carried forward by the taxpayer and used as an abatement credit in years 10 through 20 (provided that the total amount of the taxes *abated* does not exceed 90 percent of qualified rehabilitation cost.) . . .

The result of the combined exemption and abatement provisions is that the owner of the unit pays no taxes during the 20-year period following rehabilitation. This assumes that neither the applicable tax rate nor the assessed value of the unit changes. Thus, New York City foregoes $1,014 of property taxes in each of the 20 years. The present value of the property taxes foregone for 20 years discounted at 6 percent, is approximately $11,000.

SOURCE: *The Impact and Effects of Section 167(K) on the Rehabilitation of Multifamily Property*, Washington, D.C.: Touche Ross & Co., 1974 for HUD, pp. 198–201.

As of January, 1976, the city has an additional legal provision for tax abatement that gives substantial benefits to anyone who converts a commercial building to residential use. It enables developers to recoup about 60 percent of investment in any conversion by reducing real estate taxes over a period of at least nine years. Extensive renovation can result in developers not paying any taxes for up to nine years. (New York Times, 2/1/76)

Q. *You have been asked to lead a real estate discussion forum on appraisal assessment practices at a regional conference. Aside from the usual discussion of statutory provisions governing ad valorem taxation, what other points of interest should you consider presenting before an audience drawn from many states and communities?*

A. Several aspects of a recent federally sponsored study (*A Study of Property Taxes and Urban Blight,* Washington, D.C.: Arthur D. Little, Inc. for HUD, Jan. 1973) might generate interesting discussion and provide insights for more meaningful assessment of properties. For example, a continuing problem is equalization (spreading of the tax burden) among various kinds of properties in different neighborhoods. Some neighborhoods are stable, some are declining, while still other areas are ascending in demand due to new construction and/or extensive rehabilitation. Table A lists ten major cities and outlines the measures employed in making estimates of fair market value. It also indicates whether the means by which assessment offices recognize changes in neighborhoods. Some cities rely upon a cyclical reassessment policy while others employ neighborhood assessment versus sales ratios to check the validity of the assessments placed on various kinds of properties.

The assessment/sales ratio can be meaningful with the following kind of analysis:

$$Q = \frac{\text{Assessment/Sales Ratio in Blighted Neighborhood}}{\text{Assessment/Sales Ratio in Upward Transitional Neighborhood}}$$

Table B shows the results of derivations of Q for a number of cities. This involved a total of 420 multifamily properties.

An additional matter of interest might involve the assessment criteria for Section 236 housing (low and moderate income). As of the time of the study, the guidelines used were those as outlined in Table C.

Table A
Assessment standards by city

City	*Assessment Formulas*	*Neighborhood Cycle*	*Use of Neighborhood Assessment/Sales Ratios To Confirm Assessments*
Atlanta	• Gross Rent Multiplier also other criteria	No general cycle Reassess neighborhoods with greatest sales activity	No
Baltimore	• Homes: Comparable Sales • Industrial: Reproduction Costs • Rental: Variable Rent Properties • Multiplier	5 years	Yes
Chicago	• Replacement-Depreciation	4 years	No
Detroit Sales	• Replacement-Depreciation • Comparable • Capitalized Income Stream	No general cycle Reassess all neighborhoods where assessment/sales ratios out of line	Yes
Nashville	• Capitalize Standard Income Formula by Building Type	No general cycle Reassess neighborhoods with greatest sales activity	No

Oklahoma City	• Use classification formula giving cost per sq. ft. of new construction and rate of depreciation by p property type	No general cycle Last city-wide reassessment in 1952	No
Philadelphia	• No set formula	No general cycle	No
Portland	• Cost-Depreciation Neighborhood Adjustment • Comparable Sales • Capitalized Income Stream	5 years	Yes
Providence	• Replacement Cost-Depreciation • Capitalized Income Stream • Comparable Sales	No general cycle Last city-wide reassessment in 1960	No
San Francisco	• Comparable Sales • Replacement Cost-Depreciation	No general cycle Reassess all neighborhoods where assessment/sales ratios more than 6% off target	Yes

Table B
Dispersion of assessment/sales ratios by city

City	Coefficient of Dispersion, 1966*	Systematic Variation Q, 1970**
Providence	15.4	5.2
Portland	18.3	.8
Atlanta	18.3	2.2
Oklahoma City	18.7	1.1
Nashville	19.0	.8
Detroit	20.4	1.2
Baltimore	24.3	11.5
Chicago	24.5	13.2
Philadelphia	26.3	10.3
San Francisco	28.9	1.0

*Standard deviation about median.

$$**Q = \frac{\text{Assessment/Sales Ratio in Blighted Neighborhood}}{\text{Assessment/Sales Ratio in Upward Transitional Neighborhood}}$$

NOTES: Standard deviation about median is a measure of dispersion about a central value, the median. It is the sum of the squared difference between the sample median and the individual observations. The figures for 1966 are based on all single family homes for which assessment and sales information was collected by the Census of Governments. Comparison of the two columns should be guarded because of the vastly different sample sizes involved.

Table C
Criteria for assessing 236 rehab projects

City	Criteria
Atlanta	Now reviewing assessment standards, intend to increase assessments. Subsidized projects should receive no tax concessions if they can generate positive cash flow when fully taxed.
Baltimore	6% of Gross Rent
Chicago	*Ad hoc* assessments—trying to work out standards with civic groups. "We need guidelines from the Feds."
Detroit	Nonprofit groups: 10% of net shelter rent; Profit groups: "Reasonable fraction" of construction cost.
Nashville	Unknown
Oklahoma City	236 Program just starting. No concessions.
Philadelphia	Now treat as if private rentals, assessment based on project's income; "awaiting additional information from federal authorities." Have several appeals pending.
Portland	Estimate sale value on private market.
Providence	12% of Potential Gross Rent—5% vacancy allowance.
San Francisco	Use income approach, with adjustment for "lower quality" of income from 236 projects.

Q. *In undertaking any appraisals pursuant to the Bankruptcy Act (11 USCA, Sec 1), what is the value concept employed and what are some guiding parameters?*

A. The concept is "fair valuation" and is defined as the fair cash value or the fair market value of the property as between one who wants to purchase and one who wants to sell the property, or the value that can be made available within a reasonable time by the owner of the property for payment of debts (60P 2nd 979).

An important element in implementing the fair valuation concept is a determination, on the valuation date, whether the bankrupt was, in fact, a going concern (67 F. 2nd 669). If, in fact, it is established that a going concern premise is applicable, then scrap, wrecker's prices, or junk values do not apply.

"Going concern" means the value of an operation (plant, business, or the like) in successful operation; the value of a plant as a whole upon which the company is entitled to a fair return as distinguished from its bare physical value (167 P. 995). Going concern is an asset that arises from having an established or going business.

Several views prevail regarding going concern. One view holds that if the financial outlook is unfavorable, this in itself does not affect the character of the business as a going concern for the purpose of valuation. Other judicial forums regard a condition of being financially dead (bankrupt) as precluding consideration of going concern value.

Q. *As a broker I operate in a number of states searching for sites suitable for large-scale development. What basic reading and research would you suggest upon entering a new area of interest?*

A. In the last several years a number of states have enacted laws and related administrative regulations thereunder concerning land development. Depending upon the scale of the venture, location, and use, the following table outlines the various restrictions and controls on land development.

State land use programs

State	Type of State Program			Coastal Zone Management[4]	Wetlands Management[5]
	Comprehensive Permit System[1]	Coordinated Incremental[2]	Mandatory Local Planning[3]		
Alabama				X	
Alaska		X		X	
Arizona		X			
Arkansas					
California		X		X	
Colorado					
Connecticut		X		X	X
Delaware		X		X	X
Florida	X	X	X	X	X
Georgia		X		X	X
Hawaii	X	X		X	
Idaho			X		
Illinois				X	
Indiana		X		X	
Iowa					
Kansas					
Kentucky					
Louisiana				X	X
Maine	X	X	X (LTD)	X	X
Maryland		X		X	X
Massachusetts				X	X
Michigan				X	
Minnesota		X		X	X
Mississippi				X	X
Missouri					X
Montana		X	X		
Nebraska			X		
Nevada		X	X		
New Hampshire				X	X
New Jersey				X	X
New Mexico		X			
New York	X	X		X	X
North Carolina		X		X	X
North Dakota					
Ohio				X	
Oklahoma					
Oregon		X	X	X	
Pennsylvania				X	X
Rhode Island		X		X	X
South Carolina				X	
South Dakota					
Tennessee					
Texas				X	X
Utah		X			
Vermont	X	X			X
Virginia			X	X	X
Washington		X		X	X
West Virginia					
Wisconsin		X		X	X
Wyoming		X	X		

[1]State has authority to require permits for certain types of development.
[2]State-established mechanism to coordinate state land use-related problems.
[3]State requires local governments to establish a mechanism for land use planning (e.g., zoning, comprehensive plan, planning commission).
[4]State is participating in the federally funded coastal zone management program authorized by the Coastal Zone Management Act of 1972.
[5]State has authority to plan or review local plans or the ability to control land use in the wetlands.
[6]State has authority to determine the siting of power plants and related facilities.
[7]State has statutory authority to regulate surface mines. (A) State has adopted rules and regulations: (B) State has issued technical guidelines.
[8]State has established rules, or is in the process of establishing rules, regulations, and guidelines for the identification and designation of areas of critical state concern (e.g., environmentally fragile areas, areas of historical significance.

Power Plant Siting[6]	Surface Mining[7]	Designation of Critical Areas[8]	Differential Assessment Laws[9]	Floodplain Management[10]	Statewide Shorelands Act[11]
X	A			X	
X			B		
X			A	X	
X	A,B		A	X	
X	X		C	X	
X	X	X	A	X	
X			B	X	
			A		X
X	A	X	A,C		
	A,B				
X	X	X	B	X	
	X		A		
X	A,B		B	X	
	A,B		A	X	
	A,B		A	X	
	A,B				
X	A,B		B		
X	A	X	B	X	
X	A,B	X	B	X	
X		X	B	X	
	X		C	X	X
X	X	X	B	X	X
				X	
X	X		A	X	
X	A,B	X	B	X	X
X			B	X	
X		X	B		
X			B,C		
X			B	X	
X	A		A		
X	X	X	B	X	
	X		B	X	
X	A		A		
X	A		B		
	X		A	X	
X	A	X	B		
X	A	X	B		
X			B		
X	A		B		
	A	X	A		
X	A,B				
	X		B		
	A		B		
X	X		C	X	
X	A,B		B		
X	A		B	X	X
	A,B			X	
X	X	X		X	
X	A		A		

[9]State has adopted tax measure which is designed to give property tax relief to owners of agricultural or open space lands. (A) Preferential Assessment Program—Assessment of eligible land is based upon a selected formula, which is usually use-value. (B) Deferred Taxation—Assessment of eligible land is based upon a selected formula, which is usually use-value and provides for a sanction, usually the payment of back taxes, if the land is converted to a non-eligible use. (C) Restrictive Agreements—Eligible land is assessed at its use-value, a requirement that the owner sign a contract, and a sanction, usually the payment of back taxes if the owner violates the terms of the agreement.

[10]State has legislation authorizing the regulation of floodplains.

[11]State has legislation authorizing the regulation of shorelands of significant bodies of water.

SOURCE: Prepared by the Council of State Governments, based on information by the Council of State Governments. *Land Use Planning Reports 1974* and 1975; and the U.S. Department of the Interior, Office of Land Use and Water Planning; and the Resource Land Investigations Program. Data compiled October 1975.

Q. *You are asked by a group of apartment building investors to develop a proposal and plan to contest some large real estate tax increases that the owners feel are excessive. What basic framework should such an analysis follow in order to be meaningful before a taxing commission or appeals forum?*

A. First, each of the properties involved in a tax appeal must be appraised to determine the individual market values. Second, appropriate kinds of similar or competitive properties must be analyzed via share of taxes to net and gross income, on a per unit basis.

The following table illustrates the dynamics of real estate taxes (median) on a per unit basis, predicated on different price structures, for transactions between 1966 and 1970. For example, during this period in Atlanta, the highest increase (63 percent) occured on apartment properties where the sale price was in the range of $5,000–10,000 per unit; the lowest increase affected those apartment buildings selling at $10,000 or more per unit. Discriminatory, capricious, and unwarranted increase might be an allegation in such cases unless there is historical evidence that this mid-group of apartment buildings was previously underassessed. The table indicates the range of changes in the tax liabilities of owners of such properties by price class and geographical location.

Median tax as a percentage of gross rent per unit purchase price 1966–1970

	Purchase Price of Property (Per unit)								
	Less than $5,000			*$5,000–10,000*			*$10,000 and over*		
City	*1966*	*1970*	*Percent Change**	*1966*	*1970*	*Percent Change**	*1966*	*1970*	*Percent Change**
Atlanta	12.0%	18.4	+53%	8.7%	14.2	+ 63%	10.2%	12.8	+ 25%
Baltimore	15.4	14.0	− 9	16.9	16.2	− 4	15.7	14.3	− 4
Chicago	12.3	19.9	+62	13.4	14.2	+ 6	10.4	20.0	+ 92
Detroit	17.3	14.6	−16	14.8	11.9	− 20	15.3	16.2	+ 6
Nashville	7.2	8.3	+15	7.8	7.9	+ 1	8.9	9.4	+ 6
Oklahoma City	12.1	12.6	+.04	12.8	11.2	− 13	15.2	14.0	−.05
Philadelphia	10.8	10.8	0	12.2	6.8	− 44	14.3	16.2	+ 13
Portland	14.8	12.7	−14	8.2	16.8	+105	7.3	15.5	+112
San Francisco	11.2	16.9	+51	11.8	15.8	+ 34	18.8	16.7	− 11
All Cities	11.3	14.8	+31	10.6	12.3	+ 16	11.6	14.4	+ 24

*Computed by the author.

SOURCE: Basic data from "A Study of Property Taxes and Urban Blight," vol. 2, Washington, D.C.: Arthur D. Little, Inc., for HUD, January, 1973.

Q. *What forms of Federal assistance are available to people and their property in event of major disasters?*

A. The following two definitions of a disaster-emergency govern the implementation of the various categories of Federal laws.

DEFINITION OF A MAJOR DISASTER

A "major disaster" means any hurricane, tornado, storm, flood, high water, wind-driven water, tidal wave, tsunami, earthquake, volcanic eruption, landslide, mudslide, snow-storm, drought, fire, explosion or other catastrophe in any part of the United States, which, in the determination of the President, causes damage of sufficient severity and magnitude to warrant major disaster assistance by the Federal Government to supplement the efforts and resources of states, local governments, and relief organizations.

DEFINITION OF AN EMERGENCY

An "emergency" means any hurricane, tornado, storm, flood, high water, wind-driven water, tidal wave, tsunami, earthquake, volcanic eruption, landslide, mudslide, snow-storm, drought, fire, explosion, or other catastrophe in any part of the United States, which requires Federal emergency assistance to supplement state and local efforts to save lives and protect property, public health and safety or to avert or lessen the threat of a disaster.

Eight categories of disaster-emergency assistance plus preparedness and planning assistance are provided to state and local governmental units. These categories and subelements are as follows:

1. Agriculture
   Crop Insurance, Crop Loss Disaster Program, Disease and Pest Control for Plants and Animals, Emergency Conservation Measures Program, Emergency Livestock Feed Program, Emergency Loans, Forest Management and Utilization, General Information on Agricultural Assistance, Rural Electrification and Telephone Loan Adjustments, Timber Removal, Timber Sale Contracts,

2. Business
   Aid to Major Sources of Employment, Business and Industrial Development Loans, Business Repair Loans, Economic Injury Loans, Industrial Development Grants, Product Loss Loans,

3. Emergency Services
   Communications, Debris Removal, Flood Fighting and Rescue Operations, Food, Water, and Shelter, Protection, Evacuation, Search, and Rescue, Public Transportation, Victim Identification: Technical Assistance and Grants,

4. Fire Suppression
   Fire Suppression Assistance, Fire Suppression and Emergency Rehabilitation of Indian Lands,

5. Flood Prevention and Protection
   Bank Protection, Beach Erosion Control, Flood Control Projects, Flood Insurance Program, Flood Plain Management, Flood Prevention for Forest Lands, Repair or Restoration of Flood Control Works, Resource Conservation and Development, Snagging and Clearing for Flood Control, Watershed Protection and Flood Prevention Loans, Watershed Protection: Technical Assistance and Grant,

6. Health Services
   Contaminated Food and Drugs, Crisis Counseling Assistance, Health, Medical, and Sanitation, Indian Health Services, Radiological Emergency Assistance, Vector Control,

7. Housing
   Adjustments to Federal Loans: Department of Housing and Urban Development; Veterans Administration, Home Repair Loans, Insured Home Loans, Mobile Home Financing, Property Improvements, Rental Housing, Rural Housing Disaster Loans, Temporary Housing,

8. Individual and Family Assistance
   Emergency Food Stamp Program, Individual and Family Grants, Legal Services, Tax Information, Unemployment Assistance.

Q. *As a broker, I was planning on an exclusive listing of a large industrial plant. Management advised me that they had good title as they purchased the facility from the U.S. Government a number of years ago. A check of the deed at the courthouse revealed reference to a "national security clause." What is the importance of this provision?*

A. Many large and specialized industrial plants were disposed of after World War II. Some contained provisions of 50 U.S.C. 451. The basis and limitations of the law is outlined below. Whether the provision is applicable could have a bearing on the market for and marketability of the industrial facility you propose to sell.

§ 452. Definitions

As used in this chapter—

(1) The term "Secretary" means Secretary of Defense.

(2) The term "Defense Industrial Reserve" means (A) a general reserve of industrial manufacturing equipment, including machine tools, selected by the Secretary of Defense for retention for national defense or for other emergency use; (B) those industrial plants and installations held by and under the control of the Department of Defense in active or inactive status, including Government-owned/Government-operated plants and installations and Government-owned/contractor-operated plants and installations which are retained for use in their entirety, or in part, for production of military weapons systems, munitions, components, or supplies; (C) those industrial plants and installations under the control of the Secretary which are not required for the immediate need of any department or agency of the Government and which should be sold, leased, or otherwise disposed of.

(3) The term "plant equipment package" means a complement of active and idle machine tools and other industrial manufacturing equipment held by and under the control of the Department of Defense and approved by the Secretary for retention to produce particular defense material or defense supporting items at a specific level of output in the event of emergency.

As amended Nov. 16, 1973, Pub.L. 93–155, Title VIII, § 809, 87 Stat. 617.

Q. *A large real estate management firm is planning to lease several facilities to the United States Government. What is the importance of the Economy Act in such a transaction?*

A. The so-called Economy Act (40 U.S.C. 278a), which is included in all leases prepared by the Government, limits the amount of rent payable, exclusive of services, under a lease. The only exclusion is the limitation in the law and cases involving unimproved land (38 Comp. Gen. 143). The following is the kay language of this law.

§ 278a. Lease of Buildings to Government; Maximum Rental

After June 30, 1932, no appropriation shall be obligated or expended for the rent of any building or part of a building to be occupied for Government purposes at a rental in excess of the per annum rate of 15 per centum of the fair market value of the rented premises at date of the lease under which the premises are to be occupied by the Government nor for alterations, improvements, and repairs of the rented premises in excess of 25 per centum of the amount of the rent for the first year of the rental term, or for the rental term if less than one year: *Provided*, That the provisions of this section shall not apply to leases made prior to June 30, 1932, except when renewals thereof are made after such date, nor to leases of premises in foreign countries for the foreign services of the United States: *Provided further*, That the provisions of this section as applicable to rentals, shall apply only where the rental to be paid shall exceed $2,000 per annum.

June 30, 1932, c. 314, § 322, 47 Stat. 412; Mar. 3, 1933, c. 212, Title II, § 15, 47 Stat. 1517.

Q. *What is the implied warranty of habitability and how does it apply to real estate?*

A. Essentially the legal premise of habitability concerns the potential use and enjoyment of an improved property. For example, in a case where buyers agreed to have a house constructed that included the drilling of a well, a court ruled that providing an unpolluted water supply was essential to contract performance on the part of the builder. The Supreme Court of Pennsylvania stated that "a potable water supply is essential to any functioning living unit; without drinking water, the house cannot be used for the intended purpose." (Elderkin v. Gaster, 288 A2nd 771)

Q. *In recent years there has been some discussion relating to rules requiring developers of land to provide a certain percentage of completed housing units for low and moderate income households. What are some recent developments in this area?*

A. A recent Virginia case (Board of Supervisors v. De Groff Enterprises, Inc., 214 Va. 235) involved a zoning ordinance that required a developer of fifty or more units to commit himself, before rezoning or site plan approval, to the allotment of at least 15 percent of the dwelling units for low and moderate income housing. The court found the ordinance invalid stating that police power, in this instance, could not be used to accomplish the particular public purpose. In addition, the decision indicates that the court felt the ordinance exceeded the authority and intent of the state enabling legislation.

Q. *I have been working as a consultant to several developers who operate on a nationwide basis. Since a number of them specialize in nonresidential development, I have been puzzled by a number of communities that permit only single-family or residential development, that is, essentially a single urban use. What recourse, if any, is available and what have the courts been doing in this area of restricted land use control?*

A. The judiciary usually addresses itself to two key matters when a challenge is made of city or town zoning regulations. They consider the extent of conformity of the zoning ordinance to the state enabling act, and also the reasonableness of the local legislation limiting land use. A key element of the local code is the preamble. This usually outlines the objectives of the zoning ordinance, which in turn can be related to the actual implementation of the ordinance within the community since its enactment.

In a 1964 Michigan case (Gundersen v. Bingham Farms, 372 Mich 352, 126 W. 2nd 715), the court ruled invalid an ordinance that restricted property in a municipality to residential uses. The principal basis of the decision was that no enabling legislation had been passed and, therefore, the action of the community had no legal sanction. Furthermore, even with an enabling act, the reasonableness test would be applied. This test would judge the suitability of the proposed use of the land and location, in light of community objectives related to conservation and general trends in the area.

An opposite result obtained in a 1970 Missouri case (McDermott v. Calverton Park, 454 S. W. 2nd 577). Here the zoning ordinance did not provide for any commercial use while the zoning code, with certain exceptions, limited the land use to single family dwellings. The court recognized that, due to the location of the community, it was essentially a "bedroom town." The court went on to state that there was nothing in the legislative intent that required communities to zone for a multiplicity of land uses.

Basically, the decisions reflect support for restrictive zoning in more recent years. However, each case has to be treated and evaluated on its merits. Matters of location, kind and quality of land, adjacent land uses, emerging nonresidential land use developments, and so on, are pertinent matters that should bear attention in any potential contest of a restricted community zoning ordinance.

Q. *Many zoning ordinances permit schools or educational use of buildings and land in residential areas, either in specified districts or as an exception. What are the interpretations given as to what constitutes a school or educational use?*

A. A basic tenet of the courts is recognition of the fact that zoning laws are essentially in derogation of common-law real property rights. Accordingly, if the zoning law is restrictive in nature, it will be strictly construed. If the zoning provision is permissive, it will be literally construed in favor of the owners of real property interests affected. Likewise, any technical language contained in a zoning ordinance will be interpreted according to common usage and understanding in the area or community. Therefore, since the term "school" is generic in nature, its connotation must be given weight in the context of community and public perception. The following illustrate the broad array of situations involving a school or educational use of property:

1. Teaching of horsemanship was upheld as an educational function. Burgoon v. Zoning Hearing Board (1971), 277 A. 2nd 837. This is a Pennsylvania case.
2. Teaching of ceramics, painting, glazing, and so forth in a garage was held not to constitute a school under a zoning ordinance. Chicopee v. Jakubowski, 202 N. E. 2nd 913, a 1964 Massachusettts case.
3. Use of a barn to teach and conduct classes in ballet and judo was held as not constituting a "private educational institution" within the meaning of a zoning ordinance in Foos v. Lower Merian Township Zoning Board of Adjustment (1961), 26 Pa. D & C 2nd 256.
4. A dancing school operated in a home was not considered a school within the meaning of zoning ordinance provisions. Myrtle Beach v. Mayer, 181 S.E. 2nd 265, a 1971 South Carolina case.
5. Use of premises for a kindergarten and nursery school was not permitted in a Louisiana case. Parish of Jefferson v. Carl, 195 So. 2nd 401.
6. A privately owned and operated country day school, chartered by the state, was held to be within the meaning of a "school" in a village zoning ordinance. Brookville v. Paulgene Realty Corp., 180 N.E. 2nd. 905, a 1960 New York case.
7. It was held that the proposed use of a 36.85-acre estate for a religious education center was acceptable within the meaning of the zoning ordinance permitting parochial schools in residential districts. Diocese of Central New York v. Schwartzer (1960), 217 N.Y. 2nd 567.
8. Use of a 28-acre site in a residential district for a conference and leadership training center was denied. B'Nai B'Rith Foundation v. Walworth County Board of Adjustment (1973), 208 N.W. 2nd. 113, a Wisconsin case.
9. A house used as a residence by a prep school, nearby but not adjacent to the house, was construed as a school use within meaning of local laws. State v. Laurel Crest Academy 198 A. 229, a 1963 Connecticut case.

Q. *In the early part of the century, zoning was recognized as a valid instrument of the police power of the state (Euclid v. Ambler Realty Co.). During the intervening period its expansion has become evident in many forms of urban development. What are the areas and kinds of zoning activity currently prevalent in urbanized areas?*

A. The following list of kinds of zoning, as to form, substance, and objectives, is representative of present day zoning activities:

- *Impact Zoning.* A zoning system designed to provide a before-the-fact assessment of how a proposed development will affect the community in terms of community growth rate, provision of public services, costs and benefits, and impact on the environment.
- *Bonus (Incentive) Zoning.* A zoning technique that provides for flexibility in development with a built-in system for trade-offs beneficial on the one hand to the public and on the other hand to the developer.
- *Conditional Zoning.* A zoning change (rezoning) granted to a property owner subject to conditions other than those applicable to all land similarly classified. If deed restrictions or covenants are executed as a device to guarantee compliance with the stipulated conditions of rezoning, the term "contract" zoning is often used to identify such conditional zoning.
- *Back (Down, Rollback) Zoning.* A zoning change (rezoning) that reclassifies property from a higher intensity use classification to a lower intensity use classification.
- *Conservation Zoning.* Zoning regulations designed to protect and preserve, or guard against hazards to or associated with certain public facilities, or special areas or features of land development within a community. Examples of such regulations include floodplain zoning, airport area zoning, aesthetic zoning, and historic preservation zoning.
- *Performance Zoning.* A term used to identify each of the following:

  (A) A zoning regulation that includes technical standards of performance or operation applicable to all permitted uses within a given zoning district classification. Typically this type of regulation specifies maximum permitted levels for emission of noise, smoke, dust, and glare.
  (B) A zoning regulation that allows for a variety of considerations (land use, intensity, site variables, design variables, and availability of public facilities) to govern—within specified limits—permitted land use and development.

- *Floating Zone.* A zoning district classification that is included in a zoning ordinance text, but that is not (at least initially) included on the zoning ordinance map.
- *Planning Unit Development (PUD) Zoning.* A particular type of floating zone or floating district classification (1) that typically includes a minimum area requirement and provisions requiring the applicant for rezoning to submit for approval plans and specifications for development of the entire area, but (2) that allows the applicant considerable latitude in determining design, layout, and uses permitted within the area rezoned.
- *Air-rights Zoning.* Zoning regulations that are applied to uses that occupy the air space immediately above land—primarily above land occupied by public and semipublic utility or service operations.
- *Nonconforming Use Amortization.* The technique utilized in zoning ordinances to make equitable provision, over a specified period of time, for the eventual elimination of structures and uses that do not conform to the zoning district requirements of the district in which they are located at the time of adoption or amendment of the zoning ordinance.
- *Extraterritorial Zoning.* The exercise of zoning regulations by a local government in areas outside the corporate boundaries of its jurisdiction.
- *Zoning Moritoria.* A waiting period established by a local governing body during which all proposed zoning amendments, proposed zoning amendments of a particular type, and/or proposed zoning amendments within a specified geographic area are held in abeyance.
- *Transfer Development Rights Zoning.* A zoning system that permits the owner of property to transfer to other property, as "unused development rights," the difference between the density that would be allowed under existing zoning regulations and that which actually exists on any given parcel of land.
- *Subdivision Regulations.* A police power regulation of a local jurisdiction over the platting and conversion of raw land into building lots. In exchange for the privilege of recording a plat and selling lots, a developer is required to conform to the standards and requirements of the local government's subdivision regulations. Subdivisions are required to conform to the local government's site improvement standards for streets, water, sewer, drainage, lot design, and street design and must conform to local plans for major streets, utilities, drainage, schools, parks, and other public facilities.

- *Mandatory Dedication*. A land or facility acquisition technique associated with subdivision regulations, whereby the developer is required to dedicate certain properties, rights-of-way, easements and/or facilities to the local jurisdiction in which the subdivision lies. Such properties, rights-of-way, easements, and/or facilities that must be dedicated are to be an amount sufficient to meet the demand created by the development.

Q. *The preservation of historic or other kinds of special buildings has captured the imagination and interest of many groups of citizens. What are some prevailing legal mechanisms available to implement these group objectives?*

A. The following seven techniques are most frequently used. Their adoption is dependent on state and local laws.

1. *Fee Simple Acquisition*. This legal technique is almost always used by government or nonprofit agencies. Fee simple acquisition involves the sale of the structure with all legal rights attached. Due to the high cost of buying a structure, this technique is hard to implement. However, once accomplished, the organization has full rights to the property. One of the problems with this technique is that once the structure is acquired by a public or nonprofit organization, the structure is off the local real estate tax rolls.

2. *Easements*. Easements are legal restrictions imposed on the use of a parcel of land for the benefit of someone besides the owner. Easements may lower taxes for the owner because the owner is giving up some rights to his property, thereby lowering the value of the property to a new prospective owner. If the easement is donated to a charitable organization, a charitable deduction may be made on income taxes.

3. *Facade Easement*. This is a particular kind of easement where the rights to the exterior of the structure are either donated or sold to someone other than the owner.

4. *Reversions and Remainders*. This legal technique refers to action by an organization that restores a structure (usually one of considerable merit), while the present tenant remains in the structure. After the death of the tenant, the property rights will revert to the restorer. Owners may be able to receive a tax deduction by granting the structure to such an organization.

5. *Restrictive Covenants*. A restrictive covenant is a private method of controlling the use of a parcel of land. Usually a covenant restriction is written into the deed citing restrictions

designed to preserve the historical character of the land or structure.

6. *Historic District Ordinance.* An historic district is a geographically defined area that can range in size from one block to include an entire city. An historic district ordinance will cite certain restrictions that pertain to every site and structure within the district, not just to the significant ones. The ordinance is administered by an historic district commission, whose powers may include controls over alterations and additions to a structure within the district; ability to issue a stay of demolition for buildings within the district; and the ability to acquire land through gift, purchase, or even eminent domain.

7. *Landmark Commission Ordinance.* A landmark ordinance pertains to the historically, architecturally, and culturally significant structures within a given area, usually a city. A landmark commission ordinance would usually pertain to such structures as the jail, the library, city hall, some residential structures, and several churches. A landmarks commission, like an historic district commission, will have the power to impose a stay of demolition over these structures. Unlike an historic district, however, a landmarks ordinance has no control over adjacent or nearby structures.

Q. *Because of broad interest in environmental matters in recent years, attention has been focused on wetlands and marshlands. What are some of the basic issues involved?*

A. Recent controversies in the state of New Jersey can illustrate the issues and related problems. All land bordering on navigable waterways is subjected to the ebb and flow of tides. The land that is not touched by water belongs to the owner, while that entirely under water belongs to the State. The land between high and low water marks is the area of dispute. Under an old English doctrine this area belonged to the king. In the United States, some states use the mean high-tide line while others use the low-tide as a demarcation point between the sovereign interest and those of property owners. Figure 1 shows the relative position of these crucial points. In 1967, in O'Neil v. State Highway Department, 50 N.J. 307, 235 A. 2nd 1, the court ruled that the sovereign claim would be limited within the mean high-tide boundaries of a watercourse. In New Jersey this matter affects approximately 250,000 acres of land. Application of the O'Neil doctrine involves the use of titles, maps, and other historical evidence accumulated since 1664 to establish changes, in the intervening years, between the State's interest and those of private owners in their respective chains of title.

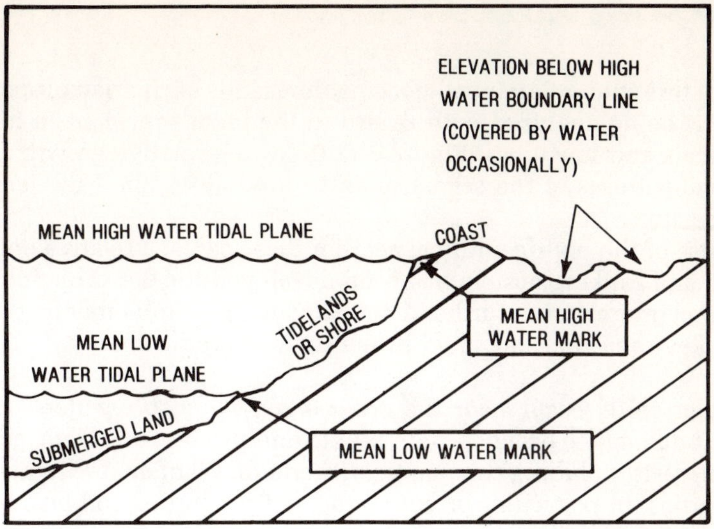

Illustration by *Gail de P. Burke*

FIG. 1. This diagram indicates both the mean high water mark and the mean low water mark. Under the present New Jersey application of the tidelands doctrine, the mean high water mark is the recognized boundary line. Previously, however, the State claimed not only the land below the mean high-tide mark, but also those areas designated on the diagram as being at an "elevation below high water boundary line."

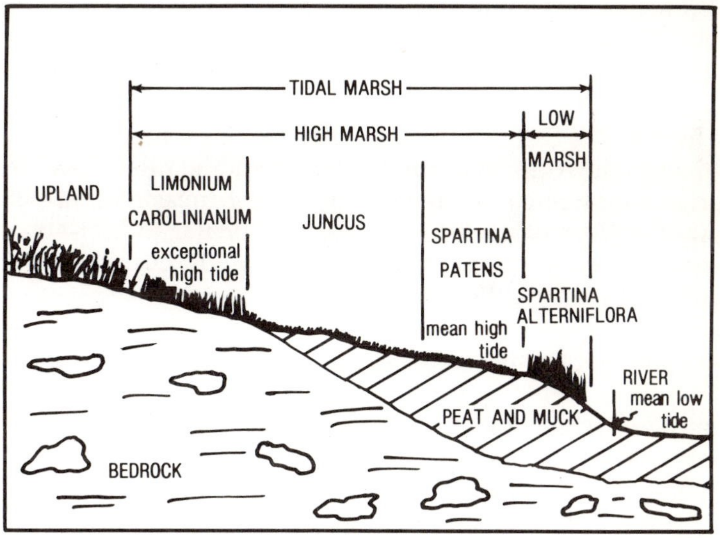

Illustration by *Gail de P. Burke*

FIG. 2.

SOURCE: Alfred A. Porro, Jr. and Lorraine S. Teleky, "Marshland Title Dilemma: A Tidal Phenomenon," *Seton Hall Law Review*, vol. 3, p. 323. Reprinted by permission of the editor, illustration by Gail de P. Burke.

Part of this evidentiary jumble facing thousands of riparian property owners is being analyzed with regard to the biota prevelant in high marshlands and low areas. Figure 2 outlines the relative growth and incidence patterns of the several plants found along the New Jersey coastline area.

Because of the multicentury aspects of these cases, a relative point, scoring, and ranking system has been developed for the valuation of the several interests. For further discussion on these and other matters, see the law review article cited in the figures' credit line.

Q. *Oil tanker spills occur near the coast or on navigable waters with resultant damage to beaches, both public and private, and damage to other interests including commercial fisherman. What are the rights of these parties, in particular private owners of properties and business establishments along beach areas?*

A. In a recent decision (1973) involving an oil spill along the coastal waters of Maine, commercial fishermen and clam diggers were affected as were a number of business firms. The latter suffered diminished business from this environmental damage.

As to the fishermen's claims, the court stated:

> Since the fishermen and clam diggers have no individual property rights with respect to the waters and marine life allegedly harmed by the oil spill, their right to recover in the present action depends upon whether they may maintain private actions for damages based upon the alleged tortious invasion of public rights which are held by the State of Maine in trust for the common benefit of all the people. As to this issue, the long standing rule of law is that a private individual can recover in tort for invasion of a public right only if he has suffered damage particular to him—that is, damage different in kind, rather than simply in degree, from that sustained by the public generally.

The court went on to state further that:

> The commercial fishermen and clam diggers in the present cases clearly have a special interest, quite apart from that of the public generally, to take fish and harvest clams from the coastal waters of the State of Maine. The injury of which they complain has resulted from defendants' alleged interference with *their* direct exercise of the public right to fish and to dig clams. It would be an incongruous result for the Court to say that a man engaged in commercial fishing or clamming, and dependent thereon for his livelihood, who may have had his business destroyed by the tortious act of another, should be denied any right to recover for his

> pecuniary loss on the ground that his injury is no different in kind from that sustained by the general public. Indeed, in substantially all of those cases in which commercial fishermen using public waters have sought damages for the pollution or other tortious invasion of those waters, they have been permitted to recover.

Concerning the claims of the business establishments, the court in disallowing any damages, presented the following reasoning:

> Unlike the commercial fishermen and clam diggers, the Old Orchard Beach businessmen do not assert any interference with *their* direct exercise of a public right. They complain only of loss of customers indirectly resulting from alleged pollution of the coastal waters and beaches in which they do not have a property interest. Although in some instances their damage may be greater in degree, the injury of which they complain, which is derivative from that of the public at large, is common to all businesses and residents of the Old Orchard Beach area. In such circumstances, the line is drawn and the courts have consistently denied recovery.

The court further supported its position in quoting a leading authority on torts, William Prosser, as follows:

> Where . . . the pecuniary loss is common to the whole community, or a large part of it, as where a whole area of a town is cut off by a viaduct, or the draining of a good fishing lake affects all the fishing camps in the vicinity, it has been regarded as no different in kind from the common misfortune, and the private action cannot be maintained. Prosser, Law of Torts, *supra*, § 88 at 591.

Q. *What is the best strategy in matters involving cases under the nuisance doctrine, concerning environmental damage to property?*

A. Most cases involving environmental damage to property are quite unique. Nevertheless, so-called comparable cases might be uncovered, providing a basis for the drawing of analogies.

Perhaps a more realistic approach to the development of a theory of a case, in contemplation of litigation, is a two-stage process. First, the kind and degree of actual and/or potential damage must be clearly established. For example, where gases and noxious odors are invading a residential property, identification of the toxic level and potential health hazards from continued use of a housing unit is paramount. From this data flows the potential measure of damages.

The second stage will involve measures of the diminution in the value of the property. From a pure market transaction point of view, it is very difficult to find evidence of a comparable nature to support positions based on "invasion by a particular nuisance." Court decisions offer some guidance, but are inconclusive in terms of the specifics of the level of nuisance damage incurred. Manifestly if, in the case of a house, human habitation is limited or precluded, a total taking or damage may be the measure of damages. Gradations in the extent of damage, from total to nominal, are what make these kinds of cases very difficult.

Q. *With the large number of shopping centers developed in many urbanized and small city areas, leasing and subleasing of space represents an active part of some brokerage offices activities. What are some of the rights and interests that tenants have in off-street parking and other common areas of shopping centers, as these areas indirectly affect the value of the leased space?*

A. There is no single answer or group of answers that can provide a clear-cut basis for evaluation. The best way to obtain an insight is to study, in detail, the existing or proposed lease, including any and all attachments or exhibits to the lease. Lease attachments may include plot plans, areas reserved or designated for parking, or areas outlined for future construction-development. The following cases highlight the extent of diversity of situations and the related judicial thinking in several jurisdictions:

1. In a Virginia case, State-Planters Bank of Commerce & Trusts v. Standard Cary Corp. (1967), 156 SE 2nd 778, the lease had a provision wherein the landlord had the right to rearrange parking and sidewalks and grant related easements. The court ruled that the tenants rights were not violated even though the owner leased to a bank a 35-foot wide strip of land (the lease provided for only 25 feet) for a drive-in banking facility; this resulted in reducing, by ten spaces, the amount of shopping center parking.

2. In one instance, the lease provisions via plot plan attachments showed an area of 50,000 sq. ft for a future building. Subsequently, a total area of 100,000 sq. ft. was used. The court, in this Michigan case, ruled in favor of the leasee. This case involved the expansion of a mall and resulted, as noted by the court, in the elimination of parking for about 250 to 300 cars. (Rogers Plaza, Inc., v. Kresge Co., 1974 189 N.W. Ind. 346.)

3. Though a lease provided that "the tenant's store shall be the last store on the easterly end of the shopping center," a New York court ruled in favor of the owner, thus permitting an extension of the building at that point. One of the controlling

facts in this case, Arralthoon v. Pergament Oceanside Corp. 281 N. Y. Ind. 263 (228 N.E. Ind. 392), was that a plot plan designating the area for parking was not attached to or made part of the tenant's lease.

4. In Gray Drug Stores Inc. v. Foto Fair International, Inc. 288 N.E. Ind. 341 (1971), the Ohio Appellate court granted injunctive relief against the owner prohibiting the construction and maintenance of a drive-in kiosk on the parking area in violation of several lease provisions that stipulated that the parking area be kept open. The owner's argument concerning the preconstruction lease agreement, relating floor areas to amount of parking provided, was rejected by the court.

5. Where a lease provided for a parking ratio of 3-to-1 (that is, three square feet of parking to one square foot of ground construction), as included in an attached plot plan and survey, the owner could not build any additional buildings without maintaining this parking ratio relationship. Thus, in Meadowdale Shopping Center, Inc. v. Meadowdale Lanes, Inc. 231 NE Ind. 466, (1967) an Illinois Appellate Court stated the owner must somehow or somewhere provide the required parking as outlined in the lease agreement.

Q. *In listing properties with riparian rights, many property owners claim additional land, over and above that described in the deed, due to accretion, that is, the process through which land is expanded along a waterway due to a gradual deposit of soil caused by the action of the contiguous waters. What's the best way to handle such cases—with the seller and with a potential buyer?*

A. Probably the best answer is that it all depends on the circumstances of the particular case. The basic rule is that accretions belong to the land they join. The same is true of the opposite development, that is, dereliction—a shrinking of the watercourse back below the usual watermark. The general rules concerning accretion are illustrated by the following case.

The facts of the case are that Hudson owns one acre of land north of Benner County Road and claims all accretion north of the road. Rozman claims part of this new land under the Massachusetts rule, that is, an equitable apportionment; the State Park Authority claims land west of the park. In addition, several other property owners have filed claims. A study of old maps by the court, some dating back to 1887, indicates that the park had frontage directly on the Pacific ocean. The court adopted the rule, prevalent in several other jurisdictions, that the owner of waterfront property

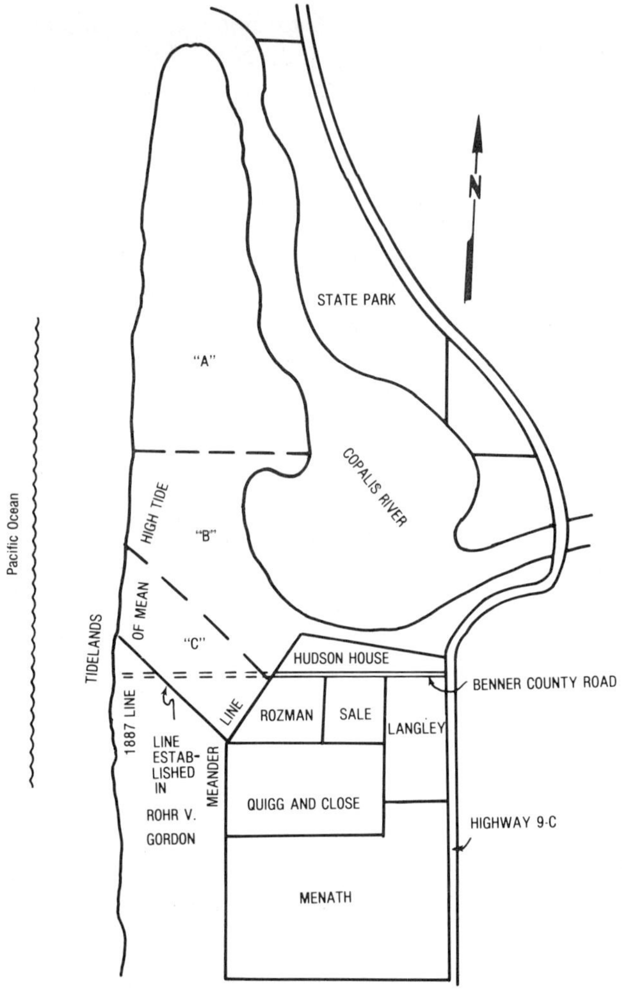

should be protected in the maintenance of access to the water. This position plus the Massachusetts equitable apportionment rule resulted in the State Park Authority getting parcel A; Hudson House received parcel B; and Rozman received parcel C. The other claims were not valid based on the court's findings. The court also stated that any claims under an adverse possession statute must be continuous, hostile, and exclusive to warrant legal cognizance and color of title sanctions.

Q. *What is a dependency ratio and how is it used in urban analysis?*

A. A dependency ratio is the relationship between the productive segment and the dependent part of a population. In a time series context, populations of those under 20 and over 65 years of age are compared with the productive element, that is, those residents between age 20 and under 65. The ratio is computed with the following formula:

$$\text{Dependency Ratio} = \frac{\text{population under 20 + 65 and over}}{\text{population 20 to 64 years}} \times 100$$

Significant changes in the birth rate, for example, have an impact five, ten, and fifteen years later on community facilities like schools, recreational facilities, and so forth. Important shifts in the dependency ratio can signal important impacts. For example, a shortage or excess of classroom space may result, thus reducing or increasing tax revenues needed to support such facilities. Escalating dependency ratios and the incidence of poverty can have a large impact on the value of the standing inventory of real property. At issue is the matter of the economics of what, when, and who is going to pay for the broad array of community services.

Q. *What is the "Rule of 72" concerning the compounding and doubling of an investment?*

A. Basically it concerns the fact that if the product of a rate of interest and a term equals 72 then that interest for that term will result in approximately doubling an initial sum. The following combinations illustrate this relationship:

Years		*Percentage Rate*	*Product*	*Capital Sum Factor*
36	×	2	72	2.039
9	×	8	72	1.99
8	×	9	72	1.9925
7	×	10.3	72	1.986
10	×	7.2	72	2.004

Q. *What segments of the population are most involved in leisure home use and/or ownership?*

A. A recent study developed a profile that highlights those segments of the population owning leisure homes. As the following table shows, higher income groups and those households owning housing with a current market value of $25,000 or more are over-represented in the ownership of leisure homes in relation to their share of total households. Other insights can be obtained from this survey concerning family size, age of head of household, and so forth.

Selected characteristics of U.S. leisure home owners and total U.S. population

	Percent of all households	Percent of leisure home owners	Leisure home owners as a percent of total households
Annual family income			
Less than $5,000	29.4	18.8	2.9
$5,000 to $9,999	30.9	24.5	3.6
$10,000 to $14,999	22.6	23.7	4.7
$15,000 to $24,999	13.2	20.9	7.2
$25,000 or more	3.9	12.1	14.1
Value of primary home			
Less than $15,000	41.3	31.3	3.4
$15,000 to $19,999	20.2	17.8	4.0
$20,000 to $24,999	14.7	13.5	4.1
$25,000 to $34,999	14.1	18.1	5.8
$35,000 to $49,999	6.5	10.7	7.4
$50,000 or more	3.2	8.6	12.2
Tenure of primary homes			
Owned	59.3	73.1	5.6
Rented	35.4	22.7	2.9
Co-op or condominium	0.5	1.1	11.0
Other	4.8	3.1	2.9
Primary residence			
Inside SMSAs	69.1	68.0	4.4
Central city	34.1	31.0	4.1
Urban balance	24.7	26.2	4.8
Remainder	10.4	10.8	4.7
Outside SMSAs	30.9	32.0	4.7
Urban	75.1	75.2	4.5
Rural	24.9	24.8	4.5
Rural-nonfarm	20.0	20.3	4.6
Rural-farm	4.9	4.5	4.1
Places 10,000 to 50,000	20.4	21.9	4.8
Age of head of household			
Less than 25 years	7.1	4.0	2.5
25 to 34 years	21.0	10.0	2.1
35 to 44 years	21.2	18.5	3.9
45 to 54 years	20.1	25.9	5.8
55 to 64 years	17.5	22.7	5.9
65 years or older	13.1	18.9	6.5
Family size			
1 person	17.6	13.3	3.4
2 persons	29.6	35.0	5.3
3 persons	17.2	18.1	4.7
4 or 5 persons	25.2	24.8	4.4
6 or more persons	10.4	8.8	3.8

SOURCE: Richard L. Ragatz Associates, *Recreational Properties: An Analysis of the Markets for Privately Owned Recreational Lots and Leisure Homes* (Springfield, Va.: National Technical Information Service, 1974).

Q. *What is reverse investment?*

A. Reverse investment relates to investment activities of foreign nations or nationals in various kinds of business, industry, or real estate ventures in the United States.

Q. *Every so often we hear about actual or potential negative equities of people who own their homes. How is this possible with a housing shortage?*

A. Negative equities develop when the property depreciates faster than the existing mortgage is being amortized. In periods and/or markets with considerable price stability (absence of very strong demand for housing), houses do depreciate.

The diagram below illustrates the reality of a stable market condition and involves a 30-year, 95 percent ratio mortgage at a 7½ percent interest rate. Assuming a straight-line depreciation of the house over a 40-year period, an owner would most likely experience a negative equity position between the fourth and twenty-fifth year. An increment of inflation, totalling about a 12½ percent increase of the value of the house, would reduce the negative equity period by about 10 years. With a 25 percent increase due to inflation or other factors, virtually no period of a negative equity prevails. Where the interest rate is high (9 percent or more) and with a longer mortgage payout term, an owner is virtually in a tenant position concerning equity accumulation.

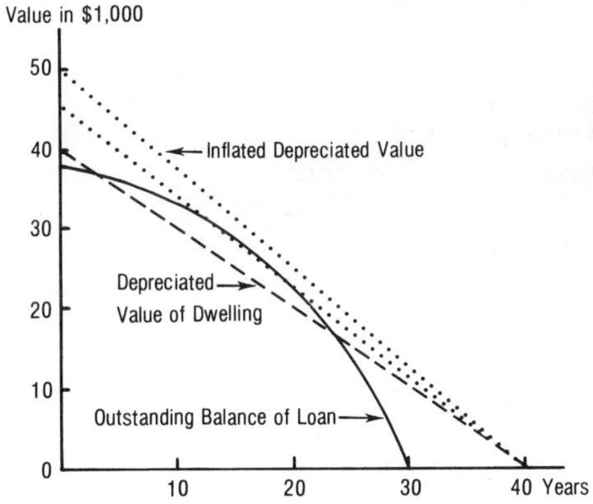

Q. *What are some energy saving design and construction features that can be incorporated in new townhouse construction to increase marketability?*

A. A study, *Residential Energy Consumption, Multifamily Housing* (HUD, June 1974) outlines several features that can be readily included in townhouse construction to reduce the energy requirements and thus reduce the cost of home ownership.

Plans for characteristic townhouse

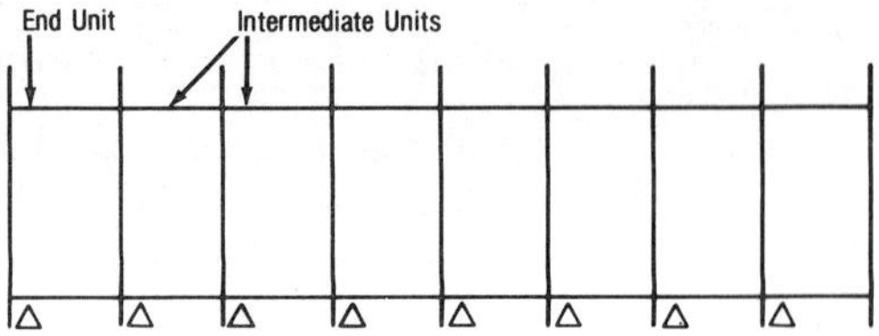

(a) Unit Arrangement

Design parameters for characteristic townhouse structure in Baltimore/Washington area

General Parameters:			
Arrangement	Rectangular structure consisting of eight townhouse units in a row.		
Number of stories	Two		
Basement	None		
Dimensional Parameters: (Areas are per townhouse unit, not per floor level)		*Intermediate Units*	*End Units*
Floor area, ft^2		1300	1300
Exterior wall area, ft^2		800	1450 (Excluding attic)
Party wall area, ft^2		1300	650 (Excluding attic)
Window glass only, % of floor area		6	8
Patio door glass, ft^2		40	40
Entrance door, ft^2		20	20
Roof area, % of floor area		57	57
Story height, ft		10	10
Construction Parameters:			
Construction type		Wall bearing	
Floors:	First	Concrete slab on grade	
	Second	Wood joist and plywood system	
Exterior walls:	Siding	Brick, four inch	
	Backup	Concrete block, four inch	
	Insulation	Air spaces (2)	
	Inside surface	Drywall, ½ inch	
Party walls:	Core	Concrete block, eight inch	
	Insulation	Air spaces (2)	
	Surfaces	Drywall, ½ inch	
Roof		Asphalt shingles	
Entrance door		Wood, solid core, 0.5 ft^2 glass pane	
Windows and patio door:	Glazing	Single	
	Frames	Aluminum	
Ceiling insulation		Loose fill blown in, five inch	
Attic		Ventilated, unheated	

continued

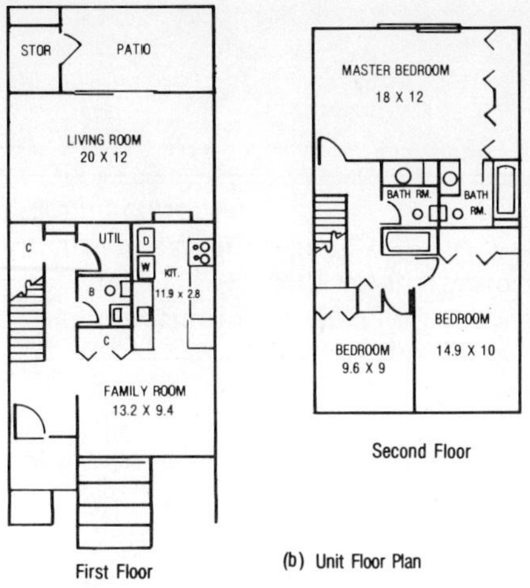

(b) Unit Floor Plan

Design parameters for characteristic townhouse structure in Baltimore/Washington area (cont.)

ENERGY CONSUMPTION PARAMETERS:	
Gas and electric metering	Individual (per townhouse)
Equipment in each townhouse:	
Heating system	Forced air, gas
Cooling system	Forced air, electric
Hot water heater	Gas
Cooking range	Gas
Refrigerator	Electric
Dishwasher	Electric
Disposal unit	Electric
Clothes washer	Electric
Clothes dryer	Gas
Lights, TV, misc. appliances	Electric
HEATING/COOLING LOAD PARAMETERS: (BASE CASE)	
Exterior glass areas	70% draped 20% shaded 10% open No awnings, no storm windows
Long (entrance) side of structure facing	North
External colors	Brown walls, white roof
External landscaping	No shading effect
People per townhouse	Two adults, two children

Parametric analyses of 8-unit townhouse
(As compared to the characteristic townhouse)

	% Change in Heating Loads	% Change in Cooling Loads	Approximate % Change in Primary Energy Consumption*
1. 25% reduction in window area	−8	−5	−7
2. 25% increase in window area	+8	+5	+7
3. Storm windows (Interlayer R=0.8)	−6	−1	−19
4. No internal shading of windows	−11	+16	−3
5. Windows with reflective glass (S.C.=0.25)	+8	−9	+2
6. Windows recessed 6″ in walls	0	−2	0
7. Windows shaded with 1-ft.-wide vertical fins	+2	−4	0
8. High insulation in ground floor (R=20)	−7	+3	−4
9. High insulation in walls (R=10.6)	−23	−2	−17
10. High insulation in roof (R=21.7)	−10	−3	−8
11. High insulation in walls & roof (#9 + #10)	−34	−5	−25
12. #11 with insulation placed close to outside	−33	−5	−25
13. Light construction	0	0	0
14. Low absorbtivity surfaces	+1	−4	0
15. House facing East-West	+8	+11	+9
16. All lighting by fluorescent lamps	+5	−6	+1
17. Combined 25% reduction in window area *plus* storm windows (#2 + #3)	−29	−6	−22
18. Combined storm windows *plus* high insulation in walls & roof (#3 + #11)	−59	−4	−43
19. Combined 25% reduction in window area *plus* storm windows *plus* high insulation in walls and roof (#1 + #3 + #11)	−63	−9	−47
20. Combined 25% reduction in window area *plus* storm windows *plus* high insulation in ground floor, walls, and roof (#1 + #3 + #8 + #11)	−69	−4	−50
21. Combined 25% reduction in window area *plus* storm windows *plus* high insulation in ground floor, walls, and roof, *plus* 25% reduction in lighting and appliance loads	−56	−25	−47

*These values assume a constant 60 percent heating system efficiency, and a cooling system performance of one Btu removed per Btu primary energy consumed.
NOTE: In this table, window area includes the patio door.

Q. *Highway administration programs require real property appraisals relating both to partial takings and to impact area studies. What are some differences between these two types of valuations?*

A. The following chart outlines the kind of reports needed, in a time-frame context, concerning highway development and its evaluation.

The similarities and differences, determined by the purposes of the reports, bear special attention.

Valuations for impact zone and partial taking cases

Some Similarities		*Some Differences*	
Impact Zone Cases	*Partial Taking Cases*	*Impact Zone Cases*	*Partial Taking Cases*
Need a valuation of the property in the absence of the highway (the "Before" value)	Need a valuation of the property in the absence of the highway (the "Before" value)	The "Before" valuation can be made some time (1 to 3 years) after highway opens	The "Before" valuation is needed at the time of right-of-way acquisition
Need a valuation of the property as affected by the highway (the "After" value)	Need a valuation of the property as affected by the highway (the "After" value)	The "After" valuation can be made some time (1 to 3 years) after highway opens	The "After" valuation is needed at the time of right-of-way acquisition

SOURCE: Federal Highway Administration, 1974.

Q. *What are some general relationships between family income and the sales price of housing?*

A. Annual family income by house value

Selling Price of House	*Mean Annual Family Income*
$10,000–11,999	$ 9,111
12,000–13,999	9,150
14,000–15,999	9,729
16,000–17,999	10,425
18,000–19,999	11,692
20,000–21,999	12,536
22,000–24,999	13,676
25,000–29,999	15,358
30,000 or more	17,680

SOURCE: HUD Statistical Yearbook, 1970.

The equation for this derived tabular data is $Y = \$3,981 + 0.407\ HV$.*

* Y = Annual family income
HV = House Value, or selling price of house.

Q. *From time to time I handle transfer cases for large corporations. The people are always interested in the relative costs of living, housing, and so forth. What is a good guide for rendering any advice?*

A. The Bureau of Labor Statistics develops cost of living indexes for a number of the larger cities. Estimates can then be made for many nearby smaller communities. The following tabulation provides a recent index for a number of the larger cities:

Comparative living costs for 1974

Area	*Rank*	*1974 Budget*	*1973–1974 Dollar Increase*	*1973–1974 Percentage Increase*	*Percent U.S. Urban Average Budget*
Honolulu	1	$17,019	2,082	13.9	119
Boston	2	16,725	1,832	12.3	117
New York-New Jersey	3	16,648	2,200	15.2	116
Buffalo	4	15,364	2,141	16.2	107
San Francisco-Oakland	5	15,127	1,749	13.1	106
Washington, D.C.	6	15,035	1,992	15.3	105
Milwaukee	7	15,024	1,813	13.7	105
Minneapolis-St. Paul	8	14,917	1,897	14.6	104
Chicago	9	14,797	1,584	12.0	103
Philadelphia	10	14,757	1,735	13.3	103
Cleveland	11	14,617	1,811	14.1	102
Seattle	12	14,487	1,820	14.4	101
Baltimore	13	14,398	1,879	15.0	100
Detroit	14	14,390	1,580	12.3	100
U.S. Urban Average		14,333	1,707	13.5	100
Los Angeles-Long Beach	15	14,068	1,548	12.4	98
San Diego	16	13,977	1,761	14.4	98
Phoenix	17	13,969	1,818	15.0	97
Kansas City, Mo.	18	13,939	1,458	11.7	97
Pittsburgh	19	13,876	1,577	12.8	97
St. Louis	20	13,859	1,469	11.9	97
Cincinnati	21	13,753	1,616	13.3	96
Atlanta	22	13,098	1,414	12.1	91
Dallas	23	12,917	1,509	13.2	90
Houston	24	12,872	1,529	13.5	90

SOURCE: U.S. figures based on April 9, 1975, U.S. Department of Labor, Bureau of Labor Statistics, news release (USDL 75-190)

Q. *You have read a Bureau of Census report and found the following table on single-family detached houses, which indicates the share of major cost items for two different time periods. What additional sense can you make of this data?*

	X Year		*Y Year*	
	Percent	*Cost*	*Percent*	*Cost*
Land	22%	5,630	25	8,950
Financing	7	1,790	10	3,580
Profit and Overhead	13	3,330	12	4,300
Other	4	1,020	5	1,790
Labor	17	4,430	15	5,370
Materials	37	9,400	33	11,810
Totals	100	25,600	100	35,800

A. One interesting analysis is done by considering the absolute dollar differences for the entire house and for its component costs. These, in turn, are compared to the total cost increase.

	Difference	*Component Percent of Total*
Land	$ 3,320	32.6%
Financing	1,790	17.6
Profit and Overhead	970	9.5
Other	770	7.4
Labor	940	9.2
Materials	2,410	23.7
Totals	$10,200	100.0%

On an absolute percentage increase basis, financing increased 100 percent, land 59 percent, labor 21 percent, etc.

Q. *What are the elements and factors to be considered in evaluating the costs of a conventional home versus that of a mobile home?*

A. The following example represents a typical comparison between the two kinds of housing facilities. Current local data and information must be obtained to clearly identify cost differences. Generally, it is estimated that the mobile home is depreciated 40 percent by the end of the tenth year and, therefore, is entirely depreciated by the twenty-fifth year.

Cost comparison—mobile home and single-family home

	Double-Wide Mobile Home	*Conventional Home*
Specifications		
Living space	1,368 sq. ft.	1,368 sq. ft.
Land included	No	Yes
Furnished	No	No
Carpeting and draperies	Yes	No
Stove and refrigerators	Yes	Yes
Simple interest rate on loan/mortgage	11%	7½%
Term of loan/mortgage	10 years	25 years
Cost		
Selling price	$12,000	$25,000
California sales tax	600	—
Closing costs	—	488
Total	$12,600	$25,488
Initial cost		
Downpayment	$ 2,452	$ 6,300
Sales tax	600	—
Closing costs	—	488
Total	$ 3,052	$ 6,788
Monthly payments		
Years 1–10		
Loan	$128	$138
License/taxes, average	9	45
Insurance	7	8
Site rent	80	—
Total	$224	$191
Years 11–25		
Loan	$ —	$138
License/taxes, average	3	45
Insurance	7	8
Site rent	80	—
Total	$ 90	$191

SOURCE: Economics and Monthly Payment Loan and Real Estate Loan Departments, Wells Fargo Bank.

Q. *A sample of 100 owner households is obtained in a neighborhood conservation area of a city. Fifty of the owners have second mortgages on their homes. Information concerning motivation and interest in rehabilitating the houses varies. You are asked to judge whether there is any association between the level and kind of indebteness (second mortgages) and likelihood of rehabilitation of properties by the various owners. The distribution of survey information by the Local Public Agency is as follows:*

		Second Mortgages		
		Yes	*No*	
Interest in Rehabilitating	High	10	35	45
	Low	40	15	55
	Totals:	50	50	100

A. One can use Guttman's Coefficient of Predictibility, Lambda, to measure any association of the above information. The equation takes on the form of:

$$\text{(Lambda) } \lambda = \frac{\Sigma f_r + \Sigma f_c - (F_r + F_c)}{2\text{ N} - (F_r + F_c)}$$

Where:

f_r = largest frequency occuring in a row
f_c = largest frequency occuring in a column
F_r = largest marginal frequency occuring among the rows
F_c = largest marginal frequency occuring among the columns
N = the number of observations

Indicated solution is:

$$\lambda = \frac{(35 + 40) + (35 + 40) - (55 + 50)}{2\ (100) - (55 + 50)}$$
$$= 45/95 = 0.47$$

The level derived, 0.47, indicates there is a moderate association.

NOTE: Nominal level data (yes, no; black, white; day, night, etc.) is required for this kind of analysis. There are no assumptions concerning the distribution of variables. This method can be utilized whenever data can be categorized as noted.

Q. *I negotiate complex real estate deals with really sharp investors. Sometimes it appears that a deal will collapse simply because neither is willing to negotiate on one of a dozen issues. These matters include closing and possession dates, treatment of personal property or intangibles included in the transaction, and so forth. What are some methods that can be used to keep matters on track and bring about a fruitful effort—closing the deal?*

A. The complexity of such transactions involves a variety of elements to test the mettle of a real estate pro. One is faced with rational and informed opponents (buyer and seller), conflicting interests, many alternatives for closing—many of which are unknown during negotiations, and, at the end of it all, the payoff (closing). All these factors are fraught with every imaginable uncertainty.

One technique for simplifying the situation is to sketch a series of scenarios (transition scenarios) as one moves from one stage of negotiations to another. Figure 1 illustrates the bounds and thresholds involving price and nonprice elements and their relative positions. These factors define a zone within which a meeting of the minds (agreement reduced to writing) can be reached. Subelements involving crucial factors may require subscenario sketches to provide a lower level decision-point for agreement between a buyer and seller. Prices, dates, or other critical factors related to a given situation can be entered on a drawing similar to Figure 1.

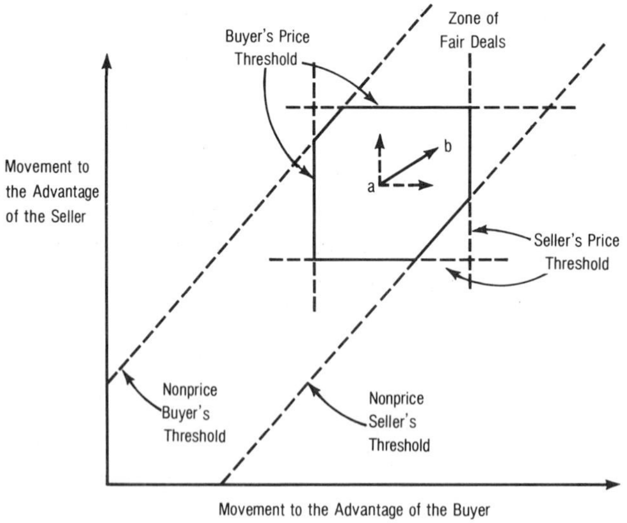

FIG. 1. Conceptual model of acquisition negotiations

SOURCE: Reprinted by permission of the publisher from Ernest C. Miller, *Advanced Techniques for Strategic Planning* (American Management Association, Inc., 1971) p. 90

Q. *What are the four different kinds of data at various levels of measurement that underlie most statistical analysis?*

A. The four kinds of data and their corresponding levels of measurement are as follows:

1. *Nominal level*—the lowest measurement level. An example would be categorizing of a population by race, religion, sex and so on; another case might be the grouping of shopping centers into two categories, in-town and out-of-town.
2. *Ordinal level*—the principal distinction of this kind of data is being able to rank the data; however, no criteria is permitted to measure how much higher or lower one ranking is from another. As an example, five shopping centers might be ranked, but measures to account for their position would not be included.
3. *Interval level*—the key attribute of this kind of data is that it measures the exact value or judgment assigned to any ranking; a scale measuring differences in quality of shopping centers illustrates the interval level of data attributes.
4. *Ratio level*—this is the highest level of data attributes and contains an absolute zero as a reference point. For example, where ranking of shopping centers is made (ordinal level) and differences in attributes accounted for (interval), we are able to arrive at a quality or weighed factor assignment (ratio level) permitting statements that are based on such ratings; that is, one shopping center is 50 percent better, or 20 percent inferior, to another.

Q. *There has been repeated discussion concerning the location, safety, and impact on the population of nuclear power plant facilities. These matters, plus recent findings concerning industrial exposure of workers, have raised some important questions relating to the safety of the area surrounding such facilities. This discussion has raised the further question of the diminution, if any, of real property values in the vicinity of such a plant. How much merit can one give to some of these reports, since they concern a commodity basic to human habitation—that is, land and improvements?*

A. Only a team of objective experts, based on the current ever-changing state of knowledge, could provide some knowledgeable parameters concerning the safety of real property in close proximity to these various kinds of industrial facilities. The word "proximity" becomes relative in terms of some of the following reported information:

1. The report on significant increases in infant mortality up to 40 miles from nuclear power plants is shown in Figures 1, 2,

and 3. The Dresden facility is at Morris, Illinois, 50 miles south of Chicago.

2. Waste materials, including disposal and storage, represent important and human endangering problems. Radioactive waste has an enormous half-life. The half-life is the time (in years) that it takes for the activity of a radioactive substance to decay to half its original strength. As an example, "reprocessing" produces highly radioactive waste in liquid form; after being boiled down it is stored in tanks. Control is by cooling. Its half-life impact is noted by Dr. I. E. Schulz, who has stated, "It is curious to think that, if highly active waste of this kind had been dumped some time in the fourteenth century, protective containers and constant supervision would still be necessary" (Verlag Karl Thiemig, "Vorkommnisse und Strahlenunfälle" in *Kerntechnischen Anlagen*, München, 1965).

3. Land used over 18 years ago (Walnut Creek area west of Denver) in connection with atomic bomb production has been found to be currently contaminated with plutonium (Washington Post, February 17, 1976). Likewise, a total of 49 sites used in the early days in connection with the nuclear weapons program are being checked for continuing radiation; these include locations at six universities, a Cook County, Illinois, forest preserve site, plus some factory buildings (Washington Star, May 6, 1976). Some current waste storage facilities exist at West Valley, New York, Oak Ridge, Tennessee, and near Idaho Falls, Idaho (Washington Star, March 3, 1976).[1]

4. In a review of a study relating to the safety of nuclear power plants, it has been estimated that the following costs would be involved in the event of a serious reactor accident at Indian Point, New York: 25,000 latent cancer fatalities, 4,000 prompt fatalities, total property damage of $17 billion, 780,000 people requiring urgent evacuation, 1,900,000 people requiring a 90-day relocation, and the affected contaminated area involving from 1,700 to 10,000 square miles (Joel Yellin, "The Nuclear Commission's Reactor Safety Study," *The Bell Journal of Economics*, Spring, 1976, p. 326).

[1]A potential multibillion dollar cost is estimated to properly manage and/or relocate the closed down facility at West Valley, N.Y., 30 miles southeast of Buffalo. (The *New York Times Magazine*, April 10, 1977). See also *Technology Review* (May 1977), pp. 20–29.

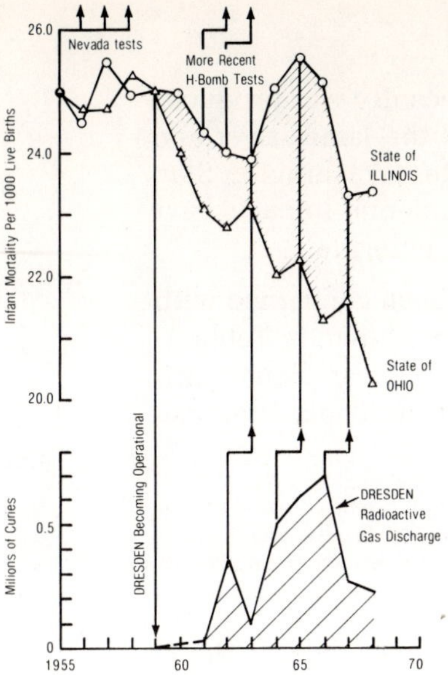

FIG. 1. Infant mortality in Ohio and Illinois, the site of the "Dresden" reactor, in the years 1955–68.

SOURCE: Reprinted from Ralph Graeub, *The Gentle Killers, Nuclear Power Stations* (London: Abelard-Schuman Limited, 1974) by permission of the publisher.

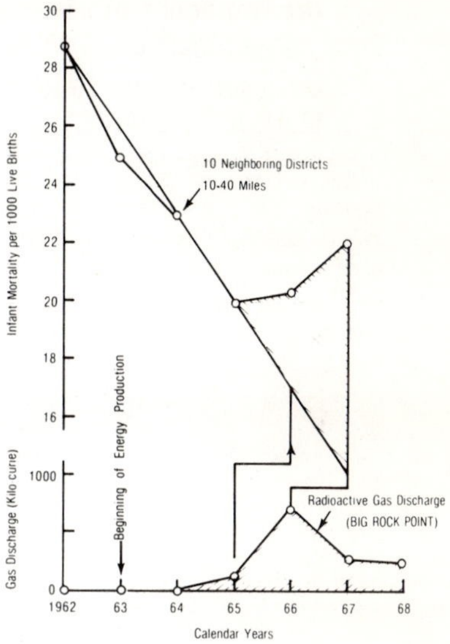

FIG. 2. Changes in infant mortality in ten districts close to the Big Rock Point Nuclear Power Station in Charlevoix, Michigan, between 1962 and 1967. The yearly discharge of radioactive gasses from fission- and activation-products is also indicated.

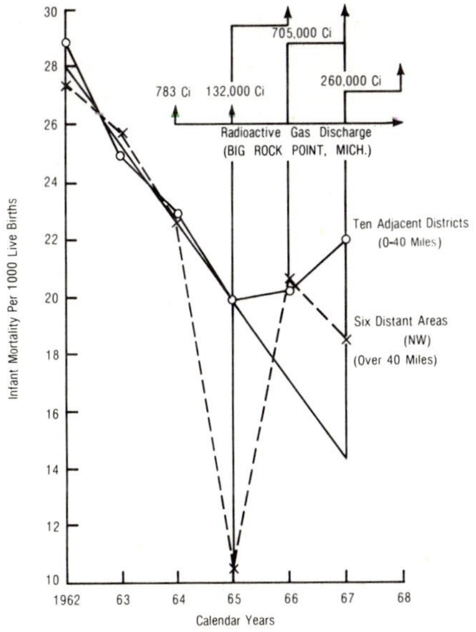

FIG. 3. Comparison of infant mortality in outlying regions in the north and northwest of the U.S.A. with rates in areas situated within a forty mile radius of the Big Rock Point reactor, Michigan.

5. Toxic pesticide (Kepone), which until recently was produced at Hopewell, Virginia has contaminated the James river and probably other connecting bodies of water (Washington Star, March 25, 1976).[2] Other adverse environmental impacts have included lead concentrations, and vinyl chloride.

6. Researchers in other countries have also been concerned with the impacts from nuclear plant facilities as shown in Table A.
   For locations and demographics of 42 nuclear plant facilities, see *Rams' Real Estate Appraising Handbook*, Prentice-Hall, Inc., 1975.

---

[2]The devastating effect is evidenced by the 940 counts against the producer, Allied Chemical Corp., along with a 13.24 million dollar fine by a Federal court. The fine was reduced (The Washington Star, February 1, 1977) by 5 million dollars because of the company's contribution to a fund established to minimize or eliminate the impact of Kepone on a vast area of Virginia.

Collective whole body doses, partial body exposures, and occupational fatality rates occurring at different stages of nuclear power production process

Stage	*Whole body exposures (man.rem/MW(e)y)*		*Partial body exposures*	*Fatal occupational accidents and diseases per 1000 MW(e)y*
	Population	*Occupational*		
Construction of installations	—	—	—	0.25
Uranium Mining	— —	External, to miners 0.1	Lung, miners	0.4
Milling and processing	—	(Probably less than 0.1)	Lung and hands slight	approx 0.1
Fabrication and enrichment	—	—	Probably slight	—
Reactor operation	Liquid wastes 0.002 Gaseous wastes 0.1	From activation and fission products (external and tritium) 2.0	—	0.02
Reprocessing plants	Liquid wastes 0.1 Gaseous wastes 0.25 C14 1.0*	From activation and fission products (mainly external) 2.0	Occupational, to lung and other tissues occasionally Public, to skin, intestine, thyroid and bone for small groups	0.02
Other fuel steps	—	0.03	—	—
Transport	0.004	0.005	—	0.003
Accidents	0.05	—	—	
Total	1.5	+4.2	See text	0.8
Total (genetically significant)	1.5	+2.7	—	

*From reactors; discharges from reprocessing plants at present uncertain. Total dose commitment to future: 0.05 in first 30 years.

SOURCE: Reprinted from Edward E. Pochin, *Estimated Population Exposure from Nuclear Power Production and Other Radiation Sources*, (Paris; Organization for Economic Cooperation and Development, 1976) by permission of editor.

Q. *What are the central elements of a tax sheltered investment and the related benefits?*

A. The following discussion provides a good outline of the several facets of a tax sheltered investment. It includes matters of deferral, leverage, and conversion.

DEFERRAL

Deferral commonly arises in situations where taxpayers make investments in activities or businesses which use the cash basis method of accounting and are permitted to take certain deductions (such as cattle feed or vineyard development costs) into account for tax purposes in the first year and the other early years of the shelter investment before the investment produces any income. Deferral also occurs where taxpayers are permitted to accelerate certain deductions (such as depreciation) to the early years of an investment transaction.

The "bunching" of deductions in the first years, rather than ratably over the life of the property, is used to offset (shelter) an individual's other income. That is, excess accelerated deductions result in losses which are then used against his other investment and earned income and may significantly reduce the individual's tax liability. However, the taxes that are reduced in the earlier years may be shifted to later years when the investment begins to generate income, and many of the offsetting deductions have been used and are thus no longer available. Taxpayers in this situation have frequently found it advantageous to invest in another tax shelter to provide a "rollover" or further deferral of the taxes.

The net effect of deferral may be viewed as an interest-free loan to the taxpayer from the Federal Government during the period of the tax deferral. Over a period of years, this "loan" can be worth a substantial amount of money. For example, if a taxpayer has $100,000 of accelerated deductions and invests the tax savings in 7% tax-exempt bonds (with interest compounded annually) his money will double in less than 11 years. In other words, deferral can be worth as much as total tax forgiveness after a period of time.

In addition, in many cases, especially where leverage is used, as discussed below, a tax shelter investment also results in a taxpayer completely recovering his investment (and in some cases more) by the acceleration of the deductions. This is often the case for taxpayers in the 50-percent or higher tax brackets. Thus, not only does the Federal Government provide an interest-free loan, but in a sense the Government provides the risk capital to high bracket taxpayers to enter into these investments.

It is important to note that this deferral treatment benefits those in the higher brackets proportionately more than it benefits those in the lower brackets. For example, for each $100 deduction, a taxpayer in the 70-percent bracket will save $70 by taking that deduction against his income. On the other hand, a taxpayer in the 20-percent bracket will save only $20 when that $100 deduction is used to offset his income. This is particularly important in a tax shelter investment because of the various risks that are involved. In other words, the interest free loan for the upper income taxpayer is $70; the interest free loan for the lower bracket taxpayer is considerably less.

It should be noted that the tax benefits from deferral are greater in some tax shelters than in others simply because the deferral is for a longer period than for other investments; that is, taxes are deferred over a longer period of time. In the case of the shorter deferrals it is possible for an individual to rollover his investment; that is, to make another tax shelter investment to provide new accelerated deductions and thus defer tax liability further into the future.

Effect of Progressive Rate Structure

One of the risks in a tax shelter is that the investment may result in a true economic loss where the taxpayer may lose his entire investment. If this were the case (not taking into account the use of borrowed money, as discussed below), a taxpayer in the 70-percent bracket would lose only $30 of his own money; whereas, a taxpayer in the 20-percent bracket would lose $80. Therefore, the high bracket taxpayer would be willing to make riskier investments because his potential net loss (that is, the tax benefit less any economic loss) is less. In effect, the Federal Government finances more of the investments, and takes more of the risks, for a high bracket taxpayer than a low bracket taxpayer.

It should be noted that in the case of a taxpayer with only "earned income" subject to a maximum tax rate of 50 percent, tax shelter deductions reduce income at the 50 percent and lower rates. However, when the tax shelter investment is disposed of at other than capital gains rates, gains may be taxed as high as 70 percent, since they will be investment income and thus not eligible for the 50 percent maximum rate on earned income.

LEVERAGE

The second element of a tax shelter investment is "leverage," which is the use of borrowed money by an individual in the investment. Generally, an individual will borrow money (or money will be borrowed on his behalf) which will equal or exceed his equity investment. There are two benefits in the use of borrowed funds, the first being an economic benefit and the second being a tax benefit. From an economic standpoint, the more that an individual can use borrowed money for an investment the more he can use his own money for other purposes (including other investments) and the more he can make on an investment which is profitable. From a tax standpoint, borrowed funds are treated in the same manner as a taxpayer's own funds that he has put up as equity in the investment. Since a taxpayer is allowed deductions not only with respect to his equity but also on the borrowed funds, he can maximize deferral by incurring deductible expenditures which exceed his equity investment.

A simple illustration of the use of leveraging in tax shelter investments is as follows: Assume the investment requires $100,000 of capital. If an individual invests $10,000 of his own money and is able to borrow $90,000 to meet the $100,000 requirement, for tax purposes he is treated as having $100,000 in the investment. This means that if there are accelerated deductions of $20,000 in the first year, the individual, if he is in the 70-percent bracket, would be reducing his tax liability by $14,000. In this case, the tax deduction in the initial year ($20,000) would be $10,000 more than the equity capital invested and his tax savings would be $4,000 more than the amount originally invested ($10,000). This individual would be financing his investment completely with what can be referred to in effect as an interest-free loan from the Federal Government. In this example above, a taxpayer in the 50-percent bracket would recover his entire investment in the initial year; that is, if he invests $10,000 of his own money and is allowed to deduct $20,000, he receives back by way of reduction of his tax liability the $10,000 he invested. This is the reason why most tax shelter investments are advertised for taxpayers in the 50-percent bracket and above.

A taxpayer in the 20-percent bracket who invests the same $10,000, as in the above example, would only receive back $4,000 from the same $20,000 tax write-off in the first year and, therefore, he is still out of pocket $6,000 in the first year. Not only is the low bracket taxpayer less likely to have the funds to invest in these investments but the Federal Government does not provide him the same subsidy as it does for the high bracket individual.

As can be seen from this example, in the initial years, the risks to a high bracket taxpayer are rather minimal because in the normal tax shelter investment, he would recover the entire amount of his own investment in the year it is made through tax deductions. It should be noted, however, that even if the investment fails, there is usually some recovery (and sometimes substantial recovery) of previous writeoffs where the investor would be liable for tax on the constructive income he is required to recognize when the shelter terminates. This is often referred to as the "phantom gain"; where there is gain for tax purposes, even though the investment does not generate economic income or positive cash flow. In other words, the taxpayer is required to repay his interest free loan from the Government at least to the extent of any nonrecourse borrowings which he was previously able to deduct. (Sometimes this repayment must be made in full, and sometimes only in part, if there is a "conversion" feature to the shelter, as discussed below.)

The use of leverage has increased significance when an investor is not even liable on the borrowed money, which is often the case in tax shelter investments. This is what is referred to as "nonrecourse financing." Where a partnership (usually a limited partnership) is being used as the investment vehicle, a loan may be made to the partnership so the partnership assets are subject to liability but the investors are not personally liable for the loan. However, under partnership tax regulations, the limited partner investor is entitled to increase his basis in his investment by the amount which is treated as his proportionate share of the liability (even though in fact he has no such liability). (A partner may deduct partnership losses to the extent of his basis.) Thus, the investor is able to take tax write-offs on account of the accelerated deductions not only for the money he invested (on which he is at risk) but, more significantly, also on his share of the nonrecourse aspects of tax shelter investments. . . .

CONVERSION OF ORDINARY INCOME INTO CAPITAL GAINS

A third aspect which is present in some tax shelter investments is referred to as "conversion," which is the process of converting ordinary income deductions into capital gains.

When a taxpayer depreciates an asset, he takes a deduction against his ordinary income (and thus reduces taxable ordinary income) for depreciation. If the asset is a capital asset when it is sold and the proceeds exceed basis, there is a taxable gain. However, even though the previous reduction in basis (depreciation) reduced ordinary income, this gain may be taxed as capital gain. When the gain is a capital gain, the effect of the sale is to convert ordinary income, that is the income which was reduced by the previous accelerated deductions at the marginal bracket of the taxpayer, to capital gains taxed at the preferential capital gains rates.

In several cases, Congress has dealt with this situation by requiring a portion of the gain on a sale or other disposition to be treated as ordinary income rather than capital gains, to the extent of accelerated depreciation deductions (and in the case of personal property, to the extent of all depreciation). This is what is referred to as "recapture." The taxes on the ordinary income that have been deferred through the taking of accelerated deductions in earlier years are recaptured at the time the property is disposed of. Although there are several recapture rules in present law today, the recapture rules do not apply to all tax shelter investments. (In addition, the "recapture" applies only to prevent the conversion of ordinary income to capital gains; it does not apply to the deferral factor.)*

*For a detailed analysis of recent tax law changes, see Stephen E. Roulac, *Real Estate Investment Under the New Tax Reform Act of 1976*, Property Press, 1976.

SOURCE: Joint Committee on Internal Revenue Taxation, *Tax Shelter Investments*, Washington, D.C., April 14, 1976.

part two

URBAN AREA—NEIGHBORHOOD STUDIES

Accelerating urbanism has brought into sharp focus matters of area and neighborhood dynamics and change. This trend, accompanied by extensive population migration, extending over the last two decades, has dramatized the linkage and interdependence of private property interests and community infrastructure. Consequently, the context of value of a property, in the private and public sectors, has drawn new attention because of the many pervasive forces at play. There has been a rediscovery of the fabric of society, and the impacts of the related socio-economic dimensions, which have been heretofore present but in a less-dominant role.

For example, a recent Bureau of Census Study (*Indicators of Housing and Neighborhood Quality*, H-150-73B, 1973) based on sample data indicates that 44 percent of households in the United States rate their neighborhood fair to poor, those in the SMSA's (Standard Metropolitan Statistical Areas) within the central city represent 50 percent of those with these ratings. Those outside the SMSA's total 35 percent of those rating their neighborhood fair to poor. This suggests that the number of households perceiving their neighborhood as being fair to poor (two other choices included excellent and good) represents a significant portion of all households.

Household mobility (moving) is perhaps another manifestation of neighborhood dissatisfaction. A companion study to the above (*Housing Characteristics of Recent Movers*, H-150-73D, 1973) reports that between April 1970 and October 1973 (3½ years) two out of five (40 percent) of all households moved. This amounts to a total of 13,284,000 households. The trend of outmigration from SMSA's continues; for the above period the overall rate was 3.5 percent, while the central cities lost 19.8 percent of households during the same period of time.

A more recent study, parallel to the first (*Advance Report for 1974*), indicates that dissatisfaction with neighborhoods is attributable to a number of factors including shopping, schools, and transportation. Again, based on sample data the findings indicate the following incidence of neighborhood dissatisfaction based on geographical location. These are households who wish to move.

	Owner Occupied	*Renter Occupied*
United States	39.8%	27.9%
Inside SMSA's	37.7	24.1
In central city	28.5	18.6
Not in central city	48.5	36.7
Outside SMSA	48.0	57.1

A study in Pennsylvania (Pittsburgh, Philadelphia, and other smaller metropolitan areas), revealed significant differences between intraurban movers and distant movers (distance to metropolitan area greater from new location than from prior location). See Table A. Based on a sample of 1,096 households, movers to nonmetropolitan areas (1) show less preference for some characteristics of the metropolitan environment, (2) have family structures that are amenable to nonmetropolitan direction moves, and (3) have social status and social aspiration levels that facilitate the decision to move away from a large city.

What is happening in the residential sector has its counterpart in retailing. Of a total of 165 shopping centers studied in the last several years, 85 percent of changes (expansion, design, population density and so forth) undertaken by management was attributable to economic factors (See Edwin M. Rams, *Analysis and Valuation of Retail Locations*, Reston Publishing Company, 1976).

These profound impacts will, over a short time-span, force a reevaluation and a reassessment of the "economic life" of many private and public real estate facilities. This, in turn, will signal important impacts on investor motivation, financing (of both private and public facilities), capital commitments, and so on.

Table A

Social and demographic characteristics of metropolitan nonmovers, nonmetropolitan direction movers, and other metropolitan area movers

	Mover Status		
Characteristics	*Nonmover*	*Nonmetropolitan Direction Mover*	*Other Movers*
Weighted N	1002	33	91
Age of head of household	50.2	33.3	34.7
Education of head (yrs. completed)	11.2	14.0	12.6
Total family income: 1973	$9,200	$10,700	$8,400
Socioeconomic status of head[1]	43.9	59.0	47.7
Household type (% nuclear family)	62.3	83.5	57.4
Average household size	3.3	3.1	3.4
Marital status (% married, spouse present)	68	87	64
Sex of head (% male)	74	92	74
Race (% nonwhite)	20	11	15
Size of area of origin[2]	1.9	2.4	1.9

[1]Criteria as outlined by Charles B. Nam, Mary G. Powers, *Social Forces* 47 (2): 158.
[2]Scale: 1 = large city; 2 = suburb of a large city, and 3 = medium-sized city.
SOURCE: *Residential Preferences and Migration Behavior*, G. F. DeJong and R. R. Sell, National Institute of Health, 1975.

Manifestly, a study of the external urban dimensions of property value and dynamics becomes an important requisite to an understanding and comprehension of real property dynamics in the marketplace. Accordingly, this part of the book treats those aspects, having impact on locational property interests. This merely attests to the necessary importance which must be afforded to externalities of property interests in a highly urbanized setting.

An operational knowledge of methods, techniques, and other action-oriented real estate formulations can provide the "edge of difference" between a novice and an experienced counselor and investment advisor. Part two of this book serves as a forum for such analysis. It places proper consideration of a real property interest in the total context of value, that is, the location and environment of such interest in the urban complex. This is an admission that value of real estate is subject to an environmental bias and is really a creature of its location.

The competitive aspects of locations and facilities at given points in an urban setting represent the fundamental data for analyzing the motivations and expectations of the various market participants—the tenants, the buyer, the seller, and the investor. They are the principal components—for without them there simply would be no market.

Q. *Residential neighborhoods seem to be changing very rapidly in some areas of large cities; the life-cycle appears to be of short duration in comparison to that of fifty or more years ago. What are some of the attributes of neighborhoods as they pass from one stage to another?*

A. This matter is of national interest and concern. Consequently, a recent government study (*The Dynamics of Neighborhood Change*, HUD, 1976) outlines five stages that a neighborhood experiences, from development to demise. They are as follows: (1) Healthy, (2) Incipient Decline, (3) Clearly Declining, (4) Accelerating Decline, and (5) Abandonment.

1

Physical

Good Property Upkeep
Sound Structural Condition
Homogeneous Housing Type
Good Location
Neighborhood Well Maintained

Social

Middle to High Social Status
Moderate to Upper Income Level
Ethnic Homogeneity
High School Graduates and Above
Family Oriented or Childless Adults
White Collar and/or Skilled Blue Collar
Pride in Neighborhood and House
Good Neighborhood Reputation
Neighborhood Perceived as Safe
Socially Cohesive

Economic

High Owner Investment
Good Property Values
Insurance Available
Conventional Financing Available
High Confidence in Future Value

Public Services

Services Efficient and Appropriate
Some Reliance on Private Service

2

Physical

Spot Maintenance Neglect
Aging Housing Stock
Some New Non-Residential Uses
Less Desirable Location

Social

Decline in Social Status
Declining Household Income
Influx of Middle Income Minorities
Decline in Education Level
Smaller Families (Widowed, Elderly)
More Semi-Skilled, Underemployed
Often Fear of Racial Transition
Decline in Neighborhood Reputation

Economic

Some Cutback in Maintenance
No Rise, Some Decline in Property Values
Increasing Insurance Costs
Some Difficulty in Getting Financing
Waning Confidence in Future Value
Property Tax Burden Increases
More Renters, in Single Family Areas

Public Services

Mismatch Between Needs and Service Provision

3
Physical

General Minor, Many Major Deficiencies
Larger Capital Improvements Needed
Higher Density Leads to Visible Wear
Relatively Poor Location
Visible Deterioration in Public Areas
Commercial Vacancies

Social

Major Decline in Social Status
Lower Incomes, More Welfare Households
Decrease in White In-Movers
Large Families, Often Female Headed
Increasing Unskilled Workers and Unemployed
Lack of Social Cohesion
Fair to Poor Neighborhood Reputation
Lack of Pride in House and Neighborhood
Increasing Fear for Safety
More Minority Children in Schools

Economic

Further Cutback on Maintenance and Repairs
Definite Decline in Property Values
Insurance Prohibitive
Serious Problems in Getting Financing
Fear for Future Value of Investment
Predominantly Renters
Revenue at Break-even Point
Increasing Operating Costs
Small Scale Investor Owners

Public Services

Perceived Decline in Service Responsiveness
Increasing Dependence on Public/Social services

4
Physical

Major Deficiencies, Deterioration Prevalent
Old Buildings Predominate
Increasing Vandalized Property
Undesirable Location
Incompatible Land Uses Allowed
Increasing Residential Vacancies
Some Abandonment

Social

Low Social Status
Predominantly Low Income/Minority Tenants
Elderly Ethnics
Increasing Multi-Problem Families
Mostly Unskilled Workers: High Unemployment
Poor Tenant-Landlord Relations
Poor Neighborhood Reputation
Absolute Decline in Population
Fear for Personal Safety
Predominantly Minority Children in Schools
Increasing Fire and Crime

Economic

Almost No Maintenance or Repairs
Lack of Buyers
Insurance Denied
Costly Non-Institutional Financing Only
Extreme Pessimism Toward Present and Future
Frequent Over-Assessment
Increasing Cash-flow Problems
Skyrocketing Operating Costs
High Proportion of Absentee Owners

Public Services

Absolute Decline in Services

5
Physical

Severe Dilapidation
Adjacent Abandoned Buildings
Voluntary/Involuntary Demolition
Noise, Abandoned Cars
Vacant Littered Lots
General Area Decay
Widespread Abandonment

Social

Lowest Social Status
Poverty Level Incomes
Squatter Population
Multi-problem Welfare Families Prevalent
Bad Neighborhood Reputation
Households With Options Leave
Fear, Apathy
High Crime and Fire Incidence

Economic

Collapsed Rental Market
Serious Rent Collection Problems
Negative Cash-flows

Public Services

Inadequate, Unresponsive to Need

Q. Since housing occupancy and use is closely tied to the family life cycle, what are some good measures for determining the "most likely" owners/tenants of single family, multifamily, and mobile housing units?

A. A recent study considering this matter developed a 30-year forecast of potential housing use by age class. The following table outlines the findings and also includes incremental occupancy rates, which can be used to calculate the overall demand for each type of unit:

Housing type occupancy rates in the United States by age class for 1960, with projections to 2020
(percent)

		Age Class							
Year	*Housing Type*	*15–19*	*20–24*	*25–29*	*30–34*	*35–44*	*45–54*	*55–64*	*65+*
1960	One-unit structures	35.6	46.4	60.0	69.1	73.9	71.8	68.3	67.5
	Multiunit structures	58.3	49.0	37.8	29.3	25.0	27.2	30.6	31.3
	Mobile units	6.9	4.6	2.2	1.6	1.1	1.0	1.1	1.2
2020	One-unit structures	12.7	23.8	40.0	55.0	69.6	68.0	60.9	56.1
	Multiunit structures	64.7	56.6	44.3	34.0	25.0	27.2	31.0	33.3
	Mobile units	22.6	19.6	15.7	11.0	5.4	4.8	8.1	10.6
		Incremental Occupancy Rates							
1970–2020	One-unit structures	0	5.0	25.0	44.5	65.0	62.7	55.2	48.2
	Multiunit structures	70.0	65.0	50.0	37.5	25.0	27.3	31.3	34.8
	Mobile units	30.0	30.0	25.0	18.0	10.0	10.0	13.5	17.0

SOURCE: Projections of Demand for Housing by Type of Unit and Region, *Agricultural Handbook No. 428*, Washington, D.C. May 1972.

Q. Replacement housing is an important element of housing demand. What are some guidelines for deriving measures of replacement housing in an urbanized area?

A. The most meaningful measure is obtained from an analysis of local data over a 5-year period. Of course, the Bureau of Census information provides a 10-year time frame for study. The statistical relationship is quite simple, being the difference in the net inventory of housing units for two periods minus the total number of units added for the same period.

In the absence of local data, reference can be made to past regional trends, profiled against aggregate housing production for the several periods, and estimates derived accordingly.

Net conventional housing replacement rates in the United States by region for 1950–56, 1957–59, and 1960–70 (percent)

Period	U.S.	Northeast	North Central	South	West
1950–56	0.46	0.27	0.33	0.76	0.49
1957–59	.85	.48	.65	1.27	1.03
1960–70	.98	.50	.93	1.33	1.00

[1]Conventional housing includes all housing except mobile homes.

SOURCES: 1950–59—U.S. Department of Commerce, Bureau of the Census, *U.S. Census of Housing: 1960*, Vol. IV *Components of Inventory Change*, 1963(37); 1960–70—Derived from data published by U.S. Department of Commerce, Bureau of the Census, *U.S. Census of Housing: 1970*, Advance Depart. HC(U1)-1, *United States General Housing Characteristics*, 1971; and from housing starts and mobile home shipments for 1960–69 published in *Construction Review*, Vol. 10(8), 1964, Vol. 13(9), 1967, and Vol. 16(10), 1970.

Another valuable adaptation of the replacement rate is in the development of measures of the economic life of older structures. Where the annual growth rate and the replacement rate are known for a given housing market area, the following equation can be used to obtain a measure of the average life of housing units:

$$n = \frac{\log\left(1 + \frac{g}{r} + \frac{g^2 + gr}{2r}\right)}{\log(1+g)}$$

where:

n = average life
g = annual rate of growth of housing stock
r = annual rate of replacement of housing stock

Q. *It is reported that the population composition and related labor force will change significantly in the next decade or two. What is a good overview of these evolving trends, which will have an impact on many sectors of the economy?*

A. The following table provides some insights into real changes in the composition of the population. As noted, the share of labor force 25 to 34 years of age increases from 19.4 percent in 1965 to 27.6 percent by 1985; between 1968 and 1980, the group between ages 24 and 35 is the most rapidly expanding segment; after 1980, the age group 16 to 24 actually decreases by 1.6 million persons for the next half decade.

Total labor force by age and sex, selected years 1955–72 and projected for 1980 and 1985

Category	Millions of Persons							
							Projected	
	1955	1965	1968	1970	1971	1972	1980	1985
Total labor force (including military)	68.1	77.2	82.3	85.9	86.9	89.0	101.8	107.7
Male labor force	47.5	50.9	53.0	54.3	54.8	55.7	62.6	66.0
16–24 years	7.7	9.8	11.0	11.8	12.1	12.6	13.5	12.5
25–34 years	11.5	10.7	11.4	12.0	12.3	12.8	17.5	19.4
35–54 years	19.7	21.6	21.5	21.3	21.2	21.1	21.8	24.4
55–64 years	6.1	6.8	7.0	7.1	7.1	7.1	7.7	7.7
65 years and over	2.5	2.1	2.2	2.2	2.1	2.0	2.1	2.1
Female labor force	20.6	26.2	29.2	31.6	32.1	33.3	39.2	41.7
16–24 years	4.2	5.9	7.2	8.1	8.4	8.9	10.3	9.7
25–34 years	4.3	4.3	5.1	5.7	5.9	6.5	9.3	10.3
35–54 years	9.0	11.4	12.0	12.5	12.5	12.6	13.4	15.1
55–64 years	2.4	3.6	3.9	4.2	4.2	4.2	5.1	5.2
65 years and over	.8	1.0	1.0	1.1	1.1	1.1	1.2	1.3

[1]Compound interest rates between terminal years.
SOURCE: *The Structure of the U.S. Economy in 1980 and 1985*, U.S. Dept. of Labor, Bureau of Labor Statistics, 1975.

Q. *I have had a number of good deals fall through on vacant close-in residential parcels of land because existing deed restrictions limited their use to single family dwellings. In some instances, there were small commercial stores down the street. Nevertheless, several buyers were told this did not matter. What are some reasonable guidelines in cases like this?*

A. Court cases present a mixed picture on the matter of enforcing deed restrictions. The courts take cognizance of changes in the neighborhood, housing patterns, traffic conditions, commercialization, and the like. The following cases highlight some trends in this area of land use.

1. In Back v. Frost (1960) 22 Pa. D & C 2nd 475, the court would not permit the construction of a pair of 17-unit apartment buildings. Evidence presented showed that only 13 of the 165 lots covered by the restriction were in violation. The court stated that where conditions in the area have so changed as to make it impossible to accomplish the purpose for which the restriction was designed, equity would not enforce the restriction.

Average Annual Rates of Change[1]					
			Projected		
1955–68	1965–72	1972–80	1968–85	1968–80	1980–85
1.47	2.06	1.69	1.60	1.79	1.13
.85	1.28	1.58	1.30	1.39	1.07
2.81	3.70	.90	.74	1.75	−1.62
−.06	2.66	3.99	3.19	3.67	2.06
.67	−.35	.37	.74	.11	2.28
1.07	.77	1.00	.55	.79	−.04
−1.22	−.75	.22	−.20	−.38	.23
2.74	3.48	2.09	2.11	2.48	1.23
4.26	6.09	1.78	1.79	3.00	−1.07
1.40	6.01	4.48	4.24	5.09	2.24
2.27	1.36	.80	1.36	.93	2.41
3.91	2.36	2.38	1.66	2.11	.61
1.92	1.52	1.68	1.65	1.81	1.26

2. The case of Dartmouth-Willow Terrace, Inc. v. MacLean (1963, Ky.) 371 S. W. 2nd 937 held that an apartment building could be built since other kinds of multifamily residential projects had been constructed, thus changing the area conditions. The deed restrictions limiting development to single family housing were held inoperative.

3. Rather than granting an injunction, damages for violation of a restriction were awarded in Wicks v. Pat Pallone Co. (1965) 265 NYS2nd 732.

4. Where change in area is fundamental and, in essence, defeats the purpose of the original restriction, courts will generally enforce a restriction as noted in Murphey v. Gray (1958), 84 Ariz. 299.

5. A restriction with no time limitations concurrent with neighborhood changes was cancelled in Realty Corp. v. Gargano (1963), 237 NYS 2nd 648.

6. Violations existing for over 50 years with no objections resulted in the negation of a restriction limiting development to

single-family residences. Noyes v. McDonnell (1965 Okla.) 398 P 2nd 838.

Q. *How would one compute the attrition rate (potential replacement demand) of housing units in an urbanized area?*

A. In computing such an attrition rate it is best to treat each geographic component separately, thus allowing for differences in net change in inventory of housing. It should be noted that removal of housing units from inventory varies from one part of a community to another. This fact is traceable to the differing reasons for such net changes, such as fire destruction, right-of way acquisition, obsolescence, decay, vandalism, and so on. The following tabulation shows one method of analysis:

Housing Units—Net Changes

	Central City	*Suburbs*	*Total SMSA*
Total Housing Units, 1975	12,000	14,000	26,000
Total Housing Units, 1970	10,800	7,200	18,000
Units Built 1970–1975	3,000	5,800	8,800
Units Lost 1970–1975*	1,800	1,000	2,800
Per Year Loss (Units)	360	200	560
Attrition Rate (%)/Year	0.33%	0.56%	0.89%

*Number of units constructed minus number of units added during period.

Q. *Three important characteristics affecting demand for housing in urbanized areas are accessibility, community amenities, and local tax expenditure levels. What impacts do changes in these characteristics have on the standing inventory of single-family housing?*

A. A study involving 46 suburban cities and towns in the Boston SMSA (1960) explored the impact of community attributes on owner-occupied single-family homes (William J. Stull, "An Essay on Externalities, Property Values and Urban Zoning," unpublished Ph.D. dissertation, MIT, 1971). Property value elasticity was estimated for several types of communities and characteristics to assess the effect of new housing construction. The following table shows the elasticity corresponding with several community attributes. For example, an increase of the ratio of local jobs to the number of single family homes results in an increase of 0.02 percent, while multifamily, industrial, and vacant land uses have a negative impact.

Other factors affecting impacts on value elasticity in single-family housing include number of rooms, median age, and lot size and condition. A one percent decrease in median age increases median property values by 0.195 percent, a 1 percent increase in average lot size increases value by 0.113 percent, while a similar increase in the proportion of structurally sound facilities increases the median value of single family homes by 0.838 percent.

As another example of impact, the addition of 52 acres of multifamily housing to a current inventory of 240 acres results in an increase of 22 percent, indicating a decrease in value of 1.95 percent. Suppose the community has 500 houses with a median value of $41,000; the estimated loss per unit is $800.00 or an aggregate $400,000 decrease in value of the single-family homes.

Elasticity of single-family home property value with respect to various community characteristics

Community Characteristic	*Elasticity%*
Accessibility:	
Road Distance to Central Business District	−0.072
Local Employment/Number of Single-Family Homes	0.023
Community Amenities:	
Land Use Pattern:*	
Proportion Land in Multi-Family Homes	−0.090
Proportion Land in Commercial Uses (retail, services, office, hotel-motel, indoor recreation and entertainment)	1.090–32.67+C
Proportion Land in Industrial Uses (manufacturing, transportation and utilities, wholesaling, mining)	−0.121
Proportion Land in Institutional Uses (Medical, religious, public buildings, colleges, cultural)	0.091
Proportion Land Vacant (forests, swamps, rivers, construction projects, military, outdoor amusements)	−0.130
Component Attributes (Single-Family Home):	
Median Number of Rooms	1.698
Median Age	−0.195
Average Lot Size	0.113
Proportion Units Sound, with All Plumbing Facilities	0.838

*Proportions are calculated on total land area minus land area devoted to roads.
+C = proportion land in commercial uses.

Q. *What is a good outline listing all the important components of a housing market analysis?*

A. The following outline lists the elements for a study of housing demand. Part II may often be omitted. The decision to omit this section would depend, of course, on the client's needs, the objective of the study, and other modifying conditions of the assignment.

Local Housing Market Analysis Outline

I. Statement of:
   A. The purpose of the analysis, and
   B. The housing market area and the geographic subareas of the market.

II. Analysis of national business conditions:
   A. The gross national product or comparable measures;
   B. Housing starts;
   C. Federal housing policy;
   D. Mortgage money availability.
      Sources:
      U.S. Dept. of Commerce: *Survey of Current Business Economic Indicators; Construction Review*
      Housing and Home Finance Agency: *Housing Statistics; Annual Report*
      Federal Reserve Board: *Federal Reserve Bulletin; Annual Report;* also, the various F. R. District Bank reports
      U.S. Savings and Loan League: various reports
      Federal Home Loan Bank Board: various reports

III. Analysis of the economic conditions of the local area:
   A. The regional setting
   B. Past and present distribution of economic activities
   C. Economic trends

IV. Basic factors in housing demand:
   A. Population trends; total population, characteristics, households, household formation, family size, and composition
   B. Migration and locational shifts of the population
   C. Distribution and trends in family income and expenditure

V. Basic factors in the housing supply; Census tract analysis:
   A. Present stock of inventory, by general characteristics
   B. Trend in the supply: new construction, conversions, and demolitions
   C. Characteristics and capacity of local home building industry
   D. Availability of mortgage money

E. Special government programs
F. Housing sales
G. Housing occupancy trends
H. Inventory of unsold new homes
I. Foreclosures.

VI. Condition of current housing market:
A. Vacancies, by price ranges, location, duration, and type of unit
B. Estimate of doubling-up factor
C. Construction cost trends
D. Availability and costs of building sites and raw land
E. Local taxes and community controls
F. Real estate activity.

VII. Effective market demand and consumer preferences analysis:
A. Locational preferences
B. House (and lot) size, type, and style preferences
C. Price ranges
D. Financial requirements
E. Ownership vs. rental trends
F. Characteristics of rental housing market

SOURCE: Subdivision Manual, State of California, 1966.

Q. *What has been the performance record of planned unit developments and new towns relating to housing development market capture rates in their respective metropolitan areas?*

A. Since only selective and limited data is available, any index of performance should, of necessity, be carefully evaluated. Furthermore, a capture rate, whether high or low in a relative sense, does not truly indicate the performance of the builder/developer or product offered. Manifestly, capture rates must be viewed as crude performance rates dependent upon a variety of factors and assumptions, such as competition, product mix, image, and so on. The following table outlines some PUD and new town capture rates and the basis of comparison. Since the market sector (last column) is highly subjective, the derivation of this factor, is, of course, conjectural.

Market performance of planned unit developments and new towns 1970–1973

Planned Unit Developments	*SMSA*	*Site Size (Acres)*	*Units Planned*
Amherst Fields	Springfield, Mass.	626	1,640 THs, Condos, SF
Bay Valley	Bay City/Saginaw, Mich.	480	2,400 Apts, THs
Talcott Village	Hartford, Conn.	164	409 Apts, THs, Condos
Flying Hills	Reading, Pa.	305	1,337 Apts. THs, SF
Mountain Park	Portland, Ore.	700	3,800 Apts, THs, SF, Condos
Greenwood Village	Cleveland/Akron, Ohio	840	4,000 Apts, THs, SF
Bay Meadows	Jacksonville, Fla.	450	3,100 Apts, THs
The Preserve	Minneapolis, Minn.	1,200	4,400 Apts, Condos, THs, SF
Edenvale	Minneapolis, Minn.	1,000	4,193 Apts, Condos, THs, SF
New Towns			
Columbia	Washington, D.C./ Baltimore, Md.	15,200	
Reston	Washington, D.C.	7,400	
Irvine Ranch	Orange County, Calif.	83,000	250,000 Apts, THs, Condos, SF

A more detailed analysis could take on the following format.

		Market Segment			
Location	*No. Available**	*Share of Inventory*	*Pace of Sales*	*Market Share*	*Absorption Coefficient*
A	20	18%	3/mo.	17%	(.17/.18) = .94
B	40	36	8/mo.	47	(.47/.36) = 1.30
C	50	45	6/mo.	35	(.35/.45) = .77

Ranking/Pace	*Ranking/Coefficient*
B	B
C	A
A	C

*Within defined time period.

Units Sold (Annual Average)	Building Permits Authorized (Annual Average)		Market Capture Rate (Annual Average)	
	SMSA	Market Sector	SMSA	Market Sector
100	4,156	1,548	2.4%	6.3%
70	3,465	1,164	2.0	6.0
102	5,328	1,881	1.9	5.4
80	1,854	1,854	3.8	3.8
240	16,490	8,894	1.5	2.7
175	16,499	4,680	1.1	3.7
275	9,137	4,454	3.0	6.1
164	20,829	6,249	0.8	2.6
350	20,829	6,249	1.7	5.6
2,002	52,305	29,048	3.8%	6.9%
1,358	32,820	11,157	4.1	12.2
1,900	29,743	29,743	6.4	6.4

Q. *As chairperson of a committee of the local real estate board, you are trying to develop some notions concerning the attractiveness of various suburban areas and the marketability of homes in these areas. What analysis can be undertaken to provide your fellow members with an index of area-attractiveness?*

A. One of the best measures, useful in analyzing both suburbs and urban neighborhoods, is an index of sales activity that ranks the geographic areas under study. By separating new houses from the existing inventory, separate rates for these two segments can be computed; or, using the combined rates, an overall rate can be developed.

The following table illustrates how such an analysis can be done, on an annual basis, for a number of cities, suburbs, or neighborhoods. Where such an analysis is done over several years, a turnover rate-pattern will be discerned for the several areas under study. Companion charting of price trends further improves the analysis and can be a basis for signalling important area dynamics.

Single-family owner occupied housing activity
April 1, 1971—March 30, 1972

		Total Sales			New Units Sold		
		(a)	(b)	(c)	(a)	(b)	(c)
Municipality	Housing Stock-1970	Number	% of Existing Stock	Rank	Number	% of Existing Stock	Rank
Mt. Vernon	8394	329	3.9	20	8	0.0953	23
New Rochelle	11070	434	3.9	19	28	0.2529	20
Peekskill	2801	77	2.7	24	1	0.0357	24
Rye (City)	5020	179	3.5	22	12	0.2390	21
White Plains	7032	289	4.1	18	19	0.2701	19
Yonkers	24347	821	3.3	23	67	0.2751	18
Bedford	3185	214	6.7	7	55	1.7268	6
Cortlandt	7290	458	6.3	9	94	1.2894	10
Eastchester	6540	270	4.12	17	23	0.35	17
Greensburgh	14425	785	5.44	13	83	0.5753	14
Harrison	3902	139	3.51	21	27	0.6919	13
Lewisboro	1540	166	10.7	3	70	4.5454	1
Mamaroneck	5775	352	6.1	10	77	1.3333	9
Mt. Pleasant	7433	447	6.0	11	53	0.7130	12
New Castle	4712	330	7.0	6	75	1.5916	8
North Castle	2185	109	4.9	16	36	1.6475	7
North Salem	857	74	8.6	5	36	4.2007	4
Ossining	5380	338	6.3	9	47	0.8730	11
Pelham	2927	152	5.2	14	6	0.2099	22
Pound Ridge	945	49	5.2	15	27	2.8847	5
Rye (Town)	1916	282	14.7	1	11	0.5741	15
Scarsdale	4888	267	5.5	12	18	0.3682	16
Somers	2115	260	12.2	2	89	4.2080	3
Yorktown	6172	557	9.0	4	263	4.2611	2

SOURCE: New York State Division of Housing and Community Renewal.

Used Units Sold				
(a)	*(b)*	*(c)*		
Number	% of Existing Stock	Rank	New Units as % of Total Sales	Rank
321	3.82	16	2.43	23
406	3.66	18	6.45	20
76	2.71	23	1.29	24
167	3.32	20	6.70	18
270	3.84	15	6.57	19
754	3.09	21	8.16	16
159	4.99	9	25.70	7
364	4.99	8	20.52	10
247	3.77	17	8.51	15
702	4.86	11	10.57	14
112	2.87	22	19.42	11
96	6.23	3	42.16	4
275	4.76	13	21.87	9
394	5.30	6	11.85	13
255	5.41	4	22.72	8
73	3.34	19	33.02	6
38	4.43	14	48.69	2
291	5.40	5	13.90	12
146	4.98	10	3.94	21
22	2.32	24	55.10	1
271	14.14	1	3.90	22
249	5.09	7	6.74	17
171	8.08	2	34.23	5
294	4.76	12	47.21	3

Q. *What are some measures to evaluate a city's level of housing adequacy that can be used either separately or in a comparative subregional context with a number of other communities?*

A. Recent studies and research provide some meaningful methods to facilitate such an analysis. Five measures of housing adequacy include plumbing, vacancy rate, overcrowding, market efficiency, and black/white overcrowding. The following table on 30 major cities and related text outline the findings and consequent implications:

Housing adequacy measures

	Plumbing			
	Index	*Rank*	*Vacancy Rate,%*	*Overcrowding (1.01 or more persons per room,%)*
Atlanta	64	9	5.3	11.0
Baltimore	46	3	5.3	8.7
Boston	171	29	6.0	7.6
Buffalo	84	14	4.8	4.7
Chicago	113	19	5.8	9.9
Cincinnati	130	22	7.5	9.6
Cleveland	75	12	6.1	7.4
Dallas	43	2	7.3	9.0
Denver	107	17	4.6	5.5
Detroit	69	11	5.9	7.5
Houston	58	6	8.2	10.2
Indianapolis	92	15	6.3	8.2
Kansas City	124	21	8.3	6.5
Los Angeles	49	4	4.6	8.3
Miami	145	24	4.0	20.7
Milwaukee	113	19	3.7	7.3
Minneapolis	145	24	3.6	5.1
Newark	159	26	4.7	14.6
New Orleans	95	16	8,2	14.3
New York	81	13	2.8	10.3
Philadelphia	61	7	4.6	6.3
Phoenix	52	5	4.6	9.2
Pittsburgh	188	30	6.3	6.4
Portland	133	23	4.6	3.5
St. Louis	168	28	9.6	12.7
San Diego	66	10	5.8	6.7
San Francisco	165	27	5.0	7.1
San Jose	35	1	3.7	7.0
Seattle	110	18	7.0	3.6
Washington, D.C.	61	7	5.4	12.2

SOURCE: Bureau of Census.

1. *Plumbing.* The lower the number for plumbing, the better the city's plumbing, and the lower the proportion of occupied housing units that have inadequate plumbing (no sink, no toilet or no bath). Using this measure, San Jose has the best plumbing, followed by Dallas, Baltimore, Los Angeles and Phoenix. The cities with the most inadequate plumbing are Pittsburgh, Boston, St. Louis, San Francisco and Newark.

Efficiency		*Black/White Overcrowding*	
Index	*Rank*	*Ratio*	*Rank*
88	22	2.00	6
108	18	3.17	26
109	17	1.80	3
221	3	2.42	16
87	21	2.65	22
69	26	2.18	14
111	16	1.84	5
76	23	3.68	28
194	5	2.06	8
113	15	2.09	10
60	27	2.65	22
96	19	2.45	17
92	20	2.56	20
131	11	1.82	4
60	27	1.64	1
185	6	2.53	19
271	2	2.07	9
73	25	1.66	2
43	29	4.37	29
173	8	2.09	10
172	9	2.41	15
118	14	2.46	18
124	13	2.11	12
310	1	3.35	27
41	30	2.63	21
128	12	3.10	25
140	10	2.11	12
177	7	2.05	7
198	4	3.03	24
76	23	4.70	30

2. *Vacancy Rates.* The vacancy rate is the percentage of sound housing units which are vacant. A high vacancy rate is good for tenants in that it provides them with more choice and allows them to bargain with landlords on rent and lease clauses.

If vacancy rates are below 8%, it means that on the average apartments are rented more than 11 months of a year, placing little pressure on landlords to compete for new tenants by offering lower rents. Using this admittedly arbitrary rule of thumb, only four cities out of the 30 in the survey have any downward pressure on rent. New York City has the lowest vacancy rate followed by Milwaukee, Minneapolis and San Jose. All are under 4%. The 30-city average is nearly 6%. St. Louis has nearly 10% of its housing units vacant and three other cities (Houston, Kansas City and New Orleans) have vacancy rates of over 8%.

3. *Overcrowding.* The overcrowding indicator measures the percentage of dwelling units with more than 1.01 persons per room. A city with many crowded units is one which has a housing shortage. The usual measures of overcrowding are density per square foot or density per room. The Census Bureau uses the latter measure, defining overcrowding as a dwelling unit in which there is more than one person per room. Miami is the most crowded city, since nearly 21% of its dwelling units are overcrowded. The least crowded city is Portland, where less than 4% of all dwelling units are overcrowded.

4. *Efficiency.* The efficiency index shows how well the housing market is functioning: if overcrowding and a high vacancy rate exist simultaneously it implies that the housing market may be segmented and inefficient. The higher the efficiency index number, the more efficient the housing market.

While crowding is a good measure of housing adequacy by itself, it is possible that crowding merely reflects a temporary situation as housing markets adjust to a sudden influx of immigrants. However, if crowding and high vacancy rates exist simultaneously, then the housing market must be considered inefficient—unresponsive to consumer demand. In the absence of evidence to place responsibility elsewhere, the presumption is that the municipality itself is at least partly to blame for any such inefficiency. The validity of this presumption is of course open to argument for individual cities. Indeed, one value of this particular indicator is to identify areas where crowding and high vacancy rates coexist and encourage further research into the reasons for this relationship. Research to date indicates that the most efficient housing markets are in Portland, Minneapolis, Buffalo, Seattle and Denver. The least efficient ones are in St. Louis, New Orleans, Miami, Houston and Cincinnati.

One explanation of housing market inefficiency is that a "dual economy" may exist: crowding in poor neighborhoods coexisting with vacancies in wealthy neighborhoods which have housing that is too expensive for poor families. While income inequality is generally beyond the control of municipalities, local policies often contribute to the widening or lessening of such inequality.

5. *Black/White Overcrowding.* Overcrowding differs for blacks and whites. The degree of difference is measured by the proportion of total black-occupied dwellings with more than one person per room divided by the proportion of total white-occupied dwellings with more than one person per room. Washington, D.C., is the most discriminatory city from the point of view of crowding, although it is the second least discriminatory in terms of how much of their income black and white tenants spend for rent, and is relatively non-discriminatory in terms of black home ownership. The other most discriminatory cities in terms of crowding are Baltimore, Portland, Dallas and New Orleans. The least discriminatory are Miami, Newark, Boston, Los Angeles and Cleveland.

SOURCE: Reprinted from John Tepper Marlin, *City Housing* (New York: Council on Municipal Performance, 1973), p. 26, by permission of the publisher.

Q. *What are some of the principal components of housing demand in an urban area?*

A. The factors most significantly contributing to housing demand include:

1. *Household additions*—the net increase of households, whether due to new household formation or inmigration of existing households attracted by such factors as employment opportunities or climate.

2. *Demolition rate*—the number and kind of units demolished for any of a number of reasons, such as public sector improvements like highway development and urban renewal or removals due to fires and other causes.

3. *Obsolescence rate*—the extent of withdrawal from the market of noncompetitive housing. The age and kind of standing inventory, technological changes, and changes in consumer preferences collectively act to impede or accellerate obsolescence. If, for example, most of the housing units in an area are quite old, the introduction into the marketplace of new, efficient, attractive housing at competitive prices can increase the rate of obsolescence of the standing inventory.

Q. *In analyzing land use allocation for a city or a segment of a large urbanized area, what kinds of data should be assembled to provide some meaningful insights into urban land economics?*

A. Several dimensions are useful in the consideration and measurement of land use allocation trends. For example, in a study of multifamily housing land use in Warren, Michigan, the city was divided into 36 area-neighborhoods. The division lines were based partly on the highway network that has, to some extent, influenced development over a period of years. In this study, three statistics were obtained for each area, as shown below. One statistic was based on the total as-

Land allocation—Assessed values, multifamily housing
Warren, Michigan

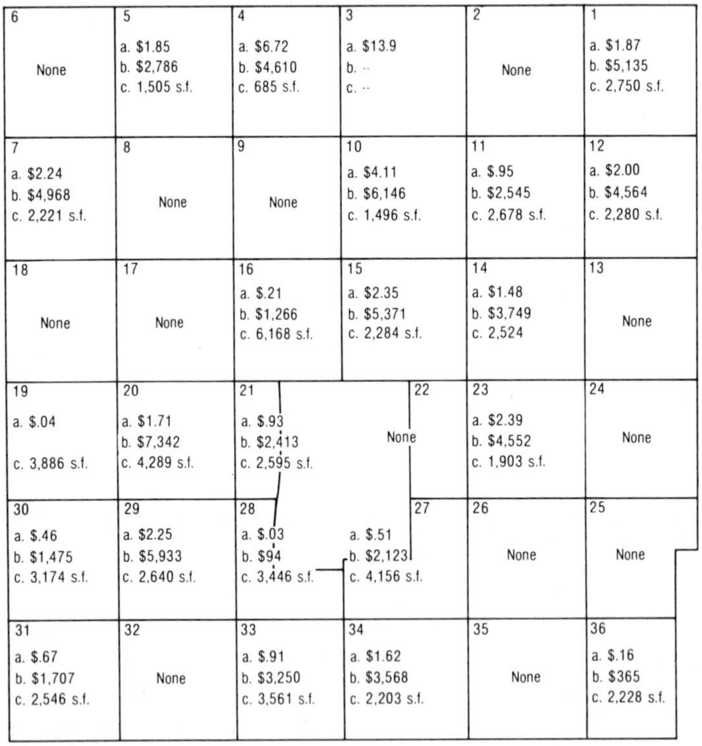

Legend:
a. Assessed Value/Square Foot of Land
b. Assessed Value/Housing Unit
c. Land Area Per Housing Unit

City-Wide Averages:
a. $1.33
b. $3,426
c. 2,579 square feet (This indicates a density of 17 units per acre.)

sessed value of the land and structure per square foot of land; this provides some insight into the relative productivity of land devoted to multifamily housing in various sectors of the city. Another statistic used was the assessed value (land and improvements) per housing unit. This provides measures of the level of tax per unit of housing. The final statistic was the amount of land per housing unit. These sector findings profiled against city-wide averages provide some guides to area performance based on land allocations.

These statistics can in turn be used in ratio form to obtain other relationships. The extent and level of research, data gathering, and analysis are essentially dictated by the scope and importance of an assignment.

Q. *What are some of the reasons for housing rent differentials between white and nonwhite areas in various urban centers?*

A. A study by Robert A. Haugen and James Heins of 82 SMSA's identified several factors accounting for such rent differentials. Part of the analysis included an index of centralization based upon a relationship between the percentage of nonwhites in the SMSA living within the center city and the size of the center city relative to the SMSA.

The value of the centralization variable for any metropolitan area *i* is u_4 from the relationship

$$y_4 = a + bx_4 + u_4$$

where

$$y_4 = \frac{\text{nonwhites in center city } (i)}{\text{nonwhites in total SMSA } (i)}$$

$$x_4 = \frac{\text{total population center city } (i)}{\text{total population SMSA } (i)}$$

SOURCE: Robert A. Haugen and James Heins, "Market Separation Theory of Rent Differentials in Metropolitan Areas," *Quarterly Journal of Economics*, Nov. 1969, pp. 660–72.

A value of u_4 equal to zero means that the SMSA has an average concentration of Blacks in the center city; a positive or negative u_4 implies a greater or less than average concentration respectively. Data for 1950 and 1960 were used and all areas studied had population in excess of 250,000. Based on a theory of market separation, the principal findings indicate that rent differentials are influenced by the following:

1. The nature of ghetto containment (physical and/or market) and the growth of ghettos within the metropolitan area.

2. Rapid growth of the nonwhite population tends to increase the relative rents paid by nonwhites.

3. A rapid rate of suburbanization, essentially by whites, tends to reduce the relative rents paid by nonwhites. This kind of spillover effect tends to reduce pressures for rent increases in any nonwhite contained areas.

Cities included in the survey were:

1. Birmingham, Alabama
2. Mobile, Alabama
3. Fresno, California
4. Los Angeles, California
5. Sacramento, California
6. San Diego, California
7. San Francisco, California
8. San Jose, California
9. Denver, Colorado
10. Bridgeport, Connecticut
11. Hartford, Connecticut
12. New Haven, Connecticut
13. Wilmington, Delaware
14. Washington, D.C.
15. Jacksonville, Florida
16. Miami, Florida
17. Orlando, Florida
18. Tampa-St. Petersburg, Florida
19. Atlanta, Georgia
20. Chicago, Illinois
21. Peoria, Illinois
22. Gary, Indiana
23. Indianapolis, Indiana
24. Des Moines, Iowa
25. Wichita, Kansas
26. Louisville, Kentucky
27. New Orleans, Louisiana
28. Shreveport, Louisiana
29. Baltimore, Maryland
30. Boston, Massachusetts
31. Detroit, Michigan
32. Flint, Michigan
33. Grand Rapids, Michigan
34. Lansing, Michigan
35. Minneapolis-St. Paul, Minnesota
36. Kansas City, Missouri-Kansas
37. St. Louis, Missouri
38. Omaha, Nebraska
39. Jersey City, New Jersey
40. Newark, New Jersey
41. Patterson, New Jersey
42. Trenton, New Jersey
43. Albuquerque, New Mexico
44. Albany, New York
45. Buffalo, New York
46. New York, New York
47. Rochester, New York
48. Syracuse, New York
49. Charlotte, North Carolina
50. Akron, Ohio
51. Canton, Ohio
52. Cincinnati, Ohio
53. Cleveland, Ohio
54. Columbus, Ohio
55. Dayton, Ohio
56. Toledo, Ohio
57. Youngstown, Ohio
58. Oklahoma City, Oklahoma
59. Tulsa, Oklahoma
60. Portland, Oregon
61. Harrisburg, Pennsylvania
62. Philadelphia, Pennsylvania
63. Pittsburgh, Pennsylvania
64. Providence, Rhode Island
65. Columbia, South Carolina
66. Chattanooga, Tennessee
67. Knoxville, Tennessee
68. Memphis, Tennessee
69. Nashville, Tennessee
70. Beaumont-Port Arthur, Texas
71. Dallas, Texas
72. El Paso, Texas
73. Fort Worth, Texas
74. Houston, Texas
75. San Antonio, Texas
76. Norfolk, Virginia
77. Richmond, Virginia
78. Seattle, Washington
79. Tacoma, Washington
80. Charleston, West Virginia
81. Huntington, West Virginia
82. Milwaukee, Wisconsin

Q. *You are reviewing a report that includes the following table of analysis. What other meaningful derivations can be obtained from the data?*

Estimated population—Rochester SMSA
1970 and 1975

County	U.S. Census 1960	U.S. Census 1970	1975 Estimate	Estimated Net Migration	Estimated Natural Increase	Change 1970–1975	Five-Year Growth Rate
Livingston	44,053	54,041	60,608	4,718	1,849	+ 6,567	+12.2%
Monroe	586,387	711,917	748,340	14,569	21,854	+36,423	+ 5.1
Ontario	68,070	78,849	88,095	6,480	2,766	+ 9,246	+11.7
Orleans	34,159	37,305	42,343	3,773	1,265	+ 5,038	+13.5
Wayne	67,989	79,404	88,870	6,426	3,040	+ 9,466	+11.9
Total SMSA	800,658	961,516	1,028,256	35,966	30,774	66,740	+ 6.9

SOURCES: U.S. Census; Estimates by Genesee/Finger Lakes Regional Information System.

A. While rate of change is meaningful, an additional analysis might be made of the share of total population involved in migration during various periods and the shares of net migration and natural increase. For example, Monroe county shows the lowest five-year growth rate (5.1 percent) when in fact it had a 40.5 percent share of total SMSA in-migration and 71.0 percent of the natural increase.

Area	Shares of Population 1960	Shares of Population 1970	Shares of Population 1975	Net Change of Shares, 1970–75: Net Migration	Net Change of Shares, 1970–75: Natural Increase
Livingston	5.5%	5.6%	5.9%	13.1%	6.0%
Monroe	73.2	74.0	72.8	40.5	71.0
Ontario	8.5	8.2	8.6	18.0	9.0
Orleans	4.3	3.9	4.1	10.5	4.1
Wayne	8.5	8.3	8.6	17.9	9.9

Q. *New annual household formations have been forecast at 6,500 per year, need for assisted housing at 1,200, replacement demand at 600, and tenure for single-family housing at 40 percent. Based on these facts, develop a schedule for the private sector to indicate the potential market in the next year for single-family housing in the subject market area, assuming, for the moment, adequate financial capabilities of the nonassisted households.*

A. New Household Formations	6,500 units
Assisted Housing	1,200
Private Sector Housing Demand	5,300
Replacement Demand	600
Total Annual Housing Demand	5,900
Tenure—Preference Share	.40
Total Forecast Single Family Housing Demand	2,360 units

Q. *A client has received a housing market study and requests some comments from you. The following table is of interest because of the significant change in the distribution of income. What does it all mean?*

			Projected to:	
Household Cash Income	X Year	Percent	Y Year	Z Year
Under $5,000	1971	19.6	23.2	18.7
Under $10,000	1971	39.0	33.3	30.6
Over $10,000	1971	41.4	50.7	74.5

A. The tabulations and findings are totally wrong. The base year (X) begins with a distribution (100.00 percent) of household incomes; by Y year the households total 107.2 percent, which of course is impossible, and by Z year the total is likewise an impossibility (123.8 percent). Furthermore, the base data is incorrectly reported; households with incomes under $10,000 really total 58.6 percent. The categories should probably read: Under $4,999, $5,000 to $9,999, and $10,000 and over.

Q. *What are the benefits, if any, to residential properties adjacent to or in the immediate area of public community parks?*

A. A study (see table credit line) of five parks in the city of Columbus, Ohio, was made to determine the effect of the park on adjacent residential property values (predominantly single-family homes). Locational qualities of houses vis-a-vis the park were as follows:

1. Hauntz, Linden, and Westgate: houses face park with street between them.

2. Audubon and Kenlawn: houses back onto park, with and without fence separation.

Externalities generated by municipal parks
Columbus, Ohio

Parks Included	Intercept	R	A	L	S_1	S_2	P_F	P_B	P_R	R^2
(1) Westgate & Hauntz #1	4446	1436	−46.62	0.8991	—	1416	1130	—	—	.720
	(910)	(412)	(33.41)	(0.2020)		(617)	(580)			
(2) Kenlawn & Audubon	12973	1319	−151.5	−0.0578	—	842.1	—	−169.3	—	.807
	(557)	(295)	(34.8)	(0.2313)		(614.4)		(556.9)		
(3) Linden	−8277	492.5	−70.24	3.783	1140	1231	—	—	−1144	.483
	(9273)	(396.8)	(38.60)	(1.575)	(704)	(585)			556)	
(4) Westgate & Hauntz #2	5365	1335	−53.45	0.8687	—	1470	1609	—	−178.3	.749
	(885)	(398)	(32.24)	(0.1944)		(593)	(604)		(840.0)	
(5) All parks combined	10660	1215	−135.2	0.2825	750.7	863.8	3434	−1030	−1057	.657
	(494)	(222)	(20.2)	(0.1422)	(422.6)	(390.7)	(526)	(656)	(422)	

Variables:

R–number of rooms in house.

A–age of house at time of sale.

L–size of lot, in square feet.

S_1–dummy variable for year of sale, taking value 1 if house was sold in 1966 or 1967, and 0 otherwise.

S_2–dummy variable for year of sale, taking value 1 if house was sold in 1968 or 1969, and 0 otherwise.

P_F–dummy variable taking value 1 if property is adjacent to park and house faces the park, and 0 otherwise.

P_B–dummy variable taking value 1 if property is adjacent to park and house backs onto the park, and 0 otherwise.

P_R–dummy variable taking value 1 if property is adjacent to park and house faces area of heavy recreational use, or park building, and 0 otherwise.

In the regression analysis, sales price was used as a dependent variable involving transactions between 1965–1969.

The following are some basic findings from this study:

1. Properties that face an adjacent park sold for approximately $1,130 more.
2. Properties backing up to a park sell for about the same as other houses in the area.
3. Properties having an obstructed view of the park (Linden) rather than a scenic view sold for $1,150 less than other immediately proximate properties.
4. Properties adjacent to Hauntz and Westgate parks sold for 7 percent more than other area properties, while those adjoining Linden Park sold for about 8 percent less.

The researchers generally concluded that the principal value impact (externally) of a public park is attributable to a combination of factors including (1) relationship of house to park, (2) view from house—scenic or otherwise, and (3) reputation of area as perceived by home owners.

As an example of the last point, both Kenlawn and Audubon parks have had reports of disturbances, drinking, and so-forth. As can be seen, the mere presence of a park is not necessarily indicative of higher property values. Rather, increased privacy and a desirable view apparently rate as significant contributors to higher property values of houses adjacent to public park areas.

From a benefit/cost analysis, the research indicated that the ratio of externalities (rents, number of lots, and the like) to opportunity costs concerning park facility investments were 8.19 percent for Westgate and 22.41 percent for Hauntz park.

SOURCE: John C. Weicher and Robert H. Zerbst, "The Externalities of Neighborhood Parks; An Empirical Investigation," *Land Economics*, 49, February 1973. Reprinted by permission of the editor.

Q. *What is the impact on the surrounding property value of electric utility power plants or similar facilities?*

A. A study of the impact of the Winnetka Power Plant in Winnetka, Illinois, provides some indications as to real or latent impact of power plants on surrounding property values. The plant has an installed generating capacity of 26 thousand kilowatts, burning 23 thousand tons of coal with the heat generated primarily derived from the burning coal.

The extent of disamenity from this kind of facility in the surrounding area is generally due to the nuisance and undesirable effects as perceived by people residing in close proximity. The technique used to measure the level of disamenity was through census block data including mean property values in the most likely affected area. The subject area is considered to be a prestige community on Lake Michigan, just north of Chicago proper.

Findings by Glenn Bloomquist ("The Effect of Electric Utility Power Plant Location on Area Property Value," *Land Economics*, February 1974) indicate that the crucial area of influence is within 11,500 feet of the power plant; that a typical property loses 0.9 percent of its value for each 10 percent move closer to the plant. Citing a study of a waste disposal site location and its effect on property value (J. Havlicek Jr., R. Richardson, and L. Davies, *University of Chicago Urban Economics Report No. 65, 1971*), Bloomquist notes a high correlation between the results of this earlier study and his own findings.

Apparently perceptions of users and buyers of housing in close proximity to such facilities are quite congruent. No generalization can be inferred however, since prevailing winds, natural or manmade obstacles can modify the extent of impact. Each situation must be individually evaluated.

Q. *What are the factors to be considered when developing estimates of the total resident population during the period between census reports?*

A. The following outline shows the elements usually included in the computation of this kind of estimate for a given geographical area:

Computation of estimated total resident population

1. Civilian resident population, April 1, 1960	271,969
2. Births, April 1, 1960 through July 1, 1967	49,393
3. Deaths, April 1, 1960 through July 1, 1967	16,177
4. Natural increase	33,216
5. Estimated net civilian migration, April 1, 1960 through July 1, 1967	+16,227
6. Net movement between civilian and military populations, April 1, 1960 through July 1, 1967	−1,422
7. Estimated civilian resident population, July 1, 1967	319,990
8. Resident military population in county, July 1, 1967	156
9. ESTIMATED TOTAL RESIDENT POPULATION, JULY 1, 1967	320,146

Line sources:
(1) Census report.
(2) Local records.
(3) Local records.
(4) Line 2—line 3.
(5) Census or local report(s).
(6) Census or local report(s).
(7) Line 1 + line 4 + line 5 + line 6.
(8) Population Division, Bureau of the Census, available on request. (Based on data from the Department of Defense.)
(9) Line 7 + line 8.

SOURCE: R-618, HUD Report, June, 1971.

Q. *In the study of population changes for different geographical areas, what is the change-in-share ratio analysis?*

A. The technique involves a comparison of a unit, such as a county unit, to a larger parent population such as a state. For example, if three counties, labeled 1, 2, and 3, formed a SMSA or State Economic Area (SEA), then the analysis indicated below would show that in 1950 the shares of state population attributable to each county would cause them to be ranked 3, 1, and 2 in descending order. By 1960 the rankings based on population changes would be the same. However, when analyzed for change in share for the decade, the counties would be 2, 3, and 1, in descending order.

Change-in-share ratios analysis

	Resident Population				
County	(1) 1950	(2) 1950 Share (%)	(3) 1960	(4) 1960 Share (%)	(5) Change-in-Share Ratio (Y)
1	85,300	2.132	98,600	2.089	0.9798
2	50,000	1.250	63,100	1.337	1.0696
3	103,100	2.577	123,400	2.614	1.0144
.	.	.	.	.	.
.	.	.	.	.	.
.	.	.	.	.	.
.	.	.	.	.	.
N					
State Total	4,001,000	100.000	4,720,000	100.000	1.0000

Columns
(1) *1950 Census of Population.*
(2) Column 1: (county population ÷ state total) × 100.
(3) *1960 Census of Population.*
(4) Column 3: (county population ÷ state total) × 100.
(5) Column 4: column 2.

SOURCE: R-618.HUD Report, June, 1971.

Q. *What steps are used in the vital rates method for estimating population?*

A. This method is based on an estimate of the annual number of births and deaths. It is assumed that this figure will be proportional to the total size of the population. The following illustrates the technique:

Population estimates by the vital rates method

1. County resident births, 1959	7,012
2. County resident births, 1960	6,928
3. County resident births, 1961	7,100
4. County resident births, centered on April 1, 1960	6,981
5. Total resident population, April 1, 1960	272,111
6. County crude birth rate, centered on April 1, 1960	25,655
7. National ratio of 1967 to 1960 crude birth rates	0.7469
8. Estimated county crude birth rate, 1967	19.162
9. County resident births, 1967	6,081
10. Total resident population, July 1, 1967, implied by birth data	317,347
11. County resident deaths, 1959	2,057
12. County resident deaths, 1960	2,152
13. County resident deaths, 1961	2,021
14. County resident deaths, centered on April 1, 1960	2,100
15. County crude death rate, centered on April 1, 1960	7,717
16. National ratio of 1967 to 1960 crude death rates	1.0267
17. Estimated county crude death rate, 1967	7.9230
18. County resident deaths, 1967	2,371
19. Total resident population, July 1, 1967, implied by death data	299,255
20. Final estimate of total resident population, July 1, 1967	308,301

Line Sources:

(1), (2), (3) Calendar year births and deaths by residence are available from the National Center for Health Statistics. All computations above should be carried out separately by race if vital statistics are so classified.

(4) Calculate as follows: [(0.75 × line 1) + (line 2) + (0.25 × line 3)] ÷ 2.0.

(5) U.S. Bureau of the Census, *1960 Census of Population*. If the total resident population base includes an appreciable resident military population, use civilian resident population instead.

(6) (Line 4 ÷ line 5) × 1,000.

(7) Calculate from data published periodically in U.S. Bureau of the Census, *Current Population Reports*. (Values used here were derived from Series P-25, No. 388, using estimates to 1966 and Series D projections for 1967.)

(8) Line 6 × line 7.

(9) See source (2).

(10) (Line 9 ÷ line 8) × 1,000.

(11), (12), (13) See source (2).

(14) Calculate as follows: [(0.75 × line 11) + (line 12) + (0.25 × line 13)] ÷ 2.0.

(15) (Line 14 ÷ line 5) × 1,000.

(16) See source (7).

(17) Line 15 × line 16.

(18) See source (2).

(19) (Line 18 ÷ line 17) × 1,000.

(20) Calculate as follows: (0.5 × line 10) + (0.5 × line 19). Alternative weights may be used where appropriate.

Q. *How is the housing unit method employed in urbanized areas to estimate current population?*

A. Four basic elements are employed when using this method. These include (1) number of households in base year, (2) number of new housing units added for period under study, (3) number of housing units demolished, and (4) average population of persons 18 years and over per household. The technique is illustrated below.

Population estimates by housing unit method

Estimate Population 18+ Per Household, 1967		
1. County population 15+, April 1, 1960		181,042
2. County population 18+, April 1, 1960		168,774
3. Ratio of population 18+ to population 15+		0.9322
4. County population 15+ in households, April 1, 1960		175,875
5. Estimated county population 18+ in households, April 1, 1960		163,951
6. County population 18+ in group quarters, April 1, 1960		4,823
7. County number of households, April 1, 1960		76,877
8. County population 18+ per household, April 1, 1960		2.1326
9. Ratio between average population 18+ per household in 1967 and 1968		0.9858
10. Estimated county population 18+ per household, July 1, 1967		2.1023
Estimate Number of Households, 1967	*Based on Utility Data*	*Based on Building Data*
11. New housing units authorized between January 1, 1960 and December 31, 1965	—	16,892
12. Occupancy rate for units constructed before 1959	—	0.9603
13. New housing units authorized between January 1, 1966 and April 1 1967	—	5,336
14. Occupancy rate for units constructed 1959 through March, 1960	—	0.8701
15. Demolitions, April 1, 1960 through July 1, 1967	—	5,912
16. Estimated net change in households, 1960 through 1967	—	+14,952
17. Estimated net change in households, 1960 through 1967	+20,800	—
18. Estimated number of households, July 1, 1967	97,677	91,829
Estimate Population 18+, 1967		
19. Estimated county population 18+ in households, July 1, 1967	205,346	193,052
20. Estimated total county population 18+ July 1, 1967	210,169	197,875

continued

Line Sources:

(1) U.S. Bureau of the Census, *1960 Census of Population.*
(2) See source (1).
(3) Line 2 ÷ line 1.
(4) *1960 Census of Population.*
(5) Line 3 × line 4.
(6) Line 2 − line 5.
(7) *1960 Census of Population.*
(8) Line 5 ÷ line 7.
(9) U.S. Bureau of the Census, *Current Population Reports,* Series P-20, No. 173.
(10) Line 8 × line 9.
(11) Sum of building permits issued, by year. Obtain locally.
(12) *1960 Census of Housing,* Table 12.
(13) See source 11.
(14) *1960 Census of Housing.*
(15) Sum of demolitions, by year. Obtain locally.
(16) (Line 11 × line 12) + (line 13 × line 14) − line 15.
(17) Electric utility residential customers, June 30, 1967 minus residential customers, April 1, 1960. Obtain locally.
(18) Line 7 + line 16 or line 17.
(19) Line 10 × line 18.
(20) Line 19 + line 6.

SOURCE: *R-618,* HUD Report, June, 1971.

Q. *Because of changes in population mix, what are some basic and realistic assumptions concerning personal consumption expenditures in the foreseeable future?*

A. A leveling of many sectors of the U.S. economy is expected during the decade from 1980 to 1990. Emerging changes in consumer consumption are anticipated because of the impact of evolving population mix as well as a probable shift in consumer needs and requirements. The table below highlights some of these probable changes.

Personal consumption expenditures, selected years 1955–72 and projected for 1980 and 1985

	Average annual rates of change[1]								
						Projected			
	1951–59	1955–68	1960–69	1965–72	1968–72	1972–80	1968–85	1968–80	1980–85
Personal consumption expenditures	3.5	4.0	4.5	4.0	3.8	4.6	4.0	4.3	3.3
Durable goods	4.1	4.9	7.4	6.6	6.5	4.5	4.5	5.2	3.1
Autos and parts	4.5	4.3	7.6	6.4	6.6	4.5	4.4	5.2	2.7
Furniture and household equipment	3.3	5.1	7.1	6.8	7.0	4.0	4.5	5.0	3.3
Other durable goods	5.2	6.9	7.7	6.5	4.7	5.9	5.0	5.5	4.0
Nondurable goods	2.9	3.2	3.5	3.1	2.8	4.1	3.4	3.7	2.8
Food and beverages	2.6	2.4	2.4	2.0	1.6	3.7	2.8	3.0	2.4
Clothing and shoes	2.4	3.6	4.3	3.8	3.5	3.3	2.9	3.4	1.9
Gasoline and oil	5.9	4.4	4.7	5.6	5.8	5.1	5.0	5.3	4.4
Other nondurable goods	3.1	4.3	4.8	4.0	3.8	5.2	4.4	4.7	3.5
Services	4.0	4.4	4.6	4.1	3.7	5.0	4.4	4.6	3.9
Housing	5.1	4.9	5.1	4.2	3.9	5.1	4.6	4.7	4.3
Household operation services	4.6	4.5	4.7	4.8	4.7	4.9	4.6	4.9	4.1
Transportation services	1.2	2.6	2.6	3.0	2.2	4.3	3.3	3.6	2.7
Other services	3.5	4.3	4.6	3.8	3.3	5.2	4.3	4.6	3.7

[1]Compound interest rates between terminal years.

SOURCE: Historical data from U.S. Department of Commerce, Bureau of Economic Analysis, converted to 1963 dollars by Bureau of Labor Statistics; projections by Bureau of Labor Statistics.

Q. *What are State Economic Areas (SEA), their attributes and uses in economic research, and how are they related to Standard Metropolitan Statistical Areas (SMSA)?*

A. State Economic Areas are relatively homogeneous subdivisions of states. They consist of single counties or groups of counties that have similar economic and social characteristics. SMSA's are basically an extension of this concept and are recognized as metropolitan versions of the State Economic Areas. In turn, State Economic Areas combine to form economic subregions.

A good basic source, which includes a list of the counties included in the various SEA's, is a Bureau of Census report, PC(2)-108, U.S. Dept of Commerce, Washington, D.C. For example, if a problem concerned the extent of population below the poverty level in Waldo County, Maine, Storey County, Nevada, and Wheeler County, Texas, the above publication would reveal that the first is an SEA of 5 counties, the second is in an SEA of 16 counties, and the last is in an SEA of 32 counties. The specifics on each county for 1970 are reported as follows.

	Area 3 (Maine)	*Area 6 (Texas)*	*Area 1 (Nevada)*
Families	$4,823	$12,114	$3,814
Percentage of all families	13.4%	18.5%	6.9%
Mean Income Deficit	$1,244	$ 1,341	$1,412
Unrelated Individuals	$5,999	$10,700	$6,574
Percentage of all unrelated individuals	50.2%	55.1%	28.8%

A variety of meaningful analyses can be undertaken involving any of many activities located within an SEA.

Q. *The dynamic changes, both positive and negative, occuring in various urban neighborhoods and adjacent urbanized areas are of immediate interest to many different segments of society, both in the public and private sectors. What is a simple method, using readily available data, to measure rates of change in areas and neighborhoods?*

A. A recent study, *Social Change Index Study Project*, (Providence, R.I.: Rhode Island Council of Community Services, Inc. June, 1974) involved an analysis of 37 census tracts in the city of Providence. Rates

Social change index (G) profile of Providence by census tract 1971

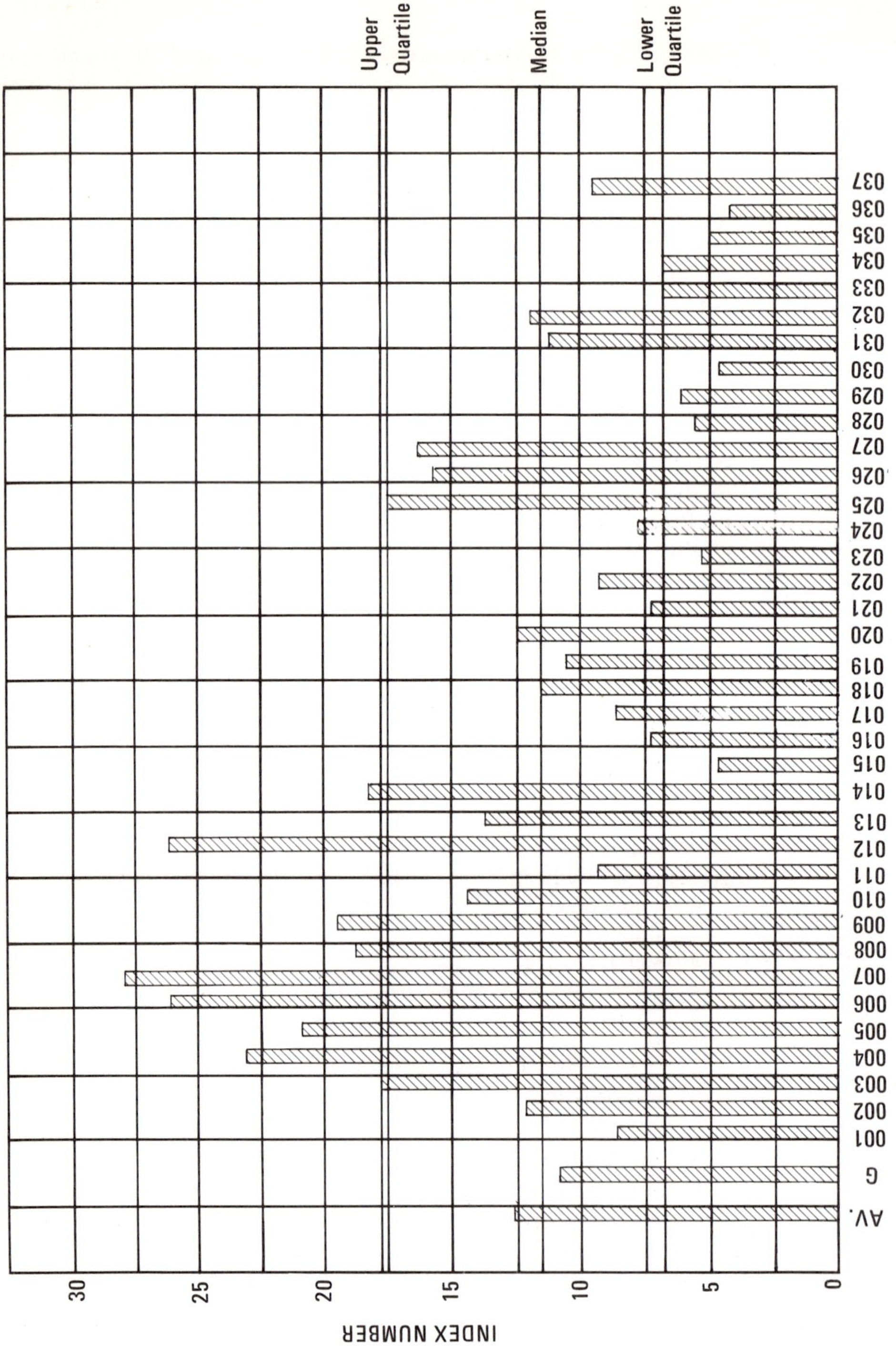

of change of six social indicators were used to compute an index of social change. They were

1. Born Out of Wedlock Children Rate
   (per thousand females in age group 15–44)
2. Low Birth Weight Infants Rate
   (per hundred live births)
3. Veneral Disease Rate
   (per thousand population)
4. Hepatitis Rate
   (per ten thousand population)
5. Death Rate
   (per thousand population)
6. Dependency Ratio
   (ratio of the total of the number of persons in the age group 0–14 and the number of persons in the age group 65+ to the number of persons in the age group 15–64)

One of the principal objectives of the study was to measure the apparent change in the level of the quality of life in the community. A geometric mean was computed for each census tract for each year, 1968 thru 1973, using the following equation for the six variables.

$$G = \sqrt[6]{x_1 \cdot x_2 \cdot x_3 \cdot x_4 \cdot x_5 \cdot x_6}$$

Twelve subareas were identified and given a rating based upon a combination of the ratings for the census tracts comprising the subarea. The result was a ranking of the 12 identified subareas as noted in the table.

An additional by-product of the data analysis was a social change index profile for each of the years by census tract. This profile, for the year 1971, is shown in the accompanying chart.

As noted in the report, "It appears that the index has potential as a predictor; in effect it seems to have predicted the geographical (home address) composition of the inmates of the prison for two years in advance" (pp. 23–24). Other measures of change in the quality of life within areas and neighborhoods are suggested by the following.

- unemployment claims
- temporary disability claims
- sales tax receipts by category
- admissions to prisons
- juvenile delinquency

Social change indices Providence subcommunities
1968—1972 comparative rankings

Subcommunity	*1968*	*1969*	*1970*	*1971*	*1972*
South Providence	1	1	1	1	1
Elmwood	5	2	2	2	2
West End	3	4	4	5	3
Smith Hill-Lower Mt. Pl.	2	3	5	4	4
Federal Hill	4	5	3	3	5
Eagle Park-Wanskuck	10	8	6	8	6
Annex-Manton	6	6	7	6	7
Washington Park	9	11	9	7	8
College Hill-Fox Point	12	10	11	11	9
Hope	7	7	8	9	10
Elmhurst-Upper Mt. Pl.	11	12	12	10	11
East Side	8	9	10	12	12

- arrests by home address of offender
- welfare recipients (by welfare classification)
- fire alarms
- school truancy
- school dropouts

Q. *What are some measurements that can be used to ascertain poverty levels in a community?*

A. Several different measures of poverty can be utilized. As an example, the 1974 Housing and Community Development Act (Table II, Section 8) defines "lower income families" as those whose incomes are at or below 80 percent of the median income for the area. Additional adjustments are made to take into account such aspects as family size, construction costs, and so forth. Further, "very low income families" are defined as those whose income does not exceed 50 percent of the median family income for the area, with adjustment for family size. Under these criteria, poverty is a relative matter based on location, cost of living index, and so on.

Another measure is based on absolute levels of income of a family, adjusted for several other related factors and family components. This statistic is based on the 1970 censes data and is given in the table opposite.

Poverty cutoffs: Criteria used in determining poverty status for 1970 census (income figures are for 1969)

		Number of Related Children Under 18 Years Old						
		None	1	2	3	4	5	6 or more
	Male Head				*Nonfarm*			
1	Under 65 years old	$1,975	—	—	—	—	—	—
	65 years old & over	1,774	—	—	—	—	—	—
2	Under 65 years old	2,469	$2,766	—	—	—	—	—
	65 years old & over	2,216	2,766	—	—	—	—	—
3	....	2,875	2,968	$3,137	—	—	—	—
4	....	3,790	3,847	3,715	$3,902	—	—	—
5	....	4,574	4,630	4,481	4,368	$4,462	—	—
6	....	5,247	5,265	5,153	5,041	4,891	$4,967	—
7	or more	6,609	6,665	6,535	6,422	6,274	6,049	$5,994
	Male Head				*Farm*			
1	Under 65 years old	$1,679	—	—	—	—	—	—
	65 years old & over	1,508	—	—	—	—	—	—
2	Under 65 years old	2,099	$2,351	—	—	—	—	—
	65 years old & over	1,884	2,351	—	—	—	—	—
3	....	2,444	2,523	$2,666	—	—	—	—
4	....	3,222	3,270	3,158	$3,317	—	—	—
5	....	3,888	3,936	3,809	3,713	$3,793	—	—
6	....	4,460	4,475	4,380	4,285	4,157	$4,222	—
7	or more	5,618	5,665	5,555	5,459	5,333	5,142	$5,095
	Female Head				*Nonfarm*			
1	Under 65 years old	$1,826	—	—	—	—	—	—
	65 years old & over	1,752	—	—	—	—	—	—
2	Under 65 years old	2,282	$2,491	—	—	—	—	—
	65 years old & over	2,190	2,491	—	—	—	—	—
3	....	2,781	2,651	$2,931	—	—	—	—
4	....	3,641	3,771	3,753	$3,715	—	—	—
5	....	4,368	4,500	4,481	4,444	$4,294	—	—
6	....	5,096	5,191	5,153	5,115	4,948	$4,798	—
7	or more	6,403	6,497	6,478	6,422	6,255	6,124	$5,825
	Female Head				*Farm*			
1	Under 65 years old	$1,552	—	—	—	—	—	—
	65 years old & over	1,489	—	—	—	—	—	—
2	Under 65 years old	1,940	$2,117	—	—	—	—	—
	65 years old & over	1,862	2,117	—	—	—	—	—
3	....	2,364	2,253	$2,491	—	—	—	—
4	....	3,095	3,205	3,190	$3,158	—	—	—
5	....	3,713	3,825	3,809	3,777	$3,650	—	—
6	....	4,332	4,412	4,380	4,348	4,206	$4,078	—
7	or more	5,443	5,522	5,506	5,459	5,317	5,205	$4,951

SOURCE: *Public Use Samples of Basic Records From the 1970 Census: Description and Technical Documentation*, Bureau of the Census April 1972, p. 122.

Q. *What is political Balkanization and how does it affect urban land development activities?*

A. The study of political Balkanization involves a determination of the optimum size of political jurisdictions from the standpoint of services. Likewise, a determination should be made of jurisdictions from the point of view of the financing of those services, such as schools, fire and police protection, social services, and so forth.

Land development in the urban context must concern itself with more than on-site costs and proximity to labor markets. The total utility of housing, for example, relates to a large bundle of external services and facilities. Proper and adequate schools have a direct impact on marketability. Manifestly, the political entity within which the land is located and the ability of such entities to provide the various urban-oriented services at a cost commensurate to the income levels of the residents is of prime importance. Such factors can have great significance when considering economic feasibility of land conversion to urban use.

Q. *In judging existing shopping areas, what are some things to look for in terms of exterior structure and immediate area characteristics?*

A. The following 11 check-points are important aspects to consider in any evaluation of existing shopping facilities.

Criteria for judgment of quality of shopping area

Pedestrian Interruptions	Interruption of the flow of pedestrian shoppers contribute to the decline of an area as a desirable place to shop. Examples of obstruction to pedestrian flow include: a. Commercial blocks containing mixtures of retail and service uses b. Dead spots, such as vacant lots and alleys which will cause the shopper to lose interest. c. Traffic, either vehicular or pedestrian, which does not generate shoppers.
Sidewalks-Poor Condition	Broken and uneven sidewalks littered with trash discourage pedestrian shopping.
Alleys-Poor Condition	Poorly maintained alleys and rear yards are a blighting influence on all types of commercial areas as well as adjacent residential property.
Inadequate Parking	Lack of parking facilities will contribute to the obsolescence of commercial structures before actual physical deterioration is evident.

continued

Criteria for judgment of quality of shopping area (cont.)

Traffic	An excess of through-traffic adds nothing to the retail shopping center; it tends to divide the area into segments and interferes with automobile and pedestrian traffic.
Inadequate Off-Street Loading	When separate loading facilities are not provided, standing trucks block streets and sidewalks and reduce the flow of traffic.
Short Blocks	Retail stores built on short blocks created by frequent street intersections suffer from disrupted flow of shoppers and excessive traffic congestion.
Obsolescence of Structures	Obsolescence due to lack of adequate floor space, inadequate site and other design features will contribute to the decline of a shopping area.
Condition of Structures	One blighted structure in an area will contribute to the decline of confidence in a shopping area, thus contributing to additional blight.
Vacant Upper Floors in Structures	A healthy vigorous center will usually have the second floor occupied. Vacant second floors will generally indicate an advanced degree of obsolescence.
Uncontrolled Signs	Uncontrolled exterior signs usually downgrade the general appearance of the entire area and in the general confusion created, will defeat their original intent. Signs will give an indication of the general condition of the area.
	Other signs which may indicate a deteriorating shopping center are: Frequent shift of occupants A noticeable number of vacancies Shift to non-retail or service areas Lack of maintenance

SOURCE: Excerpted from *Commercial Facilities: A Citywide Facts and Inventory Report, Phase 1 Community Improvement Program*. Report to the Minneapolis Planning Commission and City Council. Pub. No. 143, Community Improvement Program Series No. 4, Spring 1963.

Q. *When doing a market-feasibility study for a large office building in a large city, the matter of absorption of new office space is critical. What has been the experience and what assumptions can be made to provide a plausible basis for this kind of study?*

A. A study of the San Francisco Central Business District (CBD) revealed the sources of demand over a 15-year period and provided a forecast of the most probable demand factors of the next 15 years. The data provides a numerical accounting of the past and anticipated absorption levels attributable to the several demand factors.

Absorption of new office space in the San Francisco CBD

	1960–1974		1974–1990 Low		1974–1990 High	
	Millions of Sq. Ft.	Percent	Millions of Sq. Ft.	Percent	Millions of Sq. Ft.	Percent
Periodic Increase in Office Space Inventory (Millions of Square Feet Gross)	23.0	100%	10.0	100%	30.0	100%
Absorbed as Nonleasable Space	4.6	20%	2.0	20%	6.0	20%
Absorbed by Increase in County Employment[1]	6.3	28%	5.7	57%	9.5	32%
Absorbed by Increase in Office Job Coefficients[2]	0.9	4%	0.9	9%	2.5	8%
Absorbed by "Relocation" of Office Jobs to CBD Office Space[3]	5.6	25%	3.2	32%	5.4	18%
Absorbed by Increase in Space/Worker Requirement	3.0	13%	0	0%	5.5	19%
Accounted for by Change in Overall Vacancy Rate	2.4	11%	(1.8)[4]	(18%)[4]	0.7	2%
Total[5]	22.8	100%	10.0	100%	29.6	100%

[1]Assumes that the entire office job share (at beginning-of-period rate) of new employment locates in the CBD.

[2]Attributed to the difference between periodic increase in office jobs and the increase that would have occurred if job coefficients had remained at beginning-of-period rates.

[3]Based on the difference between the periodic increase in CBD office workers and the periodic increase in office jobs. In other words, these are jobs located outside the CBD at the beginning of the period which were either relocated to the CBD or replaced by jobs located in the CBD.

[4]A decline in overall vacancy rates from 7 percent back to the 1960 level of 2 percent will make available an additional 1.8 million square feet out of pre-1975 inventory. This space will accommodate that portion of the periodic increase in demand that exceeds post-1974 additions to inventory in scenarios 2 and 4.

[5]Totals do not always equal 100 percent due to rounding.

SOURCE: Keyser Marston Associates

Percent of new CBD office space absorbed by various factors

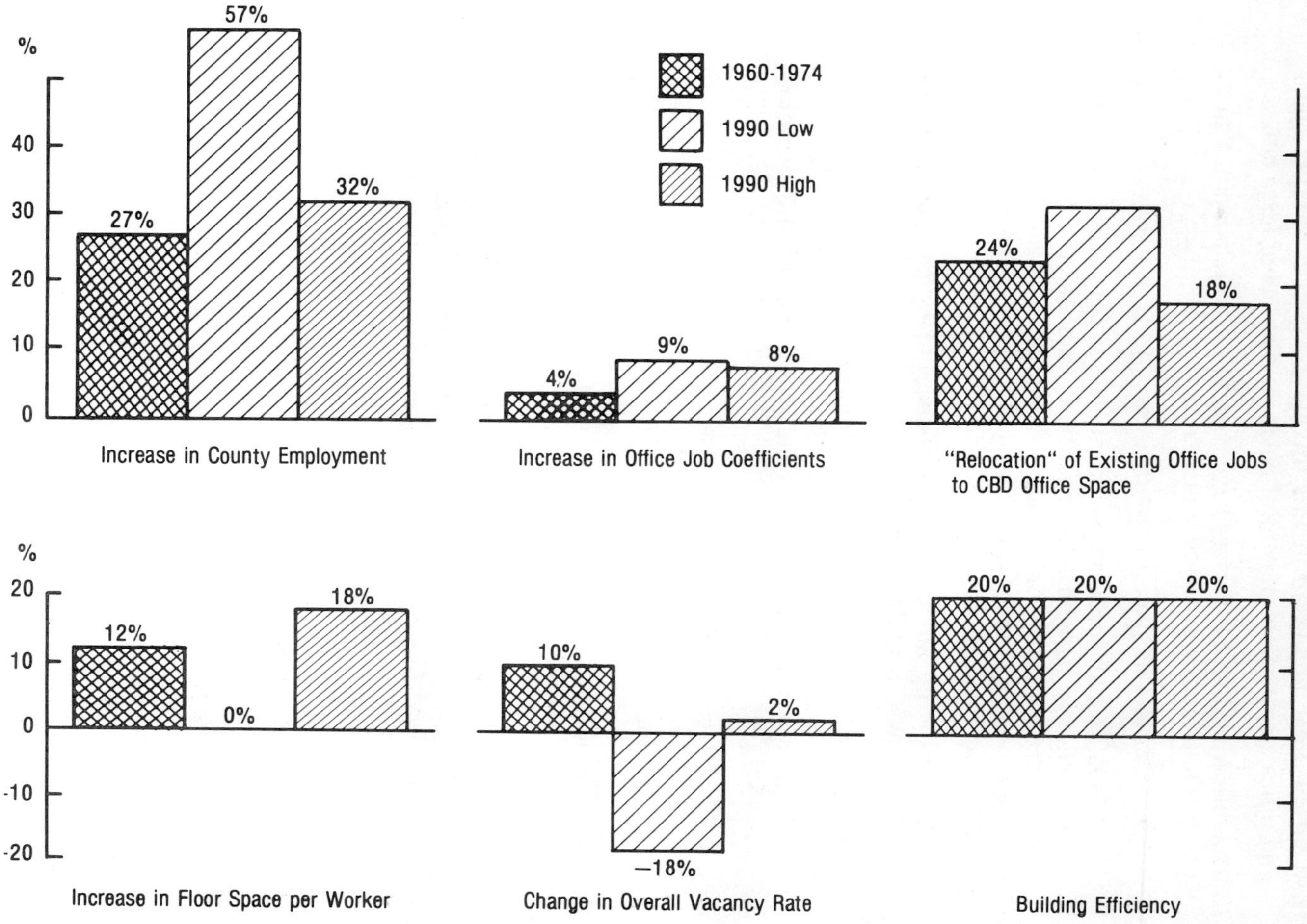

Q. *What are some important factors linking the growth of office space and office employment in central business districts of large cities?*

A. The following five key factors have been found to relate office space construction and its absorption-utilization:

1. Changes in overall vacancy rates.
2. Shifts in the occupational composition of total employment—reflecting structural changes in the national economy and the increasing preponderance of headquarters firms in the local economy—that cause office employment to grow more rapidly than total employment.
3. Changing ratios of square footage of office space actually allowed per office employee.
4. Demolition and underutilization of existing office space as firms relocate to new space, leading to new space construction at a rate in excess of the growth rate of office employment.
5. Relocation of office space users within the city resulting in greater demand for new office space within the CBD for a given employment level.

Q. *What are the various sources of data and information that can be analyzed to delineate trade areas for a city or larger urbanized area?*

A. Sources of data on consumers, extent of market penetration, and so forth include: Audit Bureau of Circulation (newspapers), American Research Bureau (television), *Survey of Buying Power* (sales management), and the *Survey of Newspaper Markets,* and *Survey of Television Markets.*

Q. *In a study of the retailing sector of an entire community, what kind of data are used to measure the productivity of this sector and its components?*

A. The following table illustrates the level of refinement necessary to obtain significant measures of productivity that can in turn be evaluated against state or regional norms. The first requirement for such an analysis is an inventory of the total gross floor area of all establishments. This information can then be used to arrive at a figure for sales per gross square foot. The statistics needed for such estimates can be found among Bureau of Census data or local and state agency information and estimates. The most precise method would utilize a matching of gross floor area of each establishment with sales tax receipts.

Retail sales: per capita and sales per square foot
Warren, Michigan

Type	Total Sales[1]	Number Square Feet[2]	Sales/ Square Foot	Per Capita Sales
Building Material, Hardware	$19,963,000	395,150	$ 51	$ 111
General Merchandise Group	59,603,000	994,000	60	331
Department Stores	52,248,000	491,300	108	290
Food Stores	68,041,000	635,791	107	378
Grocery Stores	64,235,000	579,031	111	357
Meat and Fish	423,000	4,522	94	2.35
Fruit and Vegetables	419,000	19,482	22	2.33
Candy, Nut and Confectionery	752,000	6,550	115	4.18
Retail Bakeries	1,346,000	20,598	65	7.48
Other Food Stores	866,000	5,608	154	4.81
Automotive Dealers	41,065,000	279,704	147	228
Gas Stations	20,572,000	215,440	N.A.	114
Apparel and Accessory	12,782,000	62,793	204	71
Furniture, Home Furnishings	13,660,000	331,558	41	76
Furniture—Home Furnishings	9,050,000	273,717	33	50
Household Appliances	1,785,000	31,771	56	9.90
Radio, TV, Music Stores	2,815,000	26,070	108	15.64
Eating and Drinking Places	15,968,000	332,119	48	89
Eating Places	11,996,000	233,836	51	67
Drinking Places	3,972,000	98,283	40	22
Drug Stores and Proprietary Stores	10,911,000	73,506	148	61
Miscellaneous Retail Stores				
Liquor Stores	1,306,000	19,782	66	7.25
Antiques and Secondhand Stores	496,000	13,689	36	2.75
Jewelry	864,000	7,758	111	4.80
Fuel and Ice Dealers	1,475,000	7,817	189	8.19
Florists	320,000	8,915	36	1.78

[1]Bureau of Census Report, 1967.
[2]Computer Print-Out 1968, Community Renewal Program, Warren, Michigan.

Q. *In doing a study of retail potentials, what is the first matter of inquiry after a trade area has been delineated?*

A. The first step in such a study is to measure the net changes in population and number of households. The time periods used for this study should be selected based on availability of data. As noted in the tabulation, both the primary and secondary trade areas must be considered, as any retail merchandise lines depend on their customer draw from beyond the immediate location of the retail facility.

Growth of Retail Trade Area
1960–1967

	1960	*1967*	*Percent Change*
Primary Trade Area			
Population	1,058,413	1,121,800	+6.1%
Households	322,267	340,350	+5.6%
Secondary Trade Area			
Population	574,699	648,050	+12.8%
Households	162,042	182,650	+12.7%
Total Trade Area			
Population	1,632,112	1,769,850	+8.4%
Households	484,309	523,000	+8.0%

SOURCE: Bureau of Census and Trade Association sources.

Q. *What are some guidelines for various business activities in terms of traffic volumes and road network locations?*

A. A recent study in Alabama (*Studies of Optimal Models of Interchange Development*, Alabama Highway Department, 1972) of several different kinds of businesses is shown in Tables 1 and 2.

Table 1
Roadway location preferences of business enterprises

Type of Intersecting Road	*Restaurants*	*Service Stations*	*Motels*	*Major Retail Centers*
County road	20.0	—	—	5.7
State highway	20.0	5.5	—	17.1
U.S. highway	40.0	55.5	50.0	18.5
Interstate highway	—	11.1	50.0	15.7
Beltline or circumferential highway	—	11.1	—	34.2
No preference	20.0	16.8	—	8.5
Total	100.0	100.0	100.0	99.7

Table 2
Business locations and daily traffic volumes

Necessary Volume of Traffic	Restaurants	Service Stations	Motels	Major Retail Centers
	Type of Business			
Under 5,000	—	6.2	—	—
5,001–7,500	—	12.5	—	5.8
7,501–10,000	20.0	12.5	—	25.0
10,001–15,000	20.0	31.2	—	26.9
15,001–20,000	—	31.2	—	23.1
Over 20,000	60.0	6.2	100.0	19.2
Total	100.0	99.8	100.0	100.0

Q. *Is there a study involving an estimate of expenditures by office workers in the central business district for various retail lines? What does the study indicate?*

A. An analysis of office workers in San Francisco in 1974 revealed the following distribution and level of expenditures (*Impact of Intensive High Rise Development on San Francisco*, Planning and Renewal Administration.)

CBD taxable expenditures per average office worker, 1974

Merchandise Category	Dollars
a. Groceries and Bottled Alcoholic Beverages (nontaxable, 83%)	36 (175)
b. Meals and Alcoholic Beverages Purchased in Bars/Restaurants	179
c. Cosmetics, Drugs, and Toiletries	35
d. Apparel, Footwear, and Accessories	171
e. Furniture, Home Furnishings, and Major Appliances	207
f. Miscellaneous (Newspapers, magazines, etc.) (nontaxable, 5%)	87 (5)
Total (nontaxable)	715 (180)

Q. *You have been retained by several property owners to help negotiate a new lease with major tenants: one is a department store and the other is an apparel store located in East City of North County. The tenants claim sales volume has been decreasing along with profit margins. What is your best point of inquiry on this assignment?*

A. First, analyze trends in sales volume and relative shares for various lines as noted below. Note that the share of the market in general merchandise and apparel lines has been decreasing significantly for the period under study. This evidence suggests that the tenants have probably been losing business due to shifts in consumer shopping patterns.

	1968	*1976*
County Shares of SMSA		
North County		
General Merchandise	25.2%	20.9%
Apparel	44.9	44.6
Furniture	41.5	35.1
Total GAF*	33.5	27.8
High County		
General Merchandise	71.6	76.2
Apparel	50.0	48.2
Furniture	49.3	54.2
Total GAF	61.5	67.0
City Share of County GAF		
City of East		
General Merchandise	48.2	39.8
Apparel	55.8	47.4
Furniture	45.2	34.5
Total GAF	49.5	40.7

*General merchandise, Apparel, Furniture

Q. *Gravity models depicting the attraction of shoppers to one shopping center versus another are usually based on the gross floor area of a facility (Ellwood formulation). Since a consumer usually begins his shopping trip with some clear intentions in mind as to the merchandise planned for possible purchase, is there any relationship between the type of item purchased on planned shopping trips and the incidence or concentration of convenience goods and shopper goods?*

A. The author studied this matter several years ago using questionnaire data developed by a city planning department in an SMSA with a population of about 250,000. Within a sector of a city, seven shopping centers were identified as the major areas of shopping activity. These were rated as having equal potential for shoppers based on proximity to place of residence. A questionnaire, based on a random sample taken at each center related the place of residence, purpose of trip, and so on. This so-called raw data was available for further analysis as shown below.

First, shopper responses were grouped based on the purpose of the trip, that is, to buy shopper goods, to buy convenience goods, or those where the trip represented a mixed purpose trip. Each category, therefore, represented, in fact, a homogeneous market segment. Each segment was further grouped and identified with each of the seven shopping centers. The centers, in turn, were analyzed as to the percentage of gross floor area devoted to shopper goods (General merchandise, Apparel, and Furniture—GAF). The data set is thus reduced to seven pairs of points for each of the three consumer groups identified by the principal purpose of the shopping trip. A regression analysis was undertaken with the following derivations (A *** STATPK program was used).

The three shopper groups are identified as follows:

- Group A—shopper goods—principal purpose of trip
- Group B—convenience goods—principal purpose of trip
- Group C—combined shopping for shopper goods and general shopping.

```
GROUP A        DATA MATRIX
 ROW 1
        24.000          47.000
 ROW 2
        42.000          78.000
 ROW 3
        44.000          73.000
 ROW 4
        43.000          72.000
 ROW 5
        32.000          54.000
 ROW 6
        21.000          51.000
 ROW 7
        12.000          52.000
```

Derived Equation: 33.4+.886X=Y

INTERCEPT	3.34122E+01
REGRESSION COEFFICIENT	8.85848E—01
STD. ERROR OF REG. COEF	.225
COMPUTED T-VALUE	3.942
CORRELATION COEFFICIENT	.870 (R^2 .757)
STANDARD ERROR OF ESTIMATE	6.907

ANALYSIS OF VARIANCE FOR THE REGRESSION

SOURCE OF VARIATION	D.F.	SUM OF SQ.	MEAN SQ.	F VALUE
ATTRIBUTABLE TO REGRESSION	1	741.455	741.455	15.541
DEVIATION FROM REGRESSION	5	238.545	47.709	
TOTAL	6	980.000		

TABLE OF RESIDUALS

CASE NO	Y OBSERVED	Y ESTIMATED	RESIDUAL	STD. RESIDUAL
1	47.000	54.673	-7.673	-1.111
2	78.000	70.618	7.382	1.069
3	73.000	72.389	.611	.088
4	72.000	71.504	.496	.072
5	54.000	61.759	-7.759	-1.123
6	51.000	52.015	-1.015	-.147
7	52.000	44.042	7.958	1.152

CHART FOR Y OBSERVED AND Y ESTIMATED

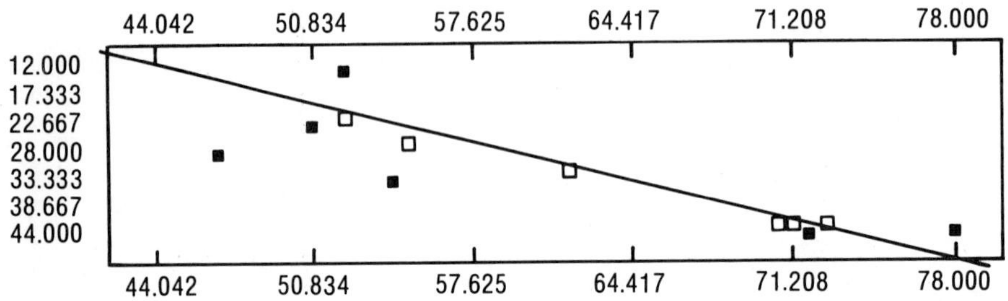

GROUP B — DATA MATRIX

ROW 1	
36.000	47.000
ROW 2	
6.000	77.000
ROW 3	
23.000	73.000
ROW 4	
21.000	71.000
ROW 5	
35.000	53.000
ROW 6	
48.000	51.000
ROW 7	
23.000	52.000

Derived Equation: $80.8-.73X=\hat{Y}$

INTERCEPT	8.08025E +01
REGRESSION COEFFICENT	−7.37591E −01
STD. ERROR OF REG. COEF	.251
COMPUTED T-VALUE	−2.938
CORRELATION COEFFICIENT	−.796 ($R^2=.633$)
STANDARD ERROR OF ESTIMATE	8.303

ANALYSIS OF VARIANCE FOR THE REGRESSION

SOURCE OF VARIATION	D.F.	SUM OF SQ.	MEAN SQ.	F VALUE
ATTRIBUTABLE TO REGRESSION	1	595.026	595.026	8.631
DEVIATION FROM REGRESSION	5	344.689	68.938	
TOTAL	6	939.714		

TABLE OF RESIDUALS

CASE NO	Y OBSERVED	Y ESTIMATED	RESIDUAL	STD. RESIDUAL
1	47.000	54.249	−7.249	−.873
2	77.000	76.377	.623	.075
3	73.000	63.838	9.162	1.103
4	71.000	65.313	5.687	.685
5	53.000	54.987	−1.987	−.239
6	51.000	45.398	5.602	.675
7	52.000	63.838	−11.838	−1.426

CHART FOR Y OBSERVED AND Y ESTIMATED

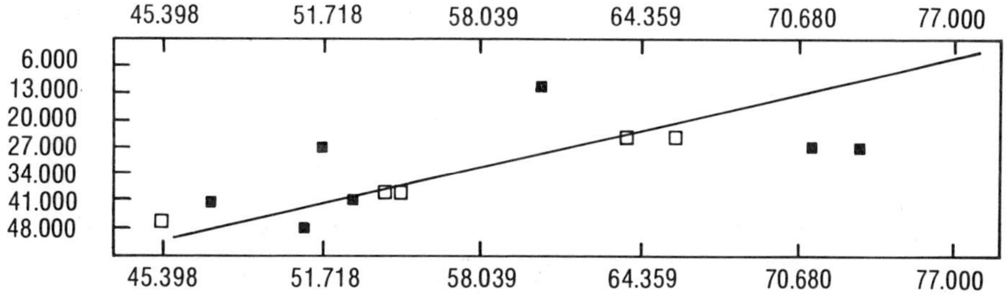

GROUP C DATA MATRIX

ROW 1
69.000 47.000

ROW 2
80.000 75.000

ROW 3
73.000 73.000

ROW 4
78.000 69.000

ROW 5
50.000 54.000

ROW 6
50.000 51.000

ROW 7
72.000 52.000

Derived Equation: $19.6 + .602X = \hat{Y}$

INTERCEPT	1.95741E+01	
REGRESSION COEFFICIENT	6.01656E−01	
STD. ERROR OF REG. COEF	.324	
COMPUTED T−VALUE	1.860	
CORRELATION COEFFICIENT	.639	($R^2 = .408$)
STANDARD ERROR OF ESTIMATE		

ANALYSIS OF VARIANCE FOR THE REGRESSION

SOURCE OF VARIATION	D.F.	SUM OF SQ.	MEAN SQ.	F VALUE
ATTRIBUTABLE TO REGRESSION	1	337.271	337.271	3.459
DEVIATION FROM REGRESSION	5	487.586	97.517	
TOTAL	6	824.857		

TABLE OF RESIDUALS

CASE NO	Y OBSERVED	Y ESTIMATED	RESIDUAL	STD. RESID.
1	47.000	61.088	-14.088	-1.427
2	75.000	67.707	7.293	.739
3	73.000	63.495	9.505	.963
4	69.000	66.503	2.497	.253
5	54.000	49.657	4.343	.440
6	51.000	49.657	1.343	.136
7	52.000	62.893	-10.893	-1.103

CHART FOR Y OBSERVED AND Y ESTIMATED

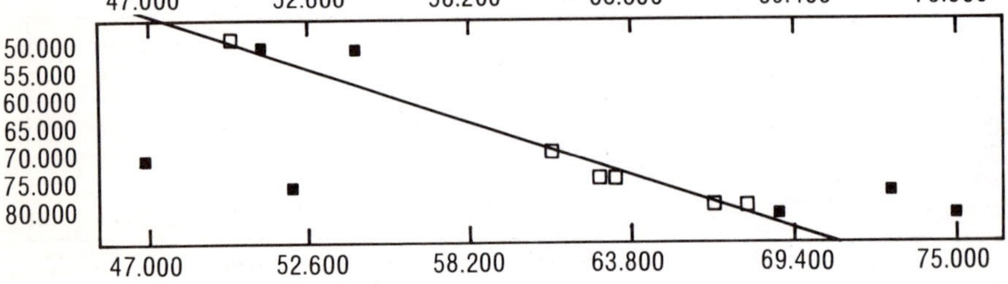

As should be noted, groups A and B are statistically significant ($R^2 = 0.757$ and $R^2 = 0.633$) while group C is less meaningful ($R^2 = 0.408$). The substance of this analysis is that there is a high correlation (particularly in groups A and B) between the intent and purpose of a consumer's shopping trip and the selection of the shopping center. Figure 1 shows the relationship of the three derived equations.

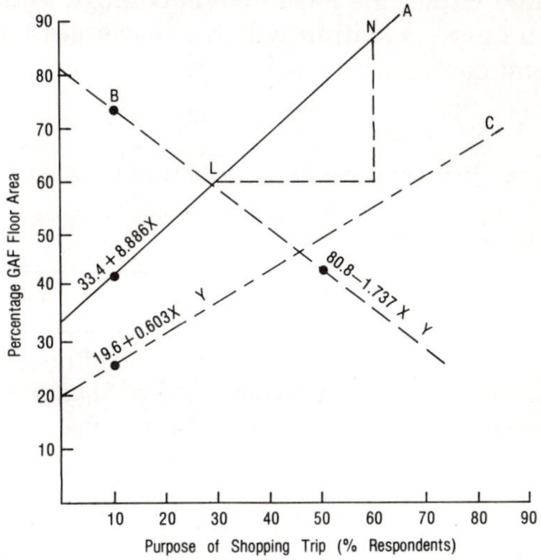

FIG. 1. Percentage GAF floor area.

One other suggested index may be derived from Figure 1 with reference to group A. It's what might be called a *consumer attraction coefficient* (CAC): the ratio of the increased attraction of a shopping center to the concentration of GAF shopping activities. The ratio, LM/MN yields an index of 1.15. This represents a positive productivity attribute of shopper goods concentration and a corresponding attractive force for the corresponding shoppers.

Q. *Potential attrition (replacement and displacement) of nonresidential facilities poses considerable difficulty when developing forecasts of future needs and requirements in terms of land and improvements. In light of this difficulty, what techniques can be developed and used to formulate plausible estimates of various urban functions?*

A. Two principal factors, aside from technological changes or expanding markets, affect locational changes of nonresidential urban land users. These are the physical age-condition of the facilities and the physical age-condition of immediate environment. For example, old and obsolete multistory industrial buildings in poor repair probably will be replaced (usually at a new location) with modern one-story structures.

In other instances, changes in roadway networks have affected access and the cost of operations. New residential developments near an industrial facility may insist on pollution controls, thereby triggering new incentives for relocation.

The following table outlines an inventory similar to that discussed. Criteria for rating of facility condition and neighborhood environment are formulated within the local market context. This kind of schedule provides a framework within which to ascertain potential short-term and long-term community needs.

Aggregate areas, nonresidential properties programmed for market withdrawal
(by gross floor and land areas)

	Environment: Fair to Good		*Environment: Poor*	
Land Use Series	*Condition 3 Square Feet*	*Condition 4 Square Feet*	*Condition 3 Square Feet*	*Condition 4 Square Feet*
200 (Manufacturing)	L 1,920 B 4,400	None	L 434,060 B 38,935	L 328,880 B 43,516
300 (Manufacturing)	L 20,750 B 3,500	None	L 515,034 B 112,237	L 185,792 B 20,374
400 (Transportation, Communications and Utilities)	L 5,520 B 1,768	None	L 182,605 B 12,432	L 144,800 B —
500 (Wholesale-Retail Trade)	L 85,750 B 20,432	L 335,384 B 22,070	L 675,160 B 112,687	L 634,214 B 33,888
600 (Services)	L 205,490 B 47,539	L 110,625 B 9,600	L 349,103 B 67,107	L 1,015,994 B 126,599
700 (Entertainment-Recreational)	None	None	L 4,200 B 1,500	None

Legend: L—Land Area
B—Gross Floor Area of Building
SOURCE: Computer Print-Out, Community Renewal Program, Warren, Michigan.

Q. *You have been asked to mediate in a dispute between area residents and the proponents of a new shopping facility. At issue are matters of traffic, congestion, and, in general, the impact of the facility on the area. What kind of background data would be helpful?*

A. Pending an on-site and area traffic engineering analysis, the following data, developed in the Chicago metropolitan area, may provide a starting point for a preliminary estimate of the potential impact of the proposed center.

Commercial Generator	*Peak Hour of Operation*	*P.M. Peak Street-Hour*
Drive-In Restaurants	257 Trips/ 1,000 Square Feet GFA[1]	108 Trips/ 1,000 Square Feet GFA
Sit-Down Restaurants	35 Trips 1,000 Square Feet GFA[1]	25 Trips 1,000 Square Feet GFA
Food Stores	14 Trips 1,000 Square Feet GFA[1]	12 Trips 1,000 Square Feet GFA
Neighborhood Shopping Centers	15 Trips 1,000 Square Feet GFA[1]	14 Trips 1,000 Square Feet GFA
Automobile Service Stations	28 Trips/Hour	23 Trips/Hour
Motels	0.8 Trips/Unit	0.6 Trips/Unit
Office Buildings	2.3 Trips/ 1,000 Square Feet GFA	2.3 Trips/ 1,000 Square Feet GFA
Hospitals	1.0 Trips/Bed	0.7 Trips/Bed

Residential Generator	*A.M. Peak*			*P.M. Total*		
	In	*Out*	*Total*	*In*	*Out*	*Total*
Single-Family Residence Subdivision	0.23	0.58	0.81 Trips/ Unit	0.60	0.40	1.00 Trips/ Unit
Multi-Family Apartments	0.08	0.49	0.57 Trips/ Unit	0.46	0.23	0.69 Trips/ Unit

[1]GFA—Gross Floor Area of Building

DEFINITION OF TERMS

The term *trip* in this study refers to a single vehicular movement (one-way) having either an origin or a destination within the study area or site.

The term *generation* refers to the total number of trips within a given time period crossing a counting station. These trips can have either an origin or destination within the study area or site. In order to facilitate its use as a factor in forecasting traffic from developments of varying size and character, generation is expressed as a rate—trips/unit of building area, trips/dwelling units, trips/hospital bed, etc. The floor area of an establishment expressed in 1,000's of square feet is usually the basis for traffic generation rates. It is, in most instances, the best identifiable characteristic of a commercial development.

Two additional terms referred to in the study are "peak hour of operation" and "peak street-hour." The *peak hour of operation* refers to the hour of the day when the highest combined in and out traffic movement was observed at the sites that were studied.

The *peak street-hour* refers to the hour during the day (usually the P.M. rush hour) that the highest traffic movements occurred on the streets adjacent to the developments that were being studied. At that time, the observed in and out traffic movements to each site were recorded.

SOURCE: *Traffic Engineering*, Washington, D.C., March 1970.

Q. *What is the SIC employment classification by two, three, or four digits?*

A. The SIC means Standard Industrial Classification and is a means for categorizing industrial and business activities including employment. The number of digits indicates the level of refinement and detail. For example, petroleum refining, 29, is a two-digit classification. Further detail at three- and four-digit levels, for example, 292 or 2,924, provides subcategories that make up the total activity under the two-digit totals. The following table lists the prevailing two-digit system as now in use in reporting statistical data:

Industrial groupings used with standard industrial classification codes

All-industry total:	
Agriculture, forestry and fisheries:	
Agriculture	01, 07
Forestry and fisheries	08, 09

continued

Industrial groupings used with standard industrial classification codes (cont.)

Mining:	
Metal	10
Coal	11, 12
Crude petroleum and natural gas	13
Nonmetallic, except fuels	14
Contract construction	15–17
Manufacturing:	
Food and kindred products	20
Textile mill products	22
Apparel and other fabric products	23
Lumber products and furniture	24, 25
Paper and allied products	26
Printing and publishing	27
Chemicals and allied products	28
Petroleum refining	29
Primary metals	33
Fabricated metals and ordnance	34, 19
Machinery, excluding electrical	35
Electrical machinery and supplies	36
Motor vehicles and equipment	371
Transportation equipment, excluding motor vehicles	37 except 371
Other manufacturing	21, 30–32, 38, 39
Transportation, communications, and public utilities:	
Railroad transportation	40
Trucking and warehousing	42
Other transportation and services	41, 44, 47
Communications	48
Utilities (electric, gas, sanitary)	49
Wholesale and retail trade	50, 52–57, 59
Finance, insurance and real estate	60–67
Services:	
Lodging places and personal services	70, 72
Business and repair services	73, 75, 76
Amusement and recreation services	78, 79
Private households	88
Professional services	80, 81, 82, 84, 86, 89
Government:	
Civilian government:	
Federal government	91 except Fed. military
State and local government	92, 93
Armed forces	Part of 91

SOURCE: Executive Office of the President, Bureau of the Budget, Standard Industrial Classification Manual, 1967.

Q. *The impact of traffic and congestion generated by large-scale developments is an emerging concern among developers and public administrators in urbanized areas. Are there any guides to assist in estimating the volume of traffic generated by different kinds of land uses within central cities?*

A. Several years ago studies were made of the traffic generation attributes of various kinds of land uses in five major American urbanized areas. Using the central business district as a focal and reference point, traffic generation schedules based on the number of "person trips" were derived. These are illustrated in the following chart.

Averages of number of person trips generated per acre for various land uses in selected cities related to number of miles from CBD

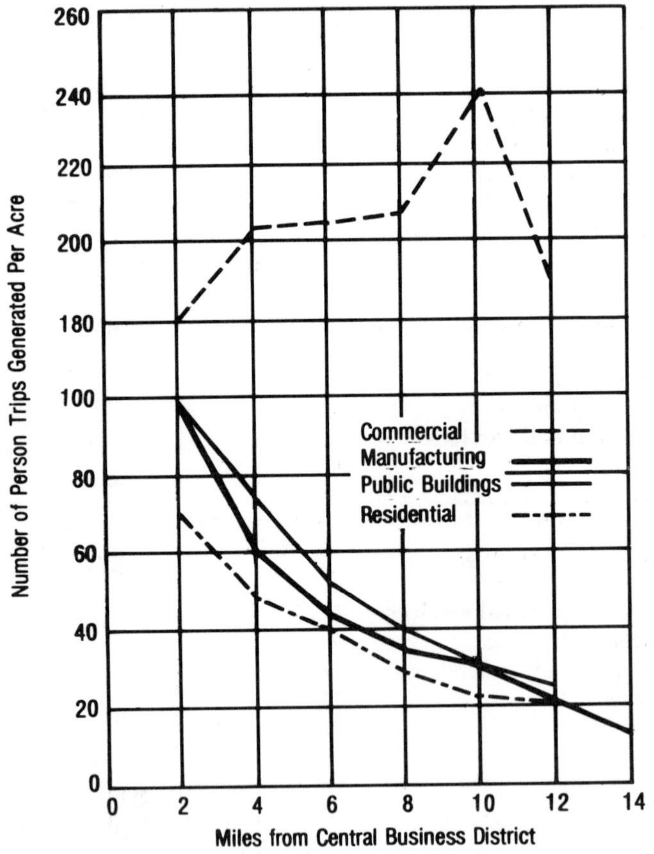

SOURCE: Averages derived from data on the Chicago, Detroit, Pittsburg, Tucson and Twin Cities transportation studies. Highway Interchange Area Development—by Floyd I. Thiel, January, 1965 page 26b.

Q. *What is a good way of monitoring employment trends and components of employment to identify turning points in the economic base of an urbanized area?*

A. The following method divides the employment base into goods-producing and services-producing employment components. This can be done on a quarterly basis and cumulative totals for the entire area can be computed and compared. As noted, prior year comparisons can signal important changes. These, in turn, have an impact upon employment, income, and potential demand for land or real estate facilities.

Employees on nonfarm payrolls
(seasonally adjusted)

		Percent Changes		
	10/75 (000)	*9/74 to 6/75*	*6/75 to 10/75*	*9/74 to 10/75*
Total	77,492	−3.2	1.5	−1.7
Goods—Producing	22,675	−10.0	2.0	−8.3
Mining	770	4.7	3.9	8.8
Contract Construction	3,387	−13.1	−0.1	−13.2
Manufacturing	18,518	−10.0	2.3	−7.9
Durable Goods	10,676	−11.9	1.4	−10.6
Nondurable Goods	7,842	−7.2	3.6	−3.9
Services—Producing	54,817	0.0	1.3	1.3
Transportation & Public Utilities	4,474	−4.6	0.1	−4.5
Wholesale & Retail Trade	17,032	−1.6	0.9	−0.6
Wholesale Trade	4,182	−2.0	0.7	−1.3
Retail Trade	12,850	−1.4	1.0	−0.4
Finance, Insurance & Real Estate	4,247	−0.5	1.1	0.5
Services	14,174	0.8	2.2	3.0
Government	14,890	2.7	1.4	4.1
Federal	2,763	−0.3	0.9	0.6
State & Local	12,127	3.5	1.5	5.0

SOURCE: Bureau of Labor Statistics.

Q. *When analyzing a labor market employment forecast for an area, what is a useful data grouping?*

A. Urban analysts frequently group employment by functional activity, such as extractive, fabricating, and services-producing, as shown below. In a time series context, net changes in the character and kind of at-place employment can be anticipated. These changes, in turn, have an impact on local resource needs and requirements.

Employment sector trends, Hamilton County, Ohio
1970–1985

	No. 1970	No. 1985	Percent Change
Extractive			
Agriculture, forestry, and fisheries	1,221	702	−42.5%
Mining	161	99	−38.5
Subtotal	1,382	801	−42.0%
Fabricating			
Manufacturing	153,130	173,655	+13.4%
Construction	21,767	29,713	+36.5
Subtotal	174,897	203,368	+16.3%
Services-Producing			
Transportation	31,144	32,211	+3.4%
Wholesale & Retail	94,196	108,799	+15.5
Finance, Insurance & Real Estate	29,015	40,398	+39.2
Service	107,865	137,680	+27.6
Public Administration	18,850	28,592	+51.7
Subtotal	281,070	347,680	23.7%
Grand Total	457,349	551,849	+20.7%

Q. *Growth of industries is clearly tied to population growth. Have there been any studies indicating the extent of this relationship and its significance, if any, for the next several decades?*

A. The following table indicates the relative responsiveness ranking (one being the most sensitive) of sixteen sectors of the economy. These are suggestive of the potential for growth for the period 1970–2000. Population estimates by the Bureau of Census (Series B and E) were profiled against previous industry growth and the forecasts were derived therefrom. The industries benefiting most from larger population include: frozen foods, domestic cars, credit, foods, and beverage. Biggest gainers include imported cars, mobile homes, dishwashers, airlines, and frozen foods. Sales of most industries should increase 10–30 percent by the year 2000 if the 20 percent population increase (an assumption) is realized. All such forecasts are underscored by the assumption that no significant changes occur in government regulations or technology.

Relative sensitivity of industries to population change

Industry	Rank							
	1948–69 data				*1959–69 data*			
	E vs. 1969		*B vs. E*		*E vs. 1969*		*B vs. E*	
	Low	*High*	*Low*	*High*	*Low*	*High*	*Low*	*High*
Railroads	16	16	12	14	16	16	13	13
Airlines	4	4	10	9	5	4	10	9
Beer	12	11	11	10	12	11	8	8
Housing starts	15	14	16	16	15	14	14	14
Mobile homes	2	2	9	11	3	3	12	12
Domestic cars	11	12	2	2	13	15	1	1
Imported cars	1	1	14	12	1	1	11	11
Men's suits	13	13	15	15	14	13	15	15
Frozen foods	5	5	5	5	2	2	9	10
Power boats	14	15	1	1	9	6	16	16
Credit	6	6	3	3	6	7	3	3
Furniture and household equipment	7	7	6	7	7	8	5	5
Foods and beverages	9	9	4	4	10	10	6	6
Clothing and shoes	8	8	8	8	8	9	7	7
Steel	10	10	13	13	11	12	2	2
Dishwashers	3	3	7	6	4	5	4	4

SOURCE: *The Commission on Population Growth and the American Future*, Vol. 2, Washington, D.C. 1972. Series B and E refer to Bureau of Census population estimates, high, and low respectively.

Q. *In analyzing the employment base of a city, what ratios can be assessed to discern meaningful trends?*

A. In a time series analysis, the following ratios, over a three- to five-year period, can provide some indicators of changes. Percentage rate of change and shares can be computed to provide further dimensions of industrial change.

Factors and Ratios	*Year* 1	2	3	4	5
1. Per Capita Personal Income					
2. Salary and Wages as Percentage of Per Capita Personal Income					
3. Total Employment					
(a) Employment Population Ratio					
(b) Annual Wages					
4. Manufacturing Employment					
(a) Employment Population Ratio					
(b) Annual Wages					

Q. *In studying place of residence vis-a-vis place of employment, how would you compute the amount of labor force retention?*

A. The following outlines the method and the appropriate facts and data necessary for this kind of analysis:

Labor force retention "X" County

	1976	*1986*
1. Total Population	48,276	52,171
2. Total Employed	16,472	17,801
3. Total Employment	14,265	12,950
4. Excluded Employment (9% of total employed)	1,482	1,602
5. Total county employment (lines 3 and 4)	15,747	14,552
6. Commutation from county (44.9% of line 2)	7,396	7,993
7. Retention of labor force (line 2 less line 6)	9,076	9,808
8. Commutation to county (line 5 less line 7)	6,671	4,744

NOTE: The above data is based on current population-employment and forecasts to terminal study year. Cross-over of labor force is obtained from Bureau of Census data reports.

Q. *How can potential growth sectors of employment be identified at the local level in absence of forecasted projections for the local economy?*

A. One has to fall back on either state, regional, or national studies. Local participation rates and employment shares in various categories (by two-, three-, or four-digit SIC) can be profiled against many aggregate studies concerning a broader area. For example, the two tables below indicate the average annual rates of change for broad economic sectors and estimates of net additions of employment opportunities in ten industries. The localization of any amount of this potential growth (or decline) must be resolved in terms of employment mix, industry dominance, and concentration.

Total employment (counting jobs rather than workers) by major sector, selected years 1955–72 and projected for 1980 and 1985.

Sector	Average Annual Rates of Change						
	1955–68	*1959–68*	*1965–72*	*1972–80*	*1968–85*	*1968–80*	*1980–85*
Total	1.6	2.0	2.0	2.2	1.7	1.9	1.2
Government	4.2	4.3	4.0	2.8	2.8	2.9	2.5
Total private	1.2	1.6	1.7	2.0	1.5	1.7	.9
Agriculture	−3.9	−4.0	−3.2	−4.9	−4.0	−4.1	−3.7
Nonagriculture	1.7	2.1	2.0	2.3	1.7	2.0	1.0
Mining	−2.0	−2.0	−.5	.2	−.1	.2	−.7
Construction	.9	1.0	1.2	1.5	1.5	1.6	1.1
Manufacturing	1.2	1.9	.6	2.2	.9	1.1	.5
Durable	1.5	2.4	.6	2.6	1.1	1.2	.8
Nondurable	.8	1.1	.7	1.6	.7	.9	.1
Transportation, communication, and public utilities	.3	.8	1.5	1.5	1.0	1.4	.2
Transportation	−.1	.5	.6	1.7	.8	1.0	.1
Communication	1.3	1.8	3.8	1.5	1.7	2.3	.2
Public utilities	.8	.8	2.0	.7	1.0	1.2	.5
Trade	1.8	2.1	2.7	2.1	1.8	2.2	.6
Wholesale	1.9	2.1	2.4	2.0	1.6	2.0	.7
Retail	1.8	2.0	2.8	2.1	1.8	2.3	.6
Finance, insurance, and real estate	2.6	2.8	3.5	2.8	2.8	3.1	2.1
Other services	3.1	3.2	2.8	3.1	2.6	2.9	1.9

[1]Changes based on compound interest rates between terminal years.

NOTE: Employment covers self-employed, unpaid family workers, and wage and salary workers. The employment is a count of jobs rather than persons holding a job. Thus, persons holding more than one job would be counted more than once.

SOURCE: Bureau of Labor Statistics.

Industries projected to show largest increases in number of jobs, 1968–1980 and 1980–1985

1968–1980

	Industry	Additional jobs (thousands)[1]
Total, 10 industries		17,024
	State and local government	4,771
105	Retail trade	3,988
112	Miscellaneous business services	1,512
119	Hospitals	1,386
118	Health services except hospitals	1,264
104	Wholesale trade	1,052
106	Finance	924
12–17	Construction	870
114	Miscellaneous professional services	649
121	Nonprofit organizations	608
Total economy		20,650
10 industries as percent of additional jobs in total economy		82.4

1980–1985

	Industry	Additional jobs (thousands)[1]
Total, 10 industries		5,302
	State and local government	2,120
112	Miscellaneous business services	628
105	Retail trade	509
119	Hospitals	460
118	Health services except hospitals	367
106	Finance	338
12–17	Construction	276
114	Miscellaneous professional services	222
121	Nonprofit organizations	205
104	Wholesale trade	177
Total economy		6,033
10 industries as percent of additional jobs in total economy		87.9

[1]Based on total employment, BLS concept.

SOURCE: *The Structure of the U.S. Economy in 1980 and 1985*, U.S. Department of Labor, Bureau of Labor Statisics, 1975.

Q. *What are some useful guidelines to be used in developing forecasts of employment in select SIC's (Standard Industrial Classifications) and related potential land requirements?*

A. The best procedure is to estimate the anticipated increase in employment, deriving floor area needs, and then translating these needs to local use based on floor area ratios (FAR's) in the particular area or community. The following table showing square feet per employee, by four-digit SIC, provides a basis for estimates, where a need exists for this level of refinement. (For further detail and adjustments for environmental factors, see original data and methods in: *Estimating Land and Floor Area Implicit in Employment Projections: How Land and Floor Area Useage Rates Vary by Industry and Site Factors,* Ide Associates, July, 1970, for the Federal Highway Administration. This study was based on a survey of 3,182 establishments).

Activity grouping and 4-digit code	*(Square feet per employee)*
1. Manufacturing—meat products; dairy products; canning and preserving of fruits, vegetables, and seafoods: 2100–2139	563
2. Manufacturing—grain mill products; bakery products; sugar; confectionary, and related products: 2140–2179	707
3. Manufacturing—beverages; other food preparations and kindred products: 2180–2199	1,491
4. Manufacturing—textile mill products: 2200–2299	496
5. Manufacturing—wearing apparel, outerwear and undergarments; hats, caps, and millinery: 2300–2359	220
6. Manufacturing—leather and leather products; fur goods; miscellaneous apparel and accessories; other fabricated textile products: 2360–2399	485
7. Manufacturing—lumber and wood products (except furniture): 2400–2499	1,325
8. Manufacturing—furniture and fixtures: 2500–2599	1,195
9. Manufacturing—paper and allied products: 2600–2699	1,021
10. Manufacturing—newspapers, periodicals, and books: publishing and printing: 2700–2739	412
11. Manufacturing—commercial printing; manifold business forms; greeting cards; bookbinding and related industries; printing trade service industries; other printing and publishing: 2740–2799	557
12. Manufacturing—chemicals and allied products: 2800–2899	857
13. Manufacturing—petroleum refining and related industries: 2900–2999	409
14. Manufacturing—rubber and miscellaneous plastic products: 3100–3199	565
15. Manufacturing—stone, clay, and glass products: 3200–3299	1,020
16. Manufacturing—primary metal industries: 3300–3399	1,043

continued

Activity grouping and 4-digit code	*(Square feet per employee)*
17. Manufacturing—ordnance and accessories; machinery (except electrical): 3400–3429	607
18. Manufacturing—electrical machinery, equipment, and supplies: 3430–3439	501
19. Manufacturing—transportation equipment: 3440–3499	478
20. Manufacturing—other fabricated metal products: 3490–3499	875
21. Manufacturing—professional, scientific and controlling instruments; photographic and optical goods; watches and clocks: 3500–3599	418
22. Manufacturing—Miscellaneous: 3900–3999	856
23. Transportation, communication, and utilities (TCU)—railroad, rapid rail transit, and street railway transportation; aircraft transportation; marine craft transportation; highway and street right-of-way; automobile parking: 4100–4199, 4300–4699	1,208
24. TCU—motor vehicle transportation: 4200–4299	717
25. TCU—communication: 4700–4799	1,152
26. TCU—utilities: 4800–4899	975
27. TCU—other transportation, communication, and utilities: 4900–4999	567
28. Trade—motor vehicles and automotive equipment, wholesale; drugs, chemicals, and allied products, wholesale; dry goods and apparel, wholesale: 5100–5139	1,668
29. Trade—groceries and related products, wholesale; farm products (raw materials), wholesale: 5140–5159	778
30. Trade—electrical goods, wholesale; hardware, plumbing, and heating equipment and supplies, wholesale: 5160–5179	907
31. Trade—machinery, equipment, and supplies, wholesale: 5180–5189	909
32. Trade—other wholesale trade: 5190–5199	1,284
33. Trade—lumber and other building materials, retail: 5200–5219	2,373
34. Trade—heating and plumbing equipment, retail; paint, glass, and wallpaper, retail; electrical supplies, retail: hardware and farm equipment, retail: 5220–5299	984
35. Trade—department stores, retail: 5300–5319	619
36. Trade—mail order houses, retail; limited price variety stores, retail; merchandise vending machine operators, retail; direct selling organizations, retail; other general merchandise, retail: 5320–5399	686
37. Trade—groceries (with or without meat), retail: 5400–5419	634
38. Trade—meats and fish, retail; fruits and vegetables, retail; candy, nut, and confectionery, retail; dairy products, retail; bakeries, retail; other food trade, retail: 5420–5499	350
39. Trade—motor vehicles, retail: 5500–5519	650
40. Trade—tires, batteries, and accessories, retail; other automotive, marine craft, aircraft, and accessories, retail: 5520–5529, 5550–5599	1,485
41. Trade—gasoline service stations: 5530–5539	591
42. Trade—men's and boys' clothing and furnishings, retail: women's ready-to-wear apparel, retail; women's accessories and specialties, retail: 5600–5639	1,639

continued

Activity grouping and 4-digit code	(Square feet per employee)
43. Trade—children's and infants' wear, retail; family clothing, retail; shoes, retail; custom tailoring; furriers and fur apparel, retail; other apparel and accessories, retail: 5640–5699	663
44. Trade—furniture, home furnishings, and equipment, retail: 5700–5719	1,370
45. Trade—household appliances, retail; radios, televisions, and music supplies, retail: 5720–5739	665
46. Trade—eating places; drinking places (alcoholic beverages): 5800–5829	452
47. Trade—drug and proprietary, retail: 5900–5919	495
48. Trade—liquor, retail; antiques and second-hand merchandise, retail; books and stationery, retail; sporting goods and bicycles, retail; farm and garden supplies, retail; jewelry, retail; fuel and ice, retail: 5920–5989	710
49. Trade—florists, retail; cigars and cigarettes, retail; newspapers and magazines, retail; cameras and photographic supplies, retail; gifts, novelties, and souvenirs, retail; optical goods, retail: 5990–5996	902
50. Trade—other retail trade: 5999	728
51. Services—banking and bank-related functions: 6100–6119	398
52. Services—credit services (other than banks); security and commodity brokers, dealers, exchanges, and services: 6120–6139	510
53. Services—insurance carriers, agents, brokers, and services: 6140–6149	228
54. Services—real estate and related services; holding and investment services; other finance, insurance, and real estate services: 6150–6199	460
55. Services—laundering, dry cleaning, and dyeing: 6200–6219	466
56. Services—photographic (including commercial); beauty and barber; funeral and crematory; cemeteries; apparel repair, alteration, and cleaning pickup; shoe repair; other personal services: 6220–6299	612
57. Services—advertising; consumer and mercantile credit reporting; adjustment and collection; duplicating, mailing and stenographic; dwelling and other building services; news syndicate, employment; warehousing and storage: 6300–6379	1,152
58. Services—other business services: 6390–6399	479
59. Services—automobile repair and services: 6400–6419	1,555
60. Services—other repair services: 6490–6499	767
61. Services—physicians', dental: 6500–6512	573
62. Services—hospital; medical laboratory: 6513–6514	439
63. Services—dental laboratory; sanitariums, convalescent, and rest home; medical clinics, out-patient; other medical and health services: 6515–6519	441
64. Services—legal; other professional services: 6520–6599	306
65. Services—building construction, general contractor: 6611	544
66. Services—other general construction contractor services: 6619	463

continued

Activity grouping and 4-digit code	*(Square feet per employee)*
67. Services—plumbing, heating, and air conditioning; painting, paper hanging and decorating; electrical: 6621–6623	548
68. Services—masonry, stonework, tile setting, and plastering; carpentering and wood flooring; roofing and sheet metal; concrete; water well drilling; other special construction trade services: 6624–6629	936
69. Services—executive, legislative and judicial functions; 6700–6719	478
70. Services—protective functions and related activities; postal; correctional institutions; military bases and reservations: 6720–6759	646
71. Services—nursery schools; secondary schools: 6810–6811, 6813	1,244
72. Services—primary (elementary) schools: 6812	1,180
73. Services—university, college, junior college, and professional school education; special training and schooling: 6820–6839	1,228
74. Services—religious activities; welfare and charitable; other miscellaneous services: 6900–6999	3,937

Q. *What are some measures of an area's vulnerability to recessions or fluctuations in the national economy?*

A. In a recent study, 31 major cities were analyzed along three important dimensions. These were: extent of diversification of local urban economic activities, the extent of self-sufficiency, and the level of share of employment in durable manufacturing. As an example, Orlando and Minneapolis are the most diversified cities; Detroit and Washington the least. Analysis indicates that the more diversified cities tend to have more equality of income among their residents and smaller city tax expenditures.

In terms of self-sufficiency, Baltimore heads the list while Washington is last. This measure is based on an index of a city's nonreliance on exports. Analysis has shown that cities ranking high on this index tend to have more nonwhites, a larger share of women in the labor force, and a higher educational level.

Durable manufacturing concentrations in urbanized areas closely correlate with below average per capita income. In addition, such concentrations correlate with fewer college graduates, highly variable unemployment rates, and higher property taxes. Cleveland has the highest concentration, ranking first, while Baton Rouge ranks last.

City	Diversification %	Diversification Rank	Self-Sufficiency %	Self-Sufficiency Rank	Employment in Durable Mfg. %	Employment in Durable Mfg. Rank
Atlanta	42.2	11	52.9	10	16.7	24
Austin	63.1	27	27.9	30	8.7	29
Baltimore	63.2	28	74.2	1	25.6	12
Baton Rouge	54.7	22	32.6	27	2.7	31
Boston	50.3	20	44.1	19	17.5	23
Buffalo	50.3	29	55.2	7	32.0	5
Chicago	35.0	3	49.8	14	32.0	5
Cincinnati	42.7	12	65.3	4	27.9	9
Cleveland	53.7	21	46.6	17	37.5	1
Dallas	45.9	15	47.8	16	20.4	19
Dayton	55.3	23	32.8	26	36.8	2
Denver	39.9	6	50.5	12	15.9	25
Detroit	85.7	31	38.4	23	35.9	3
Hartford	59.5	26	34.0	25	26.0	11
Honolulu	48.7	19	32.1	28	9.7	28
Houston	41.6	9	50.0	13	18.4	21
Indianapolis	48.6	18	53.9	9	27.9	9
Kansas City	37.4	4	59.2	6	21.2	14
Los Angeles	40.9	8	60.0	5	24.0	13
Milwaukee	58.2	25	51.8	11	34.8	21
Minneapolis	34.9	2	44.7	18	20.5	18
Nashville	44.9	13	65.5	3	21.2	15
New York	45.3	14	36.8	24	20.6	16
Orlando	33.5	1	38.7	22	10.4	27
Philadelphia	46.0	16	70.9	2	28.2	8
Pittsburgh	55.7	24	49.2	15	20.6	16
St. Louis	41.6	9	54.7	8	28.2	7
San Diego	39.5	5	41.5	20	17.7	22
San Francisco	40.6	7	29.9	29	11.7	26
Seattle	46.0	15	40.7	21	18.6	20
Washington	78.2	30	18.3	31	4.9	30

DIVERSIFICATION. Relative importance of (sum of percentage of) the three largest export industries.
ECONOMIC SELF-SUFFICIENCY. Workers in export industries relative to those not in export industries. SOURCE: Department of Commerce.
PROPORTION OF EMPLOYEES IN MANUFACTURE OF DURABLES. Workers in durable goods industries divided by all workers. Source: Bureau of the Census, "Industry of Employed Persons for Areas and Places, 1970, *U.S. Census of Population, 1970: General Social and Economic Characteristics* (Summaries for each state), Table 87.

SOURCE: Reprinted from John Tepper Marlin, *The Wealth of Cities* (New York: Council on Municipal Performance, 1974), p. 18, by permission of the publisher.

Q. *In gathering different economic indicators in various labor market areas, mention is made of different measures of unemployment. This appears confusing. What are the different means for measuring unemployment?*

A. Currently there are seven different ways in which unemployment can be measured. The following explains the differences and source of raw data for their derivation.

All series are regularly published by the BLS with the exception of U-6 and U-7, and in these cases the components are published, so they can easily be calculated by anyone who wishes to do so.

The first series, U-1, is the number of persons unemployed 15 weeks or longer as a percent of the civilian labor force. The rationale behind the selection of this series is the belief that unemployment is a more severe problem when it has lasted long enough to cause substantial financial hardship. The assumption is that shorter periods can be handled by unemployment compensation plus the use of savings and, in some cases, assistance from other family members.

The second series, U-2, is the number of persons who lost their last jobs, taken as a percent of the civilian labor force. The implication of this series is that unemployment is more serious for experienced workers, for whom the loss of a job leads to significantly lower income. Here unemployment which accompanies entry or reentry into the labor force and voluntary job-leaving would appear to be considered an inevitable but less serious matter.

U-3 is the number of household heads unemployed as a percent of all household heads in the civilian labor force. In this case, it is assumed that unemployment is more serious when it affects breadwinners. Other jobseekers, secondary workers, would presumably be supported by the heads of households while seeking employment.

U-4 is the number of unemployed persons seeking full-time jobs, as a percent of all those in the full-time labor force (including those employed part time for economic reasons). The assumption here is that a measure which is limited to those unemployed who are strongly attached to the labor force is more meaningful than one which also includes more casual and marginally attached workers. Unemployment is likely to be more serious for full-time than for part-time workers because the former are more likely to be breadwinners, will lose more income through inability to find work, and are more committed to the labor force.

U-5 is the official, regularly published unemployment rate for all workers age 16 years and over. This series represents the total number of persons not working but available for and seeking work, as a percent of the civilian labor force. It can be viewed as the base series from which each of the other six series discussed in this article is constructed through the addition or subtraction of various labor force and unemployment components. In a sense, this series reflects a consensus among the many different user groups; it involves no value judgments regarding a person's family or marital status, relative need for work, or personal characteristics. It only requires that jobseeking take place. It has had widespread support from various study groups and was recommended by the Committee to Appraise Employment and Unemployment Statistics (Gordon Committee) established by President Kennedy in 1961.

Unemployment indicators
1953 through 1975

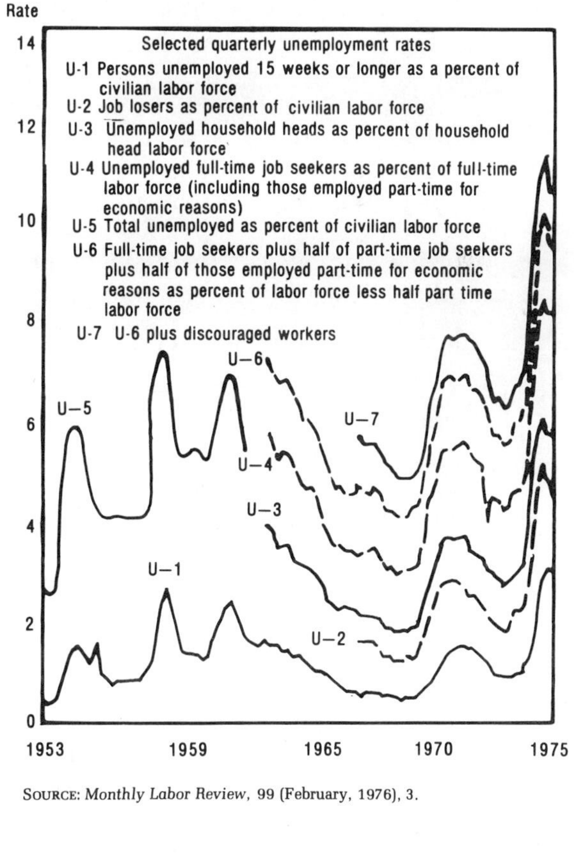

SOURCE: *Monthly Labor Review*, 99 (February, 1976), 3.

U-6 includes, as a percent of the labor force, the number of unemployed persons seeking full-time work, plus one-half of the number of unemployed persons seeking part-time work and one-half of the number of those involuntarily on part-time work schedules but desiring full-time employment (with the part-time labor force given only half weight). The rationale behind this series is that involuntary part-time workers should be counted as at least partially unemployed, and their loss of working time should be reflected in the overall measure. Similarly, it is felt that unemployed persons seeking only part-time work should be given only half weight because their employed counterparts—those employed part time voluntarily—work about half a full-time workweek; the voluntary part-time employed are also given half weight. (This indicator is comparable to the "percent of labor force time lost" series, which is regularly published.

The final series, U-7, is the same as U-6 except that the number of discouraged workers is added to both the unemployed and labor force components. This series is based on the idea that the situation of discouraged workers is essentially the same as that of the unemployed—they are jobless, want work, and presumably are available for work. The only difference is that they are not looking for jobs because they believe no work is available for them. It should be noted, however, that specific information regarding their work history and prior job-search activity is not now collected, and many of them could be reflecting only a casual interest in entering the labor market or maintaining an unrealistic desire for a prestigious job paying a high salary.

Q. *In analyzing employment trends in an urban area, what are some measures of change in the occupational composition of an area?*

A. Four measures that can be used in a time series analysis are:

- *Occupational Structure*—refers to the allocation of manpower among occupational groups, satisfying the demand for diverse services among the various sectors of the local economy. Data is analyzed by occupation according to the number of persons employed. From this an index of redistribution can be computed. This index is based on changes in the percentage of employment by occupations for each time period under study. Occupations with positive changes are termed *gaining occupations* and those with negative changes are termed *losing occupations.*

- *Industrial Structure*—refers to the distribution of the local manpower among industries. Data is analyzed by the number of persons employed according to industry.

- *Occupational Pattern*—refers to the percentage distribution of occupational employment in a given industry. Data for an industry is classified showing percentage of professional and technical workers, managers and administrators, craftsmen, clerical personnel, and so on.

- *Occupational Mix*—refers to the relative distribution of highly skilled as compared to less skilled occupations. Generally, if a large percentage of the working population is highly skilled, the area is considered as highly developed. The higher the proportions in this group, the more favorable the mix of the labor market area.

Q. *A reputable economic organization has estimated that nondurable employment in the United States will increase from 7,524,000 in 1975 to 9,743,000 by 1995, or an average annual increase of 1.475 percent. If the local urban labor market area has 18,200 jobs in this category, what assumptions will have to be made in using this data and what total net gain in employment in this sector can be anticipated?*

A. When using these national projections the assumption will be that the local economy and related labor market needs (in terms of technology, skills, etc.) will parallel that of the nation as a whole. The derivations, based on these assumptions, are as follows:

Year	*No. Employed*
Base	18,200
1	18,468
2	18,740
3	19,016
4	19,296
5	19,580

Net Gain: 19,580 − 18,200 = 1,380 jobs

Q. *In a highly urbanized area with considerable industrial activity, what kind of data, detail, and analysis will be needed to get a good picture of industrial land absorption over the last several years? Using this information, how can we arrive at a measure of demand and potential sell-out period for a proposed nearby industrial park?*

A. The following table outlines the data necessary to establish what has been happening in industrial development in a city. The instance cited, Warren, Michigan is in the Detroit SMSA, is highly industrialized, and, during the years 1967 thru 1969, evidenced extensive construction and large increases in employment.

Industrial construction–development
Warren, Michigan

	New Buildings										
	1967			1968			1969			Grand Total	
Land Use	Land Area	Floor Area	Estimated Value	Land Area	Floor Area	Estimated Value	Land Area	Floor Area	Estimated Value	Land Area	Floor Area
(21) Food & Kindred Products								75,500	35,000		75,500
(22) Textile Mill Products	936,000	49,000	375,000							936,000	49,000
(28) Chemicals & Allied Products				174,885	10,800	65,000				174,885	10,800
(33) Primary Metals	847,848	63,318	530,400		48,801	537,400				847,848	112,119
(34) Fabricated Metals	85,700	133,071	1,542,000		20,800	106,360		70,519	904,000	85,700	224,388
(39) Misc. Mfg.	117,500	24,470	210,000	108,000	68,140	1,896,000	8,256	11,002	91,000	233,757	103,540
	1,987,048	269,859	2,657,400	282,885	148,541	2,604,760	8,256	157,019	1,030,000	2,278,190	482,347
	Additions to Existing Buildings										
(22) Textile Mill Products		67,500			85,000						
(24) Lumber & Wood Products		14,400									
(28) Chemicals & Allied Products		200,000						230,000			
(33) Primary Metal Industries		795,000			245,700			1,190,600			
(34) Fabricated Metals		8,016,728			478,700			3,395,800			
(39) Misc. Mfg.					157,700			84,000			
(21) Food & Kindred Products								83,000			
(22) Textile Mill Products		26,000			4,000						
(24) Lumber & Wood Products		12,000			–0–						
(28) Chemicals & Allied Products		–0–			–0–			18,000			
(33) Primary Metal Industries		78,000			40,000			95,000			
(34) Fabricated Metals		500,000			78,000			280,000			
(39) Misc. Mfg.		20,000			45,000			21,000			
		9,729,628			1,134,100			5,397,400		16,261,128	

SOURCE: Department of Planning and Urban Renewal, Warren, Michigan. Analysis by Urban Research Associates, Washington, D.C.

Absorption of industrial land can occur in two distinct areas: current land available in the market, and land held in inventory for expansion by local industrial firms. As the tabulation and analysis indicates, over 50 acres of land were converted to use via new building construction on land held for expansion. Slightly over two million square feet of land were absorbed from the open market inventory of available sites.

The two-digit SIC provides further insight into specific growth sectors of the industrial economic base of a community. For example, fabricated metals (34) accounted for about two-thirds of all expansion for the three-year period. Land is a scarce resource, and its development for industrial use is both an expensive and, in many instances, a high-risk undertaking. Anything less than the suggested level of inquiry into the matter of industrial land absorption over the last three to five years would be inadequate to discover feasibility of a new industrial park or large acreage for industrial development. Simply stated, the effort and detail of the analysis is commensurate with the complexity of the assignment.

Q. *What is the impact of a college or university, frequently referred to as an industry without smokestacks, on a local economy?*

A. A number of studies, from different vantage points, have been made involving small and large schools.

A recent study was made of the impact of Kent State University at Kent, Ohio. This was a two-stage analysis in which the employment multiplier for the entire community was calculated at 1.82 and the university, when segmented, indicated a multiplier of 1.09. The study correctly points out that a multiplier is different for the services sector in contrast to the export sector of a local economy. This is illustrated by the following: assume that (1) average university income is $12,000, (2) average income in the service sector is $9,000 and (3) the total income multiplier has been calculated at 1.375. If the university payroll rises by $120,000, total local income will increase by $165,000, $45,000 of which will be in the service sector. Total local employment will increase by 15 (10 university and 5 service employees). Thus, the total employment multiplier is 1.5 (15/10). The services sector employment multiplier must equal 0.5 (0.375 × $12,000/$9,000). This is consistent with a total employment multiplier of 1.5 (J. H. Wilson and R. Raymond, "The Economic Impact of A University Upon the Local Community," *The Annals of Regional Science*, December, 1973).

In a study made in 1968, a sample of 200 students at the University of Pittsburgh revealed that the average student spends (in 1968 dollars) $743 per term (4 months); 30 percent or $222 is spent in Oakland,

$176 at the university, $60 (8 percent) downtown, and $285 (38.2 percent) in other areas. The place of residence influences spending patterns. It was found that home residence expenditures were $425, apartment residents outside of Oakland spent $930, those in apartments $1,041, and those in college housing $821; all figures are based on a single term of school. Based on a student population of 11,823, it was estimated that full-time students for one term resulted in expenditures of $8,800,000 (Pittsburgh Business Review, July, 1968).

In another study (sample of 75 students) involving the Greater Bangor Area with a college enrollment of 1,150 students in 1967, a multiplier of 2.9 was estimated as reflecting the impact of student and college staff expenditures. Accordingly, if $1.48 million in funds are generated by the college, the local area yielded an additional $3.14 million. This study (*New England Business Review*, Sept. 1967) contrasted the school to a hypothetical shoe factory; it indicated an employment multiplier of 1.33 for the factory and 2.33 for the college. This multiplier for the college was based on generating 83 jobs of direct employment and 117 of indirect employment in the local economy.

Q. *Having been appointed by the county as chairperson of a committee to explore the community need for a hospital, what format would facilitate development of a gross estimate of the need for such a facility?*

A. The following information is needed along with an analysis of the data as outlined. The accompanying numerical example further illustrates the method. This example covers the short-term general bed needs.

Necessary information:

- Age distribution of project population.
- Present number of patient days per 1,000 population for local area (most probable market area to be served).
- Local health planning agency recommendations on occupancy rates (city or county health departments, etc.).

1. Estimate population by major age groups for the project for a target planning year.
2. Multiply project population by patient days per 1,000 population by age group, to get total patient days.
3. Divide this total by 365 to get projected average daily census.
4. Divide average daily census by recommended occupancy rate to obtain total short-term, general beds needed for project. (The Federal Hill-Burton guidelines suggest an 80 percent occupancy factor for general hospitals and a 90 percent factor

for long-term facilities, but states and localities must develop their own guidelines.)

5. The bed needs would then be compared to existing and planned facilities to determine if a deficit exists.

6. If calculations indicate a capacity or over-capacity situation, judgment should be tempered by other measures, e.g., waiting time for treatments. Alternatives for meeting the health care needs of the project should be explored with the comprehensive health planning agency.

EXAMPLE OF CALCULATION OF BED NEEDS

1. Multiply project population by patient days for all age groups to get total projected patient days

Age	*Projected Population*		*Present Patient Days Per 1,000 Population*		*Projected Patient Days*
Under 15	500	×	315	=	158
15–24	200	×	745	=	149
25–44	350	×	700	=	245
45–64	300	×	1,350	=	405
65+	150	×	1,900	=	285
	1,500				1,242

2. Divide projected patient days by number of days in year to get projected average daily census.

$$\text{Average Daily Census} = 1{,}242 \div 365 = 3.4$$

3. Calculate projected bed need by adopting the local planning agency occupancy goal. The projected bed need is the average daily census (0.85 in this case) divided by the occupancy goal.

$$\text{Projected Bed Need} = \frac{3.4}{0.85} = 4$$

4. The total number of short-term, general beds needed by the project is therefore four.

Q. *What are some site-location criteria for service-retail establishments?*

A. A total of 14 factors related to locational attributes and site characteristics were rated by 4 different kinds of enterprises according to degree of importance, as noted.

Relative importance of selected location criteria of business enterprises

	Type of Business			
Specified Criteria	*Motels*	*Restaurants*	*Service Stations*	*Major Retail Centers*
Presence of a water system	10	8	6	10
Presence of a sewerage system	10	7	6	10
Availability of service roads	9	5	4	10
Growth potential of surrounding area	9	6	9	10
Presence of complementary highway-oriented businesses	8	5	7	9
Terrain features	8	7	7	9
Volume of through traffic	8	8	9	8
Recreational and/or cultural opportunities in the nearest urban area	7	5	5	7
Presence of zoning controls	6	5	6	7
Absence of competitors	5	6	7	6
Proximity of residential areas	4	7	9	6
Speed of traffic	4	6	6	6
Presence of competitors	4	4	6	5
Volume of local traffic	3	8	6	5

Rating Basis: In terms of median scores on a one to ten rating scale.
SOURCE: *Studies of Optimal Models of Interchange Development*, Alabama Highway Department, 1972.

Q. *Environmental impact assessments are necessary before undertaking the development of land. What are some guidelines to the kinds of information needed as a basis for environmental assessment preliminary to a project feasibility study of a tract with special features?*

A. A number of important studies are required in cases where land has special attributes. Table A outlines some guides for understanding the sequence and elements of an environmental study of various kinds of land. Table B provides an outline of information, sources, and tests to be undertaken.

Table A
Special land features environmental assessment summary table

1	2	3	4	5	6	7
Subcomponent	*Goals/Objectives*	*Impacts*	*Necessary Information*	*Methodology*	*Findings/Measurements*	*Standards/Guidelines*
Sanitary Landfills	Health and safety; property protection	Will the project be exposed to structural damage, noise, air, surface and ground water pollution or other nuisances associated with an old, active or planned sanitary landfill?	Geographic location of landfill; general geology and hydrology of area encompassing landfill	Measure distance from site to nearest sanitary landfill	Potential for negative impact of gases, litter, ground water and surface water pollution and other nuisances on project	State and local health standards, USHUD does not permit construction on landfills (L.Min)
Wetlands	Protect plant and animal life, natural water purification systems, ground water recharge and discharge areas, recreation and aesthetic values	Will the project spoil or significantly impair existing wetlands through filling, dredging, draining, waste discharges or other detrimental land use practices?	Geographic location of wetlands	Measure distance to wetlands; ascertain direction of ground and surface water flow; determine quality and quantity of underlying water	Potential for adverse impact on wetlands	State and local regulations (L.Min)
Coastal Zones/ Shorelines	Protect natural, commercial, recreational, industrial and visual resources	Will project spoil coastal management zones or shorelines through filling, dredging, draining, waste discharges or loss of visual quality?	Location of coastal zones and shorelines	Measure distance from coastal management zones or shoreline	Potential for adverse impact on coastal management zone or shoreline	State and local regulations (L.Min)
Mine Dumps/ Spoil Areas	Health and safety; property protection	Will the project be exposed to danger from unsuitable foundations, surface and ground water pollution, or landslides from existing mine dumps or dredge spoil areas?	Geographic location of mine dumps or spoil areas	Measure distance from mine dumps or spoil areas; determine chemical composition of wastes; water quality; slope stability	Potential for negative impacts from subsidence, water and soil pollution, and landslides	State and local regulations (L.Min)
Prime Agricultural Land	Mainteance of food production	Will the project be located on or near prime agricultural land?	Land capability classification	Locate site in relation to land capabilities	Consumption of prime agricultural land	State and local regulations (L.Min.L.Max)

Notes: (L.Min)—Legal Minimum Allowable, (Reco)—Recommended, a Goal, (L.Max)—Legal Maximum Allowable, (Ave)—Average or "Rule-of-Thumb" Guide.

Table B
Special land features: types of environmental information necessary for assessment

1	2	3	4	5
	Initial Screening Test		*Higher Level Tests*	
Subcomponent	*Informational Needs*	*Source*	*Informational Needs*	*Specialists*
Sanitary Landfills	Location and boundaries of abandoned, active, or planned sanitary landfills; state and local sanitary landfill regulations	Local planning agency or trash collection and disposal agency	Direction of prevailing winds; direction of surface and ground water movement; movement and impact of noxious gases and leachate	Sanitary engineer
	Location of underground utilities serving project	Local utilities company		
	Location of buildings	Developer		
Wetlands	Location of legally protected wetlands; wetland regulations	State or local natural resources agency	Any pollutants which will enter wetland from project; any alteration of water flow into wetland by project; any alteration of water table by project; project-related noise and activity which would disturb wetland's wildlife; any subdivision of wetland by project	Hydrologist; water quality specialists; ecologist
	Trends of development impacts on wetlands	Local planning or natural resources agency; site visit		
	Location of other wetlands	USGS topographic maps; site visit		
	Direction and flow of surface and ground water in project area	USGS topographic maps and Federal, state or local ground water maps		
	Waste disposal plans; any plans for dams or obstructions downstream from project	Developer		
Coastal Zones/ Shorelines	Location of legally defined coastal zones and shorelines; coastal zone/shoreline regulations	State or local natural resources agency	Characteristics of visual qualities of coastal zone or shoreline in relation to other sites	Persons familiar with project area; landscape architect
	Location and distance to any coastal zone or shoreline	USGS topographic map; local land use map; site visit		
Mine Dump/ Spoil Areas	Location of mine dumps	State bureau of mines or geologic survey	Ability of mine dumps and spoil areas to support buildings; stability of dumps and spoil areas	Soils engineer; foundation engineer
	Location of spoil areas	District office—U.S. Army Corps of Engineers		
Prime Agricultural Land	Location of project	Developer	Types of farming in area; relationship of project to other development	Agronomist
	Capability classification of land on and near site	USSCS Soils Survey		

SOURCE: Interim Guide for Environmental Assessment, HUD, 1975, Washington, D.C.

Q. *What are some of the important areas of study and analysis required under a state's environmental impact law?*

A. The following outlines the areas of consideration under the New York State Environmental Conservation Law. This example illustrates ten critical areas affecting land development.

Possible Impact Areas Considered in an Environmental Impact Assessment Pursuant to New York's Environmental Conservation Law

1. *Description of the Development*
   - Character, density of population.
   - Types of Services to be provided.
   - Number and size of lots, dwelling wants, commerce types and schedule of construction.

2. *Environmental setting and aesthetics*
   - Describe the environmental setting before and after development.
   - Describe present uses of land and the reason for selection of the site over others.
   - Discuss geology, mineral deposits, topography, vegetation, unique natural or man-made features, and visual qualities.
   - Indicate the effects of the development on the biological, sociological, ecological, historic and aesthetic resources of the development site and the surrounding area.
   - Assess the cumulative, long-term impact of the proposal, particularly relating to adverse effects or intolerable stress on the environment. Discuss permanent damage to ecosystems, scenic values, landscape and wildlife resources.
   - State proposals to restore site qualities or mitigate any and all adverse environmental qualities.
   - Discuss the extent of increased noise levels within the development area.

3. *Water Supply and Resources*
   - Describe in detail existing surface water and groundwater resources, the proposed source of the water supply, alternative sources of water supply considered, water use projections, provisions for treatment, distribution and storage. Also included should be a description of any existing county or regional comprehensive water supply or water resources plans. The integration of the development facilities with these plans must be shown.

- List all watercourses and other bodies of water within or in proximity to the development. Identify wetlands or shallow water environment. Discuss the fish and wildlife resources of these areas and the potential for enhancement or destruction.

- Describe in detail any proposed impoundment, diversion, structure or stream alteration with plans for protection and restoration of water areas, disturbed landscape and fish and wildlife. Indicate methods for dewatering the site and controlling erosion and siltation during construction.

- Present data on the amount and peak concentration of storm water and floodwaters. Describe drainage facilities and use and protection of flooded areas.

4. *Sewage*
   - Describe in detail: the method of disposal, including the quality and quantity of effluent and of surface or receiving waters; uses and biota of wter resources; use of separate sewer lines to handle storm water and miscellaneous groundwater flows; use of lands in the subdivision area or in contiguous area abutting treatment plant sites; methods of collection; use of renovated effluent for groundwater augmentation, or other reuse. Also included should be a statement of how proposed facilities fit into existing comprehensive sewage plans, if any.

5. *Industrial Wastewater Disposal*
   Describe in detail the quantity, chemical and biological quality of any industrial wastes involved and method of handling either with or without inclusion in a sewage disposal system.

6. *Solid Waste Disposal*
   Show the method and location of solid waste facilities as well as types of solid wastes. Describe the effect on surface and groundwater by leaching, air cleanliness, rodent and insect control and fire control. Discuss the use of improved land for recreational and other suitable purposes, land use patterns, traffic flow, truck haul distance, waste separation and toxic and hazardous materials and similar items. Indicate projected waste quantities and variations.

7. *Recreation*
   Discuss the effect of the new development site as well as the surrounding area, the location and size of open space or

green belt areas, and measures taken to enhance fish and wildlife values. Describe recreational facilities to be provided including a discussion of whether they are to be open to anyone other than residents of the development. Discuss the recreational facilities relative to the location and degree of treatment provided by sewage and waterworks systems and the influence of noise levels due to leisure pursuits.

8. *Air Pollution*
   - Describe the land use as it involves industrial and commercial units in relation to housing areas, regardless of local zoning and other laws. Show the methods of on-site heating, power production and industrial air pollution control.
   - Describe the effect on the development of existing and new facilities such as industry and nuclear or fossil fuel power plants outside the development.
   - Discuss the effect of pollutants in the air on plant life and animals, particularly relative to locating open space and green belt areas.

9. *Road Construction*
   Describe precautions taken in road construction and maintenance to prevent soil erosion, sedimentation, dust and possible flooding, pollution of water supply sources, streams, lakes and wildlife areas, and pollution of nearby wells, reservoirs, watersheds and recreation areas with oil and deicing chemicals. Discuss air pollution from automobile traffic and from unsuppressed noise and vibrations. Describe locations and effects of existing highway network on the development.

10. *Effects on Human Resources*
    Discuss the impact on local school systems, hospitals, fire safety, electrical power and transportation networks.

11. *Special Considerations*
    - Describe limiting conditions such as soils, excessive grade or slope, unstable ground, high water table, high pressure gas lines, high tension wires, etc., as well as proposals to assure such conditions will not cause problems. Show steps to protect terrestrial and aquatic life if blasting is to be undertaken.
    - Show land clearing and disposal methods as well as means of protection or replacement of existing vegetation.

- Discuss any proposed use of herbicides or pesticides or any other method of plant or animal control including wetland drainage or oiling.
- Identify soil borrow and disposal areas and measures to be taken to reclaim such areas.

SOURCE: Department of Environmental Conservation, "Environmental Consideration in Project Review" (Draft Guidelines): New York State.

Q. *How is the incremental method used in estimating future land demand for the several different kinds of urban uses—for example, retail, services, office, and industrial?*

A. The incremental method is based on increases over a given base period. These increases may relate to volume of retail sales, expenditures for services, or employment. The following illustrates this method for several uses:

- *Retail land needs*—Assume estimates indicate that retail sales volume will increase $1.5 million in the next five years in a city or sector of an urbanized area. If sales per square foot (average for all lines) are at $80, then the required floor area is 18,750 sq. ft. ($1,500,00/$80). If development needs indicate to 4-to-1 ratio of land area to building area, then the land requirements total 75,000 sq. ft., or 1.72 acres.
- *Retail service industries needs*—This category may include personal service, miscellaneous repair shops, and amusement establishments. Assume that space needs are resolved at 600 sq. ft. per employee and that employment will increase, for a given period, by 1,200; then the indicated additional space requirements would total 720,000 sq. ft. At a ratio of 4-to-1 of land to building, the total land required would be 2,880,000 sq. ft., or 66.12 acres.
- *Office building land*—Based on an estimated office employment increase of 5,500 for a given period and space needs of 190 sq. ft. per employee, a total of 1,045,000 sq. ft. of office space is required. At an FAR (Floor Area Ratio) of 5.0, the land needs (without parking) would total 209,000 sq. ft. or 4.8 acres.
- *Industrial land*—The predicted employment increase in manufacturing and research and development during a given period is 5,000. At a density of 35 employees per acre (this is based on local land use trends) the total land requirement would be 142.86 acres. If the density were 12 employees per acre, then the land needs requirement would increase to 416.67 acres.

Q. *A neighborhood conservation group is working with the state planning agency and is involved in developing a group of day care centers. To formulate an estimate of the final costs for the facilities, you need to know the staffing requirements of this kind of facility. How can such an estimate be made?*

A. The following chart outlines the kinds of staff normally encountered and the number of staff required to achieve three different quality levels of services. These parameters can serve as a good starting point in any discussion of staff-building needs.

Day care staffing

	Levels of Quality		
Staff	*Minimum*	*Acceptable*	*Desirable*
Classroom Professional	One per 20 children	One per 15 children	One per 15 children
Classroom Nonprofessional	Two per 20 children	Two per 15 children	Three per 15 children
Social Service Professional	one per 150 children	One per 100 children	One per 100 children
Community, Social Service, Parent, or Health Aides	None	One per 100 children	Two per 100 children
Business and Maintenance	Two per 100 children	Three per 100 children	Three per 100 children
Special Resource Personnel (Psychology, Music, Art, Consultants, etc.	Urgent need only	One per 100 children	Two per 100 children
Supervision	One per 100 children	Two per 100 children	Two per 100 children

SOURCE: This table was prepared by the Office of Child Development, HEW. The analysis was based on centers providing service 10–12 hours a day, five days a week.

Q. *It is reported that cleared urban renewal land available for redevelopment in a number of cities has failed to find a market. What are some of the reasons for this state of affairs?*

A. A recent study has determined that a number of reasons exists for the lack of sale and redevelopment of this land. The following 20 reasons, individually or in various combinations, contribute to this problem.

FREQUENT PROBLEMS ENCOUNTERED IN URBAN RENEWAL LAND DISPOSITION

1. Overpriced land
2. Inadequate interest in residential land
3. Inadequate interest in retail land
4. Inadequate interest in office land
5. Inadequate interest in hotel-motel land
6. Inadequate interest in industrial land
7. Scattered residential lots
8. Scattered nonresidential parcels
9. Inflexibility of project plan
10. Small or poorly configured parcels
11. Predisposition nonperformance by developer
12. Timing of public facility construction
13. Rehabilitation management
14. Insufficient disposition staff capabilities
15. Timing of project improvement construction
16. Selection process for multiple development proposals
17. Interim property management
18. Citizen participation
19. Whether to offer parcels to single or multiple developers
20. Determination of appropriate method of advertising disposition parcels

SOURCE: *Guidelines for Urban Renewal Land Disposition*, HUD, 1975

Q. *In current discussions of the rate of urban growth, what are some basic questions concerning the impact of growth in an urbanized area?*

A. Some basic issues concerned with urban growth involve not so much the raw quantitative aspects of such growth, but rather the relationship of the planned growth to the existing urban base. As an example, a recent study ("Costs and Revenues of Residential Growth in the City of Cupertino: A Case Study," County of Santa Clara, 1974), indicated that the addition of 300 residents to a small community would not create a significant impact. However, adding 1,020 residents via single-family housing and measuring cost-revenues over a period of subsequent years did generate financial impact. A simulation of phased single-family development in this community, located in the San Francisco Bay Area, indicated a necessity for additional expenditures for different kinds of facilities and services. As noted in the chart below, adding Phase 2 (89 units of 3–5 bedroom units) resulted, two years later, in negative cash flows from the development. In other words, predicted municipal expenses exceeded predicted revenues. These costs usually represent "chunk-like investments" and are viewed as threshold costs to be overcome in order to achieve the benefits to be derived from the additional single-family dwellings. (For further discussion on threshold analysis see *Rams' Real Estate Appraising Handbook*, Prentice-Hall, Inc., 1975.)

Development impact analysis, single family dwellings

net revenues per unit

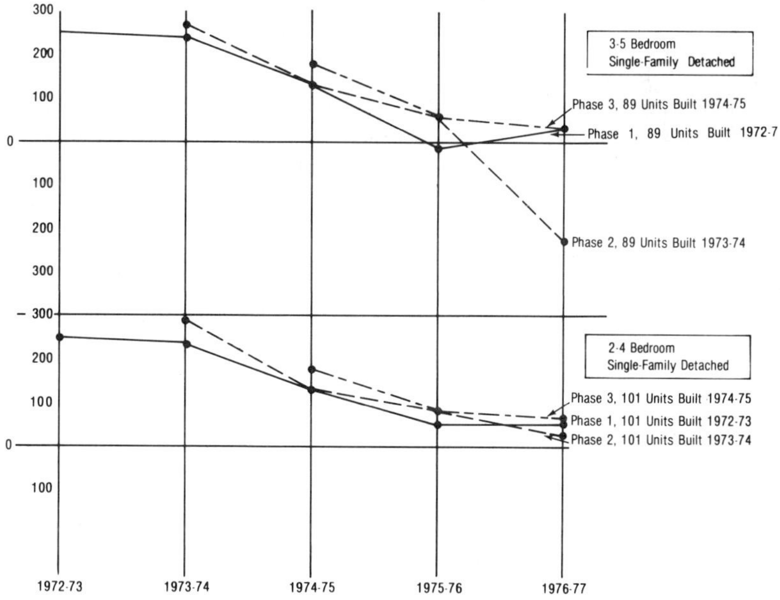

Q. *What should the real estate consultant know about the terms "Redlining" and "Urban Disinvestment?"*

A. "Redlining" is reported to have had its origin in the insurance industry and was first used to point out areas of poor risk in fire insurance policies. Later, lending institutions figuratively or literally drew a red line around those neighborhoods considered poor risk areas, refusing to make loans within the circled area because of deterioration, high unemployment, crime, and other factors that give the area a "poor economic outlook" and constitute a "bad risk." In some instances, lenders refuse to finance homes even when potential buyers—often Blacks and Mexican Americans—have the down payment and earning power to support a residential mortgage.

"Urban disinvestment" refers to withdrawal of monies from the urban structure; it is a term sometimes used interchangeably with "Redlining."

Q. *Is "Redlining" legal?*

A. To the extent that the "redlining" and "disinvestment" practices are based on racially discriminatory concepts, reasons, and processes, these practices are not legal. Such practices are made unlawful by the Civil Rights Act of 1968 (*42 U.S.C. 3601 et seq*); Title VIII—Fair Housing.

Q. *In making a study of potential absorption of various land uses in a community, how could one evaluate the competitive qualities of the available vacant land in terms of adaptability, marketability, and so forth?*

A. A total inventory (where possible) of land by zoning provides a good basis for analysis. For example, the following table outlines the vacant land by location, zoning, and size. In addition, the summary shows the gross distribution of the vacant land. Inspection of the table reveals 76 industrial sites with areas under 10,000 sq. ft. (most being less than 50 × 100 ft. in size). Except for very small industrial activities, these sites have limited utility and probable marketability. If one also eliminates from consideration those between 10,000–19,000 sq. ft., the potential of alternate, competitive, and suitable sites is further reduced. Depending on the economics of growth, expansion, and replacement of existing facilities, measures of potential absorption of new land brought on-stream (into the market) can be developed.

Size distribution of vacant land by zoning
Warren, Michigan

Zone	Number (Use)	(Numbers of Parcels) Under 10,000 Square Feet	10,000–19,000 Square Feet	20,000–49,000 Square Feet	50,000–99,000 Square Feet	100,000–200,000 Square Feet	Over 200,000 Square Feet	Over 1,000,000 Square Feet	Total Area (Acres)	Percentage of Total
6	(Multifamily)	3	2	1	7	4	2	2	102.92	8.4%
7	(Mobile Home Parks)		1				1		9.20	0.8
9	(Public, Public & Private)	4	1		2				4.34	0.4
10	(Professional Business)	1	3	6	1				7.45	0.6
11	(Office Use)		2	3					2.37	0.2
12	(Local Business Neighborhood Shops)	20	24	21	1	4	4	2	153.54	12.5
13	(Commercial Business Shopper Goods, Other)	34	9	7	7	5	6		91.02	7.4
14	(Wholesale Business)			1					0.87	0.1
15	(Light Industrial)	30	16	23	3	3	3		77.4	6.3
16	(Medium Industrial)	41	27	48	14	9	30	4	647.38	52.9
17	(Heavy Industrial)	5	5	22	2	2	2		127.03	10.4
									1,223.52	100.0%

SOURCE: Adapted by Urban Research Associates from Community Renewal Program Print-Out, Warren, Michigan.

Q. *What materials are available that describe redlining and disinvestment practices?*

A. 1. Civil Rights Act—1968—Title VIII—Fair Housing.

2. Report (May 1976) "Residential Financing Practices in the District of Columbia," by D.C. Commission on Residential Mortgage Investment, 1229 E Street, NW, Washington, D.C. 20004.

3. Report (February 1976) "The Mayor's Reinvestment Task Force;" Seattle Office of Policy Planning, 306 Cherry Street, Seattle, WA 98104.

4. Testimony, Fair Housing Public Meeting, HUD Office of Fair Housing and Equal Opportunity; Philadelphia, July 14, 15, 16, 1976 by:

   (a) W. L. Dennis, Attorney, Civil Rights Division, U.S. Department of Justice (Legal View)

   (b) Dexter D. MacBride, CAE, FASA, Executive Vice President, American Society of Appraisers (Valuation View)

5. *Desegregated Housing and Interracial Neighborhoods:* A bibliographic guide, National Neighbors Publications (Philadelphia, PA) (1975)

6. "Redlining—the Fight Against Discrimination in Mortgage Lending;" Loyola University Law Journal, Vol. 6:71 and Enforcement of Municipal Housing Codes, 78 Harv. L. Rev. 801 (1965) (note).

Q. *What are some of the impacts of highway development on adjacent and nearby land and real estate developments?*

A. The following tabulation highlights some of the impacts on use and value with reference to location and source of findings.

Studies indicating property values discounted near highways

Highway	Study or Source	Apparent Effect[1]
I-495 through Springfield, Virginia	"Community Effects of Highways" Pennsylvania State University, 1973	−5 percent (one time)
The Connecticut Turnpike	"The Connecticut Turnpike: Ribbon of Hope," University of Connecticut, 1965	−.5 percent (one time) (Annual rate of 4 percent overall less 3.9 percent abutting Turnpike for 3 years)
An Urban Highway in the Midwest	"Economic and Social Effects of Highways," 1972, page 24	−10 percent (Average for 4 properties)
I-96 in Farmington, Michigan	"Proximity Study No. 203," Michigan State Highway Commission, 1965	−16 percent (on square foot basis for small, expensive abutting lots)
Detroit-Toledo Expressway, I-280	"Expressway Traffic Noise and Residential Properties," University of Toledo, 1967	Residences within 50 feet of right-of-way declined more than more distant residences of the same age. Realtors expect abutting houses to decline 20 to 30 percent.
Ten Highway Projects in Texas	"The Effect of Access on Highway Right of Way Costs and the Determination of Special Benefits," Texas Transportation Institute, Texas A&M University, 1968	Some losses were noted abutting the highway.
I-264 in Louisville, Kentucky	"Highways and Economic and Social Changes," 1964, page 38, *Kentucky-Louisville-Watterson Expressway Study*, 1961	Property values were depressed nearby.
Several Highways in Chicago	"Highway Improvements as a Factor in Neighborhood Change," Resource Management Corporation, 1971	−5 percent near elevated highways and −1 percent near surface and depressed highways

[1]These effects are termed "apparent" because they generally result from comparing properties near or abutting a highway with nonabutting properties that have good accessibility from the highway. It is not at all clear that these properties near the highway were lowered in value compared with properties completely removed from the influence of this highway.
SOURCE: Federal Highway Administration, Washington, D.C. 1974.

Q. *I have been retained by a city to advise them on matters of impact of land development. What is an efficient and meaningful method for undertaking and completing this kind of assignment? Most of the new construction involves residential development.*

A. The following sequence of steps can provide a good measure of the impact of residential development in a community. Note that the factors relating to several aspects must be derived from the local community. They represent specific "input factors" and cannot be generalized from other geographical locations, cities, or urbanized areas.

RESIDENTIAL IMPACT ANALYSIS SYSTEM

Instructions

Section 1: Population Estimates

1. Using Table A, in the area entitled "Maximum Number of Persons," fill in the number of proposed units beside the appropriate *type of construction*.
2. Multiply the number(s) of units by the applicable factor(s) and enter the result(s) in the appropriate space provided under "Population."
3. To obtain the estimated maximum number of persons, sum the results obtained in step 2 and enter this figure in the box provided.
4. The estimated minimum number of persons is calculated by repeating steps 1–3 using the area entitled "Minimum Number of Persons," provided in Table A.

Section 2: Estimated Average Daily Trips and Peak Hour Trip Estimates

1. Using Table B, fill in the number of proposed units beside the appropriate *type of construction*.
2. Multiply the number(s) of units by the applicable factor(s) and enter the result(s) in the appropriate space provided in the column entitled Average Daily Trips.
3. Sum the numbers calculated in step 2 and enter that figure next to "Total Average Daily Trips." This number represents the estimated total number of average daily trips originating or terminating in the proposed development.

Table A
Estimated population

Maximum Number of Persons

Type of Construction	*Number of Units*		*Factor*		*Number of Persons*
Single-Family[1]	________	×	4.2	=	________
Garden Apartment[2]	________	×	2.4	=	________
Mobile Home	________	×	3.2	=	________
	MAXIMUM NUMBER OF PERSONS			=	☐

Minimum Number of Persons

Type of Construction	*Number of Units*		*Factor*		*Number of Persons*
Single-Family[1]	________	×	3.5	=	________
Garden Apartment[2]	________	×	2.0	=	________
Mobile Home	________	×	2.3	=	________
	MINIMUM NUMBER OF PERSONS			=	☐

NOTES:
1. This category includes attached, detached, row home, and townhouse units.
2. This category includes garden, low-level and high rise units.

Table B
Average daily trips

Type of Construction	*Number of Units*		*Factor*		*Average Daily Trips*
Single-family	________	×	9.5	=	________
Townhouse	________	×	8.1	=	________
Garden Apartments	________	×	6.9	=	________
High-rise Apartments	________	×	7.8	=	________
Mobile Homes	________	×	6.1	=	________
	TOTAL AVERAGE DAILY TRIPS			=	☐

An estimate of the number of peak hour trips can be found by completing Table C:

4. Beside the appropriate type of construction, fill in the number of proposed units.

5. Multiply the number(s) of units by the applicable A.M. and P.M. factor(s) and enter the result(s) in the appropriate space provided in the columns entitled either Outbound A.M. or Inbound P.M. Peak Hour Trips.

6. Sum the numbers derived in step 5 and enter the results in the appropriate "A.M." or "P.M." spaces.

Table C
Average peak hour trips

		Outbound		*Inbound*	
Type of Construction	*Number of Units*	*A.M. Factor*	*A.M. Peak Hour Trips*	*P.M. Factor*	*P.M. Peak Hour Trips*
Single-Family	______	.64	______	.77	______
Townhouse	______	.55	______	.65	______
Multifamily	______	.47	______	.55	______
High-Rise	______	.53	______	.63	______
Mobile Homes	______	.41	______	.49	______
TOTAL TRIPS		A.M. =	[ ]	P.M. =	[ ]

Section 3: Estimated Water Demand and Sewage Generation

1. Using Table D, fill in the number of proposed units beside the appropriate *type of construction.*

2. Multiply the number(s) of units by the applicable "minimum" and "maximum" factors and enter the results in the appropriate spaces.

3. Sum the number(s) derived in step 2 and enter the total "minimum" and "maximum" results in the appropriate spaces.

4. The "total" figures presented in Table D represent estimates of both the minimum and maximum number of gallons of water demanded, and the minimum and maximum number of gallons of sewage to be discharged.

Table D

Estimated water demand and sewage generation

Type of Construction	*Number of Units*		*Minimum Factor*		*Minimum Gallons*	*Maximum Factor*		*Maximum Gallons*
Single-Family Detached	_____	×	244	=	_______	311	=	_______
Single-Family Attached	_____	×	126	=	_______	183	=	_______
Garden Apartment[1]	_____	×	134	=	_______	179	=	_______
Mobile Home Park	_____	×	150	=	_______	150	=	_______
TOTAL GALLONS			MINIMUM	=	☐	MAXIMUM	=	☐

NOTE: No factors are presently available to estimate water demand and sewage generation in high-rise apartments in the Lehigh Valley.

Section 4: Summary of Impacts

Table E is provided to summarize the various impacts calculated in Table A–D.

Table E

Summary of selected impacts

Subdivision Name: ______________________________

Municipality Name: ______________________________

Type of Impact	*Impact*			
Number of Persons:	Minimum	_____	Maximum	_____
Average Daily Trips:	Total	_____		
Peak Hour Trips:	Outbound (A.M.)	_____	Inbound (P.M.)	_____
Water Demand (in gallons):	Minimum	_____	Maximum	_____
Sewage Generation (in gallons):	Minimum	_____	Maximum	_____

SOURCE: A Simplified Impact Analysis System: A Technical Report and User's Manual, Joint Planning Commission Lehigh-Northampton Counties, Pa., June, 1976.

part three
PROPERTY DYNAMICS AND ANALYSIS

The dynamics of property interests and the level of sophistication of the analysis employed determines, to a large extent, client decisions and the corresponding success matrix. Being able to discern the needs and appropriateness of methodology in given problem situations is what separates the novice from the experienced professional. For success does not rest on a formula approach: it is a result of the recognition of and drawing of distinctions in a given environment, with variations of many subset factors. Occasionally, recommended action-parameters possess unique attributes consistent with client objectives and represent professionally articulated strategies that have been formulated by consultants and investment advisors in one of the most basic resources of all human activity—the real estate industry.

An understanding of investor expectations and motivations in various kinds of real estate developments is a valuable resource for a real estate counselor. For example, as an investment advisor you might wish to develop a frame of reference for dealing with various clients concerning the possible purchase of a 70-unit walk-up garden apartment complex. Our hypothetical property was built about 20 years ago and is located in a stable area. The condition of the property is good; vacancies and collections remain typical for this kind and class of investment.

Three investors are interviewed. Investor A holds in his portfolio a number of retail store facilities and a part interest in a recently built motel near a toll road. Investor B has a history of extensive investment in different kinds of apartment complexes, and continues to look at new ventures. Investor C has built some speculative houses and has recently been involved as a general partner in a small land syndication deal. You interview investor B and she appears to be well-informed about apartment investments. She poses questions that indicate that she perceives a minimum return of 6 percent from the property (without considering financing). The perceived maximum return is 14 percent. Based on the price she would pay for the property, she feels that there would be at least a 35 percent chance for a yield of 9 percent. A figure is drawn with line MN included as shown in Figure 1.

Investor A views the property and looks at the income and expense statements for the last three years. In his judgement there is a 50 percent chance for a yield of 8 percent, a 65 percent chance for a yield of 9 percent, and a 90 percent chance for a 12 percent yield, based on what he would pay for the property.

Investor C perceives a 10 percent chance for an 8 percent yield, a 20 percent chance for a 9 percent yield, and a 60 percent chance for a 12 percent yield, based on his estimated price of the property.

All these expressions of expectations and investor preferences are plotted as shown. What the diagram shows is that investor C is risk-averse for this investment; he probably would pay the least for the property. Chances are that investor A has placed a lower value on the property than that perceived by B. In essence, he desires a risk premium

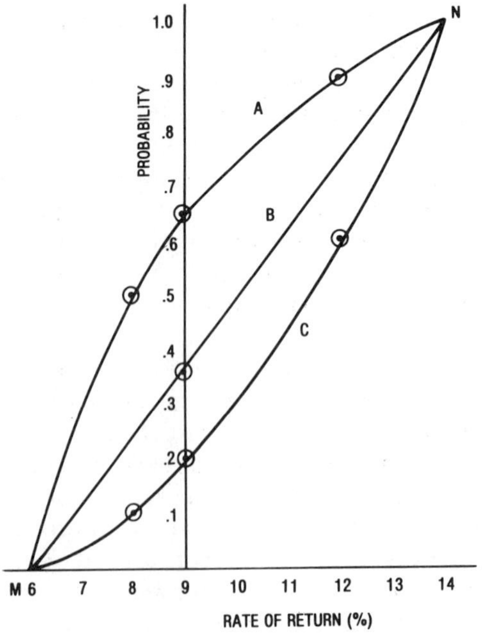

FIG. 1

if he is to undertake ownership of the property. Investor A is the gambler, with lower expectations of yield. It may be he sees certain things in the property that neither B nor C perceive. In terms of negotiating a successful deal, it should be quite obvious that the highest probability of success exists with investor C.

Since an investor's thinking always involves a number of strategies related to alternate investment opportunities, a consultant must gear his thinking and analysis to providing viable advice within the framework of client needs. Consequently, strategy formulation represents a distinguishable discipline and should be a resource of the knowledgeable investment advisor. The counselor should be particularly familiar with the use and application of probability concepts in modern decision making in business and industry. One increasingly popular application of probability concepts is Bayesian analysis (see *Rams' Real Estate Appraising Handbook,* Prentice-Hall, Inc., 1975, for applications concerning highest and best use studies).

The Bayesian probability concept rests on a subjective approach; it is based upon the personal judgement of a decision-maker concerning the probability of the occurrence of an event. This analysis can be implemented based on an informative prior distribution (real-life and market experience), or on a noninformative prior distribution (probabilities used in cases where no similar facilities have been developed in the local market area). The technique has special value in the field of real estate development because it enables the analyst to treat new innovations and ventures that exhibit a high degree of uncertainty in an organized and quantified manner. Likewise, it serves as a check on knee-jerk responses and herd syndrome, prevalent in many investment markets, while at the same time providing for inclusion of the "gut feeling" concerning new ventures.

A distinct attribute of Bayesian analysis is that it allows testing for the extent of risk. However, it does not entirely displace the classical empirical approach to notions of probability studies. In some instances, Bayesian analysis reinforces the findings based on a "track record performance" of a large sample of observed undertakings.

Several other techniques employing probability measures are gaining in popularity. These include Markov analysis and cross-impact (X-1) analysis.

MARKOV ANALYSIS

Markov Analysis concerns itself with measuring the current movement of some activity in an effort to predict its future movement. Like all applications of probability concepts, it provides a method for describing the variability of events. Principal applications of the method have encompassed the following areas:

1. Forecasting shares of retail merchandise markets.
2. Forecasting the probable market equilibrium in shares of markets of retailers and distributors.
3. Forecasting the potential gains or losses in shares of markets.
4. Evaluating advertising and promotion programs and their impacts on relative shares of markets at different levels and within different channels of distribution of goods and merchandise.

Central to this process are transition probabilities that represent the potential for a loss or gain or the probability of future events based on prior changes and the current state of affairs. The technique is particularly adaptable for analyzing short-term patterns of change such as actual changes over time of one pattern of factors versus one of several other factors.

Several underlying assumptions of the Markov process (an ordering of events in chain-like fashion) include the notion that the long-run probability of an action will be defined by the events preceding it. Accordingly, the next event or outcome in a sequence depends upon the outcome of the previous event.

A simple example will illustrate the potential of this form of analysis within a broad array of urban situations. Assume that a retail market area, contained within a county, is segmented, for study purposes, into the following three categories: (1) central business district (CBD), (2) major retail centers (MRC's), other than the central business district, and (3) the remainder of the county. Current shares of retail trade are: CBD—20 percent, MRC's—35 percent, and county—45 percent. Over the last two years, the losses and gains in share of trade are estimated to be as follows: CBD retention of 90 percent of business with a loss of 5 percent to the county and 5 percent to the MRC's; county retention of 88 percent and loss of 8 percent to the CBD and 4 percent to the MRC's; MRC trade retention of 85 percent and loss of 5 percent to the CBD and 10 percent to the county. These relationships then serve as the basis for the following transition matrix:

Retention and Loss→

$$\begin{array}{l} \\ \text{CBD} \\ \text{County} \\ \text{MRC's} \end{array} \begin{pmatrix} \textit{CBD} & \textit{County} & \textit{MRC's} \\ 0.900 & 0.050 & 0.050 \\ 0.080 & 0.880 & 0.040 \\ 0.050 & 0.100 & 0.850 \end{pmatrix} \begin{array}{c} \text{Retention} \\ \text{and} \\ \text{Gain} \\ \downarrow \end{array}$$

This matrix is then multiplied by the shares of market in the following manner:

$$(0.20 \quad 0.45 \quad 0.35)\begin{pmatrix} 0.900 & 0.050 & 0.050 \\ 0.080 & 0.880 & 0.040 \\ 0.050 & 0.100 & 0.850 \end{pmatrix}$$

That is:

Row 1	×	*Column 1*		
0.900	×	0.20	=	0.180
0.080	×	0.45	=	0.036
0.050	×	0.35	=	0.018
				0.234

Row 1	×	*Column 2*		
0.050	×	0.20	=	0.010
0.880	×	0.45	=	0.396
0.100	×	0.35	=	0.035
				0.441

Row 1	×	*Column 3*		
0.050	×	0.20	=	0.010
0.040	×	0.45	=	0.018
0.850	×	0.35	=	0.298
				0.326

The new forecast shares of retail trade from the above defined sectors in the outlined time period are

1. Central Business District—0.234 (23.4 percent)
2. County—0.441 (44.1 percent)
3. Major Retail Centers—0.326 (32.6 percent)

The above illustration is a first-order Markov chain analysis. For practical purposes involving most economic, demographic, and related data, this level of refinement is adequate. Two important conditions must be remembered when using this kind of analysis. First, so long as the transition probabilities remain the same, the respective market shares will likewise remain constant—a state of equilibrium has been reached. Second, as long as all three sectors continue to participate and derive a share of the total retail trade, regardless of periods under study, the transition matrix will not terminate. Successive incremental shifts merely result in smaller and smaller absolute differentials between shares at successive points in time.

Markov analysis can also be used to evaluate and develop different kinds of marketing strategies. It can be shown that, if the transition probabilities are changed from one period to another, the consequence is a change in relative shares of business.

Another possible area of application of Markov analysis is in the implementation of the reasonable probability doctrine in eminent domain proceedings. Here the question is when, if ever, the pressures for a change of use and zoning will reach such levels as to require a change in an area. Usually such an area has had some change prior to the proceeding. Let us assume that a public agency seeks to acquire a property that has, at present, a residential use. The surrounding area has, however, experienced some commercial development. The question is whether there is a reasonable probability that the subject, within the near future, could be rezoned and redeveloped for a commercial land use. One should note that analysis of such change, within a defined market impact area, satisfies the shares requirement, allowing for the derivation of transition probabilities similar to those illustrated. Certainly it would appear that this kind of analysis, coupled with appropriate economic and demographic studies, would provide greater credibility within a judicial proceeding than the sort of testimony that frequently passes as pure "judgemental evidence" in many litigations.

Markov analysis might be useful in determining whether or not an area has reached or is about to reach a "tipping point." "Tipping" has been defined as "that point at which a set of conditions has been created that will lead to the rapid flight of an existing class under circumstances of instability which result in the deterioration of the neighborhood environment" (Trinity Episcopal School Corp. v. Romney, 387 F. Supp. 1044 (S.D.N.Y. 1974)). The following give indications of potential tipping:

1. the gross numbers of minority group families or families in a measurable economic or social group that are likely to adversely affect Area conditions;
2. the quality of community services and facilities; and,
3. attitudes of majority group residents who might be persuaded by their subjective reactions to the first and second conditions to leave the area.

Retrospective studies of absorption of different kinds of housing units (for sectors/areas of a community) could suggest and signal the impacts on consumers of locations/products/amenity mix to forecast development potentials and developer opportunities. Markov analysis can also serve as a vehicle of measurement of the diffusion process of innovations of real estate developments.

CROSS-IMPACT (X-1) ANALYSIS

A new and challenging forecasting technique, which has captured the imagination of many scholars and researchers, is cross-impact analysis. This technique relates the probabilities of events with their structural interrelationships. The method utilizes expert opinion in forecasting evolving trends and relationships in a complex setting. The central objective of the technique is to improve the decision-making process by relating intuitive information about the socioeconomic and political environment to corresponding quantitative data and resolving these parameters into a meaningful subsystem of broadly defined problems and representative solutions.

Basically, cross-impact analysis is a futures-oriented forecasting technique that seeks to determine the future influence of an event, its likelihood, timing, and mode of impact on other events. Underlying assumptions include notions concerning likely changes in technology, values, or other important socioeconomic factors. While essentially subjective in nature, it deals with changes in the probability of occurrence of interconnected events, the timing of such events, and the mode of impact of events. The fundamental attribute of cross-impact analysis is that it allows an examination of the likely interaction of events in a probabilistic framework. A consequence of the probabilistic nature of the technique is that the resulting derivations are subject to considerable uncertainty.

A series of interconnected cross-impact studies in a time-frame context can result in the creation of a scenario. Accordingly, a complex problem can be reduced to simpler components in stated time frames. This ability to generate scenarios is one of the primary advantages of cross-impact analysis.

Several writers have drawn a distinction between events and trends, stating that events are the constituent components of a trend. For example, a market feasibility study of a proposed office building depends on events such as planning, financing, construction, leasing, and occupancy. The event of a new office building may have a series of preceding events, like the demolition of several old office buildings, a new industry locating in the community, and so forth. Manifestly, events are quantifiable and therefore arithmetic. A trend, on the other hand, is geometric—an extended time horizon with many factors and forces acting in a much larger (global) context. Real estate development is inhibited or enhanced by trends of growth or decay (a sigmoidal pattern) in the economic fabric of the relevant market area.

A very elementary example of cross-impact analysis can involve the future of retail trade in an area: at issue are trends in property values. It is estimated that the probability of further growth of an area is 0.6. The following conditional impact probabilities are related to continued growth:

1. Increasing property values in non-core area—0.3.
2. Further erosion of core area dominance—0.4.
3. Increased market competitiveness in metropolitan area due to expansion of existing firms and new entries into the market—0.2.

Supposing that event 2 has occurred, what impact does this have upon the probabilities of events 1 and 3 above?

Using the expression $p(i/j)$ to mean the probability of i if j occurs, the following relationship is found:

$$p(i/j) = p(i) + p(i)\,(1 - p(i))s$$

where

$$s = p(i/j) - p(i)/p(i)\,(1 - p(i))$$

The revised probability for one (1) above is:

$$p(j/i) = 0.3 + (0.3)\,(0.7)\,(0.833) = 0.48$$

The revised probability for three (3) above is:

$$p(j/i) = 0.2 + (0.2)\,(0.8)\,(0.833) = 0.33$$

In essence this suggests that, on the basis of a 60 percent probability of growth in the area and the occurence of event 2, the erosion of core area dominance over an identified period, the probabilities during the following period, based on prior assigned event probabilities, are as follows:

Event	*Initial Probabilities*	*Event-Impact Probabilities*
1	0.3	0.48
3	0.2	0.33

Some researchers have suggested that a prelude to "events" are omens, that is, preindications (facts with a future potential) of possible and probable events. However, a basic dimension that requires constant attention in forecasting endeavors is the element of time; for time is a vehicle of causality—the link connecting omens, events, and consequent trends. Manifestly, time becomes a basic scenario to all forecasting activities because change and rate of change is, of necessity (to be meaningful), equated over time whether one is concerned in analyzing trends through retrodiction (turning the clock back to some period in the past—starting with the present as a reference point) or postdiction (futures, the essence of forecasting).

Another variation of cross-impact analysis is through the use of a likelihood ratio. Assume the occurence of an event: what are the odds (or probability) favoring the target event? The following two relationships are used:

$$\text{odds} = \text{probability}/(1 - \text{probability})$$

$$\text{probability} = \text{odds}/(1 + \text{odds})$$

For example, assume a site is up for rezoning adjacent to one belonging to a client who would also like to have his land rezoned. Generally the odds are 1/4 (0.2 probability) for approval. However, if the neighbor obtains rezoning, it is estimated that a positive impact would occur, resulting in odds of 3/1 in favor of your client. The new probability of obtaining a rezoning would be:

$$1/4 \times 3/1 = 3/4;\ 0.75/(1 + 0.75) = 0.42\ \text{(probability)}$$

Other adaptations of cross-impact analysis include simulating the impacts of various events on trends, as a method of generating plausible scenarios and forecasting the probabilities of trends.

This part of the book outlines other problem situations and suggested solutions. Selective use of consulting activities can furnish a basis for new or different strategy formulations.

Q. *What are the five key factors that must be considered when analyzing any investment project?*

A. The factors requiring detailed analysis include:

1. *Investment Requirements*—concerns the cash outlay. Analysis in this area will include not only the down payment or cash required over a mortgage, but also any expected additional or net increases in working capital, anticipated un-capitalized expenses, analysis of the time flow of cash funds (time value of money), and a breakdown of opportunity costs (cost of capital, equity yield, and the like).

2. *Economic Life of the Investment-Development*—concerns the production of net earnings over a plausible time period. Increases in net profit may be achievable through a reduction of operating expenses or through increased productivity of the assets. An analysis of after-tax and net cash flow is also very important.

3. *Earnings Forecast*—concerns the future income and the future expenses during the contemplated holding term of an investment. Where several investments may be under consideration, differences in the anticipated level and pattern of net cash flows can serve as important criteria when matched against equity requirements.

4. *Risk*—concerns the possibility that the anticipated benefits from an investment may not be realized. Risk relates to potential shortfalls of revenues, usually related to unanticipated locational, technological, and marketplace changes. The extent of risk, both external and internal, (whether general type of improvements or special-purpose) relates to the utilization forecast of the property as developed. Errors in forecasting may affect the profitability of the venture.

5. *Liquidity–Terminal Value*—concerns the potential ease of sale and disposition for a series of holding periods under consideration, plus a forecast of probable disposition price. The extent of liquidity depends on many factors, including financing, resale equity requirements, kind, quality, and location of property; and probable demand for facilities. In some instances, liquidity analysis might include estimates of quick cash-out liquidation values in weighing both the desirability of an investment and the overall net equity yield over the holding term of the investment.

Q. *What are several different kinds of risk related to real property?*

A. Four different kinds of risk related to real property include:

1. *Functional risk*—can best be defined as a relationship between the existing use of the land and improvements and the theoretical highest and best use of the site. For example, if a current use develops a land value level of $80,000 and another use, being the best use, develops a land value of $100,000, then we will arrive at a ratio of $80,000/$100,000 or 0.80. Risk, in this case, is equal to 1 − 0.80 = 0.20, or 20 percent, directly attributable to the current program of use. Simply stated, functional risk attempts to identify the extent of property dysfunction as a joint function of land and improvements considered as a whole.

2. *Money risk*—relates to the quality of an investment at the time of purchase or refinancing due to variations in interest rates, payout terms, or simply the availability of financing. For example, one could infer a risk rate based upon the ratio of mortgage constants for investment property. Assuming two nearly identical properties for sale, the better location might warrant a mortgage at 8 percent for 20 years, at a constant of 0.1004, while the other might warrant a mortgage of 18 years at an 8.75 percent rate with a constant of 0.1106. The ratio of 0.1004 to 0.1106 equals 0.91. The relative risk is then 1 − 0.91, equalling 0.09, or 9 percent. Thus, there is an implied risk of 9 percent to the less desirably located property. Note that if the constants were equal, the ratio would be 1.00, and by definition both properties, via mortgage constant analysis, would have the same risk. (See subsequent discussion and potential applications of Rams' Mortgage Risk Tables.)

3. *Inflation/deflation risk*—relates to the impact of monetary policy, that is, the rate of inflation or deflation, upon the standing inventory of real property. Flow of mortgage funds, interest rates, mortgage ratios, and the like impact on the level of value of real property in the marketplace and its ease of liquidation and sale. Also, equities can be created via inflation and eliminated during periods of deflation. Thus the notion of a negative equity can become a reality in periods of long-term deflation.

4. *Marketability risk*—relates to the level of liquidity of different kinds of real estate improvements. Again, take two virtually

identical duplex properties. One is and has been used as designed. The other, with some minor interior changes, is being used as a rooming house. Even if the price is the same, the duplex used by two families may sell faster because it has a broader based market, i.e. better marketability. The market, in this context, consists primarily of potential owner-occupants of one of the housing units in the duplex.

Q. *What is risk-aversion and how does it manifest itself in the real estate marketplace?*

A. Risk-aversion is a basic human attribute, that is, a person in undertaking any activity wants to minimize risk and, therefore, avoid failure. Simply stated, if you reduce risk, you increase the chance of success. In real estate ventures, each buyer or investor will exhibit various levels of risk-aversion depending on the kind, quality, and location of a real estate development. For example, some buyers prefer an investment in a small retail-commercial facility over one in an apartment building. This implies that they are less risk-averse in the former instance than they are in the latter.

Studies suggest that investors want to maximize or increase their wealth position. Accordingly, as their relative wealth increases, their attitudes towards risk will change over time. Simply stated, one with wealth does not need to gamble and, hence, becomes very risk averse. Such investors simply wait until the right deal comes along. In the meantime, such an investor will feel secure because of his relative wealth position.

Q. *What is the difference between a feasibility study and a highest and best use study concerning real property interests?*

A. In the total context of the real estate marketplace they are one and the same. *Feasible* means practicable, advantageous, possible, and capable of being realized. Whether a parcel of ground is vacant or improved, the central question concerns matching the market (effective demand) with the resources (land, existing or new improvements, modernization, modification to new use, and so forth) at a given location while considering its present and anticipated overall environment. Therefore, whether you seek to determine the "most feasible development" of a vacant site, the "feasibility for continued utilization" of an existing improvement, or the "highest and best use" of an underimproved site, you are essentially attacking the same problem. In none of these instances can an assumed market demand for an identified use serve as a foundation for a feasibility study or highest and best use analysis.

Q. *Appraisers estimating the fair market value of a property, vacant or improved, mention that the value estimate is predicated on a property's "highest and best use." What is the true meaning of the term "highest and best use"?*

A. The following definitions provide some insight into the meaning of the term, "highest and best use."

- *Market Value:* the most probable price established between a willing buyer and a willing seller, both possessing a reasonable degree of knowledge of the actual and/or perceived market for the property and its potential use(s) in the forseeable future. (Rams, 1975)

- *Highest and Best Use:* A legal and perceived most profitable use, based on forecast market demand and associated risk, providing the maximum benefits, monetary and/or other, for the longest forseeable period of time. (Rams, 1974)

Thus, every estimate of market value rendered in an appraisal report should contain a judgement as to whether the subject improvements represent the highest and best use of the property. When other resources, like paint, a new heating plant, or remodeling are required to bring the property to its highest use, these should be identified and their costs estimated. The value estimate rendered should reflect the "as is value" based upon an optimum use, or, if the present use is not optimum, an alternate use should be specified.

When appraising vacant land, classifications like "commercial," in reference to the highest and best use, are redundant simply because under most zoning laws there are at least 20 or more different kinds of commercial uses that are permitted. When referring to "highest and best use" the analyst-appraiser must determine one or a combination of uses to be the optimum uses, *based on market demand* and associated risk (see above definition). Thus, optimum and best use and corresponding market value for that use are inseparable. It is obvious that a change from one use to another will very likely change the value of the land.

From a standpoint of markets and market reality, not all commercial uses can support a land value of $40 per square foot. The principal question is: Which use, if any, will support such a value? If there are none, then the best use may simply not be commercial. In some instances, where a surplus of commercial zoned land is evident, the land's potential for future commercial use must be heavily discounted.

The same kind of analysis is required concerning residential land where a broad spectrum of uses is permitted; for example, single-family, duplex, townhouse, and so forth. To say that the best use is residential is merely to state what is evident from a legal point of view under the existing zoning code. But from an economic point of view, much more needs to be said. An analysis should be made of present and future demand for residential use, be it single-family, townhouses, or a mix of several uses. When citing comparable sales transacted several years ago, it is important to remember that such sales only prove that a market need existed in the past. If the property cited remains vacant with no immediate plans for development, the sale must represent either a speculative sale, a misreading on the part of the buyer, or a purchase in which development was delayed for some other valid reason. A basic axiom might read: Value today rests on today's market demand and the outlook for the near-term future!

Simply stated, highest and best use is predicated on at-place demand, based on a market supply-demand study, with *a specificity of use*, that is, gas station, office building, single-family, walk-up apartments, etc. The corresponding and derivative value rests on market transactions involving the conversion and development of sites of the *specificied use* or vacant sites where the highest and best use is the same. Then the evidence of value is a comparison of "apples vs. apples." See the discussion concerning "Vacant Land Parity Analysis" and elements of adjustment for "test of comparability" of market transactions.

Q. *What are several important shortcomings of the so-called "replacement or reproduction" cost less depreciation as a measure of the market value of typical existing real estate developments?*

A. The foremost objection is that this method, questionably labeled an approach to value, treats only the supply side of the marketplace, that is, the cost of a particular improvement plus land. Further, a summation approach, as this approach is frequently labeled, proceeds on the premise of valuing the land as vacant (which it is not) based on its highest and best use (which may or may not be the case). To this value is added the depreciated value of the improvements. In essence, two disparate assumptions are joined in arriving at a dollar amount.

Another major objection, from economic theory and reality, is that real estate (land and structures-improvements) represent a joint product, and the relative contribution of the several components cannot be clearly ascertained. The act of taking a vacant site and building a house on it results in a particular and unique mix of land and materials, labor, and so on. The product is a new individualistic entity whose market value is based on the probable market demand at the given location.

Finally, the summation method, by its very nature, cannot and does not concern itself with the optimum allocation of scarce resources—a consideration central to all economic analysis. Merely pricing something, by whatever means, accomplishes little in an economic sense. Perhaps it is the simplicity of the method for obtaining "some kind of number" that makes its use and application so widespread, especially in the evaluation of old and obsolete properties.

Q. *In undertaking an appraisal of a property, what is the first and foremost question to be addressed if one is to provide a truly professional service in rendering an opinion of value?*

A. The central and basic question, after the legal and physical interests have been identified, concerns the matter of resource utilization. One must question whether the resources, land, improvements, and equipment, if any, are being utilized so as to maximize the aggregate and total value of the legal-physical interests under appraisal. Resource value maximization must be viewed from the vantage point of the market—not from the point of view of the appraiser's personal beliefs or bias. The basic job of a market analyst-appraiser is to interpret the market. This task includes quantifying the current and future demand for the subject property and forecasting a program of resource utilization. This information, in turn, serves as a basis for a market value estimation. For example, if an old residential property is under study, it may be established that a residential use is the best use for the next 20 years. Such a determination might be contingent upon the following assumptions: (1) certain repairs and deferred maintenance items are to be corrected immediately, (2) certain interior remodeling necessary to make the property marketable will be undertaken at this time, and (3) an outside storage facility will be built to unclutter inside use of space, allowing available space to be used for living purposes, as designed, rather than for storage purposes. This analysis should be incorporated into the appraisal. The current cost of corrections and additions is deducted from the optimum value of the property to arrive at the "as is" value of the property.

Q. *I have heard a great deal about how the allocation of resources determines the optimum use. Why not leave optimum use aside and just value what is there in terms of land and improvements, and let it go at that?*

A. In dealing with the various resources connected with a real estate venture, an investor or owner seeks to achieve the highest and best use of these resources. Accordingly, in appraising a parcel of real estate, vacant or improved, one simply does not value what is there "as is, where is." The property as developed may be a bad mistake, the wrong kind of improvement, too much building, or too little land. It is for these and other reasons that the central question for an appraiser, broker, or investor concerns the optimum specific use of the property. In some instances, analysis can reveal that demolition, even in the case of newer structures, is the best and most economical course of action. In other cases, division of the property (apartments, stores, etc.) into more marketable units might provide not only greater revenues but higher and more stable yields and stability over the longer course of the investment.

In summary, if one appraises only what is there, he will be providing something less than a professional level of service. The deception begins with the appraiser and then proceeds to manifest itself in the actions and activities of market participants as they proceed to outsmart his client. For it is basic that the real estate counselor provide advice that enables his client to achieve maximum benefit from his situations and opportunities. In some cases this means selling; in others simply holding, while in still other situations the maximum net benefits might accrue from an exchange of properties.

Q. *What is the foremost factor to consider when estimating the market value of typical properties and property interests?*

A. The foremost factor is effective demand, that is wants, needs, and desires coupled with financial ability. Under the capital theory of value and in the real world, the demand for a commodity is absolutely essential to the creation of a market that, in turn, is the foundation of property value.

While comparable sales (transactions) provide a basis of measurement, they are not evidence of demand but rather the consequence of demand. A market transaction of a year or two ago merely attests to a market demand at that time. Markets change, as do the levels of supply and demand. Values change in response to changes in markets, demand, levels of competition, and numerous other factors.

Q. *A lot of people represent themselves as appraisers, which makes it very confusing to determine as to who is qualified, and to what extent. Are there any guidelines by which to judge what, in many instances, appears to be a vast army of appraisers?*

A. A somewhat facetious classification might be as follows:

1. *Sales-jock appraisers.* The principal attribute of these is that they usually couple a massive amount of sales data information with a minimum amount of study, usually rendering reports by the pound. In court testimony they mumble through literally dozens of often irrelevant sales transactions in a vain attempt to impress the jury with their comprehensive knowledge of the market.

2. *Litany-ritual appraisers.* These follow certain pro-forma procedures regardless of whether warranted or applicable to the problem under consideration. For example, they might consider highest and best use as "commercial," when in fact the legally permissable uses may number as many as 20 different commercial uses. They usually assume that there is a demand and appear comfortable with the notion that a sale two or three years ago is ample evidence of demand today. They show a great preoccupation with manipulating and massaging numbers, lot sizes, and building dimensions. They often end a lengthy but pointless analysis by citing "judgement and experience" as the final basis of their value estimation.

3. *Market analyst-appraisers.* These utilize a broad approach concerning the economics of land utilization—they concern themselves with effective demand for property, whether improved or vacant. They expend significant time and effort on interpretation and understanding of the real estate marketplace while devoting a minimum amount of time to establishing a judgement and experience shield. The worst possible opponents in a legal proceeding, this type often send lawyers scurrying to an out-of-court settlement.

Q. *Are there any new real estate appraisal processes for the analysis of real estate and the estimation of the market value of real property interests?*

A. The real estate appraisal process shown here is a systematic new means for analyzing real property interests and estimating their market value. Because real property is a resource, its study and analysis requires more than the gathering and manipulation of prices and sales data. The ten-step method of analysis shown assures sufficient consideration of all the important factors known to influence the real estate marketplace.

The following is a brief discussion of the ten step process.

1. Identification of rights and interests that are the subject of appraisal. A concurrent activity is a physical inspection of the property, area, and perception of the locational environment. This stage also addresses itself to the legal aspects (zoning, deed restrictions, etc.) of the present, permitted, or contemplated use(s).

2. This stage involves the first proximation, or first judgement, based on an appraiser's perception of the best use (*specificity of use*) of the property. It is a hypothesis at most—subject to testing, validation, analysis, etc.

3. The next stage involves a consideration of the physical-locational-environmental attributes of the subject property, whether vacant or improved, against thirteen basic and important real property value principles. The comparison of each principle is predicated on a point of reference (which is a requirement for making all kinds of measurements) called a *value parity index*. Simply stated, a value parity index is a market derived basis that shows the attitudes and actions of the marketplace towards various property attributes and characteristics by kind and quality of property. For example, the abuttment of an old run-down and cheap house to a railroad right-of-way may be an acceptable locational factor, however marginal. On a newer and more expensive house, the market may find this either unacceptable or at most tolerable at huge discount of price. There is a market central tendency of values/prices equated out over property location-quality-condition, etc. Each of these represent value parity indexes for a particular kind of property under study.

   Experienced and knowledgeable appraisers know from the performance of various markets and market segments that value of real estate is either inhibited or propelled, depending on market attitudes, their differentiation, and the kind, quality, and location of real property. The indexes change over time, which is largely attributable to available and competitive (product-price-location) market alternatives, neighborhood changes, technological innovations, broad socioeconomic development, etc. In a contemporary context, the energy crises could, in the near future, change the mode from large spacious single-family housing life styles to more compact and densely developed energy saving housing.

4. At this step a summary of the shortcomings and positive characteristics of a parcel of real estate can be formulated. A second stage hypothesis of highest and best use can be evolved. The basis, though still tentative, has been market derived and predicated on the applicable value parity indexes. For example, a newer house in an old neighborhood might be readily marketable with some discounting of price; however, the anticipation principle, via value parity indexes, suggests a significant "downside trend," thus necessitating a much larger discounting for the implied marketability under a fair market value concept.

5. A market supply-demand study of similar and competing properties, *having the same or similar highest and best*

use(s) is made to test the marketability of the tentatively hypothesized use(s). This can signal, verify, or confirm, the extent of "upside," "no-change," or "down-side" of market trends and implications of marketability as related to the best use premise derived and the future of the property (if improved). On vacant land, modifications to the best use or change of use may be indicated along with formulating client advice concerning one of several postures, i.e., wait, develop, or sell. An analyst-appraiser must particularize both supply and demand in terms of the specific location vis-a-vis the property and its environs.

6. Step six results in a delineation of the viable best and *specific* use(s) for testing their respective economic feasibility. Factor tests might include, but are not limited to, rate of return (yield on equity cash flows, etc.), economic value, economic life, and related development/rehabilitation/property modification schemes as appropriate to the property under analysis. An important feedback concerns the legal aspects of the proposed use(s).

7. Since all futures involve risk of various kinds, a comparative study of risk (potential loss in value, failure of investment, etc.) of the highest and best use is undertaken. On improved properties, the extent of property dysfunction (functional risk) may be important; in other instances, the kind of property may reveal the principal market being constituted with largely risk-averters, thereby signalling price concessions to facilitate marketability within a reasonable period of time. In any event, a number of different measures of risk are accomplished, as appropriate, on the type of property under appraisal.

8. At this state the market best use(s) are ascertained based on: (a) the quality, kind, and locational-physical-environmental attributes of the property, (b) a realistic view of the market for and the competitive environment (supply-demand studies), (c) economic viability of the use(s), and (d) the least risk, on a comparative basis to alternate best use or uses.

9. Measures of value of the best use are utilized, which are applicable and credible. An important feedback, and as a further confirmation of market viability, are the findings derived under the market supply-demand survey. This builds a bridge between retrospective market evidence (sales transactions), current state and expectations of the market (asking prices-offers), and prospective value (market value)—all

placed within a competitive framework, i.e., market supply and demand of similar, available, and alternative properties.

10. Based on all prior data, trends, analysis, interpretation, and derivations, a market value estimate of a given property is ascertained.

The Real Estate Appraisal Process

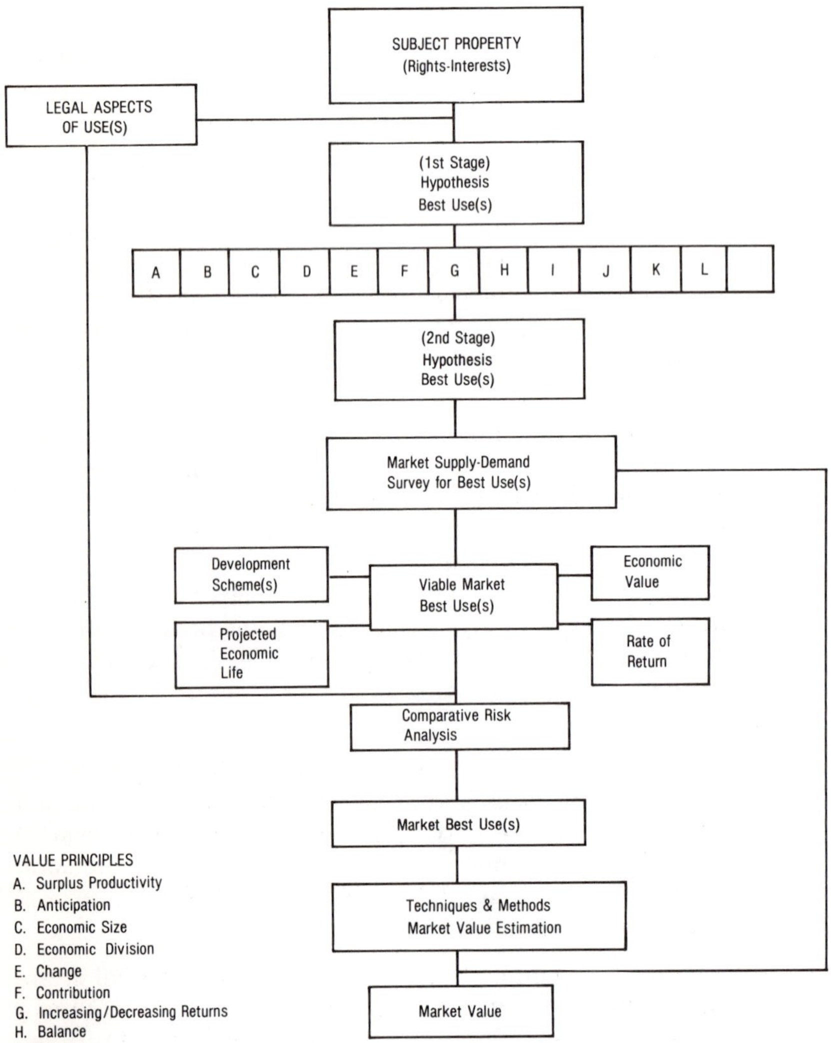

VALUE PRINCIPLES
A. Surplus Productivity
B. Anticipation
C. Economic Size
D. Economic Division
E. Change
F. Contribution
G. Increasing/Decreasing Returns
H. Balance
I. Utility
J. Conformity
K. Integration
L. Competition
M. Regression

SOURCE: Edwin M. Rams, *Rams' Real Estate Appraising Handbook*, Prentice-Hall, Inc. 1975

Q. *What is the urbanization factor and rate, as related to increasing land values?*

A. The urbanization factor relates to increases in land values that are not caused by inflation. Such increases are attributable to the density and intensity of adjacent and surrounding land use. Urbanization can be viewed as a locational benefit deriving from the site's environment. It is a factor external to the property itself.

The extent of land value increases due to urbanization must be judged within the context of competing areas and their extent of influence, since one area may be more attractive to consumers than another area. Urbanization must be viewed in a time context, in that some areas experience extensive increases in land value over a short time span while other areas literally stand still.

The following diagram illustrates the effect of urbanization in the context of density of development and potential aborting of land value increases due to locational and use obsolescence. Urban area conservation and renewal is essentially a recycling of land use and an attempt to recapture in part the positive trend of urbanization that has been dormant due to the extent of land dysfunction, resulting from fragmentary or uneconomic parcel sizes, improper and obsolete land improvements, or any of a number of other possible causes.

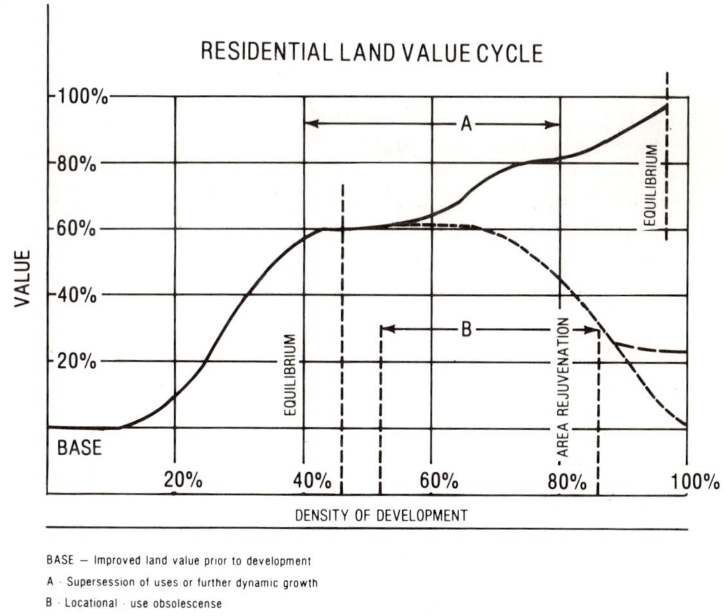

SOURCE: Edwin M. Rams, *Principles of City Land Values*, Academy Publishing Co., 1964.

Q. *Cleared urban renewal land is sold for its "fair value for use in accordance with the Urban Renewal Plan." Some reports indicate a huge discount for "pioneering." What does pioneering mean and how is it implemented in the context of the local real estate market?*

A. The so-called discount for pioneering is merely evidence of a failure to understand either the concept, the local real estate market, or the demand aspects of market viability. As for pioneering, how can this be valid when, in many cases, the sites are located a block or two from the 100 percent corner or block?

Price and value of any commodity are influenced by the basic law of supply and demand; in many communities, centrally located land probably has not been in such abundance since the founding of the city. Consequently, the ability to absorb large quantities of land has not changed simply because of clearance of run-down and dilapidated structures. *Demand is still an inseparable part of price and value,* whether the land in question results from urban renewal or is held by private parties.

The concept is indicated in Title I of the Housing Act of 1949, as amended, P. L. 171, Sec. 110(c)(4), which provides that a project may include "Disposition of any property acquired in the urban renewal area . . . at its fair value for uses in accordance with the urban renewal plan."

Attributes of the "fair value" concept as it pertains to urban renewal are derived from Title I provisions and amendments thereto, administrative regulations contained in the Urban Renewal Manual used in implementing the law, LPA letters and directives, etc., to wit:

1. All project land shall be used for only those uses set forth in the Urban Renewal Plan.
2. Purchaser must agree, in the contract for deed and the deed by reference thereto, to begin and complete construction of the improvements within a specified time.
3. Purchaser agrees to submit plans of redevelopment to the LPA for prior approval.
4. Purchaser agrees not to resell land, before constructing the improvements, for a profit, without the prior approval of the LPA.
5. Purchaser and subsequent grantees, assigns, etc., agree not to discriminate in the use or occupancy of the property because of race, color, or creed.
6. In certain transfers of stock ownership, purchaser agrees to obtain consent of sale from the LPA prior to conveyance of interests.

These factors then define the distinction between "fair value" and "fair market value." In essence, urban renewal project provisions preclude land holding, land speculation, modifications, amendments, or variances of permitted land uses, and so on.

In some instances, from a marketability viewpoint, fair value and fair market value are the same—in the marketplace as viewed by typical well informed, financially capable and interested buyers; where a strong market for land, and those permitted uses, exists, with a readily available resale market of the improved sites, the typical urban renewal restrictions do not inhibit marketability. However, where a weak demand is in evidence, these restrictions and special controls and impositions do inhibit sales, to one degree or another. Consequently, in these instances, capable and interested buyers anticipate a discount as an inducement to purchase and redevelopment.

Purchase of land in the open market requires no contractual promises, precedent or subsequent; no overt action, except that of purchase and payment, in cash or on terms is required. In urban renewal projects certain conditions, precedent and subsequent, form part of the consideration of the agreement; further, a cash purchase and payment for urban renewal land is contemplated by Title 1 of the Housing Act of 1949.

The valuation of urban renewal land, and the ascribing of its "fair value for use in accordance with the Urban Renewal Plan," must then be considered in terms of *the demand for the particular type of land, in terms of permitted uses, restrictions, immediate user requirements, etc.* The valuation process proceeds with plus and minus adjustments for factors like intensity of use, permitted uses, location, utility of the site for permitted uses, access, and the *overall productivity of the site for the possible land uses permitted by the plan.*

The following three assumptions are implicit in an appraisal of "Fair Value" of urban renewal land:

1. The area of the disposition parcels is that as set forth in the report and on the land disposition map furnished by the Local Public Agency.

2. The development of the entire renewal area will proceed in an orderly fashion in the reasonable short-term future.

3. The property being appraised is to be cleared of buildings and the streets and other site improvements are to be installed at no expense to the purchaser so that improved sites with streets and utilities in place are the subject of reuse appraisal.

Q. *What are several important factors that one must look for when trying to ascertain whether a transaction involving vacant land is truly relevant to the value of a subject parcel of land?*

A. Assuming the highest, best, and specific use of the subject land has been established *based on a market demand for that use*, the following are the critical factors concerning comparability:

1. All transactions should reflect the same or similar highest and best use. (Specificity of use—single-family, gas station, etc.)
2. The factors and forces in the marketplace that generate price (demand for best use) should be the same or similar as those prevailing at the current time.
3. The so-called comparable sales should be of properties competitive with the subject site for the same or similar highest and best use.
4. The scale of development (gross size and/or number of units to be derived should be similar to that of the subject land.
5. The physical attributes (infrastructure, roads, access, potential adaptability for highest and best use, and so forth) should be similar to those of the subject at the time of the sale.
6. If conversion of land to best use is deferred (some years delayed) the *point of market entry* should be similar to that of the subject land.
7. The market transactions must represent arm's length relationships.
8. Any financing of the land sales should be known and the price adjusted to reflect the basis on which the subject land is being offered or has been sold.

Q. *It is generally understood that when leased real estate is condemned, there is no compensation for loss of good will or going concern value to the lessee. Is this a fixed rule of the courts or are there any exceptions?*

A. The judicial viewpoint for lack of compensation usually is based on one of the following reasons: (1) the taking of the property does not in the constitutional sense mean that there is a taking of the business itself, (2) such intangible items are not property, as the term is used, and do not, therefore, require compensation for their loss, and (3) these elements are too speculative to merit consideration.

In a Michigan case in 1971 (Michigan State Highway Commission vs. L & L Concession Co., 31 Mich App. 222) the court recognized and awarded compensation. The lessee operated a concession stand at an automobile racing track. The taking of the tract resulted in the destruction of the business since the lessee "could in no way transfer his business operation to another location." The court recognized the monopoly situation of the lessee; essentially there were no alternative locations, in contrast to situations where a tenant cannot relocate simply because other firms have occupancy in all suitable buildings.

Q. *Instances have occured where a valuable and readily marketable tract of land is burdened by a life estate interest. Sale and development of such a tract (in some instances a large farm on the edge of a city) cannot be accomplished until the demise of the life tenant. What are some techniques for dealing with this kind of situation?*

A. Generally the thinking of the courts in such matters is that the economic distress of the life tenant, which can be alleviated by the sale of the property, is of primary importance. This is to preclude deterioration and waste of the property. However, a recent case, Baker vs. Weedon (1972 Miss.) 262 So 2nd. 641, expanded the criteria and stated that the propriety of the sale of property could include the "best interests" of all parties at interest, that is, life tenant and remaindermen (those who receive clear title upon the expiration of the life tenancy). The court's position was that this additional test provided more flexibility and also addressed itself to unique and unusual conditions. Even sale of part of the land could be considered, provided that sufficient funds were realized to provide for the life tenant's reasonable needs.

Q. *As an advisor on real estate ventures and investments with many different clients, why is it so important to understand risk and its many different manifestations?*

A. Understanding and mastering the application of risk concepts in dealing with a variety of clients is fundamental. It is basic to all ventures that the more one comprehends about the present and potential levels of risk, the more confidence can be placed in decisions made or recommended to clients.

Risk concerns the future and is, to some extent, uncertain—one simply does not have knowledge of the future. Because of the uncertainty in all real estate investment undertakings, an element of risk will always be present. However, risk is insurable, whereas uncertainty is not insurable. In the case of risk, modifying the purchase price of a property can be viewed as a defensive measure and perhaps an intuitive response to the element of risk. An upgrading and/or modernization of an investment property, aside from increasing rentals, is an attempt to assure that the property will remain competitive in the marketplace—in essence reducing the margin of risk.

Q. In periods of significant actual or anticipated inflation, many investors need special counseling on the impact of inflation on yields, rate of return, and the like. What means can be used to place this problem in perspective?

A. The reality of the situation is that tax rates and inflation combine to result in a synergistic effect on after-tax yields. The following tables outline the gross yield required to achieve certain after-tax yields. As an example, if an investor seeks a 12 percent after-tax return and is in the 20 percent tax rate bracket, he will need 17.5 percent gross yield at an inflation rate of 2 percent, 20 percent gross yield at an inflation rate of 4 percent, and so on. The formula for other computations is:

$$\text{Required Yield (Before)} = \frac{\text{After-tax yield} + \text{inflation rate}}{1 - \text{tax rate}}$$

After-Tax Yield (8 percent)
Inflation Rate

Tax Rate	2	4	6	8
20%	12.5%	15.0%	17.5%	20.0%
30	14.3	17.1	20.0	22.9
40	16.7	20.0	23.3	26.7
50	20.0	24.0	28.0	32.0

After-Tax Yield (10 percent)
Inflation Rate

Tax Rate	2	4	6	8
20	15.0%	17.5%	20.0%	22.5%
30	17.1	20.0	22.9	25.7
40	20.0	23.3	26.7	30.0
50	24.0	28.0	32.0	36.0

After-Tax Yield (12 percent)
Inflation Rate

Tax Rate	2	4	6	8
20	17.5%	20.0%	22.5%	25.0%
30	20.0	22.9	25.7	28.6
40	23.3	26.7	30.0	33.3
50	28.0	32.0	36.0	40.0

Q. *What are some guidelines for evaluating and possibly restructuring apartment rental units that are in trouble or on the verge of default or foreclosure?*

A. Four important components must be examined in detail before formulating plans, strategies, and related recommendations. They include a product survey, marketing survey, financial survey, and an operations survey. Specifics in each category are outlined below.

1. *Product Survey*—some key aspects include: age, condition, style and design, amenities, and typical layout of units, including kind and size. These factors are studied in comparison with currently competitive units to establish what is right and what is wrong with the subject. The advisor needs to determine what the property under study lacks that other properties have in terms of the attribute list noted above. Corrections of specific defects, whether concerned with maintenance or exterior eye appeal, can result in making the property more competitive, thus reducing potential tenant turnover and increasing rentals.

2. *Marketing Survey*—this surveys specific directly competitive properties, analyzing locational qualities, product offering techniques, management techniques for showing units, and screening applicants, and so on. A detailed study of specific units and rentals charged for similar kinds of facilities, developing price per square foot measures, is invaluable in determining whether overpricing is in fact the primary deterrent to higher occupancy. Benefits from a marketing survey include better identification of market segments and the ability to formulate a better marketing strategy with which to reach these market segments and achieve higher occupancy levels.

3. *Financial Survey*—this surveys current financing and operating capital needs, and determines the financial feasibility of the upgrading and/or modernization needed to make property competitive and viable marketwise. Benefits include better operating ratios and more realistic reserves for necessary replacement.

4. *Operating Survey*—this surveys such aspects as security, staffing, training of new personnel, and accounting systems. Benefits include a "hands-on" control of inflows and outflows of revenues, specific knowledge of expenditures, and the opportunity to undertake benefit/cost studies concerning various aspects of the operation. In some instances, curtailment of

frivolous services can be undertaken and the money resources diverted to other areas more likely to maximize appeal to occupants.

Q. *In analyzing a land market, a great deal of confusion arises concerning the relationship between the prices paid and the true value of the land. How can one begin to make sense out of literally dozens of sales of tracts that differ greatly in terms of size and features?*

A. The acreage market is extremely complex, resembling, in many ways, a huge poker game for very high stakes. Several basic steps will help make sense from the mass of market evidence that often appears quite nonsensical. Regardless of the number of transactions available, selection for use should be based on (1) similar size, (2) same or similar highest and best use, (3) similar location or adjustment for locational qualities, and (4) adjustment for financing terms (rate, payout, etc.) to estimate a cash price.

Suppose three sales (S_1, S_2, and S_3) are selected using the above criteria. As will be noted subsequently, acreage recently converted may prove to be more meaningful than sales of vacant sites. To make the price paid (after adjustments noted above) more meaningful, additional analysis is undertaken as noted in the following chart. Three basic considerations for each transaction include: at-place market demand (for the highest and best use), infrastructure (if appropriate for consideration), and actual or most likely conversion time to highest and best use. All are profiled in a time dimension context. For example, a subject at current date (T) has been analyzed, indicating demand in about 26 months (T + 2) with infrastructure required prior to site design and layout at T + 1½ years. Because the necessary infrastructure is most likely at T + 4 the "most probable actual use-conversion" is over 4 years away at T + 4½ years. In comparison, analysis of the first sale (S_1) indicates that at the time of the sale (T − 5) demand was in evidence; infrastructure was completed about 1½ years later; and shortly thereafter (T − 3) actual conversion of the land was undertaken. A similar profile exists for the second sale (S_2). The third sale (S_3) presents another situation. The sale occurred only 6 months ago. Analysis indicates that the infrastructure will be completed within a year of the sale, but at-place demand is not likely until about 4½ years from the date of sale.

Use of an asset—in this case vacant land—depends upon conversion time, which, in turn, is dictated by market demand for a site's highest and best use. The price paid for vacant land is dictated by these controlling factors, assuming, of course, that both buyers and sellers have reasonable knowledge of these important factors, which will be reflected in the agreed upon transaction price.

Discount rates often used in the real estate marketplace provide a means to adjust for the holding periods and give proper consideration to the time value of money. The eventual discount rate to be applied will depend on the final closeness and bracketing of the indicated values of the transactions. These indexes can then be applied to the subject site in terms of market demand and time of most probable market entry, that is, conversion of the land to its highest and best use.

In many instances, a sample of 20 transactions, which appear credible and relevant on first inspection, may be reduced to 4 or 5. The others may be found to represent either pure speculative purchases, with little thought given to use-conversion, or simply uninformed purchases at excessive prices. Such sales, of course, do not represent true market value.

Land sales—transaction analysis

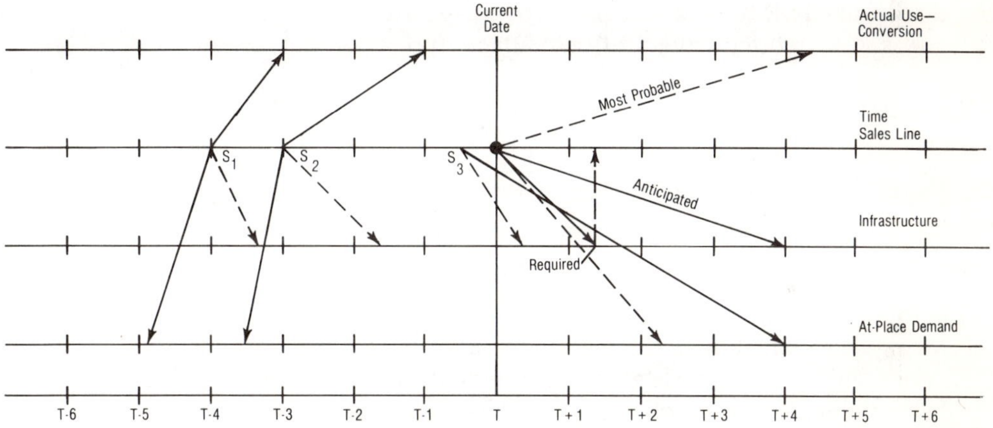

Q. *There has been a considerable amount of discussion and some legislation relating to the transfer of development rights (TDR). In such transactions a landowner may be compensated for restrictions placed on his right to develop a parcel of real estate. The compensation given reflects the potential for increased returns and profits from development. What is the outlook for a widespread use of this technique?*

A. Many clear-cut issues must be resolved before the method can be viewed as applicable on a universal basis, whether the objective is preservation, reduction of congestion, or other planning-aesthetic objective. The following recent commentary outlines some of the basic issues.

> TDR is likely to be challenged by landmark owners unless the market for development rights accurately reflects the value of their condemned development potential. A constitutional attack on TDR will probably succeed. Courts have thus far viewed preservation measures based on TDR as a taking for which just compensation is required, and have found transferable development rights inadequate as compensation. The only methods available to a municipality to salvage its TDR system will shift the cost of preservation to developers in the transfer district. Developers may find convenient precedents in subdivision exaction case law for an attack on TDR. Application of either the police power or the special assessment theory to the sale of development rights leads to the conclusion that TDR systems are, in almost all situations, unconstitutional. Because these systems are likely to be challenged and invalidated, many great landmarks may be lost if municipalities continue to rely upon TDR as a means of landmark preservation. Municipalities would be well advised, therefore, to abandon TDR in favor of landmark preservation methods that are less vulnerable to constitutional attack. (pp. 1121–2)

For a definitive analysis of the above position, see "The Unconstitutionality of Development Rights," *The Yale Law Journal*, 84 (1975), 1101.

Q. *What kind of analysis should be undertaken when significant rehabilitation is being considered by a property owner?*

A. The following brief guidelines, written by the author in 1962 for the Housing and Home Finance Agency, can serve as a format for this kind of assignment. While written in the context of urban renewal, the substitution of "owner" for "LPA" and the omission of any reference to the Urban Renewal Plan will place the subject in the framework of the private sector. The value concept considered will, of course, be fair market value.

> In the first instance, the appraiser or market analyst, as the case may be, may address himself to evaluating the extent of and the consequences of public sector investments and the elimination of blighted or deteriorating community or area influences. In this scope of analysis, it is necessary to properly measure the extent and impact of environmental changes that are contemplated, and further, that will affect to one degree or another each of the properties located within the "action area." The appraiser should not substitute broad generalities such as stating that the area will be cleaned up, dressed up, fixed up, etc., for specific data.

Within the above stated analysis, proper consideration should be given to the competitive position of the "action area" to other similar neighborhoods or areas located within the city or general community. Such a competitive position, when determined, will, to some degree, indicate the feasibility or nonfeasibility of activities contemplated in the rehabilitation of subject properties. It should be understood that since all real estate is a creature of its environment, its acceptability is largely determined by its location and its particular amenity-utility relationships to other similar and competing neighborhoods or areas. The appraiser should attempt to not only estimate the economic life of any particular property but should also extend this concept to estimating the economic life of the neighborhood *after* rehabilitation in a true relationship with the anticipated economic life of other competing areas. This will enable an appraiser to point out the differences in the quality, location, and amenity values of the area that is rehabilitated along side of other existing and known desirable areas and neighborhoods.

The evaluation considerations that enter into a rehabilitation type of appraisal are as follows:

1. The appraiser will have completed all the vital considerations in the first portion of the problem as discussed above.
2. Estimate the "fair value" of the property *for use in accordance with the Urban Renewal Plan* as though *completely rehabilitated* according to acceptable plans and specifications.
3. Estimate and/or acknowledge LPA obtained estimate of the cost in place of all of the required items of repair, replacement, etc., which are necessary to rate the property as though fully rehabilitated.
4. The difference between the estimate obtained in (3) when subtracted from the estimate in (2) above will indicate the warranted price that a well-informed buyer should be willing to pay for the property under appraisal subject to the impositions of the Urban Renewal Plan and the specified items of property rehabilitation.
5. The appraiser should comment as to the adequacy of each of the proposed items under the rehabilitation program and further indicate what might be done or not done that is feasible from a market value standpoint in order to bring the cost-value relationship into equilibrium.

6. The report shall contain a statement as to the feasibility or nonfeasibility of the proposed rehabilitation and give statements to support the findings. This final recommendation shall contain sufficient detail and be definitive to the point that the Local Public Agency will be able to undertake intelligent actions and be supported and documented by each appraisal report.

The usual requirements of an acceptable appraisal report such as maps, plats, etc., should be included in the final submittal. The appraiser should avoid delving at any length into costs as pertains to the value of the property as though fully rehabilitated. This finding should be market-oriented to the point of indicating the probable value and demand for the property when fully rehabilitated based on evidence obtained from local market conditions—past, present, and those forecast by the contract appraiser.

Q. *Leases generally have a provision requiring the lessee to obtain consent from the landlord before subleasing the premises subject to the lease. What are some basic guidelines to be used when a conflict concerning subleasing appears to be developing?*

A. In a serious and potentially protracted confrontation between a lessor and lessee, the best advice is to consult with competent legal counsel. Each case is based on particular facts and circumstances relating to the legal rights of the parties. Some state courts will assess damages to a tenant for unreasonable action by the lessor. In other instances, the courts will require the continued payment of rent by the lessee. One of the key questions that addresses the central issue is whether the consent provision in the lease is construed to be a covenant. The next question is whether the refusal of consent to sublease was reasonable or unreasonable. Other collateral questions include the matter of whether the lessee, within the factual situation, continues to be obligated under the covenant to pay rent. As in all matters that may have to be litigated, the courts look to the reasonableness of the landlord's requirements and the propriety of the corresponding responses by the tenant.

Q. *A mortgage on a small owner-occupied house is available for purchase but has a low yield interest rate of 8.5 percent. The mortgage is payable monthly and has 10 more years before final payout. A client is interested but seeks a return of 10 percent. What is the maximum he should pay to obtain this yield? The mortgage balance is $11,500.*

A. The following formula is used to compute the discount required on a mortgage balance to achieve a higher yield:

$$d = \frac{Y - r}{(1/n) + Y}$$

Where:

Y = desired annual yield percentage
r = contract interest rate
n = remaining term of mortgage in years
d = discount rate on balance due

$$d = \frac{0.10 - 0.085}{(1/10) + 0.085} = \frac{0.015}{0.20}$$

$= 8.1\%$ or \$931.50 discount

Maximum purchase price: \$11,500 − \$931.50 = \$10,568.50

Q. *What are some rules of thumb that can be used in developing estimates of lot yield per acre for single-family development?*

A. The following tables can serve as preliminary guides for such rough estimates:

Approximate Lot Size (square feet)	*Lots Per Acre*
6,000–8,000	4.5
8,000–10,000	3.5
10,000–12,500	3.0
12,500–15,000	2.7
15,000–20,000	2.3
20,000–25,000	1.5

Where slope of land is a factor, the following provides modifications to lot yield per acre:

Slope of Land	*Lots Per Acre*
0.5%	4.61
10.0	4.27
15.0	3.82
20.0	3.40
25.0	3.20

Other important factors include extent of green areas, width of right-of-ways, block lengths, curved streets, cul-de-sacs, and positioning of streets in relation to land contours. The following table provides additional yield information relating to depth of lot, block length, and width of street. Current local costs for streets and infrastructure for the indicated street length, plus an allowance for connector streets, can provide a rough cost approximation for this segment of a land development undertaking.

Lot yield per acre—land development*

Lot Depth (in feet)	Block Length (in feet)	Street Width (in feet)	Allocation (%) Land for Streets	Balance for Development	Street Length	Street Length Per Acre Land Developed
		40	20.6	79.4	224	282
100	800	50	24.7	75.3	216	287
		60	28.5	71.5	205	292
		40	20.2	79.8	220	277
	900	50	24.2	75.8	211	280
		60	27.9	72.1	203	282
		40	18.5	81.5	202	248
	700	50	22.2	77.8	194	251
		60	25.8	74.2	188	253
		40	17.9	82.1	195	239
125	800	50	21.6	78.4	188	241
		60	25.0	75.0	182	243
		40	17.5	82.5	191	232
	900	50	21.1	78.9	184	233
		60	24.4	75.6	177	234
		40	17.2	82.2	185	224
	700	50	20.0	80.0	173	226
		60	23.2	76.8	169	230
		40	16.0	84.0	174	207
150	800	50	19.4	80.6	170	210
		60	22.5	77.5	164	212
		40	15.5	84.5	170	201
	900	50	18.8	81.2	164	202
		60	21.9	78.1	159	203

*Assumes essentially a flat terrain.

Q. *Based on share of market demand studies, you have estimated at-place demand for the subject acreage to be 1,000 housing units over the next 5 years with a uniform annual absorption rate. At a mix of 60 percent single-family and 40 percent multifamily and respective densities of 2.6 and 8.0 units per acre, what is the annual absorption rate of the land and what is the aggregate demand over the next 5 years?*

A. *Total annual demand:* 200 units per year

60/40 Mix: 120 single-family units
80 multifamily units

Annual Acreage Absorption:

Single Family: 120/2.6 = 46.2 acres
Multifamily: 80/8 = 10.0 acres

Aggregate 5-Year Demand for Land:

5 × 46.2 = 231.0
5 × 10.0 = 50.0

Total: 281.0 acres

Q. *A small investment property has a mortgage balance of $146,700 with annual payments of $12,200. Net income after expenses is $22,500. If equity yield is 10 percent, what is a likely index of the value of the property?*

A. Income attributable to equity is $10,300, which is the difference between the net income from the property and annual debt charges of $12,200.

Equity interest is capitalized as follows:	
$10,300/0.10 =	$103,000
Add mortgage balance =	146,700
Approximate value based on equity income =	$249,700

Q. *As an investment advisor, you have been discussing a number of potential investments with Mr. Smith. During the course of these meetings he evidenced some interest in an apartment building, but with some reservations. Based on his tax bracket and other investment situations you have surmised his investment thinking and attitude towards the risk involved in an apartment property to be as follows: at least a 20 percent chance of a yield of 15 percent or more on his equity and a 90 percent chance that his losses (negative cash flow) will not exceed 5 percent.*

Recently a property has been offered, and based on its location and competitive position among other similar apartment developments, you have analyzed four possible levels of net cash flow including your perceived probability for several rates of return on a purchaser's equity position as noted below.

Consultant's estimates of net return to equity

(1) Outcome	(2) Probability of Outcome	(3) Net Return	(4) Rate of Return	(5) Probability Return Will be Greater Than Given Rate
1	0.10	$6,200	−10%	1 − (0.10) = 0.90
2	0.30	10,000	10	1 − (0.10 + 0.30) = 0.60
3	0.40	11,500	20	1 − (0.10 + 0.30 + 0.40) = 0.20
4	0.20	12,000	30	1 − (0.10 + 0.30 + 0.40 + 0.20) = 0.0

What is a quick way of screening this proposal to ascertain whether Mr. Smith might be interested?

A. A simple drawing may help out in this kind of situation. The first thing to do is to draw a graph representing the limitations of Mr. Smith's risk profile as noted in the above estimate. Point B, which might be called a loss coefficient, represents an accepted probability and the minimum rate of return that is acceptable (maximum 5 percent loss with a 90 percent probability). Point C, which might be called a payoff coefficient, represents the achievable desired yield (15 percent or more with at least a one in five change—20 percent probability). These two points on the graph are connected and represent a basic utility curve outlining the limits of risk. All cases falling to the right of this line ABCD are in the acceptance area, those to the left represent the rejection area of the investor's risk criteria.

The computations derived from columns (4) and (5) are plotted as dashed lines on this diagram. Since the connecting line crosses into the rejection area, you conclude that the apartment investment proposal does not meet Mr. Smith's investment standards and attitudes towards risk.

As a matter of interest you make one more computation—the expected value (average of random variables) of return. The expected value, using columns (2) and (4) is as follows:

$$\text{Expected Value} = (0.20)(30\%) + (0.40)(20\%) + (0.30)(10\%) + (0.10)(-0.10\%)$$
$$= 0.06 + 0.08 + 0.03 + (-0.01) = 16\%$$

Therefore, even though the expected value exceeds a given payoff level (15 percent) for an investment, the investment's potential for losses is critical in the decision-making process. You conclude Mr. Smith would not be interested in the subject apartment building as an investment.

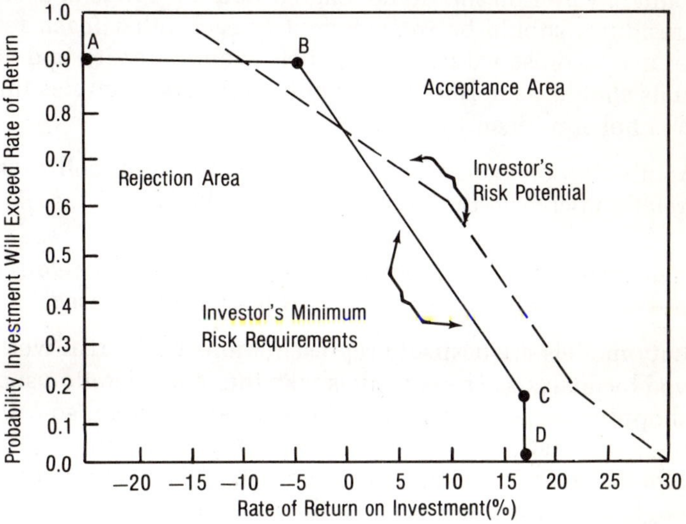

Q. *Your client has had a rental-potential study made of a one-story 67,000 sq. ft. warehouse property. The study included a full regression analysis, including measures of the mean, standard deviation, and so forth. You have been asked to comment on the report. You note that the mean building area is around 14,000 sq. ft. A quick analysis of the raw data (comparables) utilized revealed the following: 11 properties have more than one story; 16 properties have areas of 10,000 sq. ft. or less; 6 properties have areas over 10,000 sq. ft. but less than 30,000 sq. ft., and 3 have areas over 30,000 sq. ft.*

A. Based on the facts listed, the study is meaningless and worthless. First, one cannot compare the utility and function of two-, three-, or four-story buildings with the utility of a one-story warehouse. Further, only 3 properties (those over 30,000 square feet) could be remotely comparable while 22 properties included in the analysis are clearly noncomparable. Obtaining a mean—and standard deviation via regression analysis—does not, in and of itself, prove very much if the input data is inappropriate. A regression relationship is merely a mathematical relationship between a set of numbers. The validity of the input data determines the validity of any so-called "regression analysis findings." *Note:* Regression analysis is like any other mathematical model or technique; its findings are worthwhile only if the technique has been applied. Four basic assumptions (conditions) should prevail in its application. They are (1) the dependent variable must be linearly related to each of the independent variables, (2) the amount of variation should not change over the range of observations, (3) residuals should be independent of each other (each residual in reference to those values coming before and after it), and (4) the residuals should be normally distributed (on large samples this restriction is not significant).

Another problem arises when we encounter multicollinearity (high correlation between the independent variables).

Q. *I have heard about gravity models being used in retail potential analysis. What are these models and how are they used?*

A. Gravity models are basically representations of the real world as perceived by analysts. These models take into consideration such factors as shopping areas, distances, and consumers. Several so-called "laws of retail gravitation" have been formulated incorporating these basic factors. As an example, the market potential of a town can be estimated through the application of the following formula:

$$M_x = \sum \frac{P \cdot a}{D}$$

Where:

a = mean per capita income of the region and/or surrounding potential trade area

P = population of the region or potential trade area

D* = the distance between the town (x) and the median center of the regional population and distance based on the long axis of the region.

M_x = the market potential of town (x)

---

*Computed as follows:

$$D = 1/2\,(d_1 + d_2)$$

where:

d_1 is the distance from the town to the median center of population

d_2 is the length of one half the distance along the long axis of the region.

This derivation provides for a one-way influence rather than a two-way interaction. This is because only one "P" is used in the equation. In an intraurban analysis involving one or several competing centers, the following relationships can be used:

$$\text{Attraction of a Retail Center} = S/D^2$$

Where:

S = area concentration (total square feet) of retail facilities
D^2 = driving-time distance (calculated in five minute driving-time units)

To derive a breaking point between two centers, A and B, the following can be used:

$$\text{Breaking Point (B.P.)}^* = \frac{\text{Distance from A to B}}{1 + \sqrt{\dfrac{\text{size A (Sq. Ft.)}}{\text{size B (Sq. Ft.)}}}}$$

*Point of equal probability

Q. *An investor paid $325,000 for a property that has a firm lease with a utility company for a balance of 25 years. The overall capitalization rate for this kind of investment is 9 percent. What is the anticipated annual income flow from the investment?*

A. The present worth of one dollar per annum factor is:

9.823, at 9% for 25 years
Thus: $325,000/9.823 = $33,085.62 per year

Q. *If an investor paid $325,000 for an anticipated annual income flow of $40,000 for 20 years, what is the indicated capitalization rate?*

A. The ratio of value to cash flow is $325,000/$40,000 = 8.13. Locate this factor in the table of Present Worth of One Dollar Per Annum to determine the capitalization rate. The number does not appear in the twenty-year row and must be calculated as follows:

10%, 20 years factor:	8.514
11%, 20 years factor:	−7.963
Difference:	0.551

The factor 8.13 (derived above), lies between these two factors, with the difference being:

$$\begin{array}{r} 8.514 \\ -8.130 \\ \hline 0.384 \end{array}$$

Then the ratio of

$$384/551 = 70\% \times 1\% \ (11\text{-}10) = 0.7\%$$
$$10\% + 0.7\% = 10.7\%$$

The capitalization rate is 10.7%

Q. *What are three important components that must be accounted for when analyzing trends and activities in any land market?*

A. Generally, the land market is composed of (1) speculators, (2) investors who land bank for personal conversion or for sale to third parties, and (3) immediate users. The raw facts of a transaction usually reflect only the consideration. Expectations, motivations, or financing terms may, in some instances, be more important than the price paid for a parcel of land. Where possible, a separation of sales into three categories based on the above market components provides very important information concerning the direction of the land market and corresponding land values.

Q. *What is a valid basis for developing estimates of the value of reserves in the extractive industries, like coal, oil, and ore?*

A. The best method is the production-development analysis technique. This takes into account: (1) the demand for the raw material at given market prices over time, (2) the costs associated with the actual extractive process, (3) the residual value of the deposit or reserve in its present state, and (4) the recognition of the time value of money. The judiciary, in condemnation and other proceedings has, on numerable occasions, recognized this method as valid and admissible.

The following examples outline methods and factors for consideration for several kinds of typical problems involving extractive industry valuation problems.

I. VALUE OF AN OPERATING MINE

$$V = P.W.\ (O.R.) + R\ (C)$$

Value = Present Worth of "Operation Returns" plus "Reserves" as an annuity to extinguish "original cost" of property.

Important Factors in Mine Valuation:

(a) Determine adequacy of existing plant and necessity for additional investment to continue operations at the desired output.

(b) Determine the quality and quantity of the remaining ore or mineral deposit.

(c) Determine and estimate the probable annual gross receipts during the remainder of the enterprise.

(d) Determine and estimate the probable operating costs during the remainder of the enterprise.

(e) Capitalize the anticipated net annual return at a commensurate rate-of-return.

II. OIL-WELL VALUATION

(1) Annual production, gross barrels $________

(2) Less royalty, net barrels $________

(3) Annual net production (1–2) $________

(4) Annual expenses:
- (a) Production cost
- (b) Taxes and overhead cost
- (c) Miscellaneous (land, geophysical studies, etc.)

(5) Total annual expenses $________

(6) Annual gross receipts (3 × Sale Price/bbl.) $________

(7) Annual operating return (6–5) $________

(8) Value of operation: $________

P.W. of (7) for projected operations period.* $________

*Normally computations are made for each separate year over the anticipated period of oil production.

III. ORE RESERVE VALUATION

(1)	Annual gross receipts	$______
(2)	Annual operating expenses	
	(a) Mining—underground and open pit	$______
	(b) Transportation	$______
	(c) Insurance	$______
	(d) Miscellaneous	$______
	(e) Selling commission	$______
	(f) Development costs	$______
	(g) Taxes	$______
	(h) Interest on working capital	$______
	Total	$______
(3)	Annual return needed to amortize development costs and taxes paid during deferment period	$______
(4)	Total chargeable operations cost (2 + 3)	$______
(5)	Annual return for returns on investment and amortization of investment (Item 1 – Item 4)	$______
(6)	Warranted investment in the undertaking (present worth of Item 5 at appropriate rate)	$______
(7)	Warranted ore reserve investment: Item 6 minus present worth of capital investments to put undertaking in full operation.	$______

Q. *What should usually be included in the deed for a condominium unit?*

A. The following items generally are included (from the New York State Condominium Act).

1. Description of the land and the page and date of recording the condominium declaration;
2. The unit designation given the unit in the declaration and the other data necessary for its proper identification;
3. Statement of the use for which the unit is intended;
4. The common interest appertaining to the unit; and
5. Any further details the grantor and grantee may deem desirable to set forth.

Q. *What are some of the elements that should be included in a declaration concerning a condominium development?*

A. Inclusion of the following elements and provisions is customary:

1. A description of the land and/or interests in real property included within the project.
2. A description of the building, if any, stating the number of stories and basements and the number of units and the principal materials of which it is or is to be constructed and a description of all other significant improvements contained or to be contained in the project.
3. The unit number of each unit and any other data necessary to its proper identification.
4. A description of the common areas and facilities.
5. A description of the limited common areas and facilities, if any, stating to which units such use is reserved. Any shutter, awnings, window boxes, door steps, porches, balconies, patios, or other apparatus intended to serve a single unit, but located outside the boundaries thereof, shall constitute a limited common area and facility appertaining to that unit exclusively, whether or not the declaration so provides.
6. The percentage or fraction of undivided interest in the common areas and facilities appertenant to each unit and its owner for all purposes, including voting, derived and allocated in accordance with provisions of state law.
7. A statement of the purposes for which the units are intended and restricted as to use, if any use restrictions are to apply.
8. The name of a person to receive service of process, in the cases hereinafter provided, together with the residence or place of business of such person which shall be within the city or county in which the property is located.
9. The method by which the declaration may be amended consistent with the provisions of this act.
10. Any further matters in connection with the property which the person or persons executing the declaration may deem desirable to set forth consistent with this act.

The record of survey recorded with the declaration may provide or supplement the information required under items 1, 2, 3, 4, and 5 of this subsection.

Q. *What are the experiences in the private sector concerning cash flow and tax shelter characteristics of low- and moderate-income housing financed under various Federal and State programs?*

A. The following comparative analysis of several hundred multifamily housing developments provides a basis for study. The sample size and locations are noted in this compilation.

Median operating data for section 167(K) projects*
(all cities—all projects)

	Federally Insured					
	Section 221 (d) (3) BMIR		*Section 236*		*Section 221 (d) (3) Rent Supp.*	
	%	*$ per unit*	%	*$ per unit*	%	*$ per unit*
Gross Rent at Full Occupancy	85.0	1,735	67.6	1,362	47.8	974
Less Vacancy Losses	2.3	48	3.4	68	5.0	100
Rental Income	82.0	1,688	63.3	1,273	43.1	816
Subsidy Income (Federal or State)	4.0	82	34.7	730	56.1	1,043
Other Income	1.8	37	0.0	1	0.0	0
Total Project Income	100.0	1,862	100.0	2,028	100.0	2,005
Property Taxes	14.3	274	11.3	215	3.6	73
Interest and Mortgage Insurance	33.3	684	52.4	1,055	478.4	896
Operating/Maintenance Expense	40.6	734	28.4	579	49.1	786
Depreciation	81.6	1,527	104.1	2,150	97.4	1,654
Total Expense	171.7	3,226	196.0	3,956	191.7	3,318
Taxable Income (Loss)	(71.7)	(1,275)	(96.0)	(1,926)	(91.7)	(1,722)
Add Back Depreciation	81.6	1,527	104.1	2,150	97.4	1,654
Cash Flow From Operations	9.9	186	8.9	174	3.5	76
Less Amortization of Loan	3.0	59	3.3	70	2.5	50
Less Replacement Reserves	1.9	37	2.5	48	2.4	47
Less Other Cash Outlays.	0.0	0	0.0	0	0.0	0
Cash Available for Distribution	4.4	95	3.2	61	−0.9	−19
Properties in sample:	6		77		27	

NOTE: Because data are medians, details may not add to totals
*Located in the following cities: Boston, New York, Baltimore, Washington, Chicago, Detroit, Cincinnati, Cleveland, Los Angeles, and San Francisco.
SOURCE: *The Impact and Effects of Section 167 (K) on the Rehabilitation of Multifamily Property*, Touche Ross & Co. for HUD 1974.

State and Local Agency		*Conventionally Financed*		*All Types*	
%	*$ per unit*	*%*	*$ per unit*	*%*	*$ per unit*
74.5	1,633	102.6	1,555	68.1	1,261
3.3	81	2.6	39	3.4	63
70.4	1,512	100.0	1,224	64.0	1,188
29.4	755	0.0	0	34.4	657
0.0	0	0.0	0	0.0	0
100.0	2,304	100.0	1,395	100.0	1,883
6.8	173	14.6	192	10.6	85
43.5	1,016	25.3	389	48.9	905
39.7	875	32.3	548	32.0	559
131.2	3,087	65.0	1,046	107.9	1,695
216.7	4,972	138.4	2,223	198.6	3,463
(116.7)	(2,787)	(38.4)	(608)	(98.6)	(1,594)
131.2	3,087	65.0	1,046	107.9	1,695
10.8	237	32.1	427	8.9	135
2.9	68	3.4	47	3.1	56
1.8	44	0.0	0	2.4	40
0.0	0	0.0	0	0.0	0
4.4	107	28.3	397	3.4	29
37		6		153	

Q. *What are some facts concerning the economics of new housing construction and energy saving features?*

A. The following findings highlight the features, initial cost and annual savings.

Annual savings for energy conservative modifications
(as added to new construction)

Modification	First Cost of Modification (or Incremental Cost), Dollars (1973)	Annual Energy Savings of Residences, Therms	Annual Savings in Residence Energy Costs. Dollars (1973)*
(1) Storm windows and storm doors	430	163	52.00
(2) Increased wall insulation (R7 to R11) incremental cost	15	48	15.00
(3) Improved gas range	25	24	4.80
(4) High performance furnace Incremental cost	100	120	24.00
(5) Furnace flue damper	90	100	20.00
(6) Improved gas water heater Incremental cost	20	27	5.40
(7) High performance air conditioner. Incremental cost	150	60	70.00
(8) Open air cycle control device	75	10	11.70
(9) Insulation of exposed basement wall. Incremental cost	105	50	10.00

*Based on gas costs of 20¢ per therm, and electricity costs of 4¢ per Kw-hr. (Washington, D.C. Area).
SOURCE: *Residential Energy Consumption, Single Family Housing*, HUD, March 1973.

Q. *I have been asked to speak to a consumer's group on the economics of owning a condominium versus renting. How could this be illustrated?*

A. The following two illustrations represent typical situations and should provide a good explanation.

Comparison of annual housing expenses
conversion unit owner vs. tenant

		Own	Rent
Sales Price	$50,000		
Down payment	10,000		
Balance	$40,000		
Rent ($400/month)			$4,800
Interest on mortgage @ 9%–25 yrs. (annual avg.)		2,428	
Common expense assessments		700	
Property taxes		800	
Economic rent on down payments @7%		700	
		$4,628	$4,800
Tax deductions			
Interest	$ 2,428		
Taxes	800		
Economic rent	700		
	$ 3,928		
50% tax bracket		1,964	0
Net cost (before appreciation)		$2,664	$4,800
Equity increase (annual avg.)		1,600	0
Cash flow		$4,264	$4,800
Assumption: Increase in property values—approximately 3% per year		1,500	0
Net Cost		$2,764	$4,800

		Own	Rent
Sales price	$30,000		
Down payment	6,000		
Balance	$24,000		
Rent ($250/month)			$3,000
Interest on mortgage @9%–25 yrs. (annual avg.)		1,457	
Common expense assessments		480	
Property taxes		600	
Economic rent on down payments @7%		420	
		$3,957	$3,000
Tax deductions			
Interest	$ 1,457		
Taxes	600		
Economic rent	420		
	$ 2,477		
20% tax bracket		495	0
Net cost (before appreciation)		$2,462	$3,000
Equity increase (annual avg.)		960	0
Cash flow		$3,422	$3,000
Assumption: Increase in property values—approximately 3% per year		900	0
Net Cost		$2,522	$3,000

Q. *What are the various depreciation methods that can be used on real estate investment properties and how are they computed on an annual basis?*

A. Three basic methods of depreciation for allowed or allowable annual deductors include (1) straight line, (2) declining balance, (3) sum of the years' digits. The methods are applicable as follows:

Optimum depreciation methods

Type of Property	*Straight Line*	*Declining Balance*	*S-Digits*
New Residential-Original User		x(200%)	x
New Nonresidential		x(150%)	
Used Residential (Useful life of 20 or more years)		x(125%)	
Used Residential (Useful life less than 20 years)	x		

Assuming improvements of $100,000 on a new apartment rental unit, the following would represent the annual depreciation sums:

1. *Straight Line*

$100,000   30 yrs. = $3,333.33 per year for each of the 30 years

2. *Declining Balance Rate*

Straight Line Rate × 200% = Annual Rate

3.33% × 200% = 6.66% per year

Year	*Balance*		*Depreciation*
1	100,000 × 6.66%	=	$6,660.00 per year
2	93,340 × 6.66%	=	6,216.44 per year
3	87,123.56 × 6.66%	=	5,750.15 per year

The same method is used with 150 percent and 125 percent as applicable.

3. *Sum of the Years' Digits*

$$\text{Sum} = \frac{\text{Useful Life} \times (1 + \text{Useful Life})}{2}$$

$$\text{Sum} = \frac{30 \times (1 + 30)}{2} = 465$$

Year	*Balance*				*Depreciation*
1	\$100,000	×	$\frac{30}{465}$	=	\$6,451.61
2	93,548.39	×	$\frac{29}{465}$	=	\$5,834.20
3	87,714.19	×	$\frac{28}{465}$	=	\$5,281.71

This illustrates the computations for 3 years only. The same method is used for each of the 30 years of the useful life of improvements. If a salvage value is anticipated, then that sum must be deducted from the current depreciable property value to arrive at a base sum subject to annual depreciation.

Q. *Several investors I know have paid special attention to construction features of office buildings constructed throughout the U.S. between 1958 and 1970. They report certain environmental hazards in some of the buildings. What should be carefully inspected in such buildings?*

A. In many office buildings asbestos is used as fire-retarding wrapping for steel beams. The asbestos is applied by spraying a mixture of asbestos with water or cement. When water is used, the asbestos fibers eventually come loose and are introduced into the air conditioning and heating systems. The result, from studies conducted by Mt. Sinai School of Medicine, is a level of asbestos fibers in the inside air averaging three times higher than the level in the outside air. The Washington Post (December 10, 1975) reported that in New York alone 700 tons of asbestos were sprayed as fireproofing in 1969 and 1970. The Occupational Safety and Health Administration proposes that asbestos levels in work areas be lowered from 5 fibers per cubic centimeter to 0.55 fibers per cubic centimeter.

The implications on value are self-evident. Where corrective measures may be required to meet state or Federal standards, the costs could be significant.

Q. *Frequently we hear of new real estate ventures that involve negative cash flows for the first year or two. Aside from the tax shelter aspects, what are some facts concerning the financial integrity of such an investment that might be helpful in discussion with potential investors?*

A. Let us assume, for illustrative purposes, that there is a one dollar loss at the end of the first year, that is, expenses exceed gross income by one dollar. If we go on the basis that the second year will be the "catch-up" year, it will take $1.12 at a discount rate of 12 percent the second year to cover the one dollar loss of the first year; at a 15 percent discount rate it would take $1.15.

The following tabulation shows the additional money needed to be earned for each of seven years to offset a first-year deficit of one dollar:

Year	*12% Discount*	*15% Discount*
1	$1.00(Loss)	$1.00(Loss)
2	1.12	1.15
3	1.25	1.32
4	1.41	1.52
5	1.58	1.75
6	1.76	2.01
7	1.98	2.31

If the first two years each had a one dollar loss, then, at a discount rate of 12 percent, the third-year recoupment would reach a level of $1.12 + $1.25 or $2.37. These relationships highlight the value of money over time.

Q. *How are air rights and development rights assessed when they are held separately and apart from the fee (land) interest?*

A. Only one recent case is reported in the legal case law involving the assessment of air rights only (Macht vs. Department of Assessments, 1972, 266 Md. 602, 296 A 2nd 162). In this case, an air rights lease was drawn up for 98 years and 9 months for the use of airspace above an altitude of 124 feet of the taxpayer's property. The lease had no provision for extension or renewal and the rent was fixed at twice the annual real estate taxes levied on the taxpayer's entire property (land, improvements, and air space) less any increase in taxes attributable to improvements made by any predecessor. Within the maximum and minimum rents, the agreement permitted the purchase of the airspace at the termination of the lease for a specified price with adjustments for purchasing power and so forth. The assessor valued the air rights at $50,700, which in turn resulted in litigation. The court's reasoning was as follows: as long as a property owner makes no use of the airspace over his property, the airspace cannot be subject to assessment. However, once he denies himself the use (present or potential) of the airpsace through vesting of such interests in another party, the interests (airspace) take on a value for purposes of assessment. The value of the airspace prevails whether separated out or included in the valuation of the fee for assessment purposes. One basic rule governs this: the aggregate value of the components cannot exceed the value of the whole.

Q. *What is amenity rent and what are some of the factors that can be considered as reliable measures of its presence or absence?*

A. One measure utilized to determine amenity rent is the differential in land values. In one study, the supply aspect of the market was found to be related to zoning, socioeconomic class, and tenancy. On the demand side, significant factors included family size, income, and the kind and quality of housing as measures of the market evaluation of amenity rent.

Q. *You are asked to provide a quick overview for a client who is considering opening a discount store in a small city of 10,000 people in a county with a total population of 16,320. For practical purposes the county is the trade area for all retail merchants.*

A. Four quick calculations include (1) trade area family income, (2) retail share of personal income, (3) trade area retail buying power, and (4) retail strength. Computations of each are illustrated as follows:

1. Number of households × average household income = $51,581,800

2. Ratio of retail sales to personal income:

   $19,926,000/$51,581,800= 38.6%

3. County retail share × city trade area income

   45%× $51,581,800 = $23,211,810

   (Similar and adjoining areas indicate an expenditure level somewhat above the subject area)

4. Ratio of actual retail sales to trade area retail buying power

   $19,926,000/$23,211,810 = 85.5%

The difference between actual sales and trade area retail buying power is equal to the amount of external sales ($3,285,000). These external sales represent an important potential target market for any new local market entry.

Q. *You have been retained to advise on a rehabilitation program on a commercial building. Some new building equipment is required. Type A costs $20,000 with a 10-year life and an annual operating cost of $1,500. Type B is 20 percent cheaper, has the same life expectancy with operating costs of $2,000 per year. Which equipment would you recommend be installed? Required return is 12 percent.*

A. Given equal life expectancy, the actual cost of the equipment is computed by adding the acquisition cost to the present worth of the anticipated operating costs at the required rate of return, as follows:

Actual cost (A) = $20,000 + $1,500 × 5.650 (P.W. factor)
= 20,000 + 8,475
= $28,475

Actual cost (B) = $16,000 + $2,000 × 5.650
= 16,000 + 11,300
= $27,300

The cheaper equipment (B) should be recommended.

Q. *I have heard a great deal about the mortgage-equity method of capitalization in contrast to the price-earnings ratio and gross income multiple (GIM) methods. What are the advantages of the mortgage-equity method of capitalization and how do you go about computing a rate?*

A. The mortgage-equity capitalization technique takes into consideration the extent of mortgage financing, mortgage terms, and payout period. Further, the system recognizes the equity built up during the course of ownership, and the potential net appreciation or depreciation of the property at the end of the holding period of the investment. This latter aspect duly recognizes the anticipated level of reversionary interest at disposition of the investment property. Manifestly, the mortgage-equity method provides an investment model of the key determinants of an investment.

Principal factors having a direct impact on the overall capitalization rate are shown in Table A. Included is the factual data on the contemplated mortgage basis, the contemplated holding period, the target equity yield, and the forecast appreciation or depreciation of the property over the holding term. The table data provides the mathematical relationships of the above information based upon the time value of money—one of the distinctive advantages of this method over several other means of capitalization.

Table A
Capitalization rate computation
(Investment Capital Structure)

1

Loan Ratio* x A
0.90 x 0.10531
= 0.0948

4

[1] x C
0.0948 x 5.21612
= 0.4945

FACTUAL DATA

1. Mortgage Ratio, Rate, Term
   90%, 10%, 30 yrs. monthly
2. Holding Period 10 Yrs.
3. Equity Yield 14%
4. Terminal Value/Holding Period
   A) Appreciation None
   B) Depreciation None

TABLE DATA

A. Constant 0.10531

*B. P.W. $\frac{1}{p}$ @ X yrs. @ Mtg. Rate ÷ 12
(X=Loan-Holding Periods) 8.635

C. P.W. $\frac{1}{p}$ @ Holding Term @ Equity Rate
(Annual Basis) 5.21612

D. P.W. 1 @ Holding Term @ Equity Rate
(Annual Basis) 0.26974

*Divisor changed if payments made on other than monthly basis.

2

[1] x B
0.0948 x 8.635
= 0.8186

3

SALE AS % OF UNITY - [2]
1.00 - 0.8186
= 0.1814

5

[3] x D
0.1814 x 0.26974
= 0.0489

6

[4] - [5]
0.4945 - 0.0489
= 0.4456

7

EQUITY RATIO + [6]
0.10 + 0.4456
= 0.5456

8

[7] ÷ C
0.5456 ÷ 5.21612
= 0.10459

CAPITALIZATION RATE: 10.5%

*Loan ratio is the ratio of mortgage to sale or acquisition price of property.

Q. *A method frequently used by investors is to compute the number of years it will take them to recover their initial equity investment based on the net cash flow from a property—a payback method and approach. A shortcoming of this technique is that it does not measure the time value of money. Is there any shortcut method that incorporates the simplicity of the payback notion and yet recognizes the time value of money?*

A. The following table is a simplified version of a discounted cash flow model. As an example, if the holding period is six years and equity requirements are 10 percent (top line of table), it will take about four years (body of table) to recoup the equity investment and obtain the targeted yield. This assumes the property will sell for an amount equal to the mortgage balance at the end of the five-year holding period.

The table provides a quick approximation of the factors of equity yield and recapture over any one of a number of holding periods. In the table the actual and correct present worth (of one per period) factors have been rounded. For a detailed estimate, the applicable discounting tables should be consulted and used.

Estimated Holding Period	*Estimated Discount Rate*																	
	5	6	7	8	9	10	11	12	13	14	15	16	17	18	19	20	21	22
2	1	1	1	1	1	1	1	1	1	1	1	1	1	1	1	1	1	1
3	2	2	2	2	2	2	2	2	2	2	2	2	2	2	2	2	2	2
4	3	3	3	3	3	3	3	3	2	2	2	2	2	2	2	2	2	2
5	4	4	4	3	3	3	3	3	3	3	3	3	3	3	3	2	2	2
6	5	4	4	4	4	4	4	4	3	3	3	3	3	3	3	3	3	3
7	5	5	5	5	5	4	4	4	4	4	4	4	3	3	3	3	3	3
8	6	6	5	5	5	5	5	4	4	4	4	4	4	4	3	3	3	3
9	7	6	6	6	5	5	5	5	5	4	4	4	4	4	4	4	3	3
10	7	7	7	6	6	6	5	5	5	5	5	4	4	4	4	4	4	3
11	8	7	7	7	6	6	6	5	5	5	5	5	4	4	4	4	4	4
12	8	8	7	7	7	6	6	6	5	5	5	5	4	4	4	4	4	4
13	9	8	8	7	7	7	6	6	6	5	5	5	5	4	4	4	4	4
14	9	9	8	8	7	7	6	6	6	6	5	5	5	5	4	4	4	4
15	10	9	9	8	8	7	7	6	6	6	5	5	5	5	4	4	4	4

Q. *What are some different types of financing and capital structure that can be used to put a deal together?*

A. The following examples illustrate the numerous variations that can be used. The subject property involves a shopping center with 100,000 sq. ft. of gross leasable area. The basic structure or "givens" in this illustration are outlined in Table 1, which assumes a free and clear ownership. The extent and changes in financial leverage should be noted as the "financial package" is changed from one situation to another. The degree of tolerable leverage that an investor and/or mortgagee is willing to assume depends largely on the assumption of risk and the quality and location of an investment property. The concept of "perceived risk" on the part of an investor or developer is applicable in every real estate investment venture.

Table 1

Assumptions

Land Cost	$ 100,000
Total Cost	1,900,000
Total Market Value	2,100,000
Gross Income ($3.50 per square foot)	350,000
Expenses and Taxes ($1.25 per square foot)	125,000
Net Operating Income ($2.25 per square foot)	225,000
First Mortgage Interest Rate	10.25%
Overall Capitalization Rate (N.O.I. divided by market value)	10.71%

Table 2

Straight first-mortgage financing

Loan to Value Percent	75%
Loan Amount	$1,575,000
Mortgage Constant (10.25%, 28 years)	10.88%
Annual Debt Service	$ 171,360
Net Operating Income	$ 225,000
Cash Flow	$ 53,640

Cash Flow Returns:

10.2% on Value Equity of $525,000
16.5% on Cost Equity of $325,000

Contingent Interest Alternatives:

- 15% of gross rents in excess of $350,000 (the gross income in Table 1).
- 25% of net operating income in excess of $225,000.
- 2% of total gross income ($7,000 or .44% additional interest).
- 25% of all percentage rents.

Table 3

Land purchase leaseback—leasehold loan

Lender buys land for $200,000 and leases it back @ 11% for 40 years.

Lender makes 75% leasehold loan, $1,425,000 @ 10.25%, 28 years, 10.88% constant.

Total Financing	$1,625,000
Annual Ground Rent	22,000
Annual Debt Service	155,040
Total Debt Service	177,040
Net Operating Income	225,000
Cash Flow	47,960

Cash Flow Returns:
10.1% on Value Equity of $475,000
17.4% on Cost Equity of $275,000

Table 4

Subordinated land purchase-leaseback—first-mortgage loan

75% Loan	$1,575,000,	10.25%, 28 yrs. (10.88% constant)
Subordinated Land Purchase	200,000,	12%, 40 yr. Ground Lease
Total Financing	$1,775,000	

Annual Ground Rent	$ 24,000
Annual Debt Service	171,360
Total Debt Service	195,360
Net Operating Income	225,000
Cash Flow	29,640

Cash Flow Returns:
9.1% on Value Equity of $325,000
23.7% on Cost Equity of $125,000

Table 5
Combined first mortgage and second mortgage financing

First Mortgage	$1,575,000,	10.25%, 28 yrs. (10.88% constant)
Second Mortgage	200,000,	14%, 10 yrs. (19.17% constant)
Total Financing	$1,775,000	
First Mortgage Debt Service		$171,360
Second Mortgage Debt Service		38,340
Total Mortgage Debt Service		209,700
Net Operating Income		225,000
Cash Flow		15,300

Cash Flow Returns:
4.7% on Value Equity of $325,000
12.2% on Cost Equity of $125,000

Table 6
Wraparound financing

Lender *A* makes wraparound loan	$1,775,000,	11%, 28 yrs. (11.54% constant)
Around Lender *B*'s first mortgage loan	$1,575,000,	10.25%, 28 yrs. (10.88% constant)
Additional Money	$ 200,000	
Total Debt Service		$204,835
Net Operating Income		225,000
Cash Flow		20,165

Cash Flow Returns:
6.2% on Value Equity of $325,000
16% on Cost Equity of $125,000

NOTE: Lender *A* collects $204,835 annually and pays $171,360 to Lender *B*. The balance of $33,475 pays Lender *A* debt service of 16.7% on the $200,000 additional investment.

Table 7
Purchase-leaseback of entire property

Price—$2,100,000, leased back @ 10.25% rental, 28 yrs.	
Annual Rental	$215,000
Net Operating Income	225,000
Cash Flow	9,480
Cash Flow returns infinite yield on no equity.	

Table 8
Purchase-saleback of entire property

Net Operating Income	$225,000
Annual Debt Service (on repurchase contract)	225,000
Net Operating Income	225,000
Cash Flow	0

Table 9
Joint venture financing

First Mortgage	$1,575,000,	10.25%, 28 yrs. (10.88% constant)
Lender Equity Contribution	250,000	
Total Financing	$1,825,000	
Annual Debt Service		$171,360
Net Operating Income		225,000
Cash Flow		53,640

50% of Cash Flow ($26,820) to Lender returns 10.7% on lender's $250,000 Equity.

50% of Cash Flow ($26,820) to developer returns:
9.7% on Value Equity of $275,000
35.8% on Cost Equity of $75,000

Table 10

Joint venture financing

First Mortgage	$1,575,000,	10.25%, 28 yrs. (10.88% constant)
Lender Equity Contribution	425,000	
Total Financing	$2,000,000	
Annual Debt Service		$171,360
Net Operating Income		225,000
Cash Flow		53,640

90% of Cash Flow ($48,276) to Lender until $425,000 equity contribution recaptured (8 yrs.); then 50-50. This returns 11.4% on lender's equity of $425,000.

10% of Cash Flow ($5,364) to Developer returns:

5.4% return on Value Equity of $100,000
Infinite return on zero Cash Equity
Developer pockets $100,000 front-end profit.

SOURCE: Reprinted from *The Mortgage and Real Estate Executives Report*, Vol. 7, No. 20, December 16, 1974 by permission of the editor.

Q. *With the great concern about energy, the following costs and savings of insulation are reported on a proposed new housing project of over 1,000 units:*

Insulation (inches) Thickness	*Initial Cost*	*Annual Heat Loss*	*Annual Savings*
0	0	$275	0
1.0	$275	200	$75
2.25	350	140	60
3.00	475	100	45
3.25	600	80	35

How should this data be analyzed to indicate the proper level of insulation for the proposed project? Assume an 8 percent return and a 25-year usable period for the insulation?

A. The above data should be retabulated as follows:

Insulation Thickness	*Initial Cost*	*Extra Investment*	*Annual Heat Loss*	*Annual Saving*	*Present Worth of Benefit of Added Investment*
0	0	0	$275	0	0
1.0	$275	$275	200	75	$525.63
2.25	350	75	140	60	565.50
3.00	470	125	100	45	355.38
3.25	600	125	80	35	248.63

The value added by the given investment in insulation is computed as follows:

Present Worth of one per year at 8 percent for 25 years = 10.675

P.W. of Annual Savings − Cost = Value Added

$800.63 ($75 × 10.675) − $275 = $525.63

The highest value added thus derived will correspond to the thickness of insulation that should be used.

Q. *In developing annual repair and maintenance costs on a newly finished commercial building, you are asked by the owners to advise them concerning the selection of paint to be used on portions of the exterior. Paint A has a 5-year life and will cost $4,000; paint B will cost $2,800 and is expected to last 3 years. If their minimum rate of return is 30 percent, what would you recommend from an annual-cost analysis? Assume that application costs will be the same for both paints.*

A. This calculation involves the use of a factor to determine annual capital recovery of an investment—the annual amount payable that will result in a given capital sum at the end of a given period.

Paint A = $4,000 × 0.41058 (Capital Recovery factor)
= $1,642.32 (Annual Cost)

Paint B = $2,800 × 0.55063 (Capital Recovery factor)
= $1,541.76 (Annual Cost)

Paint B should be recommended based on the above facts.

Q. *A city is proposing to convert part of its central business district into a mall-type shopping facility. The mall will cost $6,000,000 and is to be financed with a bond issue with interest payable annually at 7 percent and a sinking fund payment of 5 percent for 20 years. What is the city's annual obligation under this proposal?*

A. This computation involves adding the annual interest payment to the sinking fund payment that will yield the principal amount at the end of 20 years.

$$\begin{aligned}\text{Annual payment} &= \text{Annual Interest} + \text{Sinking Fund Payment}\\ &= (\$6{,}000{,}000 \times 0.07) + (\$6{,}000{,}000 \times 0.03024)\\ &= \$420{,}000 + \$181{,}440\\ &= \$601{,}440\end{aligned}$$

Q. *An architect has drawn up plans for a developer for a small services-oriented building. Three plans are proposed: a three-story structure that will cost $255,000 and have an income of $63,000 and expenses of $28,000; a four-story building with a cost of $315,000 and an income of $92,000 with expenses of $38,000; and a five-story building costing $410,000 with an income of $110,000 and expenses of $45,000. Assuming the income and expense forecasts are realistic and the economic life of each is 30 years, what is the best development if the rate of return is 16 percent and the site, which will cost $45,000, is expected to have a value of $52,000 at the end of the proposed use?*

A. This is really a determination of highest and best use via differential analysis. The respective costs and benefits are compared over the time horizon (economic life) of 30 years. The present worth of net income stream plus reversionary value is discounted and this sum is compared with the capital cost. Disregarding the reversion value, since it is nominal, the following analysis is undertaken.

$$\begin{aligned}\text{P.W.} &= \text{P.W. (of net income)} - \text{cost}\\ \text{P.W. (Three-story)} &= (\$35{,}000 \times 6.177) - \$255{,}000\\ &= -\ \$38{,}805\\ \text{P.W. (Four-story)} &= (\$54{,}000 \times 6.177) - \$315{,}000\\ &= +\ \$18{,}258\\ \text{P.W. (Five-story)} &= (\$65{,}000 \times 6.177) - \$410{,}000\\ &= -\ \$8{,}495\end{aligned}$$

Based on the stated facts and assumptions, the four-story building should be built because this is the only one that develops a positive present worth.

Q. *How would one develop a basic economic-demographic analysis to assist the proper location of a supermarket facility with respect to the important aspects of trade area potential?*

A. The following cites sources of data and illustrates their application for preliminary studies related to a location analysis for a new supermarket facility:

FREEMANS' SUPERMARKET, INCORPORATED

Objective:

To select a county in the Syracuse, New York, Standard Metropolitan Statistical Area to locate new supermarkets. The area is composed of Madison, Onondaga and Oswego counties.

Kind of Business:

A firm operating a local chain of supermarkets.

Problem:

Freemans' wished to explore the possibility of expanding their operations into the Syracuse metropolitan area. The company had experienced rapid growth in the area they operated and felt that the territory was saturated with supermarkets. In selecting an area within the SMSA the firm wanted to choose the county which had experienced the greatest economic growth rate and appeared to have future development characteristics.

Source of Data:

(1) *Census of Housing; 1960 and 1970—Detailed Housing Characteristics.*

(2) *Census of Population; 1960 and 1970—General Population Characteristics.*

(3) *Census of Population; 1960 and 1970—General Social and Economic Characteristics.*

(4) *Census of Business; Retail Trade—1963 and 1972.*

Assumption:

Freemans' marketing department held preliminary discussions with firm's management to determine which economic growth factors would most affect grocery store sales. Based upon its knowledge, and that of management's, the marketing department assumed that greatest growth market indicators are population, income, housing units, car ownership, and grocery store sales. Since the *Census of Business, Retail Sales,* shows sales of establishments with and without payroll, the marketing department chose those with payroll, because those without accounted for only 6.2 percent of sales in the metropolitan area.

Procedure:

(See calculations on Table which follows.)

(1) Oswego County showed the greatest growth in population and the number of families (columns 1 and 2) in 1970 over 1960 than either Madison or Onondaga Counties.

(2) When examining median family income (column 3) Oswego County grew 3.3 percent more rapidly than either of the other counties.

(3) Oswego County also had the greatest percent increase in housing units (column 4) and continued to maintain the largest share of units occupied by owners (column 5). While median rent in Oswego and Onondaga Counties increased by the same percentage (column 6) it was felt that Oswego had a better growth potential due to its land development possibilities.

(4) Column 7 shows that Oswego County had the greatest decline in number of housing units without automobiles, which is also an indication of economic growth.

(5) Upon analyzing grocery store sales Oswego also displayed the greatest growth. Based on percentage increase (column 8) it grew 10 percent more than its nearest rival, Madison County.

Conclusion:

The market factors analyzed clearly reveal that Oswego County had the greatest growth and should continue to offer future development potential. Selection of an exact site for each supermarket within the county will be determined by an analysis of data in *Census Tract Reports, Major Retail Center Reports* (both published by the Bureau of the Census), the usual onsite survey, and other sources and methods to be determined by management.

Market factors for evaluating location factors of a food store in Syracuse, New York, smsa

County	Population[1] (number)	Families[1] (number)	Family median income[2] (dollars)	Occupied housing units[3] (number)	Percent owner occupied[3]	Median rent[3] (dollars)	Housing units without automobiles (number)[3]	Grocery store sales ($1,000)
	(1)	(2)	(3)	(4)	(5)	(6)	(7)	(8)
Madison								
1960	54,635	13,282	5,451	15,236	74.4	70	11.5	
1970	62,864	14,660	7,123	17,741	74.6	108	11.3	
Percent change	15.1	10.4	30.7	16.4	0.2	54.3	1.7	
1963								17,694
1972								28,116
Percent change								58.9
Onondaga								
1960	423,028	06,065	6,691	124,090	64.5	81	18.4	
1970	472,746	14,707	8,208	145,322	62.6	121	16.7	
Percentage change	11.8	8.1	22.7	17.1	2.9	49.3	9.2	
1963								137,345
1972								190,158
Percentage change								38.4
Oswego								
1960	86,118	21,063	5,580	24,323	76.0	69	17.9	
1970	100,897	24,057	7,479	29,179	76.1	103	12.6	
Percentage change	17.2	14.2	34.0	20.0	0.1	49.3	29.6	
1963								28,548
1972								48,152
Percentage change								68.7

[1]*Census of Population, 1960 and 1970–General Population Characteristics.* U.S. Department of Commerce.
[2]*Census of Population, 1960 and 1970–General and Social Economic Characteristics.* U.S. Department of Commerce.
[3]*Census of Housing, 1960 and 1970–Detailed Housing Characteristics.* U.S. Department of Commerce.
[4]Census of Business, 1963 and 1972—Retail Trade. U.S. Department of Commerce.
SOURCE: *Measuring Markets*, U.S. Dept. of Commerce, Washington, D.C. 1974.

Q. *I keep a pretty good running account of walk-up apartment land sales. Since the advent of new zoning codes, a variety of densities are permitted and, in many cases, sites are developed at less than the permitted density. How can this array of information be managed in a meaningful way to assist my work as a counselor to local investors?*

A. Let us suppose you want some value insight concerning a parcel of land that is either zoned or proposed for utilization at a development density of 14 units per acre. Four very recent sales are available in similar locations ranging in density from 12 to 20 units.

First, all transactions should be adjusted to the subject for time and location as appropriate. These adjusted prices and densities are then plotted as shown. What emerges is a transformation line, ABCDE. Feasible price levels, at the indicated density per acre, appear on the line and below it. Based on this transformation, which is a market-derived index, plausible prices per unit at various densities can be estimated. For each new case a new group must be drawn based on the procedure outlined. What emerges, over a period of time, is a series of transformation lines indicating the changes of price levels for each location under study. Also, any relative steepness or flattening of a line will suggest an important market trend concerning that particular kind of land. It's merely a simple market monitoring device.

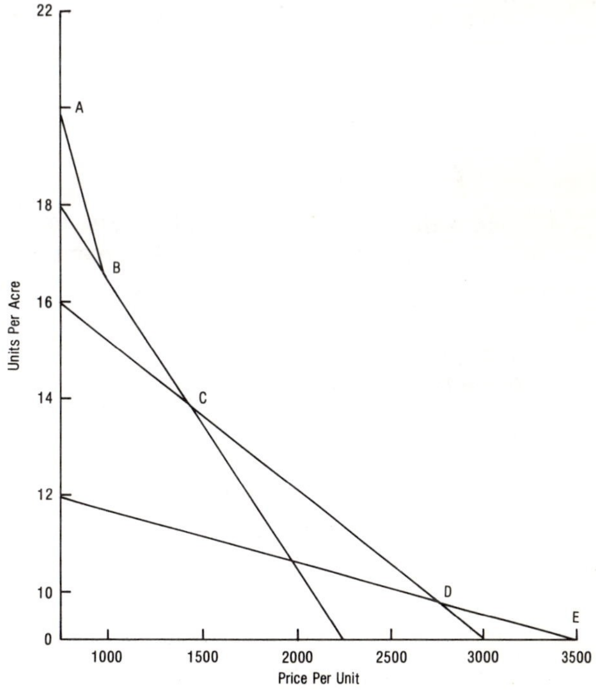

Q. *An investor has two opportunities to take over unexpired leases and in turn sublease them to tenants with good credit ratings. Proposition A involves an obligation of $110,000 for the lease term with the present worth of rents to be received being $140,000. Proposal B concerns a lease obligation of $70,000 with a present worth of rentals to be received of $92,000. Which is the better deal if all other factors are perceived to be equal?*

A. A profit-investment ratio analysis can be made to arrive at a plausible decision based on the following relationship:

$$\text{Profit/Investment Ratio} = \frac{DE - C}{C}$$

Where:

D = present worth factor (discount rate)
E = Net Income
C = cost of the undertaking

Case A

$$P/I = \frac{\$140{,}000 - \$110{,}000}{\$110{,}000} = 0.27$$

Case B

$$P/I = \frac{\$92{,}000 - \$70{,}000}{\$70{,}000} = 0.31$$

In case A the $110,000 potential investment increased by 27 percent, while in case B the increase is 31 percent. Case B would be the preferred venture based on the facts outlined.

Q. *You are asked to advise from a standpoint of yield in the choice between the following two situations in a contemplated purchase of a mortgage:*

Case 1—The mortgage has an $18,200 balance due at 9.5 percent annual interest, payable monthly with 15 years remaining and is offered at a discount of $2,000.

Case 2—The mortgage has a $16,500 balance due at 9.0 percent annual interest, payable monthly, with 10 years remaining and is offered at a discount of $1,200.

A. The two problems are solved using the following relationship to compute yield:

$$Y = \frac{r + (d/n)}{P - d}$$

Where:

P = principal balance (1)
n = remaining term of mortgage (years)
r = current mortgage interest rate (percent)
d = discount rate from balance due (percent)
Y = yield to maturity

Case 1

$$Y = \frac{0.095 + (0.11/15)}{1 - 0.11} = \frac{0.095 + 0.00733}{0.89}$$

$$= \frac{0.10233}{0.89} = 11.5\%$$

Case 2

$$Y = \frac{0.090 + (0.0727/10)}{1 - 0.0727} = \frac{0.090 + 0.00727}{0.9273}$$

$$= \frac{0.09727}{0.9273} = 10.5\%$$

The first proposal will provide the higher return to maturity based on the stated facts.

Q. *Two locations for a specialty ready-to-wear shop have been analyzed with the following estimated monthly gross sales for each location. Probability estimates for each location have also been developed.*

Sales	*Location 1*	*Location 2*
$130,000	0.20	0.20
150,000	0.50	0.60
200,000	0.30	0.20
	1.00	1.00

Which location is superior based on expected sales? Note: the expected value represents the average of a random variable; a concept used in statistics.

A. This problem involves computing the expected volume for each location. Estimated gross sales are multiplied by the corresponding probability and the totals summed for each location. The location with the higher sum is preferable from the standpoint of maximization of expected profit.

Location 1

$$
\begin{aligned}
\$130{,}000 \times 0.20 &= \$26{,}000\\
150{,}000 \times 0.50 &= 75{,}000\\
200{,}000 \times 0.30 &= 60{,}000\\
\hline
&\$161{,}000
\end{aligned}
$$

Location 2

$$
\begin{aligned}
\$130{,}000 \times 0.20 &= \$26{,}000\\
150{,}000 \times 0.60 &= 90{,}000\\
200{,}000 \times 0.20 &= 40{,}000\\
\hline
&\$156{,}000
\end{aligned}
$$

Based on this analysis, location 1 should be selected.

Q. *An investment property with a net annual income of $24,600 was financed by an 80 percent loan over 25 years at an interest rate of 8 percent. Discussion with the owner indicates a contemplated holding period of 10 years, after which he anticipates the property will sell for 10 percent below its acquisition cost. These assumptions appear reasonable based on area trends. What method can be used to ascertain the equity yield rate to the owner?*

A. The following format can be used to derive the equity yield rate. Each of the components is explained as follows:

FACTUAL DATA

I. The loan ratio is 80 percent of purchase price as indicated.
II. The loan constant, based on capital structure, is 0.09262.
III. The indicated overall capitalization rate is 0.11 ($24,600/$224,000).

IV. The loan balance at the end of the 10-year holding period is 81 percent of the principal sum.

V. The property is expected to depreciate 10 percent during the 10-year holding period, resulting in a resale price of $201,000.

Factor A—The product of the loan ratio and the mortgage constant.

Factor B—The overall rate less Factor A.

Factor C—The product of the loan ratio and the percentage loan balance remaining at the end of the holding period.

Factor D—Since the property is forecast to depreciate 10 percent by the end of the holding period, this decimal equivalent is subtracted from unity (1.00). If a property were expected to appreciate, this percentage would be added to unity. From this sum/difference is subtracted Factor C.

Factor E—Two components must be derived that have a total equal to the percent of equity investment, in this case 20 percent (0.20). This involves a trial and error method of selecting the factors of the present worth of one per period (PW 1/p) and the present worth of one (PW 1) at the end of the 10-year holding period. This process usually results in a bracketing of the eventual answer. Two trials are shown, one at 16 percent with a resulting sum of 0.231 (which is too high); the second trial, at the higher rate of 20 percent, results in a sum of 0.192, which indicates that the rate is less than 20 percent.

The following interpolation is done, resulting in an indicated discount rate of 19.2 percent.

	Bracket difference:
0.200 (target)	0.231
0.192	0.192
0.008	0.039

The ratio of 8/39 of 0.04 = 0.20 × 0.04 = 0.008; thus, 0.200 less 0.008 = 0.192 or 19.2 percent.

EQUITY DISCOUNT RATE DERIVATION

Address of Property 23 BYE St. Net Income $24,600 Sale Price/Cost $224,000
Est. Holding Period 10 Yrs., Mortgage: Rate 8% Term 25 Yrs. Amount $179,200

FACTUAL DATA

I. Loan Ratio 0.80
II. Loan Constant* 0.9262
III. Overall Rate 0.11

IV. Loan Balance End of Holding Period 81% (%)
V. Prop. Appreciation/Depreciation (%) 1.00 ± (-) 10%

A	I x II
	0.80 x 0.09262 = 0.074

B	III - [A]
	0.11 - 0.074 = 0.036

C	I x IV
	0.80 x 0.81 = 0.648

D	V - [C]
	0.90 - 0.648 = 0.252

E					
	[B] x	P.W. i/p			
	0.036 x	4.83 (4.19)	=	0.174 (0.151)	→ 16% → (20%)
	[D] x	P.W.I			
	0.252 x	0.227 (0.162)	=	0.057 (0.041)	
	(Summation):			0.231 (0.192)	

F	Range/[E] Est.	0.231
		0.192
	Equity (decimal)	0.20
	Indicated Rate:	19.2%

*Loan Constant represents the total annual payments of principal and interest (level payment amortization) as a percentage of the initial principal amount of loan.

Q. *Mr. Brown has received a proposal for his 50-acre parcel of land. Time payments are involved, as shown in Proposals I and II, with interest at 8 percent. Since he plans a maximum of a 5-year holding period for this contract for deed, what are the implications of this proposal and the best situation for him assuming a rate of return on risk money of about 12 percent for the land sale?*

Proposal I

	Principal	Total Payment	Balance
1.	$200,000	$16,000	$200,000
2.	200,000	16,000	200,000
3.	200,000	16,000	200,000
4.	200,000	16,000	200,000
5.	200,000	16,000	200,000

Proposal II

	Principal	Total Payment	Balance
1.	$ 2,000	$ 2,160	$198,000
2.	4,000	4,640	194,000
3.	6,000	7,440	188,000
4.	8,000	10,560	180,000
5.	10,000	14,000	170,000

A. Proposal I involves the payment of interest only for the 5 years under consideration with no reduction in principal. The alternative is what is known in the trade as *reverse interest*, that is, payment of interest on the payment amount only: 8% × $2,000 = $160 plus $2,000 = $2,160, and so forth. To properly evaluate the two proposals, a present value analysis is undertaken as follows:

Proposal I

	Cash In-Flow	Discount Rate	Present Value
1.	$16,000	0.8929	$14,286.40
2.	16,000	0.7972	12,755.20
3.	16,000	0.7118	11,388.80
4.	16,000	0.6355	10,168.00
5.	16,000	0.5674	9,078.40
			$57,626.80

Plus balance at end of fifth year principal:

$200,000 × 0.5674 = $113,480.00

Total Present Value: $171,156.80

Proposal II

	Cash In-Flow	Discount Rate	Present Value
1.	$ 2,160	0.8929	$ 1,928.66
2.	4,640	0.7972	3,699.01
3.	7,440	0.7118	5,295.79
4.	10,560	0.6355	6,710.88
5.	14,000	0.5674	7,943.60
Plus balance end of fifth year:			$ 25,577.94
	$170,000 × 0.5674		$ 96,458.00
		Total Present Value:	$122,035.94

Difference between present values: $49,120.86

Clearly, Proposal I is far superior based on a present value study, even though there is no reduction in the capital sum. On reverse interest, no payment of interest is made on the outstanding balance, which is the main reason for the significant difference in computed present values.

Q. *A low ratio (to value) mortgage of $60,000 on a small retail facility leased for a firm remaining term of 10 years is offered at $65,000, thus reflecting a premium of $5,000. The mortgage rate is 9.6 percent with 12 years remaining for full payment. If purchased, what would the yield be to an investor?*

A. The following equation provides a solution to this problem:

$$Y = \frac{r - (p/n)}{P + p}$$

Where:

P = principal balance (1)
Y = yield to maturity (percent)
n = remaining term of mortgage (years)
r = contract interest rate (percent)

Solution:

$$Y = \frac{0.09 - (0.0833/12)}{1 + 0.0833} = \frac{0.09 - 0.00694}{1.0833}$$

$$= \frac{0.08306}{1.0833} = 7.7\%$$

Q. *A client comes to you concerning his interest in acquiring a small retail store in a declining neighborhood scheduled for purchase by the redevelopment authority. A local bank trust department is liquidating the investment and the asking price is $60,000; the income is $10,000 per year after expenses. The store is vacant, but inquiry reveals that a prime tenant with a firm lease continues to pay rent, with 6 years remaining on the lease. The tenant ceased retail operations about 3 years ago because of the changing neighborhood, declining gross sales, and so on. The date of probable acquisition is uncertain but will occur prior to the expiration of the lease. The reversion value of the property after 6 years is estimated at $45,000. What kind of advice do you give the client?*

A. Your research indicates that judicial decisions on such cases have been mixed: some treated such leases as in-rem contracts (undivided fee rule) that convey with the property. Others have been treated as in-personam contracts (personal contractual relationships) that may be voided at sale. Study of risk in these kinds of cases indicates a discount rate in excess of 12 percent. A 14 percent rate appears plausible and supportable.

In Rem Treatment

Cash Flow Value:	
P.W. $10,000 for 6 yrs. @ 14% (3.888668)	= $38,886
Reversion Value:	= 20,500
$45,000 in 6 yrs. @ 14% (0.455587)	$59,386

In Personam Treatment

Economic Rent a maximum of $7,000/yr after expenses:	
Cash Flow Value: P.W. $7,000 for 6 yrs. @ 14%	= $27,200
Reversion Value: $45,000 in 6 yrs. @ 14% (0.455587)	= 20,500
	$47,700

Suggest that the client offer $52,500 for the property. The following are added considerations of your analysis:

Offer:	$52,500
Reversion Value:	20,500
P.W. Cash Flow:	$32,000

Then: $32,000/$10,000 (contract income) = 3.2, or a discount factor of 21%

Overall discount factor:
Ratio of P.W. of Cash Flow in total price: \$32,000/\$52,500 = 61%
= 61%

$$\text{Ratio of Reversion value to total: } \left(1 - \frac{\text{P.W. Cash Flow}}{\text{Total price}}\right) = 39\%$$

The weighed rate is as follows:

61% @ 21% = 0.1281

39% @ 14% = 0.0546

0.1827 or 18.3%

Because of the added risk from the uncertainty of a judicial decree, the cash flow imputed value bears a discount of 21 percent, the reversion 14 percent, or an overall discount rate of 18.3 percent, if the client's offer of \$52,500 is accepted.

Q. *A ground lease with an AAA tenant as lessee was negotiated a number of years ago with an annual net yield of \$15,000. The lease has 12 years remaining and the land value today is estimated at \$100,000, after demolition of the obsolete improvements. The land is estimated to increase at an annual rate of 3 percent per year for the balance of the term. What is the value of the property if investment money is worth 12 percent?*

A. The value of this property is equal to the present worth of the anticipated cash flow plus the present worth of the value of the property at reversion. This is computed as follows:

P.W. of 1 per period for 12 years, @ 12% = 6.194374	
Present Worth of cash flow:	
6.194374 × \$15,000 =	\$92,915
Value of land 12 years hence:	
Compounding @ 3% for 12 years: 1.425761	
\$100,000 × 1.425761 = \$142,576	
Present value of land based on reversion:	
Discount factor @ 12%, 12 years: 0.256675	
\$142,576 × 0.256675 =	36,595
Value of cash flow reversion:	\$129,510

Q. *A tenant has a firm lease on a store property with a balance of 7 years remaining at an annual rental of $12,000 per year. He has the right to sublease; he subleases the premises for a firm term of 5 years at $16,000 per year. What is the value of the leasehold estate he has generated through this course of action? Risk rates indicate that the anticipated return on a prime lease would be 12 percent with a sublease rate at 14 percent.*

A. This problem indicates the use of a level annuity (present worth of one per year) with the following rate factors:

P.W. 12%, 5 years (Prime lease): 3.605

$$3.605 \times \$12{,}000 = \$43{,}260$$

P.W. 14%, 5 years (sublease): 3.433

$$3.433 \times \$16{,}000 = \$54{,}928$$

Difference: $54,928 − $43,260 = $11,668 (Value of leasehold estate)

Q. *What is sensitivity analysis and how is it used in the study of real estate investment properties and alternatives?*

A. The technique is based on changing various inputs, such as the allocation of resources or levels of expectations, to assess the impact of these changes on the feasibility and viability of an investment property. The following cases illustrate the use of sensitivity analysis involving a warehouse, shopping center, motel development, office building, and a multifamily residential development. In each illustration, note the impact of changes in a single factor (land cost, occupancy, building cost, etc.) with all other factors remaining unchanged.

The absence or inadequacy of demand studies for the particular development at a given location would represent a significant impact factor; in some cases it is crucial, bordering on being disastrous. Without relating any schedule and/or financial development scheme to the reality of the marketplace (supply/demand studies) sensitivity analysis can become merely a numbers game—heavily postulated with assumptions and not very useful for intelligent decision making.

I.
Investment analysis of projected multi-lease warehouse/office facility (80,000 sq. ft. facility)

A. *Investment*		
Land Value @ $1.00/Sq.Ft.		$217,800
Construction Costs @ $7.00/Sq.Ft. (including site improvements and retaining wall)		560,000
	Total Investment	$777,800
B. *Cash Flow Before Income Tax*		
Effective Gross Income (Average $1.50/Sq.Ft. Gross)		$114,000
Gross Potential Income	$120,000	
Less: Vacancy and Rental Loss at 5%	6,000	
Expenses:		25,400
Leasing Fee and Management Cost @ 5% of Effective Gross Income	$ 5,300	
Insurance @ 2½¢/Sq.Ft.	2,000	
Maintenance and Repair @ 3½¢/Sq.Ft.	2,800	
Real Estate Taxes (rate $5.615 per $100 of assessed valuation, or $272,300 × .05615)	15,300	
Net Annual Income		$ 88,600
Yield on Total Investment ($88,600 ÷ $777,800)−11.39%		
Annual Debt Charges		
$777,800 × 75% = $583,350 loan @ 9½% for 25 yrs.; Factor .1049		61,190
Cash Flow Before Income Tax		$ 27,410
C. *Rate of Return Before Tax*		
Equity Investment ($777,800 − $583,350)		$194,450
Rate of Return on Investment ($27,410 ÷ $194,450)		14.1%

Assumptions for the Example:
- Five acres cleared land @ $1.00 Per Square Foot
- An 80,000 Square Foot Facility @ $7.00 Per Square Foot
- A 75% loan @ 9½% for 25 years

Table 1
Effect of changes in cost per square foot of land on total cost and return on equity

Land Cost Per Sq.Ft.	Total Cost	Cash Flow Before Income Tax	Equity Return
$ .50	$668,900	$39,480	19.7%
.75	$723,350	$31,690	17.5%
*1.00	$777,800	$27,410	14.1%
1.25	$832,250	$23,120	11.1%
1.50	$886,700	$18,840	8.5%

Table 2
Effect of changes in construction cost on total cost and return on equity

Construction Cost Per Sq.Ft.	Total Cost Incl. Land	Cash Flow Before Income Tax	Equity Return
$6.00	$697,800	$33,700	19.3%
6.50	$737,800	$30,550	16.5%
*7.00	$777,800	$27,410	14.1%
7.50	$817,800	$24,260	11.9%
8.00	$857,800	$21,110	9.8%

Table 3
Effect of changes in average occupancy on income and return on equity

Average Occupancy Rate	Gross Income	Cash Flow Before Income Tax	Equity Return
100%	$120,000	$33,410	17.2%
* 95%	$114,000	$27,410	14.1%
90%	$108,000	$21,410	11.0%
85%	$102,000	$15,410	7.9%
80%	$ 96,000	$ 9,410	4.8%

*Based on calculations in preceding investment analysis.

II

Investment analysis of projected shopping center
(130,000 gross sq. ft. facility)

A. *Investment*		
Land Value @ $1.50/Sq.Ft.		$ 718,740
Construction Costs @ $27.00/Sq.Ft., including parking, lighting, site preparation, etc.)		3,510,000
	Total Investment	$4,218,740
B. *Cash Flow Before Income Tax*		
Effective Gross Income		$ 648,370
Gross Potential Income @ $5.25/Sq.Ft.	$682,500	
Less: Vacancy and Collection Losses @ 5%	34,130	
Expenses:		169,850
Management @ 4%	$ 23,600	
Advertising & Promotion $250/Mo.	3,000	
Legal & Accounting	3,000	
Insurance	5,000	
Real Estate Taxes	107,000	
Utilities	5,000	
Maintenance and Repairs	20,000	
Reserve (2.5¢/Sq.Ft.)	3,250	
Net Annual Income		$ 478,520
Yield on Total Investment ($478,520 ÷ $4,218,740) – 11.34%		
Annual Debt Charges ($4,218,740 × 75% = $3,164,060 loan @ 9½% for 25 yrs.; Factor .1049)		331,910
Cash Flow Before Income Tax		$ 146,610
C. *Rate of Return Before Tax*		
Equity Investment ($4,218,740 – $3,164,060)		$1,054,680
Rate of Return on Investment ($146,610 ÷ $1,054,680)		13.9%

Assumptions for the Example:

- Eleven acres cleared land @ $1.50 Per Square Foot
- A 130,000 Square Foot Shopping Center @ $27.00 Per Square Foot
- A 75% loan 9½% for 25 years

Table 1

Effect of changes in cost per square foot of land on total cost and return on equity

Land Cost Per Sq.Ft.	Total Cost	Cash Flow Before Income Tax	Equity Return
$ .50	$3,749,580	$183,520	19.57%
$1.00	$3,989,160	$164,670	16.51%
*$1.50	$4,218,740	$146,610	13.9%
$2.00	$4,468,320	$126,970	11.36%
$2.50	$4,707,900	$108,130	9.18%

Table 2

Effect of changes in construction cost on total cost and return on equity

Construction Costs Per Sq.Ft.	Total Cost Incl. Land	Cash Flow Before Income Tax	Equity Return
$25.00	$3,968,740	$166,280	16.75%
$26.00	$4,098,740	$156,050	15.22%
*$27.00	$4,218,740	$146,610	13.9%
$28.00	$4,358,740	$135,600	12.44%
$29.00	$4,488,740	$125,370	11.17%

Table 3

Effect of changes in average occupancy on income and return on equity

Average Occupancy Rate	Gross Income	Cash Flow Before Income Tax	Equity Return
100%	$682,500	$180,740	17.13%
* 95%	$648,370	$146,610	13.9%
90%	$614,250	$112,490	10.66%
85%	$580,130	$ 78,370	7.43%
80%	$546,000	$ 44,240	4.19%

*Based on calculations used in preceding investment analysis.

III

Investment analysis of projected motel facility—165 rooms
(100,000 sq. ft. facility)

A. *Investment*		
Land Value @ $5.50/Sq.Ft.		$ 479,160
Construction Costs @ $22.00/Sq.Ft.		2,200,000
Furnishings & Equipment @ $1,500/Unit for 165 Units		247,500
Site Improvements @ $1.00/Sq.Ft.		65,340
Total Investment		$2,992,000
B. *Cash Flow Before Income Tax*		
Effective Gross Income		
Gross Potential Income @ $14,37/Sq.Ft. Gross	$1,437,000	
Expenses		
Administrative & General	$ 143,500	
Advertising & Promotion	46,000	
Heat, Light and Power	49,200	
Repairs & Maintenance	51,300	
Room Department	221,150	
Food & Beverage	454,900	
Telephone	50,000	
Fire & Insurance	13,500	
Real Estate Taxes	36,500	
Personal Property	3,000	
Net Annual Income		$ 367,950
Less: Amortization for Furnishings & Equipment		40,000
Net Available for Debt Service		$ 327,950
Yield on Total Investment ($367,950 ÷ $2,992,000) – 12.29%		
Annual Debt Charges ($2,992,000 × 75% – $2,244,000 loan @ 9½% for 25 yrs.; Factor .1049)		235,400
Cash Flow Before Income Tax		$ 92,550
C. *Rate of Return Before Tax*		
Equity Investment ($2,992,000 – $2,244,000)		$ 748,000
Rate of Return on Investment ($92,550 ÷ $748,000)		12.3%

Assumptions for the Example:

- Two acres cleared land @ $5.50 Per Square Foot
- A 100,000 Square Foot Facility @ $22 Per Square Foot (incl., restaurant, cocktail lounge, coffee shop, etc.)
- Site Improvements @ $1.00 Per Square Foot; assumes building coverage of ½ acre
- A 75% loan @ 9½% for 25 years; excludes amortization of furnishings and equipment

Table 1

Effect of changes in cost per square foot of land on total cost and return on equity

Land Cost Per Sq.Ft.	Total Cost	Cash Flow Before Income Tax	Equity Return
$3.50	$2,817,760	$106,260	15.08%
$4.50	$2,904,880	$ 99,410	13.68%
$5.50	$2,992,000	$ 92,550	12.37%
$6.50	$3,079,120	$ 85,700	11.13%
$7.50	$3,166,240	$ 78,850	9.96%

Table 2

Effect of changes per square foot site improvements on total cost and return on equity

Site Improvement Cost Per Sq.Ft.	Total Cost	Cash Flow Before Income Tax	Equity Return
$ .25	$2,943,000	$ 96,410	13.1%
$1.00	$2,992,000	$ 92,550	12.37%
$1.75	$3,041,010	$ 88,700	11.66%
$2.50	$3,090,010	$ 84,840	10.98%

Table 3

Effect of changes in construction cost per square foot on total cost and return on equity

Construction Cost Per Sq.Ft.	Total Cost	Cash Flow Before Income Tax	Equity Return
$20.00	$2,792,000	$108,290	15.51%
$21.00	$2,892,000	$100,420	13.88%
$22.00	$2,992,000	$ 92,550	12.37%
$23.00	$3,092,000	$ 84,690	10.95%
$24.00	$3,192,000	$ 76,820	9.62%

*Based on calculations used in preceding investment analysis.

IV

Investment analysis of projected office facility
(36,000 net rentable sq. ft.)

A. *Investment*		
Land Value @ $2.50/sq. ft.		$ 215,500
Construction Cost: 42,350 gross sq. ft. @ $25/sq. ft.		1,058,750
Site Improvements (including parking and landscaping)		42,000
	Total Investment	$1,316,250
B. *Cash Flow Before Income Tax*		
Effective Gross Income		$ 242,300
Gross Potential Income: 36,000 net rentable sq. ft. @ $6.50 per sq. ft.	$234,000	
Gross Potential Parking Income: 100 spaces @ $20 per month for each space	20,000	
Less: Vacancy and Rental Loss at 5%	11,700	
Expenses		97,320
Includes operating expenses, utilities, leasing fee, management, insurance, maintenance, repair, and taxes @ 40.5% of effective gross income.		
Net Annual Income		$ 144,980
Yield on Total Investment ($144,980 ÷ $1,316,250)	11.01%	
Annual Debt Charges ($1,316,250 × 75% = $987,190 loan @ 9½% for 25 years; Factor .1049)		103,560
Cash Flow before Income Tax		$ 41,420
C. *Rate of Return Before Tax*		
Equity Investment ($1,316,250 − $987,190)		$ 329,060
Cash on Cash Return on Investment ($41,420 ÷ $329,060)		12.58%

Assumptions for the Example:

- 86,200 Sq. Ft. of cleared land @ $2.50/Sq. Ft.
- A 42,350 Gross Square Foot Office Facility @ $2.50/Sq. Ft.
- 100 surface parking spaces @ $20 monthly rental per space
- A 75% loan @ 9½% for 25 years.

Table 1

Effect of changes in cost per square foot of land on total cost and return on equity

Land Cost Per Sq. Ft.	Total Cost	Cash Flow Before Income Tax	Equity Return
$1.50	$1,230,050	$48,210	14.67%
2.00	$1,273,150	$44,810	14.07%
2.50	$1,316,250	$41,420	12.58%
3.00	$1,359,350	$38,030	11.19%
3.50	$1,402,450	$34,640	9.87%

Table 2

Effect of changes in cost of site improvements on total cost and return on equity

Cost of Site Improvements Including Surface Parking & Landscaping	Total Cost	Cash Flow Before Income Tax	Equity Return
$ 22,000	$1,296,250	$43,000	13.26%
$ 42,000	$1,316,250	$41,420	12.58%
$ 62,000	$1,336,250	$39,850	11.92%
$ 82,000	$1,356,250	$38,280	11.29%
$102,000	$1,376,250	$36,700	10.66%

Table 3

Effect of changes in average occupancy on income and return on equity

Average Occupancy Rate	Gross Income	Cash Flow Before Income Tax	Equity Return
100%	$254,000	$53,120	16.14%
95%	$242,300	$41,420	12.58%
90%	$230,600	$29,720	9.03%
85%	$218,900	$18,020	5.47%
80%	$207,200	$ 6,320	1.92%

V

Investment analysis of projected multi-family residential development

A. *Investment*		
Land Value @ 60¢/Sq. Ft.		$ 392,040
Construction Costs @ $16/Sq. Ft. for 300 units, 1,000 Sq. Ft. average		4,800,000
	Total Investment	$5,192,040
B. *Cash Flow Before Income Tax*		
Effective Gross Income		$ 803,700
Rental Income @ $235/unit	$846,000	
Less Vacancy and Less Allowance 5%	42,300	
Expenses:		229,600
Management & Leasing @ 5%	$ 34,200	
Salaries & Wages	19,500	
Utilities	7,200	
Water	6,000	
Painting & Decorating	7,200	
Maintenance & Repairs	12,600	
Refuse Removal	6,050	
Real Estate Taxes	89,750	
Insurance @ $45/unit	13,400	
Swimming Pool	1,000	
Supplies	6,000	
Sinking Fund	26,700	
Net Annual Income		$ 574,100
Yield on Total Investment ($574,100 ÷ $5,192,040) – 11.1%		
Annual Debt Charges $5,192,040 × 75% = $3,894,030 loan @ 9½% for 25 years; Factor .1049		408,480
Cash Flow Before Income Tax		$ 165;620
C. *Rate of Return Before Tax*		
Equity Investment ($5,192,040–$3,894,030)		$1,298,010
Rate of Return on Investment ($165,620 ÷ $1,298,010)		12.76%

Assumptions for the Example:
- Fifteen acres cleared land @ 60¢ Per Square Foot
- Three hundred units of 1,000 Square Foot Facility @ $16 Per Square foot
- Density of 20 Units Per Acre
- A 75% loan @ 9½% for 25 years

Table 1
Effect of changes in land cost on total cost and equity return

Land Cost Per Sq. Ft.	Total Cost	Cash Flow Before Income Tax	Equity Return
$ .40	$5,061,360	$175,900	13.90%
.50	$5,126,700	$170,760	13.32%
* .60	$5,192,040	$165,620	12.76%
.70	$5,257,380	$160,480	12.20%
.80	$5,322,720	$155,340	11.67%

Table 2
Effect of changes in construction cost on total cost and equity return

Construction Cost Per Sq. Ft.	Total Cost	Cash Flow Before Income Tax	Equity Return
$15.00	$4,892,040	$189,220	15.47%
15.50	$4,942,040	$185,290	14.99%
*16.00	$5,192,040	$165,620	12.76%
16.50	$5,342,040	$153,820	11.51%
17.00	$5,492,040	$142,010	10.34%

Table 3
Effect of changes in density on total cost and equity return[1]

Units Per Acre	No. of Units	Total Cost	Cash Flow Before Income Tax	Equity Return
10	150	$2,792,040	$ 67,390	9.65%
15	225	$3,992,040	$116,500	11.67%
*20	300	$5,192,040	$165,620	12.76%
25	375	$6,392,040	$214,740	13.44%
30	450	$7,592,040	$263,450	13.88%

*Based on calculations used in preceding investment analysis.
[1]Expenses adjusted proportionately for changes in density.

SOURCE: *Guidelines for Urban Renewal Land Disposition*, HUD, 1975, Washington, D.C.

Q. *Mrs. Smith has been offered six residential lots as a package at $6,500 each. Lots in this middle-range development have been selling quite briskly for the last several years at $10,000. The builder has over-developed and has a large inventory. Mrs. Smith was advised that if she acts quickly—in the next three days—the seller will finance with 20 percent down, interest for five years at 11 percent, and no liability for balance in case of default. You have been asked to advise Mrs. Smith on this matter.*

A. Study of the market demand *at this location,* considering household formation, existing inventory in the subject development, and other housing coming on-stream indicates absorption of the subject lots in about five to six years. Even then, the anticipated sale price of the lots is judged to be at $10,000 each. Inquiry into the local market also reveals that *for the risk involved* in this kind of venture, even with a no-liability provision, a minimum of 16 percent should be derived on the equity investment. The estimated discount rate is computed as follows:

80% @ 11% =	0.088
20% @ 16% =	0.032
Total:	0.120

Using a 12 percent discount, the indicated present value of a lot over various holding periods is:

Year	*12% Discount*	*Present Value*
1	0.893	$8,930
2	0.797	7,970
3	0.712	7,120
4	0.636	6,360
5	0.567	5,670
6	0.507	5,070
7	0.452	4,520

Based on the above, the maximum Mrs. Smith should pay for each lot is in the range of $5,000 to $5,700. Since the asking price is too high, a counter-offer may be in order.

Q. *Your client has been contemplating investing in land for two different uses and, based on his calculations, he figures to achieve the following net profits in the next several years on each venture. Much depends on the anticipated level of economic growth; he feels the chances are about 60 percent for stable conditions to prevail.*

	Parcel A	*Parcel B*
Stable economy	15%	10%
Dynamic economy	20%	40%

Your opinion is solicited. What will you tell him based on the above information submitted?

A. The problem is basically one of investment alternatives based on probabilities. Since your client forecast the probability of a stable economy at 60 percent (0.6), the chances of dynamic growth are 0.4 (1 − 0.6). The data can be arranged in a 2 × 2 matrix as follows:

Economic conditions alternatives

		Stable	*Dynamic*
Investment	A	15%	20%
Alternatives	B	10%	40%

If stable (S) and dynamic (D) probabilities are equated with returns, a set of indifference probabilities can be derived, that is, the point at which the chances are the client will be equally as well off with either investment A or B. S and D can be viewed as coefficients with the following derived equations:

$$15\ S + 20\ D = \text{potential parcel A}$$
$$10\ S + 40\ D = \text{potential parcel B}$$

The same potential exists when:

$$15\ S + 20\ D = 10S + 40D$$

Solving for S we get:

$$15\ S - 10\ S = 40D - 20D$$
$$5\ S = 20D$$
$$S = 4D$$

Since D = (1-S)

$$S = 4(1\text{-}S) = 4 - 4S$$
$$5\ S = 4$$
$$S = 4/5 = 0.80;\ \text{then}\ 0 = 0.20$$

We have then the following:

	Stable Economy	*Dynamic Economy*
Forecast probabilities	0.60	0.40
Indifference probabilities	0.80	0.20

The proper choice is always the alternative that has a higher forecast probability than indifference probability. Under the stated facts, the client should purchase parcel B as an investment.

Q. *An investment is being formulated for a client involving a warehouse with sales office space to be occupied by a single tenant under an initial 5-year firm lease. An option on the site has been obtained; land cost including site preparation is $75,000. A mortgage of 60 percent of economic value can be obtained with a mortgage constant of 0.10904. The overall capitalization rate on this class of investments for this location is 10 percent. Vacancy and expenses are estimated at $7,500 for the 18,000 sq. ft. net lease area based on provisional lease conditions. Rental will be $2.50 per sq. ft. per year.*

A budget for the cost of construction has to be formulated to determine if development is feasible. In addition, estimates of return on equity, after taxes, are needed for presentation to the client. The investor is in the 40 percent tax bracket. A 40-year straight line depreciation is planned for the improvements. What is a good format for working out this proposal?

A. The following form provides a simple and direct basis for completing this kind of analysis. It uses a four-stage process to compute economic value based on gross and net rentals, and most likely financing. Next is an analysis of the economics of project development, which indicates the most likely budget for improvements, followed by derivations of the amount of tax shelter, and finally an estimate of the after-tax cash flow as related to equity requirements.

PROJECT DEVELOPMENT ANALYSIS

Section	Item	Value	Operator	Item	Value	Result	Value
Economic Value and Capital Structure	Rent/Sq. Ft.	2.50	×	Net Lease Area	18,000	Gross Rent	$45,000
	Gross Rent	45,000	−	Vacancy + Expenses	7,500	Net Income	$37,500
	Net Income	37,500	÷	Cap Rate	.100	Economic Value	375,000
	Economic Value	$375,000	×	Mortgage Ratio	.60	Mortgage Loan	$225,000
	Mortgage Loan	225,000	×	Debt Constant	.10904	Debt Service	24,534
	Economic Value	375,000	−	Mortgage Loan	225,000	Equity	$150,000
Project Development	Net Income	37,500	−	Debt Service	$24,534	Cash Flow Before Tax	12,966
	Economic Value	375,000	−	Land, Cost, Fees, etc.	75,000	Building Budget	300,000
	Building Budget	300,000	÷	Building Gross Area	18,600	Budget Per Sq. Ft.	$16.13
Tax Shelter	Interest	22,404	+	Depreciation	7,500	Income Shelter	$29,904
	Net Income	37,500	×	Marginal Tax Rate	.40	Loss Gain	$15,000 (G)
	Income Shelter	29,904	−	Loss/Gain	15,000 (G)	∓ Income Tax	14,904 (Shelter)
Cash Flow Equity Return	Cash Flow Before Taxes	$12,966	+	Income Tax	$14,904 (Shelter)	Cash Flow After Tax	$27,870
	Cash Flow After Tax	$27,870	÷	Equity	$150,000	Return on Investment	18.6%

Q. When analyzing office building transactions for possible use in estimating the value of a subject building and facility, why is it important to establish both the gross areas and the net rentable areas?

A. The importance lies in the relationship between these areas and building efficiency and consequent productivity. Simply stated, a poorly designed office building costs more to maintain, clean, heat, light, and so forth. The basic generating unit of gross and net income is the net rentable area, assuming multiple occupancy of all floors.

From a transaction analysis point of view, the following illustration highlights some of these differences and their relative importance. Three recent sales are examined for comparison to a subject property that has 8 floors, and 44,000 sq. ft. Assume no adjustment for age, time, location, or condition. All have multiple occupancy tenants.

Sale	*No. Floors*	*Gross Area (square feet)*	*Net Rent Area (square feet)*	*Bldg. Efficiency*	*Sale Price*
1	10	38,000	26,000	68%	$468,000
2	6	42,000	37,000	88%	819,000
3	5	40,000	34,000	85%	705,000

Subject property efficiency (net to gross floor area) is 85 percent.

An analysis of sales price per gross square foot of floor area for each transaction indicates the following:

Sale	*Price/Gross Floor Area*
1	$12.32
2	19.50
3	17.64

The average is $16.20; the lowest is 75 percent of the average and the highest is 120 percent of the average. In other words, there is a total range of 45 percent from the average price per gross square foot of building area. If building efficiency is considered, the transactions are translated in the following manner:

Sale	*Price/Gross Floor Area*
1	$18.00
2	22.14
3	20.75

The average is $20.30; the lowest is 89 percent of the average and the highest is 109 percent, with a range of 20 percent above and below the average. Thus, the transactions not only are more meaningful when put in terms of building efficiency, but also the transaction price becomes more credible as the range (in this instance related to the average) is reduced over one half.

Q. *You have read two nationwide surveys of buyers and builders as shown below. In the 1975 study, the following questions were asked:*

- *Buyer Question:* What general features are most important to you when selecting a home? (Ranked in order of importance)
- *Builder Question:* Which general features are most important as standard or optional inclusions in your best selling model home? (Ranked in order of importance).

In the 1976 survey, the following questions were posed.

- *Buyer Question:* What features are most important to you when selecting a home?
- *Builder Question:* What features are standard in your best selling model home? Both buyers and builders were asked to rank the items in order of importance.

After having studied the tables of responses, you note a general lack of agreement and perception concerning the relative importance of house features. What other analysis can be undertaken to provide more insight into the extent of agreement/disagreement and relative priorities between buyers and builders on these two studies?

A. A statistical technique called Kendall's Rank Correlation Coefficient can be computed. It is most appropriate, since it provides for ties and shows the extent of association of rankings. The following are the computed coefficients. For example, (1975 study) item 8 (Builder, Central part of the U.S.) shows a reasonable correspondence of 0.703 for buyer and 0.851 for builder on houses in the $35–44,999 range. In contrast, the 1976 survey shows a reasonable association (item 4, Builder, Eastern part of U.S.) concerning houses in the $25–34,999 price range. As a whole, the coefficients suggest a significant difference between buyers and builders as to the relative importance of various house attributes and amenity-neighborhood features (1975). Additionally, the impact of potential consumer preferences for new housing in various price ranges transcends the immediate new housing market. These trends, assuming they are not short-term or transient in nature, impact on the marketability and value of the standing inventory of housing. Major changes in preferences accelerate obsolescence and dysfunction of existing and competitive properties in terms of price, potential utility, location, and so forth. Essentially, this represents a *shift in the parity value indexes* of housing along the lines of defined housing attributes and characteristics. Relating national and regional survey data to micro-markets (at county or metro area level) is one of the challenging aspects of real estate market analysis.

1975—Buyer and builder survey

					REGION							
	Detached		*Attached*		*East*		*Central*		*South*		*West*	
	BUYER	BUILDER	BUYER	BUILDER	BUYER	BUILDER	BUYER	BUILDER	BUYER	BUILDER	BUYER	BUILDER
Carpeted Floors	1	1	2	1	4	3	1	1	2	1	1	1
Separate Family Room	2	3	10	14	2	2	4	4	3	6	3	5
Insulated Windows Dbl. Glazed	3	11	6	10	3	13	2	3	4	16	9	14
Separate Dining Room	4	4	4	6	1	1	6	5	9	8	4	7
Fireplace	5	6	12	13	6	7	7	7	6	9	2	3
Air Conditioning	6	9	1	5	11	9	5	10	1	2	7	9
Heavy Duty Security Locks	7	14	5	9	7	15	9	16	8	13	5	11
Sep. Storm Windows & Screens	8	15	3	21	5	14	3	9	10	18	15	20
Den/Guest Room	9	10	8	11	8	12	11	14	11	10	6	10
Complete Landscaping	10	12	7	4	10	6	10	15	12	11	11	16
Patio or Balcony	11	7	9	3	12	8	13	11	7	4	8	4
Wall Paneling	12	5	13	12	13	5	15	6	5	3	12	8
Hardwood Floors	13	16	14	22	9	11	14	17	18	20	14	19
Humidifier	14	18	11	24	14	18	8	12	14	19	18	21
Patio, Balcony Slid. Glass Door	15	2	15	2	15	4	16	2	15	7	10	2
Water Softener	16	22	17	28	17	23	12	20	19	22	13	18
Wall Mirrors	17	8	19	7	19	10	20	8	13	5	16	6
Enclosed/Screened Porch	18	23	18	27	16	21	21	23	20	23	24	25
Children's Playground	19	26	23	17	18	26	17	26	17	28	22	29
Electronic Air Cleaner	20	21	20	25	21	22	18	19	16	21	19	22
Garage Door Opener	21	13	21	18	22	16	19	13	21	15	17	12
Swimming Facilities	22	25	16	8	20	25	22	25	23	25	20	23
Intercom/Security Sys.	23	19	22	16	23	19	23	21	24	14	23	15
Central Vacuum System	24	20	24	23	24	17	24	22	22	17	25	17
Wet Bar	25	17	27	19	25	20	25	18	26	12	21	13
Atrium	26	24	28	26	26	24	26	24	28	24	26	24
Tennis Facilities	27	28	26	20	27	28	27	28	25	27	27	27
Golf Facilities	28	29	29	29	28	29	28	29	27	29	28	28
Club House	29	27	25	15	29	27	29	27	29	26	29	26
Item:	1	2	3	4	5	6	7	8	9	10	11	12

HOME PRICE RANGE											
Under $25,000		$25,000–$34,999		$35,000–$44,999		$45,000–$54,999		$55,000–$64,999		$65,000 & Over	
BUYER	BUILDER	BUYER	BUILDER	BUYER	BUILDER	BUYER	BUILDER	BUYER	BUILDER	BUYER	BUILDER
2	1	1	1	2	1	4	3	4	5	7	8
7	9	3	4	1	3	1	1	1	2	2	2
1	11	2	11	3	10	5	11	7	11	9	16
5	8	7	5	4	4	2	2	3	1	1	1
8	10	5	9	5	5	3	5	2	3	3	3
4	4	6	7	6	9	7	8	8	9	6	9
6	12	8	15	9	14	6	12	5	14	10	12
3	13	4	12	11	13	12	19	15	20	21	20
11	6	9	13	8	11	8	10	6	10	4	10
12	7	10	10	10	12	11	13	11	16	13	15
14	14	11	8	7	6	9	7	10	7	8	6
9	3	12	3	13	7	10	6	9	6	12	5
10	15	13	16	15	16	13	16	16	15	16	14
13	21	15	17	14	18	14	15	19	17	14	17
19	2	14	2	12	2	15	4	13	4	11	4
16	20	16	21	16	21	17	22	17	22	15	22
18	5	19	6	17	8	16	9	14	8	17	7
17	23	18	23	20	23	25	23	23	23	20	23
15	26	17	25	23	26	22	26	20	29	25	28
20	22	20	22	18	22	18	21	22	10	19	21
22	17	21	14	19	15	23	14	12	12	5	11
21	25	22	26	21	25	20	25	21	25	22	25
25	16	24	18	22	19	19	18	24	18	23	18
23	19	23	20	24	20	24	20	27	21	24	19
26	18	26	19	25	17	21	17	18	13	19	13
24	24	25	24	26	24	27	24	28	24	26	24
28	28	27	27	27	28	26	28	25	27	28	27
27	29	28	29	28	29	28	29	26	28	27	29
29	27	29	28	29	27	29	27	29	26	29	26
13	14	15	16	17	18	19	20	21	22	23	24

1976—Buyer and builder survey

	Region										Home Price Range									
	Totals		East		Central		South		West		Under $25,000		$25,000–$34,999		$35,000–$44,999		$45,000–$54,999		$55,000–plus	
	BUYER	BUILDER	BUYER	BUILDER	BUYER	BUILDER	BUYER	BUILDER	BUYER	BUILDER	BUYER	BUILDER	BUYER	BUILDER	BUYER	BUILDER	BUYER	BUILDER	BUYER	BUILDER
Range/oven	1	2	1	1	1	3	1	2	1	2	1	2	1	2	1	3	1	2	1	1
Refrigerator	2	10	2	7	2	9	2	9	2	10	2	8	2	9	2	10	2	10	3	11
Carpeting	3	1	4	5	3	1	5	1	3	1	3	1	3	1	3	1	4	4	4	6
Dishwasher	4	4	3	3	5	5	4	5	5	5	6	7	5	5	4	4	3	3	2	2
Range hood with exhaust fan	5	3	5	2	4	2	6	4	6	4	4	3	4	3	5	2	6	1	6	3
Fireplace	6	6	6	4	8	6	8	7	4	6	7	9	6	7	6	6	8	5	8	4
Central air conditioning	7	7	8	8	6	7	3	3	8	8	5	5	8	6	7	7	7	7	7	7
Garbage disposal	8	5	7	6	7	4	7	6	7	3	8	4	7	4	8	5	5	6	5	5
Burglar/fire detector system	9	9	9	10	10	11	9	8	9	7	9	6	9	8	9	8	11	9	10	9
Power humidifier	10	12	11	11	9	10	12	14	15	15	12	13	10	13	10	11	10	12	12	13
Electronic air filter	11	15	13	15	11	13	10	15	12	14	13	15	11	15	11	15	9	15	11	15
Trash compactor	12	13	12	14	13	14	11	12	10	11	10	11	13	14	12	13	12	13	15	12
Central vacuum cleaner	13	14	10	12	14	15	13	13	13	13	11	14	14	11	13	14	14	14	13	14
Garage door operator	14	8	14	9	12	8	15	10	11	9	14	10	12	10	14	9	13	8	9	8
Intercom	15	11	15	13	15	12	14	11	14	12	15	12	15	12	15	12	15	11	14	10
Item:	1	2	3	4	5	6	7	8	9	10	11	12	13	14	15	16	17	18	19	20

SOURCE: Reprinted from *Professional Builder*, January, 1975, and January, 1976 issues, by permission of the editor.

1975—Kendall rank correlation coefficients

	Detached		Attached		East		Central		South		West		<T 25 K		< 35 K		< 45 K		< 55 K		< 65 K		≥ 65 K		
	BY	*BL*	*BY*	*BL*	*BY*	*BL*	*BY*	*BL*	*BY*	*BL*	*BY*	*BL*	*BY*	*BL*	*BY*	*BL*	*BY*	*BL*	*BY*	*BL*	*BY*	*BL*	*BY*	*BL*	
	1	2	3	4	5	6	7	8	9	10	11	12	13	14	15	16	17	18	19	20	21	22	23	24	
1	.000	.616	.793	.369	.901	.601	.872	.655	.818	.501	.806	.506	.806	.571	.935	.619	.910	.654	.846	.619	.759	.560	.703	.525	1
2		.000	.488	.537	.527	.867	.507	.862	.621	.806	.698	.821	.496	.837	.560	.910	.688	.954	.663	.930	.690	.880	.688	.846	2
3			.000	.438	.764	.512	.764	.537	.700	.446	.693	.412	.737	.522	.797	.510	.752	.535	.708	.501	.611	.441	.570	.427	3
4				.000	.330	.512	.310	.438	.394	.560	.456	.540	.284	.562	.353	.530	.412	.540	.417	.506	.424	.471	.353	.461	4
5					.000	.571	.823	.576	.719	.412	.718	.417	.856	.493	.880	.540	.821	.575	.806	.550	.719	.510	.654	.476	5
6						.000	.502	.759	.596	.723	.654	.718	.520	.803	.565	.841	.663	.861	.639	.875	.626	.811	.644	.801	6
7							.000	.616	.739	.422	.732	.412	.816	.483	.890	.540	.811	.555	.747	.520	.670	.451	.624	.417	7
8								.000	.650	.688	.649	.693	.565	.749	.624	.841	.703	.851	.649	.816	.640	.762	.644	.723	8
9									.000	.580	.747	.506	.732	.567	.801	.634	.806	.629	.752	.624	.714	.555	.614	.530	9
10										.000	.607	.810	.385	.792	.464	.790	.568	.795	.563	.800	.584	.760	.573	.780	10
11											.000	.672	.662	.649	.785	.667	.835	.726	.820	.711	.821	.652	.790	.627	11
12												.000	.370	.723	.464	.741	.578	.825	.563	.810	.609	.810	.627	.805	12
13													.000	.461	.874	.509	.756	.523	.731	.499	.644	.459	.573	.425	13
14														.000	.535	.851	.599	.836	.604	.792	.606	.732	.565	.718	14
15															.000	.583	.854	.607	.790	.563	.723	.504	.647	.469	15
16																.000	.667	.914	.642	.859	.644	.793	.632	.775	16
17																	.000	.723	.857	.709	.767	.642	.785	.605	17
18																		.000	.699	.916	.698	.849	.691	.822	18
19																			.000	.684	.821	.637	.751	.600	19
20																				.000	.703	.914	.736	.886	20
21																					.000	.663	.777	.639	21
22																						.000	.721	.928	22
23																							.000	.681	23
24																								.000	24

BY = Buyer
BL = Builder

1976—Kendall rank correlation coefficients

	Totals		East		Central		South		West		<T 25 K		< 35 K		< 45 K		< 55 K		⩾ 55 K		
	BY	BL	BY	BL	BY	BL	BY	BL	BY	BL	BY	BL	BY	BL	BY	BL	BY	BL	BY	BL	
	1	2	3	4	5	6	7	8	9	10	11	12	13	14	15	16	17	18	19	20	
1	.000	.562	.886	.619	.886	.581	.829	.524	.790	.486	.867	.524	.924	.543	.000	.581	.829	.543	.733	.505	1
2		.000	.562	.790	.600	.867	.429	.848	.581	.848	.543	.810	.638	.867	.562	.943	.505	.905	.638	.829	2
3			.000	.695	.771	.505	.752	.524	.790	.524	.867	.524	.848	.619	.886	.581	.790	.581	.733	.543	3
4				.000	.619	.733	.486	.676	.600	.638	.600	.638	.695	.771	.619	.771	.562	.848	.733	.810	4
5					.000	.657	.790	.600	.714	.524	.829	.600	.924	.619	.886	.619	.867	.543	.771	.467	5
6						.000	.448	.714	.524	.752	.486	.714	.657	.771	.581	.886	.562	.810	.657	.695	6
7							.000	.543	.695	.429	.810	.505	.752	.448	.829	.448	.810	.410	.714	.410	7
8								.000	.581	.810	.657	.848	.562	.867	.524	.829	.467	.752	.562	.714	8
9									.000	.619	.771	.581	.790	.600	.790	.562	.733	.562	.714	.562	9
10										.000	.543	.810	.562	.829	.486	.829	.505	.752	.562	.714	10
11											.000	.619	.829	.600	.867	.562	.733	.524	.638	.486	11
12												.000	.600	.829	.524	.790	.505	.714	.562	.676	12
13													.000	.619	.924	.657	.829	.619	.771	.543	13
14														.000	.543	.848	.524	.771	.657	.695	14
15															.000	.581	.829	.543	.733	.505	15
16																.000	.524	.886	.619	.771	16
17																	.000	.486	.829	.448	17
18																		.000	.619	.886	18
19																			.000	.581	19
20																				.000	20

BY = Buyer
BL = Builder

Q. *A small commercial building is estimated, based on leases and current occupancy, to have a net income of $16,000 for the next 7 years. For tax depreciation purposes the improvements are valued at $120,000, with an estimated remaining economic life of 20 years. A new purchaser just obtained a $100,000 mortgage at 9.25 percent for a term of 15 years, payable semiannually. A 20-year straight line depreciation of the improvements is contemplated. If the property is held for 4 years, what is the after-tax cash flow if owner is in the 50 percent tax bracket?*

A. The schedule that can be prepared would appear as follows:

Year	(1) Net Income	(2) Depreciation	(3) Interest	(4) Taxable Cash Flow	(5) Cash Flow	(6) Income Taxes	(7) After-Tax Cash FLow
1	$16,000	$6,000	$9,176	$824	$3,541	$412	$3,129
2	16,000	6,000	8,865	1,135	3,541	568	2,973
3	16,000	6,000	8,525	1,475	3,541	738	2,803
4	16,000	6,000	8,152	1,848	3,541	924	2,617

Computations:
Column 2 = $120,000 / 20 = $6,000
Column 4 = Columns 1 − 2 − 3
Column 5 = Column 1 less debt service

Q. *You have appraised an investment property at $1,300,000. You estimate its minimum value in a downward market at about $1,000,000, and its maximum value in a better market at $1,500,000. Since you wish to give your client as much guidance as possible, what other realistic and sound analysis can be made using these estimates?*

A. Given these three discrete estimates of the potential investment value of the property, a series of probability statements could be made that might help the client in his decision-making process. A technique that can be used is the triangular density function. This has the attributes of a normal distribution, but eliminates skewness as a problem. Further, in the subject case, there is an assumed probability of zero that the value will be less than $1,000,000 or more than $1,500,000. The triangle generated by this technique is an envelope that includes all probable values as of a given time.

FIG. 1

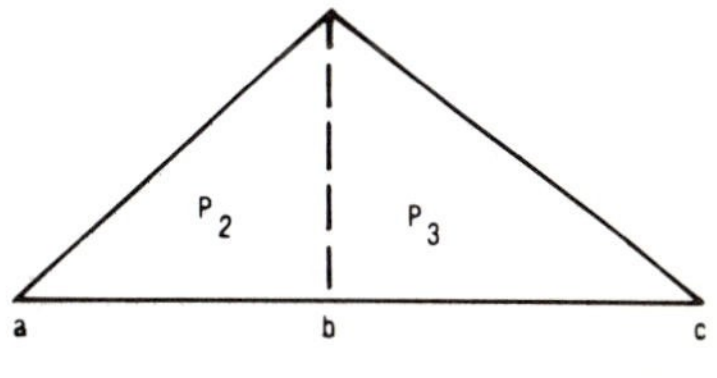

The indicated capitalization rates are as follows: at $1,000,000 the rate is 13 percent; at $1,300,000 it is 10 percent; and at $1,500,000 it is 9 percent, based on a forecast stable net income of $130,000 for the property. The applicable formulas are noted below where $a = 0.09$, $b = 0.10$, and $c = 0.13$.

$$\text{(Mean)}\ m = \frac{a + b + c}{3}$$

$$\text{(Probabilities)}\ p_2 = \frac{b - a}{c - a}$$

$$p_3 = \frac{c - b}{c - a}$$

$$\text{(Variance)}\ \sigma^2 = \frac{(c - a)^2}{18}(1 - p_2 p_3)$$

$$\text{(Standard Deviation)}\ \sigma = \sqrt{\sigma^2}$$

Substituting our data into the equation results in the following answers:

$$\begin{aligned} m &= .10667 \\ p_2 &= .25 \text{ or } 25\% \\ p_3 &= .75 \text{ or } 75\% \\ \text{Variance} &= 0.000072 \\ \text{Standard Deviation} &= 0.01 \end{aligned}$$

The findings indicate, based on the capitalization rate parameters, that a probability of 25 percent exists that the rate is 0.10 or less; that a 75 percent probability that the rate is greater than 0.10. The standard deviation indicates that the rate can vary above or below the mean by 0.01.

Cumulative probabilities can be computed with the following formulas:

$$F = 1 - p_3 \left(\frac{c - X}{c - b}\right)^2$$

If $X = 11$, then:

$$F = 1 - 0.75 \left(\frac{0.13 - 0.11}{0.13 - 0.10}\right)^2 = 0.667$$

$$F = p_2 \left(\frac{X - a}{b - a}\right)^2$$

If X = 0.095, then:

$$F = 0.25 \left(\frac{0.095 - 0.09}{0.10 - 0.09} \right)^2 = 0.13$$

A computation of a series of these values results in a cumulative chart as shown in Figure 2. From this we can see the probabilities of the capitalization rate being more than or less than a given rate. For example, the graph indicates that if there is a cumulative probability of 50 percent (0.50) the rate will be 0.106 or less.

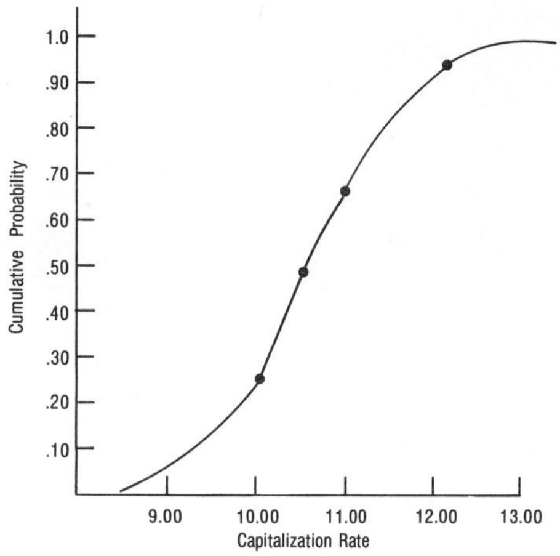

FIG. 2

Q. *A client is considering the construction of a free-standing one-story building for a retail discount outlet. This would be a new kind of venture in the area. The proposal he has received from the potential lessee would result in rentals about 50 percent above the typical percentage of gross receipts rental. The only problem is that there is no guarantee of minimum rent. In-depth market studies of trade areas, disposable income, and consumer expenditures show that there is a 60 percent chance that a rental of $60,000 per year can be realized. An additional $12,000 per year in rental income is plausible, $18,000 is optimistically achievable, and up to $30,000 is within the realm of possibility. What further analysis or comments can be made based on this information provided by the client?*

A. One could use a variation of the triangular density function. This takes on a modified form that includes a "spike" as noted in Figure 1. The mean, which is representative of an average or expectancy, is computed as follows:

$$\text{(Mean) } m = p_1 X_1 + (1 - p_1) \frac{(a + b + c)}{3}$$

Where:

$p_1 = 0.60$
$X_1 = \$60{,}000$
$a = \$72{,}000$
$b = \$78{,}000$
$c = \$90{,}000$

Substituting the data into the equation, the mean is computed as:

$$m = (0.60)\,(\$60{,}000) + (1 - 0.60)\;\frac{\$72{,}000 + \$78{,}000 + \$90{,}000}{3}$$
$$= \$68{,}000$$

Both p_2 (probability of a return greater than \$60,000 but less than \$78,000) and p_3 (probability of a return greater than \$60,000 but less than \$90,000) are computed with the following formulas:

$$p_2 = (1 - p_1)\left(\frac{b - a}{c - a}\right)$$

$$= (1 - 0.60)\left(\frac{\$78{,}000 - \$72{,}000}{\$90{,}000 - \$72{,}000}\right)$$

$$= (0.40)\left(\frac{6{,}000}{18{,}000}\right) = 0.40 \times 1/3 = 0.13$$

$$p_3 = (1 - p_1)\left(\frac{c - b}{c - a}\right)$$

$$= (1 - 0.60)\left(\frac{\$90{,}000 - \$78{,}000}{\$90{,}000 - \$72{,}000}\right)$$

$$= (0.40)\left(\frac{\$12{,}000}{\$18{,}000}\right)$$

$$= 0.40 \times 2/3 = 0.27$$

These derivations suggest that there exists a 73 percent chance (0.60 + 0.13) that the rental will be less than \$78,000 and almost 9 chances out of 10 (0.60 + 0.27) that the rental receipts will not reach the level of \$90,000 per year. It should be noted that if the initial subjective judgment of 60 percent is reduced, say to 40 percent, then the mean or average expected value will be closer to the "spike value" of \$60,000.

The variance in this modified triangular density method can be computed with the following formula:

$$(\text{Variance})\ \sigma^2 = \frac{p_1}{1-p_1}(m - X_1) + \frac{(c-a)^2}{18}\left(1 - p_1 - \frac{p_2 p_3}{1-p_1}\right)$$

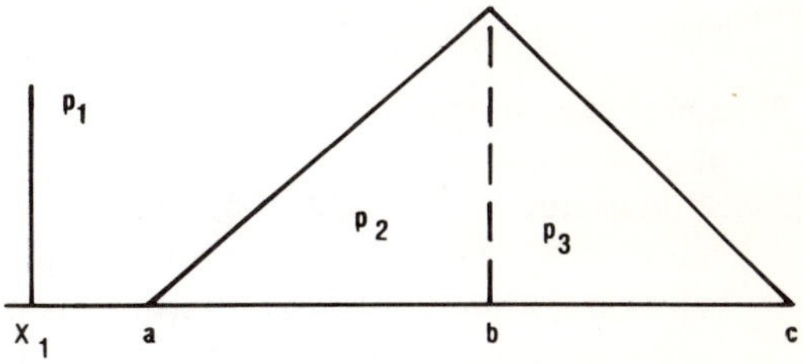

FIG. 1

Q. *A client just closed a deal on a small commercial storeroom building taking back a second mortgage for a face amount of $20,000 payable in ten equal annual payments of $2,000 plus accrued interest at 8 percent. He would like to know what the value of this obligation is in today's market. While the mortgage has good security, property, and borrower, the client needs the money for other purposes. Recent activity in second mortgages indicates a discount of 15 percent is appropriate for good risk situations.*

A. There are several ways to compute the discounted value of this security note. In some markets, a flat discount of 15 percent of the capital sum would indicate a present value of $17,000; in other markets, the following method might be used. This technique more clearly measures the time value of money.

Year	*Interest*	*Principal*	*Total*	*Discount*	*Present Value*
1	$1,600	$2,000	$3,600	0.8696	$3,130.56
2	1,440	2,000	3,440	0.7561	2,600.98
3	1,280	2,000	3,280	0.6575	2,156.60
4	1,120	2,000	3,120	0.5718	1,784.02
5	960	2,000	2,960	0.4972	1,471.71
6	800	2,000	2,800	0.4323	1,210.44
7	640	2,000	2,640	0.3759	992.38
8	480	2,000	2,480	0.3269	810.71
9	320	2,000	2,320	0.2843	659.58
10	160	2,000	2,160	0.2472	533.95
				Total:	$15,350.93

Current value of the second mortgage at a 15 percent rate is estimated at $15,350.

Q. *A bank is handling the sale of some acreage held in a trust for a client who asks you to comment on the following, which was recommended as the typical sale price per acre. Assuming all the facts as stated are plausible, what are your probable recommendations based on this data compiled by an appraiser? The purpose of such an analysis is to show the economics of development.*

A. Based on the factual data outlined, the analysis is wrong. The appraiser was carried away with the usable land-to-gross land ratio. If a typical acre will produce 3.5 single-family lots yielding a total retail value of $21,000, then any further reduction of the "net per net acre before profit and carrying charges" is unnecessary. The true indicated value per gross acre under the facts stated is $13,400, not $10,721.

Data and Analysis

Typical parcel size (acreage)	20.0 acres
Average price per lot	$6,000
Lots per acre (acreage)	3.5
Usable acreage (terrain, soil, etc.)	80%
Infrasructure connection, off-site (gross acre)	$2,500
On-site development costs	$3,000 per lot

Imputed Land Value to Developer (Per Acre Basis)

Retail Value Per Net Acre		$21,000
Less Selling Costs (10% of retail)		2,100
		$18,900
Development Costs:		
Off-site	$2,500	
On-site	3,000	
	$5,500	5,500
Net Per Net Acre before profit and carrying charges		$13,400
Net per gross acre at 80% usable		$10,720

Q. *You have completed a detailed market analysis for a feasibility study of a large marina development. Part of the analysis includes engineering studies provided by a subcontractor engineer who reports two plans for the bulkhead development. Plan A will cost $300,000 with* *probable reconstruction in about 30 years at a cost of $100,000. Maintenance costs will be $25,000 for the first 15 years and $40,000 for the next 15 years. Plan B requires an investment of $550,000 and a reconstruction in the same period at a cost of $50,000; annual maintenance will be $15,000. Developers figure their rate of return at a minimum of 15 percent. Which is the better design from a present worth basis of analysis?*

A. The analysis is accomplished as follows:

Plan A = Present Cost + (Annual Maintenance Cost) (P.W. Annuity Factor) + (Reconstruction Cost)
(Sinking Fund Factor) (P.W. Annuity Factor)
= $300,000 + ($25,000) (5.8474) + ($100,000)(0.00230)(6.56598)
= $300,000 + $146,185 + $1,510.18
= $447,695.18

Plan B = $550,000 + ($15,000) (5.8474) + ($50,000)(0.00230)(6.56598)
= $550,000 + $87,711 + $755
= $638,466

Based on the data outlined, plan A should be recommended.

Q. *You are analyzing some listings of acreage suitable for single-family development. Some are being offered on a cash basis while others, for tax reasons, are offered with terms. The following per-acre prices of nearly identical adjoining sites are being considered by a client and he would like to know what's the best deal when all adjustments for terms are made. How would you rank them?*

	Site #1	*Site #2*	*Site #3*	*Site #4*
Asking Price	$9,500/A	$12,000/A	$11,000/A	$12,500/A
Terms	cash	25% down	15% down	10% down
Interest only	na	5 yrs.	3 yrs.	2 yrs.
Interest Rate	na	8%	9%	12%
Balance Payout	na	5 yrs.	4 yrs.	3 yrs.

A. Sites 2, 3, and 4 are analyzed in the following manner to determine their equivalent cash asking price.

Site #2

Year	Interest	Principal	Total	Discount (15%*)	Present Value
1	$720	—	$720	0.8696	$626.12
2	720	—	720	0.7561	544.39
3	720	—	720	0.6575	473.40
4	720	—	720	0.5718	411.70
5	720	—	720	0.4972	357.98
6	720	1,800	2,520	0.4323	1,089.40
7	576	1,800	2,376	0.3759	893.14
8	432	1,800	2,232	0.3269	729.64
9	288	1,800	2,088	0.2843	593.62
10	144	1,800	1,944	0.2472	480.56
				Total:	$6,199.95

*Based on competitive yields for risk involved.

Down Payment:	$3,000.00
Present Value Future Payments:	6,199.95
Equivalent Cash Asking Price:	$9,199.95 per acre

Site # 3

Year	Interest	Principal	Total	Discount Factor	Present Value
1	$841.50	—	$841.50	0.8696	$731.77
2	841.50	—	841.50	0.7561	636.26
3	841.50	—	841.50	0.6575	553.29
4	841.50	$2,337.50	3,179.00	0.5718	1,817.75
5	631.13	2,337.50	2,968.63	0.4972	1,476.00
6	420.75	2,337.50	2,758.25	0.4323	1,192.39
7	210.38	2,337.50	2,547.88	0.3759	957.75
				Total	$7,365.21

Down Payment:	$1,650.00
Present Value Future Payments:	7,365.21
Equivalent Cash Asking Price:	$9,015.21 per acre

Site #4

Year	Interest	Principal	Total	Discount Rate	Present Value
1	$1,350	—	$1,350	0.8698	$1,173.96
2	1,350	—	1,350	0.7561	1,020.74
3	1,350	$3,750	5,100	0.6575	3,353.25
4	900	3,750	4,650	0.5718	2,658.87
5	450	3,750	4,200	0.4972	2,088.24
				Total:	$10,295.06

Down Payment: $1,250
Present Value Future Payments: 10,295
Equivalent Cash Asking Price: $11,545 per acre

The equivalent cash prices for the several sites, on a per acre basis, would be ranked as follows:

Site #3 ($9,000/A)
Site #2 ($9,200/A)
Site #1 ($9,500/A)
Site #4 ($11,500/A)

Q. *You are negotiating for the purchase of a business site 100 × 110 (11,000 sq. ft.) an inside parcel, zoned business, and adaptable for use by your client as a site for a franchised carry-out food drive-in facility. The listing broker tells you the asking price is $26,400 (firm) and that the price, at $2.40 per sq. ft., is fair and competitive. To support his position he gives you the following data and information. Since the locations are comparable and the sales have taken place in the last year or two, no adjustments for these factors need be considered. Do you think that your client should pay $26,400 for the site?*

No.	Use	Size	Area (sq. ft.)	Position	Price	Price/sq. ft.
1	Vacant	60×125	7,500	corner	$19,500(A)	$2.60
2	Parking	125×125	15,625	inside	31,500(S)	2.00
3	Stores	75×110	8,250	inside	20,300(S)	2.46
4	Drive-In Cleaner	65×150	9,750	inside	22,400(S)	2.30

(A) asking price
(S) sale price

A. The central question is adaptability for the proposed use—a drive-in and carry-out franchised food facility. From criteria and standards for similar developments, only sale 2 would be suitable and adaptable for the intended use, that is, the intended highest and best use. The other sales (3 and 4) reflect different kinds of business uses with different physical site requirements. What was paid may be irrelevant. To have comparability, a site must be suitable and adaptable for the same use.

To give credence to sales 3 and 4 and to the offer (No. 1) is to say in essence that one would build the contemplated facility (saving on land) and end up with a functionally obsolete development! The fact that all sites are zoned for business only tells you that the proposed use is permitted—nothing else. Consequently, the most suitable site is No. 2, which would be adaptable for the intended use. Based on this kind of presentation to the broker, the price should be negotiated at around $2.00 per sq. ft., which would reflect a realistic offer for the planned development.

Q. *An owner of a small office building can obtain a firm 6-year lease on a block of space if he installs a package air conditioner costing $10,000. Additional rent is to be paid, above the basic rent, if the unit is installed. This additional rent will be $1,300 per year for 3 years and $1,600 for the remaining 3 years. The tenant will pay for maintenance and operation. If the unit has a 15-year physical life, what will be the deficit, if any, at the end of 6 years? What will the owner have to charge on an annual basis if he figures a 10-year payout for this particular improvement? Investment capital to the owner is capitalized at 10 percent.*

A. The present value of these cash flows at 10 percent for the 6-year lease term is $6,220.80 and was computed in the following manner.

Year	*Income*	*Discount Factor*	*Present Value*
1	$1,300	0.909	$1,181.70
2	1,300	0.826	1,073.80
3	1,300	0.751	976.30
4	1,600	0.683	1,092.80
5	1,600	0.621	993.60
6	1,600	0.564	902.40
			$6,220.80

Remaining value at the end of the sixth year is (1–6/15) or 3/5.

3/5 × 10,000 = $6,000	
P.W. of Remaining Value: $6,000 × 0.564:	$3,384.00
P.W. of Cash Flow:	6,220.80
Total P.W.:	$9,604.80

Deficit is $10,000 − 9,604.80 = $395.20

To compute the rent necessary to recapture the investment in years 7 through 10 requires a present value of future rents equal to $3,779.20 ($10,000 − $6,220.80).

Averaging the discount rates for these years (0.513 + 0.467 + 0.424 + 0.386)/4 yields 0.4475.

Then $3,779.20 ÷ 0.4475 = $8,445; $8,445÷ 4 (years remaining) = $2,111. Computing present value of $2,111 per year for seventh through the tenth year yields:

Year 7	$2,111 × 0.513 =	$1,082.94
Year 8	$2,111 × 0.467 =	985.84
Year 9	$2,111 × 0.424 =	895.06
Year 10	$2,111 × 0.386 =	814.85
		$3,878.69

The result, $3,878.69, approximates the present value deficit of $3,779.20. Therefore, the rental necessary to achieve a payout in 10 years must be equal to or exceed $2,111 per year for the seventh through tenth years.

Q. *A truck terminal is being constructed and it is anticipated that expansion will take place in about 10 years. A complete self-contained sewage and water system for current needs costs $32,000 with annual maintenance costs of about $4,800; an identical system can be added for the same cost in 10 years. As an alternate design, a potential full capacity system costs $48,000 with annual operating costs of $6,000 for the first 10 years, and after expansion the costs will increase to $9,000 per year. If rate of return is 13 percent and the economic life from installation date is 20 years, what is the optimum course of action?*

A. Table data required @ 13 percent rate:

Discount factor–10 years	= 0.2946
P.W. Annuity–10 years	= 5.4262
Capital Recovery–20 years	= 0.1424

P.W. (Two-stage) = 32,000 + (4,800 · 5.4262) + (9,600 · 5.4262 · 0.2946)
+ (32,000 · 0.1424 · 5.4262 · 0.2946)
= 32,000 + 26,045.76 + 15,346.16 + 7,284.31
= 80,676.23

P.W. (Full System) = 48,000 + (6,000 · 5.1446) + (9,000 · 5.1446 · 0.2946)
48 + 30,867.70 + 13,640.30
= 92,508.09

The difference, $11,831.86, indicates two-stage development is advantageous because it represents the least cost (lowest present value) based on the factual information provided.

Q. *A feasibility study, which includes a detailed study of at-place demand for retail stores, shows a very strong demand above and beyond that currently planned for construction. While the site is more than adequate, terrain and subsoil conditions present some excess costs of construction. An architect has submitted the following information for expansion of the facility.*

Plan	*Additional Investment*
1	$ 400,000
2	900,000
3	1,700,000
4	2,500,000
5	3,400,000

Analysis indicates that the additional net annual income to be anticipated under each expansion plan is as follows:

(1) $100,000, (2) $225,000, (3) $320,000, (4) $400,000 and (5) $475,000.

How should this be analyzed and what is the optimum expansion plan based on this factual data? Risk of venture dictates a 16 percent return and the owners plan to hold the investment for 10 years.

A. This can be solved via incremental analysis—costs versus cash flows discounted to present worth. For example, the present worth benefit of Plan 1 is derived as follows:

P.W. (Benefit) = [$100,000 (Income) · 4.833 (16%, 10 yrs.)] −$400,000
P.W. (Benefit) = $83,300

Plan	*Additional Investment*	*Excess Investment*	*Net Income*	*Excess Income*	*P.W. of Additional Investment*
1	$ 400,000	$400,000	$100,000	$100,000	$ 83,300
2	900,000	500,000	225,000	125,000	104,125
3	1,700,000	800,000	320,000	90,000	−365,030
4	2,500,000	800,000	400,000	80,000	−413,360
5	3,400,000	900,000	475,000	75,000	−537,525

Plan II should be implemented.

Plan II should be implemented.

Q. *In connection with domestic energy development, some rather specialized land improvements are being constructed. The local bank's trust department offers a client two propositions for an investment. Proposal X involves an investment of $300,000, which will yield a gross annual income of $125,000 with expenses estimated at $45,000 and salvage value at the end of 20 years estimated at $90,000. Proposal Y involves an investment of $190,000, annual income of $100,000, expenses of $60,000, and an estimated salvage value of $75,000 at the end of 20 years. Considering risk in terms of location and kind of activity, investors figure the minimum return should be about 18 percent. Which investment should be seriously considered?*

A. The present worth of each alternative is computed as follows:

P.W. = (Net Income − 20 year P.W. Annuity) + (P.W. of Salvage Value) − Cost
P.W.(X) = (125,000 − 45,000) 5.353 + (90,000 0.0365) − 300,000
= 80,000 5.353 + 3,285 − 300,000
= 426,085 − 300,000 = $126,085

P.W.(Y) = (100,000 − 60,000) 5.353 + (75,000 0.0365) − $190,000
= 40,000 5.353 + 2,737.50 − $190,000
= 216,857.50 − 190,000 = $26,857.50

Proposal X, having the higher net present value, should be recommended.

Suppose the investor now states that the risk is much higher than previously perceived and his return should be at least 30 percent. Does this change the recommendation?

P.W.(X) = 80,000 (3.316 + 90,000) .0053 −300,000
265,280 + 477 − 300,000 = −$34,343

P.W.(Y) = 40,000 (3.316 + 75,000) .0053 −190,000
132,640 + 397.50 − $190,000 = −$56,962.50

Based on this new rate of return requirement, neither of the investments should be undertaken since each net present value is negative, indicating that the cost/revenue matrix does not satisfy this new rate.

Q. *A leasehold improvement is to be financed by an owner on a firm 3-year lease and she is offered the following two proposals for repayment. Proposal X involves a cash outlay of $7,200 with payments, annually in arrears, of $3,000, $4,000, and $5,000. Proposal Y involves a cost of $7,700 with payments in similar fashion of $3,500, $3,800, and $5,300. If the owner's discount rate is 10 percent, which is the best proposal for the owner to accept, and why?*

A. This is a problem involving an analysis of (DBCR) discounted benefit/cost ratios—the ratio of the benefits discounted to present day to the cost or investment required. The first steps involved are as follows:

Year	*10% Factor*	*X Proposal ($7,200)*	P.V. (X)
1	0.909	3,000	2,727
2	0.826	4,000	3,304
3	0.751	5,000	3,755
			9,786

$$\text{DBCR} = \frac{9{,}786}{7{,}200} = 1.36$$

Year	*10% Factor*	*Y Proposal ($7,700)*	P.V. (Y)
1	0.909	3,500	2,389
2	0.826	3,800	3,138
3	0.751	5,300	3,980
			9,507

$$\text{DBCR} = \frac{9{,}507}{7{,}700} = 1.23$$

Since both ratios exceed unity, the higher ratio would suggest the better proposition—the X proposal. However, an additional check can be made via incremental analysis by determining the DBCR for the difference between the cash flows under X and Y, resulting from the additional $500 investment. The differences, Y − X, are as follows:

PV (Y − X)
$454
−165
225
$514

$$DBCR = \frac{514}{500} = 1.03$$

This indicates that the Y proposal should be selected because the additional investment is attractive, having a DBCR of 1.03 at the owners discount rate.

Q. *You are reviewing an appraisal for a client who is deciding whether or not to buy a parcel of unimproved land that has only electricity and roads. You find the following tabulation used to suggest a value for the land. What are your conclusions? Land values generally have not increased in the area. (Subject = 100.00 for comparison purposes.)*

Sale	*Price*	*Date*	*Location*	*Physical**	*Total Adjustment Factor*	*Indicated Value*
A	$1,500	2 years	1.00	1.00(R.E)	none	$1,500
B	2,000	Offer	0.90	1.15(R.E.S.W.)	1.03	2,060
C	1,200	1 year	0.60	1.00(R.E.)	0.00	720
D	1,800	1 year	1.00	1.15(R.E.S.W.)	1.15	2,070
E	1,400	6 months	1.20	1.00(R.E.)	1.20	1,680
					Esimated Value:	$2,000

*R—Road,
E—Electricity
S—Sewer,
W—Water

A. The conclusion is wrong because of improper evidence of value. Sales B and D have sewer and water. Attempting to extract these land attributes on a cost basis from market value (assumed via sales) is completely wrong; one simply cannot deduct an item of cost from value and call the remainder value. Based on the three other sales (A, C, E) the land is probably worth about $1,600; the estimate is about 25 percent high.

Q. *You are asked to estimate the market value of a 40-acre site whose highest and best use is for single-family development. Three very recent sales of properties with the same highest and best use have been selected for analysis. No time adjustment is necessary. The following information is known about the transactions:*

Transaction	*Consideration*	*Number of Acres*	*Probable/Planned Conversion Time*	*Location Rating*
1	$ 65,000	26	2 years	Similar
2	88,000	48	5 years	Inferior
3	147,000	60	4 years	Inferior

Conversion time period is based on an in-depth market supply-demand study. Assuming no other adjustments are necessary, and applicable discount rates are 10 percent (#1), 12 percent (#2), and 13 percent (#3), how can these sales be used to formulate a meaningful index of value of the subject 40-acre tract?

A. Based on the probable and planned conversion time and utilization of the sites, the following derivations give some insight into present value. The sale price is divided by the present worth factor based upon conversion time. The result is the approximate value if conversion were possible immediately.

Transaction	*Location Rating*	*Subject Value Index*	
		Gross Price	*Per Acre*
1	10% discount ($65,000 ÷ .826) =	$ 78,924	$3,035
2	12% discount ($88,000 ÷ .567) =	$155,200	$3,233
3	13% discount ($147,000 ÷ .613 =	$239,804	$4,000

Subject estimate of value: 40 acres @ $3,500/A = $140,000

If a percentage adjustment technique were used, the following gross percentage adjustments would be necessary; their level exceeds substantially any acceptable supportable criteria.

Transaction	*Market Consideration*	*Estimated Value*	*Difference*	*Percent*
1	$2,500/A	$3,500/A	$1,000/A	40%
2	1,833/A	$3,500/A	1,667/A	91%
3	2,450/A	$3,500‘A	980/A	40%

Q. *In analyzing resources and their allocation in an existing or contemplated real estate development, how can profiling and development analysis be helpful?*

A. Resource allocation is one of the most important aspects of value of a real estate venture—existing or planned. A study of resource allocation is basic to highest and best use analysis; it also signals the extent of a property's dysfunction, that is, the presence and extent of functional risk. Formulating resource utilization profiles of existing similar ventures will provide insights into market thinking and activity. More importantly, such profiles provide a basis for evaluating the performance and productivity of such resources in the marketplace.

Based on locational trends, economies of scale, consumer tastes, and investor expectations, a profiling study may signal a need for reallocation or reorientation of the amount and kind of resources. For example, many drive-in and carry-out food service facilities are developed with given standards for such factors as off-street parking. An in-depth study of going concerns might reveal inherent defects of design and planning, causing a loss of business simply because of deficient resources that limit the efficiency of service and flow of trade. In other cases, competition and market preemption by potential competitors may not have been fully analyzed.

An important fact that should be kept in mind is that successful ventures tell us something in terms of the allocation of resources and level of competition that must be matched to succeed.

The following tables outline and highlight some basic relationships discovered in four types of successful going concern investments:

Small medical clinics

	Land Value Ratio	*Property Operating Ratio*	*Net Income/ Property Value*	*Net Rentable Area*	*Kind of Facility*
1	13%	19%	0.09	13,870	2 story(E)
2	21%	32%	0.08	8,100	1 story
3	14%	32%	0.09	7,396	1 story
4	18%	27%	0.08	21,150	2 story(E)
5	16%	51%	0.10	5,690	1 story
6	19%	37%	0.08	6,725	1 story
7	8%	31%	0.09	13,100	2 story(E)
8	19%	26%	0.08	15,250	3 story(E)
9	4%	28%	0.09	23,200	3 story(E)
10	19%	41%	0.10	21,500	3 story(E)

(E) Elevator

Industrial buildings—one story

	Site Size (acres)	*Land Value Ratio*	*Owner's Operating Ratio*	*Net Income/ Property Value*	*Building Site (square feet)*
1	51.0	22%	—	—	492,000
2	23.0	13%	8%	0.09	139,000
3	11.7	15%	—	0.08	54,200
4	7.8	11%	10%	0.01	70,600
5	2.5	47%	—	0.10	47,500
6	15.0	2%	7%	0.10	96,500
7	1.5	19%	7%	0.07	34,000
8	1.94	25%	6%	0.09	77,000
9	18.2	7%	11%	0.10	168,600
10	2.13	44%	—	0.09	25,000
11	2.25	16%	8%	0.08	30,050
12	5.0	8%	—	—	81,250
13	3.5	22%	4%	0.09	59,400
14	5.4	17%	—	—	32,000
15	10.6	16%	26%	0.09	212,100

*Facilities studied are new or recently constructed.

Small retail stores[1]
(main retail area)

	Land Value Ratio	*Gross Floor Area*	*Owner's Operating Ratio*[2]	*Net Income/ Property Value*
1	30%	18,850	0.09	0.08
2	20%	24,300	0.07	0.08
3	24%	12,900	0.08	0.08
4	21%	12,150	0.06	0.07
5	36%	12,500	0.05	0.09
6	50%	22,500	0.07	0.07
7	39%	—	0.07	0.07
8	56%	6,600	—	—
9	42%	13,200	—	—
10	42%	10,480	—	0.08

[1]All one-story except case 5. Prime or nearly prime locations in medium or large urban areas.
[2]Very low ratio because many cases represent net leases.

Elmira, New York, truck terminals

	Location	Land Area (acres)	Number of Doors	Land Area/Door (square feet)
1	Big Flats Road	1.75	20	3,811
2	Franklin Street	0.3	2	6,534
3	Philo Road	1.6	22	3,168
4	Philo Road	1.5	23	2,841
5	Sears Road	2.3	27	3,710
6	Ithaca Road	11.0	8	59,895*
7	Holding Point	3.7	20	8,058
8	Grand Central Ave.	3.25	26	5,445
9	Sheridan Ave.	6.0	24	10,890
10	Sheridan Ave.	1.0	10	4,356
11	Grand Central Ave.	1.5	8	8,167
12	Grand Central Ave.	3.0	33	3,960
13	Lackawanna Ave.	1.2	44	1,188

*Underdeveloped site with excess land.
SOURCE: Elmira Area Truck Study, December, 1974

Q. *An assignment involves an analysis of apartment properties. Five properties have been studied and the following ratings have been made based on the items noted:*

Property	Location	Aesthetic Appeal	Quality of Tenants	Rank Sum
A	1	2	1	4
B	3	4	5	12
C	5	3	4	12
D	4	5	2	11
E	2	1	3	6

How can this data be analyzed in a meaningful manner?

A. One could use Kendall's Coefficient of Concordance, W, as a means of determining whether there is any agreement between the rankings. Where there is perfect agreement between the rankings of the properties on the above attributes, then the rank sum would be as follows.

Property	*Location*	*Aesthetic Appeal*	*Quality of Tenants*	*Rank Sum*
A	1	1	1	3
B	2	2	2	6
C	3	3	3	9
D	4	4	4	12
E	5	5	5	15

If there were no agreement between the properties on these variables, each would have a total (this is the expected sum of the rankings) rank score of 9 (i.e., 45/5). A null hypothesis is as follows:

H_0 : No valid association exists between these properties based on quality evaluation of items.

H_1 : Association exists between the properties based on the quality evaluation used.

W is computed as follows:

$$W = \frac{S}{(1/12)\, k^2\, (N^3 - N)}$$

S = sum of the squares of the observed deviation from the expected sum of ranks.
k = number of variables ranked.
N = number of properties in the sample being ranked.

The computations are as follows:

$$\begin{aligned} &A\ (4 - 9)^2 = 25 \\ &B\ (12 - 9)^2 = 9 \\ &C\ (12 - 9)^2 = 9 \\ &D\ (11 - 9)^2 = 4 \\ &E\ (6 - 9)^2 = 9 \\ &\overline{56} \end{aligned}$$

$$W = \frac{56}{(1/12)(3)^2\,(5^3 - 5)}$$

$$= \frac{56}{(1/12)(9)(125\text{-}5)} = \frac{56}{(1/12)(9)(120)} = 56/90$$

$$= 0.62 \text{ or } 62\%$$

The computation indicates a fair degree of association between the five properties rated on the attributes of location, aesthetic appeal, and quality of tenants. Note: the variable must be at the ordinal level.

Q. *I do not have access to a computer to simulate a situation, but I understand that this can be done with a table of random numbers. How can this be applied in real estate analysis?*

A. Simulation with random numbers can be undertaken on a select basis assuming limitations of time and energy. For example, in estimating the potential absorption rate for single-family lots in various competing areas, in comparison to a subject acreage site, the following absorption is noted and cumulative probabilities are computed for income segment A in a section of an urbanized area:

Units Per Yr. Absorbed	*Cumulative Probability*
30	1.00
20	0.90
21	0.75
20	0.60
18	0.20

The data can be arranged in the following manner. The second line of the table represents differences between the cumulative table items.

	A	B	C	D	E
Sale X	18	20	21	24	30
P (X=x)	0.20	0.40	0.15	0.15	0.10

To provide for the drawing of random numbers, the interval 0 to 1 is divided into one hundredths as follows: A = 0.01 – 20, B = 0.21 – 0.60, C = 0.61 – 0.75, D = 0.76 – 0.90, and C = 0.91 – 1.00. Using the last two numbers in columns 13 and 14 of the table of random numbers, the distribution derived in percentage distribution is as follows (based on actual count of numbers drawn):

Probability of 18 Lot Sales Per Year
A = 21%
B = 34%
C = 23%
D = 11%
E = 11%

Comparison of the two distributions, one market-derived and the other simulated, indicates a 75–78 percent probability that at least 21 lots per year will be absorbed. The probability derived is based on the assumption that a demand study of this income segment indicates sufficient depth based on household formation, consumer preferences, and reasonable expectations of consumer acceptance of the location of the subject site.

	Cumulative Probabilities				
	A	B	C	D	E
Market Derived	20	60	75	90	1.00
Simulated	21	55	78	89	1.00

Other applications might include the need for a random sample of current households (by socioeconomic attributes) from census tracts. With the number of households known, for example, 9,000 with a sample of 200 targeted random numbers can be drawn from a table to correspond by some design to house addresses. The households thus identified would constitute the sample.

One could also simulate the arrival and departure of shoppers and the related intensity of use of parking facilities. This technique is helpful in many other similar situations involving utilization of land developments and ancillary services.

Q. *Inspection of a site for a multi-million dollar warehouse indicate some potential drainage and soil erosion problems. Plans and specifications indicate a proposed new design method for dealing with this situation. A net saving in construction costs is $310,000; the conventional design methods cost $365,000, while the new method will cost $55,000. Inquiry among informed architects and contractors indicates a 60 percent chance for success with the new design. If it simply does not do the job, about $10,000 worth of construction will be adaptable to the conventional method.*

Since a number of important factors are involved, including matters of property security, time (if conversion to the conventional method is required) etc., what is the risk involved and what would be your recommendation?

Random numbers

Col. / Line	(1)	(2)	(3)	(4)	(5)	(6)	(7)	(8)	(9)	(10)	(11)	(12)	(13)	(14)
551	31630	67734	78201	94545	00152	62327	83165	31035	82295	11824	06765	29501	62849	50419
552	25101	98983	36993	40026	58036	14075	05980	57094	45527	18766	77741	12985	14112	65058
553	86207	09805	46240	70644	76012	37000	98321	97197	30645	56169	09363	44394	29087	96569
554	31611	47643	28795	48115	17223	63161	29677	69820	77189	20762	94296	94528	82984	71418
555	10649	89132	59781	12373	35999	30832	02508	93055	57173	79848	25439	18861	86742	54970
556	68210	16228	34801	40972	22887	89759	09095	00587	03998	13659	64179	98567	69313	84637
557	32367	69587	66162	44358	69844	73042	88091	07288	74971	47066	36927	53520	58309	58605
558	14684	42446	01751	37459	31945	03627	47690	97813	45272	42789	99315	26662	15833	37246
559	64260	04661	39957	01200	84800	27930	98937	76108	11043	29101	01767	78894	92922	66537
560	66035	77943	70861	32037	96699	56314	75755	68667	04730	15256	13957	52743	42306	87515
561	20966	71492	32323	11867	47583	24094	23334	78839	81588	67374	43855	24512	81956	75721
562	20498	68176	02027	22358	15907	13247	44784	82937	53009	73379	44093	58405	38515	85531
563	56320	79875	60634	17556	52153	63549	03661	78290	96447	04192	30157	63198	75932	02367
564	50559	90270	33571	88091	34749	56784	98486	06018	27447	00884	29564	51522	35571	69208
565	49366	90095	73459	12225	28483	35358	99941	63054	54358	80748	54049	85937	64718	21466
566	29022	19268	03003	96622	30239	20482	50028	16638	57708	78559	70241	47977	78645	48550
567	77212	76531	68842	37777	20085	38703	31753	18608	52524	08585	91711	63572	57007	11379
568	41121	90499	83459	71424	27596	74645	68790	66478	78885	53799	02026	24596	88692	55936
569	06613	95412	94751	60763	56611	73508	88479	86151	78563	31633	92321	23304	77153	86639
570	66430	95324	60108	42377	56350	67861	47478	11961	78516	95316	64393	52020	44994	88205
571	39380	09648	47285	62864	03421	34292	36084	39604	89838	03635	30064	72710	26327	65521
572	27595	63289	75149	03348	91237	28372	65330	00966	73904	17477	34953	08975	83142	48425
573	43525	45549	58819	48478	14007	11384	19576	66158	30774	51892	24711	78537	18360	95682
574	60024	79858	72015	01236	27444	47010	80938	15828	86484	92753	04322	27171	41828	79025
575	35914	73076	05158	40190	41294	72776	38528	22272	34709	34561	65554	53461	61776	03585
576	58253	32995	54370	34437	98365	17630	42196	49736	39619	16731	71792	38047	85559	56700
577	85887	54618	23538	73621	80904	05950	63441	86109	79900	14063	03152	39235	74289	42342
578	98988	60426	34636	40601	57718	93925	67763	67671	21739	87534	83385	91492	45796	04621
579	65381	17333	32358	49608	36893	43453	38580	27639	52832	01522	11108	59992	23168	04414
580	20214	88406	06098	07770	51679	64857	36998	95796	46745	36780	56791	34690	61634	85411
581	04970	56425	74303	94793	55055	44762	22800	02663	91182	13102	07408	50545	21312	11365
582	87556	31521	19669	16311	01767	67301	63016	01227	29273	79256	50368	88633	23329	86500
583	34615	85796	30299	56090	41453	82886	33077	99791	86553	64640	61529	88660	66941	15936
584	95769	07371	49569	42262	74097	44317	40304	05346	90342	73324	81555	62769	83559	55238
585	57338	58325	53918	08075	69395	08189	66668	11663	84858	93146	87188	34936	97867	63996
586	08882	30762	14602	54767	67683	57818	98756	49119	91258	71916	65948	94841	38607	39412
587	62644	32814	31337	06011	80623	36021	81846	71868	98242	72307	25917	56240	73499	45106
588	55358	48010	24440	51092	89263	82352	95072	68828	28001	48991	19201	90963	34192	63336
589	02254	43319	79888	86311	57615	69666	60651	49084	39681	66415	10201	33931	44245	42050
590	61023	48494	57279	47133	89534	37085	28495	39162	89121	52021	23143	14829	55792	84641
591	41900	90881	96080	35258	70734	59465	49227	01431	90694	96186	57811	54512	30108	01861
592	94500	19764	94752	73077	74726	86176	31623	14569	89225	09606	73432	95276	21237	36807
593	66375	34653	37125	84780	92759	09781	06912	96802	92502	97497	67702	49763	25930	49924
594	27141	20939	02318	57546	45467	06653	99212	60612	26046	53553	39737	70491	69632	46009
595	25670	88933	19316	57014	52797	83779	56495	33104	86858	07668	41253	97688	76883	29444
596	06590	67256	81117	69351	98168	81043	86682	00063	96223	30436	21987	15450	56874	45011
597	36429	99750	38004	64992	25021	45680	46501	92943	99165	20707	43410	53746	54716	17090
598	52011	93461	06334	83801	34422	13722	35016	80605	86628	21689	34082	26035	11928	41817
599	09443	77694	26882	15663	45983	29425	12085	96233	29036	91135	28238	27709	90674	09705
600	25862	81855	15254	28462	95680	42433	70311	09702	71615	72628	85922	58369	89734	08750

Source: Interstate Commerce Commission. Table of 105,000 Random Decimal Digits. Washington, D.C. May 1949.

A. The Bayesian concept for minimizing losses can be utilized and is of the following general relationship.

$$\text{risk/gain ratio} = \frac{\left(\begin{array}{c}\text{potential losses}\\ \text{from new design}\end{array}\right)\left(\begin{array}{c}\text{Probability}\\ \text{of failure}\end{array}\right)}{\left(\begin{array}{c}\text{potential savings}\\ \text{by using new design}\end{array}\right)\left(\begin{array}{c}\text{Probability}\\ \text{of success}\end{array}\right)}$$

In equation form, this relationship is as follows:

$$r = \frac{(C_1 + C_5 + C_3 - C_4 - C_2)(1 - p)}{(C_2 + C_6 - C_1)\,p}$$

Where:

C_1 = new design/equipment investment (dollars)
C_2 = conventional design/equipment investment (dollars)
C_3 = modification cost if new design/equipment fails (dollars)
C_4 = salvage from the new design/equipment if not operational (dollars).
C_5 = net revenue losses if new design/equipment fails (dollars).
C_6 = net revenue losses, if any, from using conventional design/equipment (dollars).
p = probability of new design succeeding.

Substituting in the equation, the following is derived:

$$r = \frac{(55{,}000 + 0 + 365{,}000 - 10{,}000 - 365{,}000)(1 - 0.60)}{(365{,}000 + 0 - 55{,}000)(0.60)}$$

$$r = \frac{(45{,}000)(0.40)}{(310{,}000)(0.60)} = 0.10$$

Since the risk/gain ratio (r) is only 0.10, the new design should be used. If the ratio turns out to be 1.00, the indifference point, either design would be a matter of choice. Where the ratio exceeds unity (1.0), the new design should not be utilized. From a pragmatic point of view, the risk ratio should be less than 0.5 to be seriously considered. Computations of C_5 and C_6 can be accomplished, where applicable, with the following equations.

$$C_5 = N_1 (R_1 + Y_1)(1 - t) - t\,Y_2$$

$$C_6 = N_2 (R_2 - Y_1)(1 - t) + t\,Y_2$$

Where:

N_1 = number of years required to modify/replace new design/equipment
N_2 = payout time for old design/equipment (years)
R_1 = net operating profit lost, if new method fails, dollars/year
R_2 = net operating profit lost by continuing old design/equipment, in dollars per year
Y_1 = difference in annual maintenance, property taxes, insurance, etc., between new and conventional,eequipment
Y_2 = difference in depreciation, new minus conventional, in dollars per year
t = income tax rate (fraction).

Q. *You have been retained by a large life insurance company as a consultant and you are faced with the evaluation of a multi-million dollar office building proposal requesting a loan for the full legal limit. One of the problems your client has had in the last several years has been cost overruns, resulting in projects ending up partly completed and/or forced into foreclosure because of less than realistic development costs. This, in turn, has resulted in substantial equity depletion where overruns required additional developer contributions. Total cost of improvements has been estimated by the developer to be $1,750,000. Subsequent documentation submitted by the proposed mortgagor reveals the following concerning the cost to build the structure:*

	In units of ten thousand dollars
1. Pilings, foundation, excavation work	51 to 76
2. Exterior walls, floors, roof	69 to 103
3. Equipment (elevators, A/A, etc.)	16 to 29
4. Interior finish	20 to 25

What further analysis can be undertaken to test for the plausibility of the estimate submitted? Should it be increased and, if so, by what amount?

A. Realizing that a point estimate (one number) is very dangerous, you develop additional estimates with an architect, calling them "most likely cost" estimates. The estimates take on the following form:

Item	*Optimistic*	*Most Likely*	*Pessimistic*
1.	51	60	76
2.	69	80	103
3.	16	20	29
4.	20	21	25
Total:	156	181	233

A beta distribution is used to analyze this bid data. To properly utilize this technique the following computations are made:

$$\text{(Standardized mode) } r = \frac{m\text{-}o}{p\text{-}o}$$

where: m = most likely estimate
p = pessimistic estimate
o = optimistic estimate

$$r = \frac{181 - 156}{233 - 156} = \frac{25}{77} = 0.32$$

The submitted cost estimate (t) is analyzed to determine whether the costs in fact can be less than the stated amount. For this test X_t is computed.

$$X_t = \frac{t - o}{p - o} = \frac{175 - 156}{233 - 156} = \frac{19}{77} = 0.25$$

We locate the intersection of $r = 0.32$ and $X_t = 0.25$ on the Beta Curve Area Chart and read down to the indicated probability of 25 percent that the construction costs will be less than $1,750,000.

Suppose that management wants a 70 percent confidence probability that the costs will be less than a selected estimate. As indicated on the chart, this probability would require an X_t equal to about 0.45. Substituting this figure into the prior equation, we have

$$0.45 = \frac{t - 156}{233 - 156} = \frac{t - 156}{77} = 0.45(77) = t - 156$$

$$34.6 + 156 = t = 190.6$$

Based on this data, if $1,906,000 is taken as a realistic cost estimate for the structure, there is a 70 percent probability that costs will be less than this estimate.

Suppose there is still some uncertainty due to subsoil conditions and a 15 percent safety factor is desired. Then the estimate at the same probability (70%) would take form as follows:

	$1,906,000
(15% @ 70% confidence level)	285,900
	$2,191,900

The difference between the submitted point estimate and the above at a 70 percent confidence interval is $441,900, representing a 25 percent increase in construction costs that should probably be recognized in any mortgage loan negotiation. (Note: If r and X_t exceed 0.50, then their reciprocals may be used in connection with the chart.)

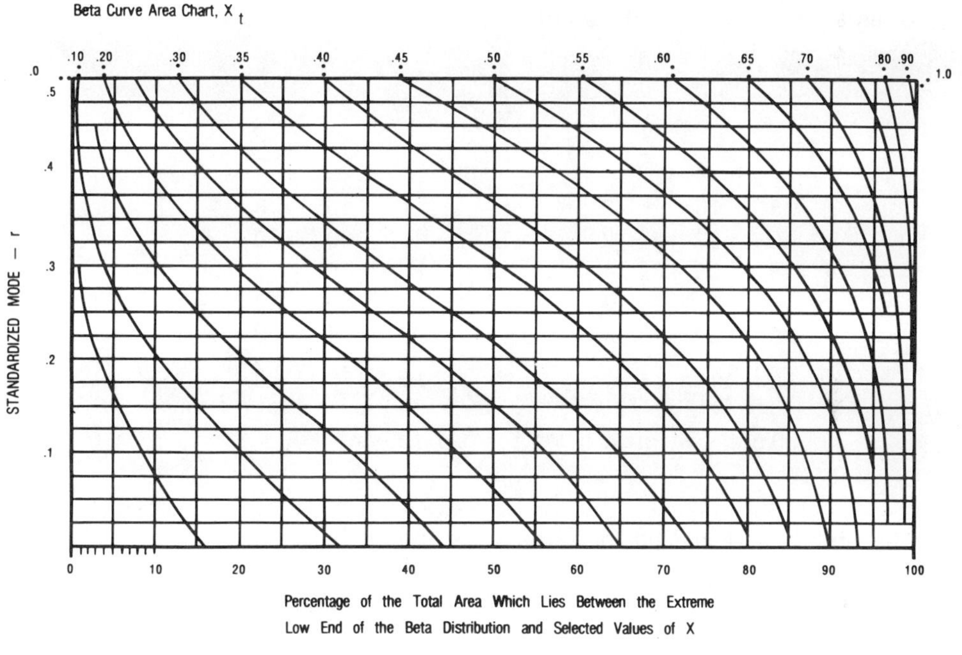

Q. *Five small housing developments are identified as competitive with a builder's proposed new subdivision. The following data has been obtained based on year of market entry, annual absorption of single-family housing units, scale of venture, and percentage of subdivision that is sold out:*

Year	*Absorption Rate/Year*	*Percentage Sold*
1975	8	18
1974	12	32
1974	15	25
1975	6	15
1975	10	20

What further analysis can be made to determine if there is any relationship between the rate of absorption and the extent of utilization of the standing inventory of the planned subdivisions?

A. A rather simple test is to calculate the extent of correlation between these two data sets since the time periods of start-up of the subdivisions are rather close. The solution is as follows:

		x	y			
X	Y	$(X - \bar{X})$	$(Y - \bar{Y})$	x^2	y^2	$x \cdot y$
8	18	−2	−4	4	16	8
12	32	2	10	4	100	20
14	25	4	3	16	9	12
6	15	−4	7	16	49	28
10	20	0	−2	0	4	0
50	110			40	178	68

$50/5 = \bar{X}$ (mean); $110/5 = \bar{Y}$ (mean)

The Standard Deviation for x and y are then calculated:

$$\sigma x = \sqrt{\frac{\Sigma x^2}{N}} = \sqrt{40/5} = \sqrt{8} = 2.83$$

$$\sigma y = \sqrt{\frac{\Sigma y^2}{N}} = \sqrt{178/5} = \sqrt{35.6} = 5.96$$

$$\text{(correlation) } r = \frac{\Sigma x\, y}{N\sigma x\, \sigma y} = 68/5(2.83)(5.96) = 68/84.34 = 0.806 = 80.6\%$$

$$r = \frac{\Sigma xy}{N\sigma_x\sigma_y} = 68/5(2.83)(5.96) = 68/84.34 = 0.806 = 80.6\%$$

The correlation, using this simple "Pearson product moment" correlation coefficient (80.6 percent) indicates a good correlation. As a rule, r is meaningful within the following limitations:

- greater than 0.90—high degree of correlation
- between 0.80 and 0.90—good correlation
- between 0.60 and 0.80—some degree of correlation
- between 0.30 and 0.60—slight chance of correlation
- less than 0.30—no relationship exists

Q. *What is a good format for use in analyzing land development activities (subdivision analysis) that will allow the proper treatment of revenues, expenses, and profits, while giving proper recognition to the time value of money?*

A. The following pro-forma "Economic Market Financial Simulation Model" is adaptable for use in all different kinds of land development activities. Two methods of analysis are integrated to enable the measurement of profit based on gross revenues (from land sales) over the forecast sell-out period. Further, this format recognizes all the development and predevelopment cost elements, allowing their proper discounting based on cash-flow analysis. For example, if single-family lots are proposed for development (this being the best and specific use of the acreage site), the following sequence of steps and analyses must be completed.

1. Analysis of demographic and economic factors in the relevant market area (area of influence on the subject acreage) to forecast the rate of household formation, the extent of surplus or deficit construction of single-family housing, and the growth and distribution of family and household incomes.
2. Analysis of the viability of housing market price segments to determine the appropriate price range of housing for the location and the housing segment that has sufficient depth for absorption of the proposed site.
3. Analysis of the current inventory of competitive sites in the identified market segment, the prices of sites, and the rate of absorption.

These three elements provide the basis for answering the basic questions concerning development of an acreage for a given use. This analysis provides the input for use in the pro-forma simulation model. The first step in the simulation is the estimation of gross revenue of

ECONOMIC — MARKET — FINANCIAL — SIMULATION MODEL

Method A

	Pre-development	Year 1	Year 2	Year 3	Year 4
GROSS SALES REVENUE					
EXPENSES					
A. PRE-DEVELOPMENT					
Planning					
Engineering					
Market Analysis					
R.E. Taxes					
Envir. Impact Study					
Cost of Options					
Land Interest Costs					
Zoning-Variance Costs					
Appraisal(s)					
Other					
B. DEVELOPMENT					
Land Development Costs					
Interest/Development Costs					
Engineering					
Legal/Title/Surveys					
Admn.-Management					
Sales Expenses (____%)					
Promotion (____%)					
Contingencies-Other					
Real Estate Taxes					
C. PROFIT (____%)					
NET TOTAL	( )				
NET CASH FLOW					
DISCOUNT FACTORS (Rate ____%)	* (1)	(2)	(3)	(4)	(5)
PRESENT VALUE (Land Only)					

Method B

1. NET CASH FLOW — PROFIT (C)	( )				
2. DISCOUNT FACTORS					
3. PRESENT VALUE (Land Value & Profit)	( )				
4. LESS P.V. LAND VALUE (Above)					
5. PRESENT VALUE PROFIT					
6. RATIO (Totals), Line 5 to Line 3					
7. INDICATED (P.V.) PROFIT SHARE	____ PERCENT				

( ) Indicates negative cash flow/value

* On large-scale projects, the pre-development period may be 2-3 yrs. in length

sales based on potential absorption, i.e., total potential future need for sites (top line of schedule).

Next, all predevelopment expenses (Item A) are estimated or derived and entered; this entry represents year one for present value discounting purposes and always reflects a negative cash flow because no sites have yet been sold. Item B covers the actual costs involved in the physical production of the sites (infrastructure), sales expenses, carrying charges, and so forth. Item C is profit, which is a percentage of gross sales. Items B and C are totals that are subtracted from gross revenues; the remainder is then discounted at an appropriate risk rate. Summation of present values (positive and negative) indicates the present value of the land (acreage) under the outlined program of utilization. Thus, under Method A, profit is an explicit expense item as a percentage of gross retail sales, year by year.

Method B proceeds in similar fashion to Method A except that profit is not explicitly deducted as an expense item. Rather, all other expenses are deducted from the annual revenues with profit flowing through to be discounted (Lines 1 and 2), resulting in a total present value of profit and land (Line 3). From this is deducted the heretofore derived present value of land only (Line 4) to indicate the present value of profit (Line 5). Line 6 derives a percentage relationship between profits and the total of profit and land value. Thus, what is indicated under Method B is the share of profit as opposed to the treatment of profit as an expense item under Method A. Both these rates and ratios are critical and must be derived from the local market of the subject property.

Where negative cash flows are anticipated during the early years of the sell-out period (post predevelopment), Method A should be used, deleting the treatment of profit. Gross revenues and Item B will be used in conjunction with Method B to arrive at an estimate of raw land value under the premised land utilization program. This is to avoid a distortion of the indicated land value, which would result from the increase in the level of negative cash flows due to the addition of profit as an expense (Item C). One simply cannot have a profit as part of a negative (before profit) cash flow.

The economic value of the raw land can be further analyzed for specific programmed land uses (where multiple uses are involved) by disaggregating by land use the components of the land development analysis—essentially a benefit/cost assessment. Profitability ratios can be computed between the discounted present values (by land use) and specific site and/or average land costs. This can provide insights concerning the extent of land cost subsidy between uses, if present, and also the marginality of certain targeted land utilization schemes. It could serve as an additional decision basis for implementing the highest and best use criterion standard. (For further discussion, see Edwin M. Rams, "Simulating Land Development As A Measure of Just

Pro-forma feasibility, condominium conversion

Pre-Sale Activities		YEAR Sales Revenue	(1) (25 units)	(2) (40 units)	(3) (35 units)
Rehabilitation			(0.80)($1,200,000)=	(0.90)($1,480,000)=	(0.60)($1,330,000)=
(0.70)($5,000/unit)=$3,500			$960,000	$1,332,000	$798,000
(0.30)(7,000/unit)= 2,100			(0.20)($1,400,000)=	(0.10)($1,300,000)=	(0.40)($1,200,000)=
5,600			$280,000	$130,000	$480,000
100 units × $5,600 =	$560,000		$1,240,000	$1,462,000	$1,278,000
Management-Supervision					
(0.90)($40,000)=$36,000					
(0.10)(55,000)= 5,500		*Expenses:*			
	$41,500	*Promotion/Sales*			
Financing Costs			(0.85)($105,000)=	(0.90)($115,000)=	(0.70)($90,000)=
80% Mortgage @ 12% of $1,280,000			$89,250	$103,500	$63,000
of acquisition cost of $1,600,000			(0.15)($90,000)=	(0.10)($135,000)=	(0.30)($110,000)=
			$13,500	$13,500	$33,000
	$153,600		$102,750	$117,000	$96,000
$560,00 rehab @ 12% (6 mos. avg.)	$33,600				
		Mortgage Interest:	$115,000	$76,800	$38,400
NET CASH FLOW	($788,700)		$1,022,050	$1,268,200	$1,143,600
	(1)		(2)	(3)	(4)
DISCOUNT RATE (12%)	0.893		0.797	0.712	0.636
PRESENT VALUE	($704,309)		$814,574	$902,958	$727,330

TOTAL NET PRESENT VALUE: $1,740,553

Compensation," presented before the Legal Resources Group, Transportation Research Board, 56th Annual Meeting, National Academy of Sciences, January 26, 1977, Washington, D.C.)

Q. *An investor is considering buying an existing 100 rental-unit apartment project for conversion to a condominium. Rehabilitation will take at least a year, during which time the cash flow from occupied units will pay operating expenses, taxes, and insurance. A mortgage of 80 percent of the purchase price of $1,600,000 at 12 percent is available to finance the venture. Considering location factors, extent of rehabilitation work on the units, and fluctuating cost schedules, what is a suitable format for analyzing such an investment?*

A. Conversion of existing apartment units to a condominium involves a number of uncertainties, that is, the cash inflows and outflows relating to rehabilitation, management, and promotion costs, and the retail value and absorption time of the units to be marketed. One way to manage the various uncertainties is to assign probabilities to the numerous line items, like expenditures and revenues, based on "most likely" and high and low estimates. As noted in the pro-forma outline, contractor estimates for rehabilitation are firm at $5,000 per unit but they could go as high as $7,000 per unit. Accordingly, the illustrated case suggests a probability of 70 percent that the costs will be at the $5,000 per unit level; a 30 percent chance has been estimated that the costs could reach a unit cost of $7,000. The weighted average shows a unit cost of $5,600 which has been utilized in the cash-flow feasibility analysis. As noted, all elements, except cost of financing, have been treated as subject to variance (as random variables within established and realistic limits).

This kind of format permits several derivations that can then be evaluated based on the quantity and quality of information available. The discount rate used is pegged at the cost of capital (12 percent). All profit revenues flow through to indicate the present value of net cash flows. In the subject case, a potential profit of $140,553 is indicated. Based on an equity of $320,000, the indicated rate of return ($140,553/$320,000) is 44 percent, if the financial-market development model for the conversion performs as outlined.

Q. *A large-scale land development is under study involving nearly 500 acres of land. Based on in-depth market supply/demand studies, including absorption rates and land development costs, two net cash flows are postulated following about a year of site preparation. Cash flow "A" indicates a sell-out period of 7 years. Cash flow "B" indicates a sell-out period of 6 years if the developer will build a community recreational center at his own cost. Detailed estimates indicate the cost of the center to be $4,000,000.*

Year	*Cash Flow "A"*	*Cash Flow "B"*	*Cash Flow-Community Center*
1	−$500,000	−$ 580,000	−$ 10,000
2	620,000	720,000	− 15,000
3	630,000	860,000	− 30,000
4	700,000	1,700,000	40,000
5	725,000	1,900,000	60,000
6	810,000	1,300,000	85,000
7	600,000	—	100,000
8	—	—	120,000
9	—	—	150,000

The best judgment is that the community center recreational facilities will be worth $6,000,000 at the end of the ninth year, at which time the developer plans to sell them. At a discount rate of 10 percent, in the treatment of all net cash flows, what combination, if any, should be seriously considered?

A. To obtain a better perspective, all the cash flows should be discounted to present value at the indicated rate.

Cash flow "A"

Year	*Amount*	*Discount Factor*	*Present Value*
1	−$500,000	0.909	−$ 454,500
2	620,000	0.826	512,120
3	630,000	0.751	473,130
4	700,000	0.683	478,100
5	725,000	0.621	450,225
6	810,000	0.564	456,840
7	600,000	0.513	307,800
			$2,678,215

Cash flow "B"

Year	*Amount*	*Discount Factor*	*Present Value*
1	−$ 580,000	0.909	−$ 527,220
2	720,000	0.826	594,720
3	860,000	0.751	645,860
4	1,700,000	0.683	1,161,100
5	1,900,000	0.621	1,179,900
6	1,300,000	0.564	733,200
			$4,314,780

Cash flow community center

Year	Amount	Discount Factor	Present Value
1	−$ 10,000	0.909	−$ 9,090
2	− 15,000	0.826	− 12,390
3	− 30,000	0.751	− 22,530
4	40,000	0.683	27,320
5	60,000	0.621	37,260
6	85,000	0.564	47,940
7	100,000	0.513	51,300
8	120,000	0.467	56,040
9	150,000	0.424	63,600
		Net Present Value of Cash Flow:	$239,450

Present Value of Reversion:		
9 years @ 10% (0.424)		
$6,000,000 × 0.424 =		$2,544,000
Present Value of Cash Flow Plus Reversion:		$2,783,450
Net Benefit—Plan A	$2,678,215	
Net Benefit—Plan B	4,314,780	
Plus Present Value of Community Center	+2,783,450	
Total Benefit—Plan B	$7,098,230	
Less Community Center Cost	−4,000,000	
Total Net Benefit—Plan B	$3,098,230	

Difference between Plan A and Plan B:

$3,098,230	
2,678,215	
$ 420,015	(Excess benefit—Plan B over Plan A)

Q. *A national bank has foreclosed on an office building under construction in a central area of a medium-sized city. They are offering it to your client for $1,110,000 "as is" and will provide long-term financing immediately at closing. The bank has stated that the land cost*

$200,000 and that the building, when completed, would be worth $2,000,000. Their estimates indicate a cost of $500,000 to complete construction. The bank's numbers look like this:

Value on completion:	*$2,000,000.*
less land cost:	*200,000*
	1,800,000
less $500,000 for completion:	*500,000*
	$1,300,000
Extra discount:	*200,000*
	$1,100,000

A client asks you to evaluate this offer as she is seriously considering purchasing the building and undertaking completion of the construction. What do you advise?

A. You undertake and complete a detailed and in-depth market supply/demand analysis covering the next five to seven years and develop estimates of office space demand, competitiveness of the subject building when complete, and rental rate structures and services offered at various locations. From this you derive the following plausible estimates of cash flows. Considering the impact of current economic conditions, you believe a 12 percent discount rate is warranted in terms of risk of venture and the rate of the permanent financing.

Year	*Cash Flow*	*Discount*	*Present Value*
1	−$40,000	0.893	−$35,720
2	− 15,000	0.797	− 11,955
3	112,000	0.712	79,744

Assuming efficient completion of several of the floors in the first year, partial rentals can be achieved. However, the loss at the end of the year is estimated at $40,000. By the end of the fourth year, the building should achieve a 92 percent occupancy—or a vacancy rate of 8 percent. Permanent financing and the probable holding term by your client indicates an overall capitalization rate of 10.6 percent, thus indicating a value of the completed and occupied building of $2,136,849 by the end of the fourth year. Your other calculations indicate the following.

$2,136,849 × 0.636 (12 percent discount)	= $1,359,036
Net value of cash flows, first three years:	32,069
	$1,391,105
Less cost to complete, plus 10 percent for contingencies:	550,000
	$841,105
Less cost of leasing-up building:	16,000
	$825,105

You tell your client that she should pay a maximum of about $800,000 to $825,000 for the partially completed office building. The client seems confused; she indicates that the banks' numbers look realistic and she would like to have some additional explanation as she would not like to miss a good deal. In response you offer the following:

1. While the bank stated the value on completion was $2,000,000, what they probably meant was that the cost of land and building, when finished, would total this amount. Since cost and value are not always synonymous, the derived numbers indicate that, in reality, the building will have more value than its actual cost; but this situation is four years away.
2. Since there will be losses during the first two years due to lack of demand, and a less than optimum rent during the third year, someone has to absorb these losses. Obviously the losses must be reflected in the capital asset value.
3. Since the building will have a capital value of $2,136,849 at the end of the fourth year, all future values and intervening profits and losses must be discounted (time value of money) to the present time. From this discounted value are deducted the estimated present costs (completion of building and leasing-up) to be expended to achieve the capital value indicated.
4. The extra discount offered by the bank is not adequate in terms of what has yet to be done in the future to obtain a viable on-going investment property. A modest 10 percent additional discount of estimated completion costs was taken to cover unforeseen overruns.

Q. *An investor has been offered a property for $1,500,000 with a down payment of $300,000 with the balance in the form of a first mortgage at 9 percent interest (constant of 0.1007). You are given the factual and financial information as shown in Table A prepared by the client and his tax advisor. Questions posed to you are: What are the pre-tax* *and after-tax cash flows for each of the 5 years of the contemplated holding term assuming that the net annual income is sustained for each period? What will be the cash reversion value after taxes but before disposition (sales) costs? Also, is the purchase price fair based on the financial outlook for the property and the client's tax position?*

A. This problem involves a cash flow analysis for each of the 5 years as developed in Table B. The computer analysis indicates that with the outlined financial factors (mortgage, rate, term, equity yield, etc.), the maximum investment value of the property is $1,341,085, with an equity of $141,085 to provide a 12 percent equity yield. The after-tax cash flows plus the after-tax cash reversion (end of fifth year) discounted at 12 percent is equal to the initial equity investment.

Table A

Yield (on equity)	.12
Average Federal income tax bracket	.40
Proposed ownership term in years	5.00
Net property resale value, end of term	$1,300,000.00
1st mortgage ($ amt. or % of prop. value)	$1,200,000.00
1st mortgage annual interest rate (%)	.09
1st mortgage debt serv. (constant)	.1007
Year 1st mortgage starts	1.00
Asset #1 ($ amt. or % of prop. value)	$1,350,000.00
Asset #1 life in years	35.00
Asset #1 depreciation (% of straight line)	1.50
Year Asset #1 starts	1.00

Year	*Net Income Before Real Estate Taxes*
1	$128,571
2	129,000
3	130,000
4	130,000
5	132,000

Table B

Year	(1)	(2)	(3)	(4)	(5)
Mortgage interest	107,457	106,201	104,828	103,326	101,683
Book depreciation	57,857	55,378	53,004	50,733	48,558
Taxable income	−36,743	−32,579	−27,832	−24,059	−18,242
Income taxes	−14,697	−13,032	−11,133	−9,624	−7,297
Pre-Tax cash flow	7,731	8,160	9,160	9,160	11,160
After-Tax cash flow	22,428	21,192	20,293	18,784	18,457

Table C

Cash reversion before taxes	$180,704
Taxes on recaptured excess depreciation	29,069
Capital gain taxes	30,354
Tax preference taxes	1,823
Cash reversion after taxes	119,457

Q. *You are retained as a counselor to a large corporation with considerable real estate holdings. Early discussions indicate that they have a broad and flexible approach to problems and solutions. Single point answers are seldom used, as the company relies instead upon a series of plausible solutions to any problem at hand. Although the Ellwood analysis provides one method of depicting alternatives, you would like to do more. What are some options?*

A. One meaningful way to extend the Ellwood analysis is via simulation. The following can serve as an example using the familiar Ellwood equation:

$$R = (Y - mc) \frac{\text{depreciation} \cdot 1/S_n}{\text{appreciation} \cdot 1/S_n}$$

Assuming a 10-year holding period, a 9 percent, 25-year mortgage, and a desired 14 percent equity yield, the constant in the equation is 0.10385 (Y − mc). If the extent of appreciation or depreciation of the property at the end of ten years is highly uncertain, a simulation program (*** QIKSIM) can be undertaken. The program assumes a normal probability distribution of R (capitalization rate) with a mean of zero and a standard deviation of 0.02 (assumes a 40 percent appreciation/depreciation for each standard deviation). The simulation produces the following range of values based upon a net income stream of $200,000.

Mean (0.0977452)—$2,046,100
Max. Value (0.05711)— 3,502,000
Min. Value (0.14288)— 1,399,800

Table A shows the distribution of values and cumulative probabilities. A value of less than $2,384,800 has a probability of 75 percent (1 − 0.25), whereas a value of less than $1,853,200 has a probability of 30 percent (1 − 0.70). These capitalization rates and corresponding probabilities are plotted in Figure 1. The histogram, Figure 2, provides notions of the "most likely value" based on various capitalization rates. The highest three bars (16 + 16 + 15) indicate a 47

Table A

TABULAR SUMMARY OF Y=X1+.10385

	Y(I)	PROB. OF Y(I-1) TO Y(I)	CUMULATIVE PROBABILITY	INDICATED VALUE
1	6.55255E-2	.05	.05	$3,052,200
2	7.12535E-2	.05	.1	2,806,900
3	7.63414E-2	.05	.15	2,619,800
4	8.13431E-2	.05	.2	2,458,700
5	8.38628E-2	.05	.25	2,384,800
6	8.63196E-2	.05	.3	2,317,000
7	8.88838E-2	.05	.35	2,250,100
8	9.14628E-2	.05	.4	2,186,700
9	9.45315E-2	.05	.45	2,116,000
10	9.69346E-2	.05	.5	2,063,200
11	9.94594E-2	.05	.55	2,010,900
12	.103183	.05	.6	1,938,300
13	.104354	.05	.65	1,916,500
14	.107922	.05	.7	1,853.200
15	.111482	.05	.75	1,794,000
16	.112986	.05	.8	1,770,100
17	.118921	.05	.85	1,681.800
18	.121652	.05	.9	1,644,000
19	.131004	.05	.95	1,526,700
20	.14288	.05	1.	1,399,800

CUMULATIVE FREQUENCY PLOT OF Y = X1 + .10385

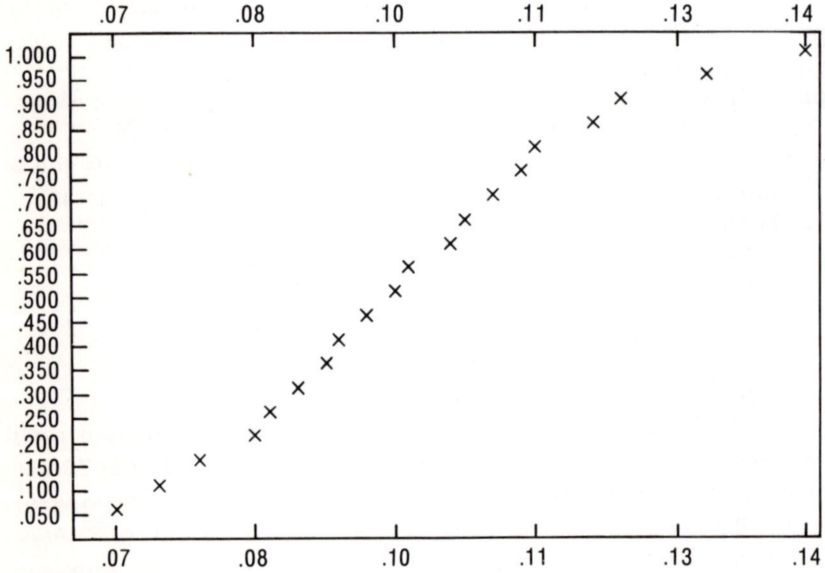

FIG. 1

HISTOGRAM OF Y=X1+.10385

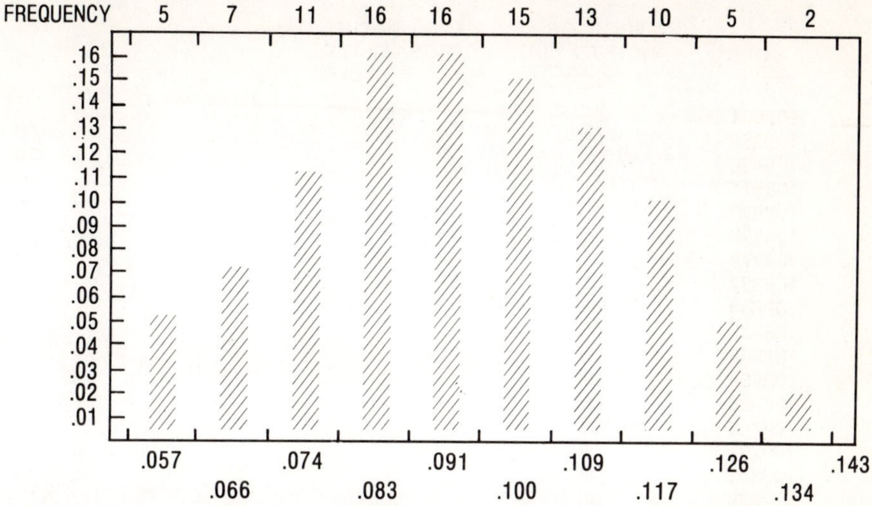

FIG. 2

percent chance (47/100) that the rate is between 0.083 and 0.108 or, in terms of value, between $1,851,800 and $2,409,600 with a mean value of $2,046,100.

If there is still considerable uncertainty, the analyst may want to take a more defensive or "downside position" via a simulation analysis. The $1/S_n$ factor is selected at 0.00517 for a depreciation of 10 percent and a standard deviation of 0.0005, which results in a mean capitilization rate of 0.108941 ($1,835,800), a minimum value of $1,819,100 (0.109944) and a maximum value of $1,852,300 (0.107974). The cumulative probability schedule is shown in Table B.

Based on these simulations and related outputs, a counselor should be able to provide a client with a series of scenarios concerning contemplated investments or divestments of real estate interests. Simulation does not provide answers to problems; what simulation really does is sharpen analysis and provide insight into a range of plausible probabilities, providing a much clearer picture of risk and capital value in real estate ventures.

Table B

TABULAR SUMMARY OF Y=X1+.10385

	Y(I)	PROB. OF Y(I-1) TO Y(I)	CUMULATIVE PROBABILITY
1	.107994	.05	.05
2	.108252	.05	.1
3	.108458	.05	.15
4	.108511	.05	.2
5	.108679	.05	.25
6	.108728	.05	.3
7	.108779	.05	.35
8	.108837	.05	.4
9	.108861	.05	.45
10	.108935	.05	.5
11	.108949	.05	.55
12	.108964	.05	.6
13	.108986	.05	.65
14	.109089	.05	.7
15	.10923	.05	.75
16	.109342	.05	.8
17	.109458	.05	.85
18	.109494	.05	.9
19	.109562	.05	.95
20	.109941	.05	1.

Q. *In the past several years I have read about seminars dealing with projections concerning land use, housing, retail sales, and so forth. Likewise, I have read about the need to forecast and the importance of turning points. Frankly, I'm confused and would like to know what methods to consider using.*

A. Suppose the following represents data from a small community whose retail trade area is, for simplicity's sake, assumed to be the SMSA.

Retail sales trends
(In millions)

Geographic Unit	*1965*	*1970*	*1975*
SMSA	$50	$62	$80
City	35	32	34
CBD	28	25	22

This data has been drawn on Figure 1. Two illustrations of projection (or trending) are shown by the dotted extension of line AB and HI. A trend-projection will not show a turning point (point F); rather it assumes that the future, including the future rate of change, will be like

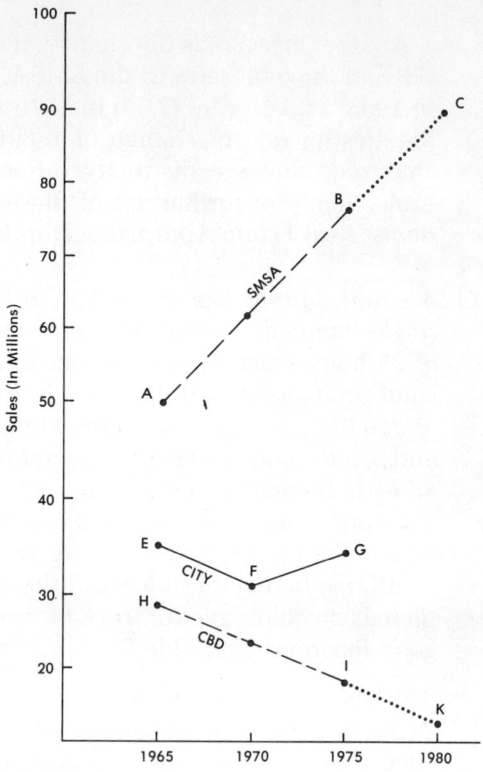

FIG. 1

the past. This projection assumes that in 1980 the SMSA total retail sales would reach $90,000,000 and sales in the CBD (central business district) of about $12,000,000. Such assumptions are questionable and would be hard to support.

A forecast, on the other hand, not only contemplates turning points but includes other dimensions of the problem, that is, factors, forces, and changes external to the retailing sector. These could include the location (near CBD, city, or outside the city) of new housing, the amount of land available and suitable for retailing functions, and recent new developments (food chains, fashion stores, etc.). The data in the above table could be further analyzed to suggest some of the following trends, shifts, and corresponding turning points.

CBD share of:	*SMSA*	*CITY*
1965	56%	80%
1970	38.5%	78.1%
1975	27.5%	64.7%

Rate of Change:	*1965–70*	*1970–75*
SMSA	24%	22.5%
City	− 8.6%	6.3%
CBD	−10.7%	−12.0%

Another measure is the change, if any, in the city's share (excluding CBD) of the total sales in the SMSA. This share was 20 percent (7/35) in 1965, 21.9 percent (7/32) in 1970, and 35.3 percent (12/34) in 1975. Manifestly, rate of change of relative shares, when computed and analyzed, shows a distinctly different picture than a simple trend projection. (For further use of these techniques, see Edwin M. Rams, *Rams' Real Estate Appraising Handbook*, Prentice-Hall, 1975).

Q. *A small builder has an option to buy a 100-acre tract suitable for single-family development. As the town is a modest size, construction of 25 houses per year would make him the biggest builder in town. Land productivity will be at 2.5 units per acre, yielding a retail value of $10,000 per acre. Development costs, including taxes, overhead, and profit come to 50 percent, leaving a residual value today of $5,000 an acre. He has an option to buy all or some of the land. Based on an absorption rate of 25 units (10 acres) per year, what is the maximum amount of land that the builder should buy if: (1) land prices have continued to remain stable and the outlook remains the same; and (2) there is an abundance of truck farming land, worth $2,500 per acre, in good locations available for conversion to urban use?*

A. The basic question concerns the amount of land inventory that should be maintained based on the facts and taking into consideration the time value of money. Assuming a 10-year sell-out for the subject parcel, the following analysis is developed using a 10 percent discount, which is considered competitive in light of the risks involved.

Year	*Residual Value*	*Discount Factor*	*Present Value*
1	$5,000	0.909	$4,545/A
2	5,000	0.826	4,130
3	5,000	0.751	3,755
4	5,000	0.683	3,415
5	5,000	0.621	3,105
6	5,000	0.564	2,820
7	5,000	0.513	2,565
8	5,000	0.467	2,335
9	5,000	0.424	2,120
10	5,000	0.386	1,930

The table shows that, at an absorption rate of 10 acres per year, 70 acres would have a present value greater than their value as farmland, if held until sold. The remaining 30 acres, if held for development, would have a present value less than their value as truck farm land.

Based on this analysis, the highest and best use of the subject site is for a 70-acre single-family development with the balance—30 acres—being used for a number of years as a small truck farm. Advice might include the following: buy only 70 acres unless the price can be negotiated downward on the 30 remaining acres, or buy the entire 100 acres and immediately lease the least desirable 30 acres (from a development/marketing standpoint) for truck farming use.

An alternate method for handling this kind of problem follows.

> Demand for farm real estate is a derived demand, generated by the demand for products produced on the land and future uses of the land. Consequently, farm real estate values differ between regions and over time, based on differences in product demand and land productivity as well as anticipated land use. However, substantial differences in perceived value also result from varying assumptions about the size and distribution of the future stream of annual returns from land, as well as from expected changes in land value. Additionally, attitudes of farmers and ranchers toward land ownership provide support for land values, at any given level of net returns to land. Finally, technological innovation and economies of scale that reduce per unit costs of production provide a powerful upward bias—at a farm firm level—to farm real estate values. As a consequence, different prospective purchasers may compute substantially different capitalized values for a given tract of land offered for sale.

TECHNICAL APPENDIX

The formula used to compute the present value of a stream of future income is:

(1) $$N = \frac{A_1}{(1 + r)^1} + \frac{A_2}{(1 + r)^2} + \ldots + \frac{A_n}{(1 + r)^n}$$

where:

V = present value
A = net return to land
r = interest rate used to discount future earnings
n = number of years over which returns are discounted.

When it can be assumed that the net returns to land remain constant over time, that the discounted rate does not change, and that a very long investment period is considered, the formula reduces to the familiar:

$$V = \frac{A}{r} \tag{2}$$

Though equation (2) is the more common formula, it is clearly not the appropriate one when net returns and land prices are changing. If a once and for all change occurs and returns are expected to continue at that new level in the future, the value of A can be adjusted to reflect this expectation. If, however, the value of A is expected to increase at a constant arithmetic rate, the formula becomes:

$$V = \frac{A}{r} + \frac{I}{r^2} \tag{3}$$

where I is the average expected annual increment of increased returns to land and A is the present average net return to land. It may, however, be more realistic to expect either an increase or decrease in the returns to land to continue for a specified number of years into the future. In that event, the formula becomes:

$$V = \frac{A}{r} + \frac{I_1}{(1 + r)^1} + \frac{I_2}{(1 + r)^2} + \ldots + \frac{I_n}{(1 + r)^n} \tag{4}$$

Here, I assumes a specific value for each year in question ($I_1, \ldots I_n$).

The capitalization formula could be further modified to account for an increase or decrease in the future value of the property itself, in the event the buyer intended to resell after a specified time period. The general form of the discounting formula

$$V = \sum_{t=1}^{n} \frac{A_t}{(1 + r)^t} + \frac{V_{o+n}}{(1 + r)^n} \tag{5}$$

can be modified. If the net rent is expected to change by S percent each year, the A_t term can be replaced by A_0 $(1 + S)_t$ where A_0 is the net rent at the beginning of year 1. Rents are assumed to be received at the end of the year. If the property value is increasing at a constant annual rate U, the term V_o can be replaced by $V_o(1 + U)^n$, where n is the number of years the property is held.

SOURCE: Monthly Review, Federal Reserve Bank of Kansas City, January, 1977.

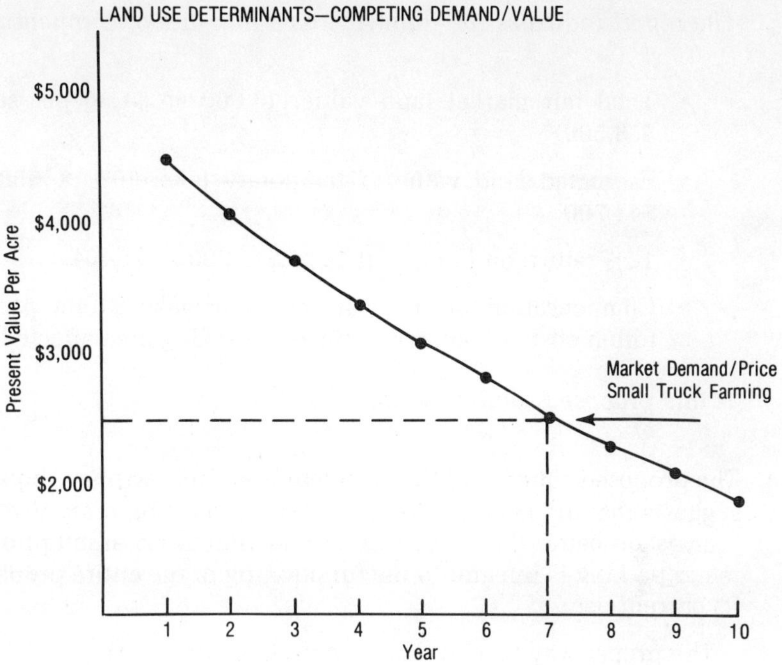

Q. *A local county, in concert with the state highway department, is widening several county and state roads. In this connection they are acquiring temporary rights-of-way over parts of a number of parcels. Your case of interest is a small shopping center. The temporary take is shown in the drawing; it affects 7 parking spaces out of a total of 20. The county has had appraisals made to establish compensation for the use of this land for a period of one year.*

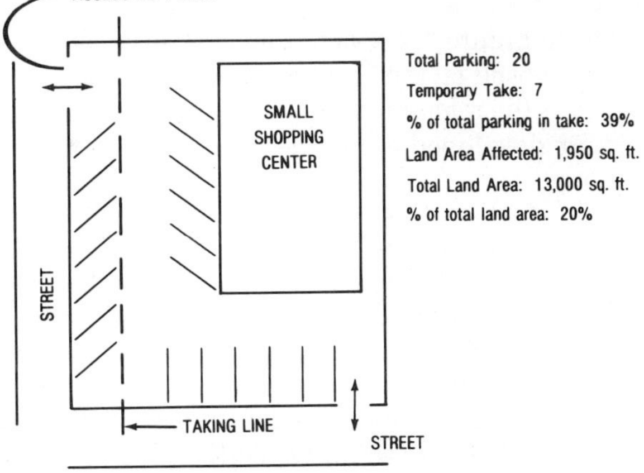

The report indicates the following as a measure of compensation:

- Total fair market land value: 13,000 @ $4.50 per sq. ft. = $58,500.
- Estimated land value of temporary take: 20% × $58,500 = $11,700.
- 12% return on land, or 0.12 × $11,700 = $1,404.
- Compensation for one year, temporary take: $1,400 plus restoration cost of blacktop surface in parking area affected.

Is this proposed solution valid?

A. The proposed solution of this problem is entirely wrong. The solution suggests that the land in question, subject to a temporary use for one year, is no better than a vacant site—a ridiculous assumption. Customer parking is integral to the functioning of the entire property, for its current use.

The proper way to treat damages from temporary take is to estimate the value of the entire property, then estimate the value during the temporary take. The difference, based on the period involved (one, two, or three years), will establish the value of the take, to which is added restoration cost, if any.

Q. *What are some basic valuation guidelines in partial taking cases involving condemnation of private property for public use?*

A. The following two illustrations outline the techniques and related considerations used in developing estimates of the amount of just compensation in partial taking cases.

In Figure 1, a 4-acre tract of vacant land is located on X Street. The proposed taking involves a rear triangular portion totalling 0.80 acres, thus the remainder or after amount of land is 3.2 acres. Value estimates are developed along the following lines.

- *Value Before Take*—Value of the entire 4.0 acre tract based on its highest and best use within zoning and deed restriction limitations (an exception might fall within the reasonable probability legal doctrine). Estimate of delineated specific use must be based on a market supply/demand study. Market transactions, properly analyzed, will aid in giving direction and substance to current present value based on demand for identified best and specified use.

- *Value After Take*—Value of the remainder of 3.2 acres based on its highest and specified best use; the specified use may be different than that of the before take value. However, whatever use is designated, it also must be based on a market analysis (supply/demand) study. Estimate of the amount of compensation is the difference between the value before and value after derivations.

  Value before: ________

  less value after: ________

  Equals value of the part taken (0.80 acres) including damage to the remainder, if any.

In Figure 2, the entire before tract totals 4.0 acres; the take is for a new connecting street to X street, the location of the subject vacant parcel of land. The areas are as follows: Before: 4.0 acres; After: Parcel 1—0.50 acres; Parcel 2—2.50 acres. Value estimates are developed along the following lines:

- *Value Before Take*—Value of the entire 4.0 acre tract of land based on its highest and best and specified use. Use selected must be predicated on a market supply/demand study. Market transactions are properly analyzed, considering supply/demand parameters, and estimate of value vacant site is derived.

- *Value After Take*—The specified highest and best use based on a market supply/demand study is outlined for parcels 1 and 2; in some cases the best use may be different from the original parcel. Based on delineated specific use(s) of both remainder

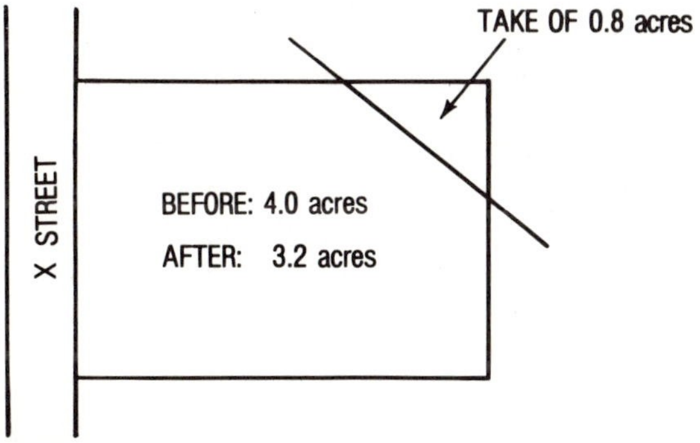

FIG. 1

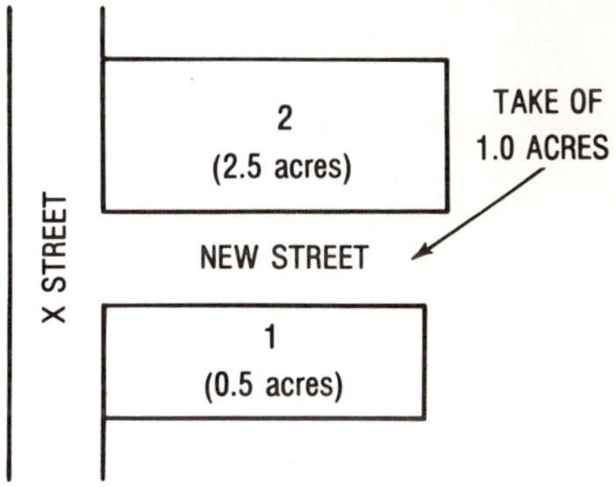

FIG. 2

parcels, market transaction evidence is synthesized with supply/demand findings to derive an estimate of value of each of the remainder parcels. The estimate of the amount of compensation is the difference between the before and after value derivations.

Value before: ________

less value after Parcel 1: ________

Parcel 2: ________

Equals value of part taken (1.0 acres) including damage to the remainders, if any, less any permitted offsetting of special benefits.

All market transactions used as supporting evidence of values before or after take must represent the same or similar specified highest and best use as that identified and delineated. For example, merely assigning "commercial" as the best use is neither meaningful nor satisfactory, even assuming the parcel is zoned "commercial." Instead, one must select, identify (specificity of use), and show market support for any one of 10 or 20 different uses permitted under a typical zoning code. Suppose an office building is selected as the best use based on an in-depth market supply/demand study showing adequate at-place demand within the next year or two. Then market transactions in the competitive market of the subject site for land with office building use as the highest and best use must be utilized in the estimation of the value of the subject site.

For example, in illustration B, the market supply/demand study might indicate the 4.0 acres before the take had a highest and best use for single-family development, while after the take parcel 1 was best for retail stores and parcel 2 was best for apartments. In this event, supporting market transactions must be obtained for these three different uses. All transactions, as noted earlier, must in fact represent the same highest and best use to properly merit comparison and application as an index of value of each of the three parcels (an "apples vs. apples" comparison).

Another point to remember is that any special benefits deriving from the take must be offset against any severance damage. In illustration B such special benefits might result from the creation of frontage along the new street. In some instances, such benefits may be offset against the value of the part taken. In this area of damages, legal counsel advice should be obtained to clearly outline the compensable and noncompensable elements.*

*For a more detailed discussion see Edwin M. Rams, "Markets, Market Value, and Just Compensation," *Valuation*, vol. 22 (October/November, 1975), American Society of Appraisers.

Q. *A client owns a valuable vacant downtown parcel that he intends to develop. Design, lease negotiations, settlement with several heirs having partial interests, and other matters will take about three years before actual ground breaking. Several proposals for off-street parking during the interim have been received and evaluated by the client and his tax advisor. After allowing for a 7 percent return on the estimated value of the site, the after-tax cash flows for each of three years from two final proposals have been calculated. Both are owner-tenant participation ventures, having no minimum rent. Some site preparation is required ($15,000). A judgment must be made as to the probability of achieving minimum and maximum after-tax cash flows based on each lease operator's experience in this kind of operation. You are asked to make an analysis and provide recommendations. Cost of capital is taken at 12 percent for this case.*

	Proposal X		*Proposal Y*	
Year	*After-Tax Flow*	*Probability*	*After-Tax Flow*	*Probability*
1	$4,500	0.45	$5,000	0.50
	6,000	0.55	5,800	0.50
2	6,200	0.70	6,500	0.40
	7,500	0.30	9,000	0.60
3	7,000	0.80	7,200	0.60
	10,000	0.20	12,000	0.40

A. This being essentially a joint venture for a short term, it involves a question of risk in terms of expenditures of money and most likely returns. There are several ways to evaluate risk on a comparative basis, between the two proposals, as outlined below. These include (1) a profitability index, which is a ratio of the present value of any net cash benefits to the present value of the net cash outlay; (2) standard deviation to estimate the extent of variation and dispersion of the anticipated cash flows; and (3) coefficient of variation to compare the degree of dispersion with the dollar value of the likely returns, relating the variance (standard deviation) with the probabilities of most likely cash flows. The probability estimates are integrated into the findings as illustrated. The technique provides a weighed-average basis for each of the indexes of risk; it also incorporates decision tree techniques (probabilities of alternate courses of action) with standard measures of risk.

I. PROFITABILITY INDEX COMPUTATION

A profitability index is computed for each year based on the expected value average based on probabilities, discounted at 12 percent.

Year	Proposal X	Proposal Y
1	($4,500)(0.893)(0.45) = $1,808	($5,000)(0.893)(0.50) = $2,232
	($6,000)(0.893)(0.55) = 2,947	($5,800)(0.893)(0.50) = 2,589
	$4,755	$4,821
2	($6,200)(0.797)(0.70) = 3,458	($6,500)(0.797)(0.40) = 2,072
	($7,500)(0.797)(0.30) = 1,793	($6,500)(0.797)(0.60) = 4,303
	$5,251	$6,375
3	($7,000)(0.712)(0.80) = 3,987	($7,200)(0.712)(0.60) = 3,075
	(10,000)(0.712)(0.20) = 1,424	(12,000)(0.712)(0.40) = 3,417
	$5,411	$6,492
Present Value:	$15,417	$17,688
Profitability Index:	$15,417/15,000 = 1.03	$17,688 / 15,000 = 1.18

II. TARGET VALUE COMPUTATIONS

Year	Proposal X	Proposal Y
1	($4,500)(0.45) + ($6,000)(0.55) = $5,325	($5,000)(0.50) + ($5,800)(0.50) = $5,400
2	(6,200)(0.70) + (7,500)(0.30) = 6,590	(6,500)(0.40) + (9,000)(0.60) = 8,000
3	(7,000)(0.80) + (10,000)(0.20) = 7,600	(7,200)(0.60) + (12,000)(0.40) = 9,120

III. STANDARD DEVIATION COMPUTATIONS

Year	Proposal X	Proposal Y
1	$\sigma^2 = (4{,}500 - 5{,}325)^2 (0.45) + (6{,}000 - 5{,}325)^2 (0.55)$	$\sigma^2 = (5{,}000 - 5{,}400)^2 (0.50) + (5{,}800 - 5{,}400)^2 (0.50)$
	$\sigma = \sqrt{309{,}374} = 556$	$\sigma = \sqrt{160{,}000} = 400$
2	$\sigma^2 = (6{,}200 - 6{,}590)^2 (0.70) + (7{,}500 - 6{,}590)^2 (0.30)$	$\sigma^2 = (6{,}500 - 8{,}000)^2 (0.40) + (9{,}000 - 8{,}000)^2 (0.60)$
	$\sigma = \sqrt{354{,}950} = 595$	$\sigma = \sqrt{1{,}500{,}000} = 1{,}224$
3	$\sigma^2 = (7{,}000 - 7{,}600)^2 (0.80) + (10{,}000 - 7{,}600)^2 (0.20)$	$\sigma^2 = (7{,}200 - 9{,}120)^2 (0.60) + (12{,}000 - 9{,}120)^2 (0.40)$
	$\sigma = 1{,}440{,}000 = 1{,}200$	$\sigma = 5{,}529{,}600 = 2{,}351$

IV. STANDARD DEVIATION FOR EACH PROPOSAL

$$\sigma_x = \frac{556 + 595 + 1{,}200}{3} = 783 \qquad \sigma_y = \frac{400 + 1{,}224 + 2{,}351}{3} = 1{,}325$$

(e) *Coefficient of Variation Computation*

$$R = \frac{5{,}325 + 6{,}590 + 7{,}600}{3} = 6{,}505 \qquad R = \frac{5{,}400 + 8{,}000 + 9{,}120}{3} = 7{,}506$$

$$V = \sigma_x / R = 783/6{,}505 = 0.12 \qquad V = \sigma_y / R = 1{,}325/7{,}506 = 0.18$$

Summary of analysis indicates that:

1. Profitability Index: Project X : 1.03
   Project Y : 1.18
2. Standard Deviation: Project X : 783
   Project Y : 1325
3. Coefficient of variation: Project X : 0.12
   Project Y : 0.18

While project Y has a higher profitability index, it also indicates a greater vulnerability and uncertainty in the cash flows. If management tends to be risk-averse, the best bet is likely to be project X, which is still profitable based on the PI.

Q. *As neighborhoods appear to be changing much more than they did several decades ago, what methods can be used to evaluate such changes at the census tract unit level of measurement?*

A. The following two examples demonstrate the use of such methods:

1. Suppose an analyst wants to compare the racial or ethnic diversity of census tracts X and Y. The composition of each, at the nominal level of data, is as follows:

Kind of Residents	*Tract X*	*Tract Y*
White	30	40
Oriental	12	10
Mexican	8	10
	50	60

An Index of Qualitative Variation (IQV) as shown below can be computed for each tract to indicate "within tract variation" with the index indicating the extent of diversity.

$$\text{IQV} = \frac{\Sigma n_i\, n_j}{\frac{k(k-1)}{2}(N/k)^2}$$

$$\text{(Tract X) IQV} = \frac{(30 \times 12) + (30 \times 8) + (12 \times 8)}{\frac{3(3-1)}{2}\quad (50/3)^2} = 0.84$$

$$\text{(Tract Y) IQV} = \frac{(40 \times 10) + (40 \times 10) + (10 \times 10)}{\frac{3(3-1)}{2}\quad (60/3)^2} = 0.75$$

Based on these derivations, the findings indicate that there is less diversity in tract Y than in tract X. The closer the index (which is always less than unity) is to zero, the less diversity prevails, and vice-versa.

2. Another readily usable and rather simple computation is the coefficient of variation (CV) for the standard deviation. The relationship is

$$\text{CV} = (\text{S.D.}/\overline{X}) \times 100$$

Where: S.D. is the standard deviation and the $\overline{X}$ the mean.

Interval level data is necessary for the use of this measure of relative dispersion. As before, the index is between zero and unity, and the closer to zero, the less dispersion is in evidence, and vice versa. For example, the value of owner-occupied houses in two census tracts may be analyzed; if the CV is 0.48 in one and 0.64 in another, the values have less dispersion in the former and more in the latter.

NOTE: The usual formula is used to compute the S.D. for a derivation of CV.

Q. *What are some of the "economics of industrial land development"?*

A. This is a very complex subject. Several insights from a recent analysis may provide some guidance in this area of land utilization and development. A study by the Economic Development Administration of three distinct areas (development costs/park size, aspects of age and rate of utilization, and locational attributes based on proximity to an SMSA and county population) provides some interesting information. A total of 53 industrial parks were analyzed based on a stratified sample (based on park size).

As noted in Table A, the optimum (least cost per acre) sized industrial park is one with 100 to 150 acres, on both a gross and net usable acreage basis.

Table A
Cost measures by park size

Developed Acres	*Total Cost Per Developed Acre*	*Total Cost Per Job Provided*	*Total Cost Per Occupied Acre*
50	$18,520	$2,241	$26,834
51–100	$11,908	$2,114	$19,964
101–150	$ 4,787	$1,833	$ 9,323
151–300	$ 5,888	$1,828	$12,632
300+	$ 5,335	$5,145	$38,160

For the period 1971–74, of the 53 parks studied, the best performing, in terms of rate of utilization, were parks of 100–150 acres; those with 300 or more acres had the least attractive absorption rate. These net changes based on size of park, including their failure rate, are outlined in Table B.

Because land in an industrial park is a product being offered in a generally competitive spatially-dimensioned framework, the extent of attraction of buyers/lessees and users is related to the time function. As noted in Figure 1, the longer the time period since initial development, the more likely it is that utilization has progressed beyond what might be called the "pioneer stage." As Table C shows, when age of the parks is used along with size differentials, parks with 50 acres demonstrate considerable viability in contrast to those with the optimum 100–150 acres, heretofore discussed. This may in part be attributed to location, identity, and/or parcelization.

Table B

Performance measures by park size

(averages)

Developed Acres	Utilization 1971	Utilization 1974	Percent Change 1971–74	Employment 1971	Employment 1974	Percent Change 1971–74	Number Of Firms 1971	Number Of Firms 1974	Percent Change 1971–74	Failure Rate 1971	Failure Rate 1974
50	42%	66%	57%	78	213	173%	1.3	3.0	131%	35%	15%
51–100	36%	52%	44%	193	327	69%	1.3	2.6	100%	36%	18%
100–150	25%	52%	108%	165	355	115%	3.1	4.6	48%	0	0
150–300	39%	47%	21%	481	748	56%	2.8	5.0	79%	0	0
300+	23%	23%	0	440	1,079	145%	4.4	8.0	82%	0	0

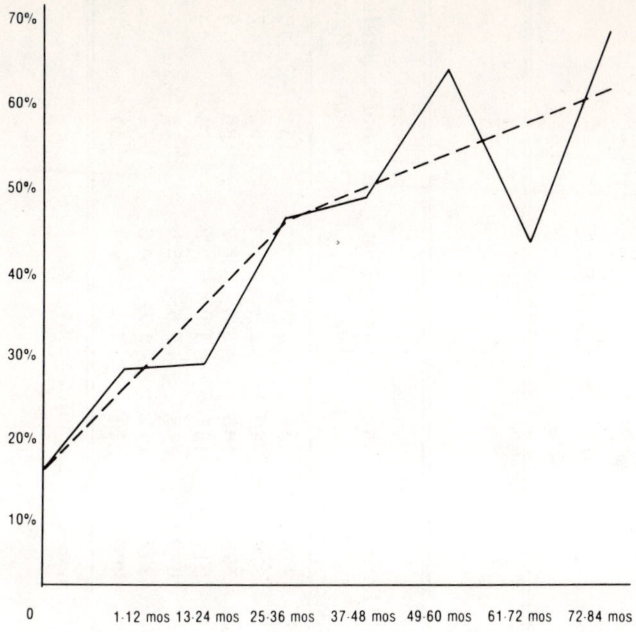

FIG. 1. Park utilization vs. age.

Table C
Park utilization and age

	Number of Months in Operation	
Acres	More Than Average (% Utilization)	Less Than Average (% Utilization)
50	68	65
51–100	35	73
100–150	52	52
150	28	36

Finally, the EDA study concluded that an initial "proximity hypothesis" was valid, that is, the "success" of industrial parks decreases as the distance to the nearest SMSA increases. Success is inversely related to distance from an SMSA up to about 100 miles. Parks located more than this distance from an SMSA appear to reverse the downward trend and are rated as successful. This appears to be attributable to different market orientations and perhaps represents a threshold point where product markets/materials/distribution resources of an SMSA are negligible. The data outlined in Table E,

Table D

Performance of industrial parks by distance to nearest SMSA

	Developed Acres 1974	Average % Utilization 1971	Average % Utilization 1974 (% Change 1971–74)	Employment 1971	Employment 1974 (% Change 1971–74)	Firms 1971	Firms 1974 (% Change 1971–74)	"Failure Rate"
In SMSA	139	40	51 (28%)	254	635 (150%)	3.0	5.4 (80%)	7%
In ADJ County	115	29	50 (72%)	156	313 (101%)	1.9	3.4 (79%)	11%
Up To 50 Miles	116	34	67 (97%)	201	397 (98%)	1.3	3.7 (185%)	0%
51–99 Miles	174	35	44 (26%)	227	403 (78%)	2.1	3.6 (71%)	20%
100+ Miles	65	37	67 (81%)	101	240 (138%)	2.0	4.0 (100%)	0%

Table E

Park characteristics by county population

County Population	Developed Acres	Utilization Rate 1971	Utilization Rate 1974	% Change in Utilization	Employ 1971	Employ 1974	% Change in Utilization	Firms 1971	Firms 1974	% Change In Number Of Firms	Failure Rate
<25K	112	27	60	122	145	339	134	1.6	3.7	131	16%
25–50K	91	38	55	45	196	276	40	2.1	3.4	62	7%
50–75K	318	13	34	162	202	578	186	3.3	6.2	88	0%
75–100K	125	23	37	61	134	211	157	1.9	3.3	74	14%
>100K(a)	110	42	47	12	359	879	145	2.6	5.6	115	
(b)	52	36	44	22	158	333	111	1.7	4.6	171	
(c)	54	39	40	03	163	206	26	3.3	4.3	30	13%

a) 8 parks b) Rancho Bernardo I.P. (San Diego Co., CA) deleted c) Rancho Bernardo and Lynwood, CA (Los Angeles) deleted relating county population and rate of utilization presents a mixed picture. No doubt other factors modified and contributed to either a rapid or a slow rate of absorption-utilization.

SOURCE: *An Updated Evaluation of EDA-Funded Industrial Parks 1968–1974*, Economic Development Administration, June, 1974.

Q. *In structuring a real estate tax shelter situation, what are some of the advantages of a limited partnership over that of a corporate form of operation?*

A. The form of entity most commonly chosen to maximize tax benefits in a tax shelter investment has been the limited partnership, which, upon meeting certain requirements, is subject to the partnership rules of the Internal Revenue Code. In general, a partnership is not considered a separate entity for tax purposes; rather the individual partners are taxed currently on their share of the partnership gains and can deduct partnership losses to the extent of the basis of their partnership interest.

When an investor enters a partnerhsip, his basis in the partnership generally includes the amount he invested and his share, if any, of the partnership liabilities. In this regard, the income tax regulations (Regs. § 1.752-1(e)) provide that a limited partner may include in the basis of his partnership interest his share of the nonrecourse loans to the partnership even though he is not personally liable on the debt. (Such loans usually are secured only by the partnership property.) Nonrecourse financing facilitates the use of limited partnerships for tax shelter investments because the investor is able to limit his liability to the amount he has actually invested but use nonrecourse loans obtained by the partnership to substantially increase his basis and thus increase his tax deductions.

More specifically, these general principles apply to limited partnerships in tax shelter investments.

1. The limited partnership is not a taxpaying entity, but instead is a tax conduit, the partners reporting their distributive shares of partnership income or loss.

2. Subject to the restriction that its purpose not be to avoid or evade tax, a limited partnership agreement may provide for the manner in which the partnership's items of income, gain, loss, deduction or credit will be allocated among the partners.

3. The amount of losses which a partner may deduct for a particular year is limited to the amount of the adjusted basis of

> his partnership interest as of the end of the year. At the inception of a partnership, the adjusted basis of the partner's partnership interest equals the sum of his capital contribution to the partnership plus his share, if any, of partnership liabilities. In the case of a limited partnership, a limited partner's share of the partnership liabilities is his pro rata share (the same proportion in which he shares profits) of all liabilities with respect to which there is no personal liability ("nonrecourse liability"). This rule, where a limited partner's adjusted basis in his partnership interest is increased by a pro rata amount of nonrecourse liability, is one of the cornerstones of tax shelter investments, allowing the investor, in many cases, to currently deduct amounts in excess of his actual investment.

The limited partnership is generally preferred over the general partnership because the limited partners, who are passive investors in most cases, have limited liability for the debts of or claims against the partnership.

The corporate form of doing business generally does not lend itself to tax shelter investments by individuals since the corporation is the taxpaying entity and, therefore, the tax incidents of its operation remain at the corporate level and do not pass through to its shareholders. The one exception to this treatment is for Subchapter S corporations. To a great extent, the tax incidents of a Subchapter S corporation's operations pass through to its shareholders. However, there are certain tax limitations applicable to the Subchapter S corporation (and to its shareholders) which are not imposed upon a limited partnership under the partnership provisions. These limitations generally make Subchapter S corporations less attractive as a vehicle for tax shelter investments.

As previously noted, one of the principal tax shelter benefits obtained under the partnership tax provisions is that the adjusted basis of an individual partner in his partnership interest not only includes his cash investment but also a pro rata share of any nonrecourse liability of the partnership. By contrast, the adjusted basis of the shareholders of a Subchapter S corporation in their stock includes their investment in the stock and any loans they may have made to the corporation, but, most significantly, does not include any portion of the corporation's liabilities. In both cases, that of the Subchapter S corporation shareholder and the limited partner, it is the adjusted basis in partnership interest or stock, as the case may be, which serves as the upper limit on the amount of loss that may be deducted by the shareholder (partner) in a given year. Thus, in comparison to the limited partner, the Subchapter S corporation shareholder is severely limited in terms of the amount of losses, and therefore tax shelter, available.

Other limitations which apply only to Subchapter S corporations are: (1) A Subchapter S corporation may not have more than ten shareholders; (2) Trusts may not be shareholders of a Subchapter S corporation; (3) A Subchapter S corporation may not have two or more classes of stock; (4) No more than 20 percent of a Subchapter S corporation's gross receipts may be derived from passive investment income, which includes, among other things, certain types of rental income; (5) No provision may be made for special allocation of losses and other items to the shareholders, these items being allocated strictly in proportion to stock ownership. (Tax treatment of some items changed by Tax Reform Act of 1976, Public Law 94-455.)

SOURCE: *Tax Shelter Investments*, Joint Committee on Internal Revenue Taxation, April 14, 1976, Washington, D.C.

Q. *What is a reliable and acceptable format that can be used as an alternative to a detailed Land Development (simulation) Analysis for estimating the value of vacant acreage for its highest and best use?*

A. The new "Vacant Land Value Parity Analysis," employing the semantic differential technique, provides a plausible basis for analyzing "comparable sales" that serve as an index of value of vacant or de-facto vacant land. De-facto vacant land is a site with current dysfunctional improvements that are not consistent with a site's highest and best use. The following elements highlight the parity analysis format.

1. Recognition of dysfunctional improvements for highest and best use—This precludes confusion between current use and best use and also provides an adjustment for demolition of existing improvements.
2. Qualitative evaluation profile of seventeen property attributes in direct comparison to subject property.
3. Maximum lump sum adjustment of plus and minus 30 percent of a comparable-to-the-subject site under study (Item A under Valuation Analysis).
4. Parity (cost) adjustment for tie-in of sewer/water (if applicable).
5. Adjustment of comparables to cash basis (if appropriate) or terms to subject site.
6. Specificity of use, in contrast to meaningless statements like "residential" or "commercial," concerning highest and best use.

7. Time adjustment treated separately (Item B) to target and indicate value trends to specific highest and best use, i.e., gas station site, shopping center land, etc.

8. Demand for specific use—market entry (Item C) to interface with subject site. Deferred conversion can be due to rezoning (additional cost adjustment element), market conditions, or growth policy at the local level. This last point can be illustrated in the case of the Minneapolis–St. Paul Metro Area wherein a "Developing Ring" and "Outlying Area" have been identified; future growth till 1990 in urban service areas. Essentially a moratorium on sewer-water, which directs growth in some areas and precludes development in other areas—thus impacting on present value of land for its highest and best use.

SOURCE: Development Framework, Metropolitan Council, St. Paul, Minn. September, 1975.

Vacant Land Value Parity Analysis

Sale 3 Location/Address 26 PINE STREET Dysfunctional Improvements: Yes ✓ No

Highest & Best Use (i.e. Walk-up apts., Hi-Rise, Gas Station, etc.) SINGLE FAMILY

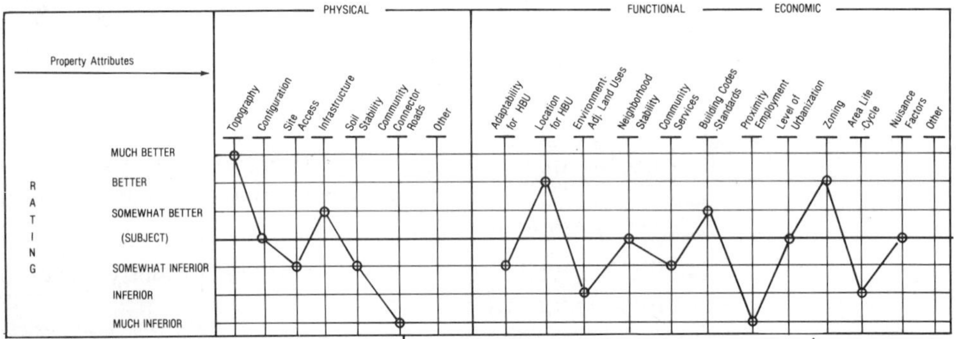

TRANSACTION DATA

Date of Sale 2/1/75

PropertySize 10 ACRES

Zoning SINGLE FAMILY

Grantor R. JONES

Grantee K. C. M. BROWN

Price $38,000

Terms CASH

Adjusted Price for Terms —

Demand HBU Time of Sale: Similar ✓ Different

Legal/Physical Development Potential (No. apts., Gross Leasable area, houses/acre) MAXIMUM 2.5 UNITS/ACRE

Water ✓ Sewer Electricity ✓ Gas ✓ Street paved ✓ Not paved

Proximity of schools, churches, shopping fire/police protection, etc.

HBU: Allowed ✓ Need Rezoning Revision Deed Restrictions

VALUATION ANALYSIS

A. Parity Adjustment
Estimated Value Per Physical/Functional/Economic Attributes 30,000
Loss Removal Costs of Dysfunctional Improvements 1,000
Less Infrastructure Access Cost(200 ft.(if applicable) 1,000
Net Total: (a) 28,000

B. Time Adjustment
(a) 28,000 x 1.03% = $28,850 (b)

C. Market Entry Adjstment
Forecast Conversion/Utilization 2 yrs. (Growth Policy Market) ✓
Discount/Holding Costs(12%): .797 x 28,850 (b) = 22,993

PRESENT VALUE PARITY INDEX: $23,000

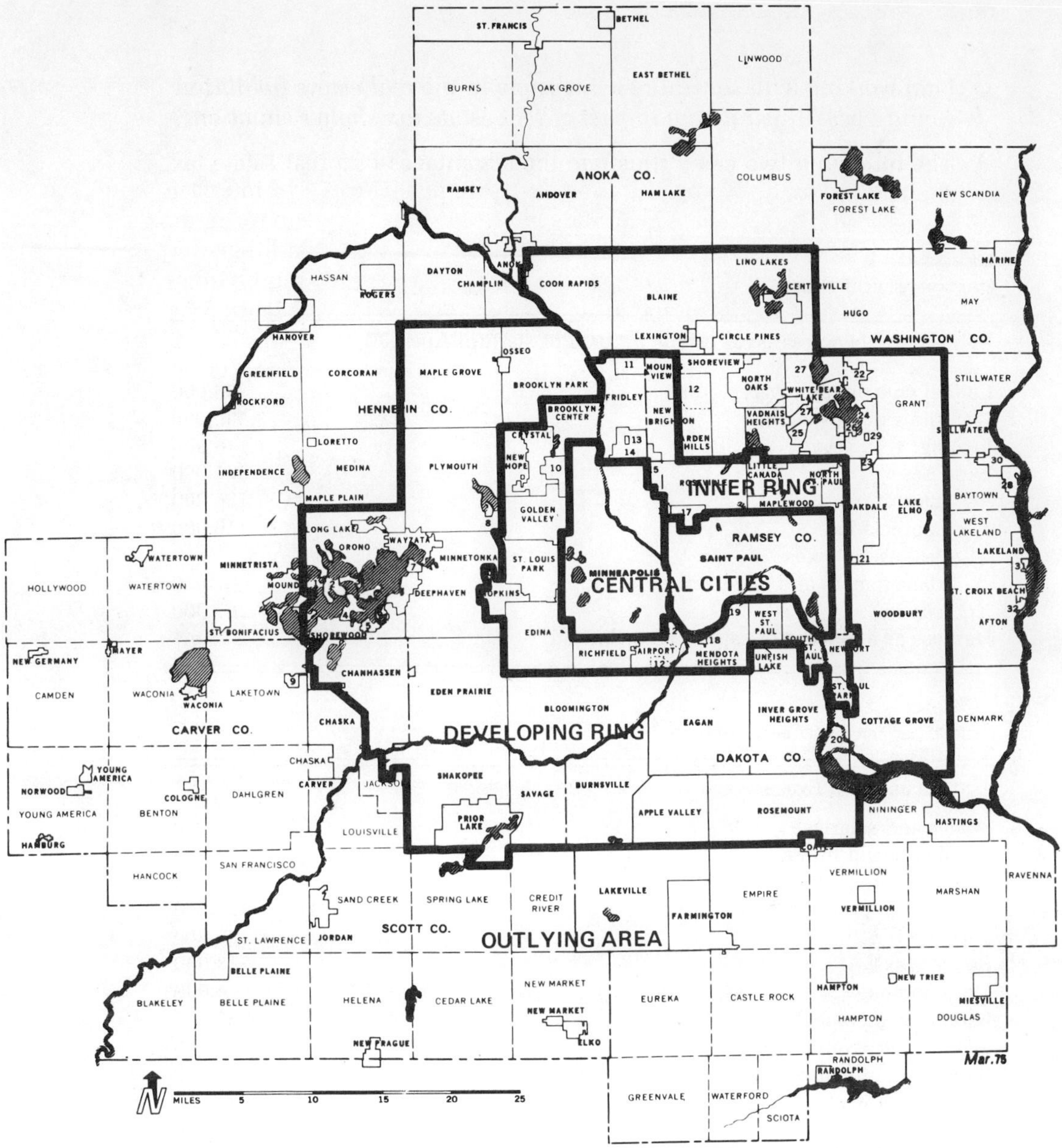

FORECAST RINGS

1 SPRING PARK
2 ORONO
3 MINNETONKA BEACH
4 TONKA BAY
5 EXCELSIOR
6 GREENWOOD
7 WOODLAND
8 MEDICINE LAKE
9 VICTORIA
10 ROBBINSDALE
11 SPRING LAKE PARK
12 U. S. GOVT.
13 HILLTOP
14 COLUMBIA HEIGHTS
15 ST. ANTHONY
16 LAUDERDALE
17 FALCON HEIGHTS
18 MENDOTA
19 LILYDALE
20 GREY CLOUD
21 LANDFALL
22 DELLWOOD
23 PINE SPRINGS
24 MAHTOMEDI
25 GEM LAKE
26 BIRCHWOOD
27 WHITE BEAR
28 BAYPORT
29 WILLERNIE
30 OAK PARK HEIGHTS
31 LAKELAND SHORES
32 ST. MARY'S POINT

ANOKA — County Boundary
ORONO — Municipal Boundary
CAMDEN — Township Boundary

Q. *I am working with several new investors in the real estate field. How would I best illustrate the impact of real estate tax shelter situations?*

A. The following two cases illustrate the advantages of a real estate tax shelter:

Case No. 1

Partnership return

Type of business: Real estate	Date of startup: April 30
Capital contributed by partners	53,000
Liabilities of partnership	3,420,000
Income	118,000
Expenses	321,000
Interest	186,000
Depreciation	116,000
Real estate taxes	0
Management and syndication fees	0
Net loss	203,000
Net loss as a percent of capital contribution	383.0%

Individual income tax return

Occupation: Executive	
Wages and salaries	100,000
Dividends and interest	51,000
Capital gains (100%)	0
Partnership profit and loss: Real estate	−127,000
Farming income	97,000
Rental loss	−13,000
Other income	4,000
Economic income	252,000
Adjusted gross income	112,000
Itemized deductions	35,000
Taxable income	74,000
Income tax	30,000
Minimum tax	0
Tax credits	0
Total tax after credits	30,000
Tax as a percent of economic income	11.9%

Analysis

This partnership, which is building and operating a store, is highly leveraged. Partners contributed capital of $53,000 to finance assets of

$3,280,000. In the first year, the partnership threw off a loss of $203,000, almost four times the investment by the partners. Deductions were for interest $186,000, amortization of the financing fee $19,000, and depreciation $116,000.

The executive who invested in this store had a large salary, dividends and interest and also had sizable income from a farm. The farm income consisted of a profit on the sale of cattle and feed grain. This executive used the 50-percent maximum tax method to compute his income tax.

Case No. 2

Partnership return

Type of business: Real estate
Date: Second year of operation

Capital contributed by partners	[1]
Liabilities of partnership	1,968,000
Income	102,000
Expenses	303,000
Interest	121,000
Depreciation	104,000
Real estate taxes	0
Management and syndication fees	13,000
Net loss	201,000
Net loss as a percent of capital contribution	[1]

[1]Not available.

Individual income tax return

Occupation: Businessperson

Wages and salaries	62,000
Dividends and interest	4,000
Capital gains (100%)	1,000
Partnership profit and loss: Real estate	−14,000
Other income	3,000
Economic income	70,000
Adjusted gross income	57,000
Itemized deductions	7,000
Taxable income	47,000
Income tax	15,000
Minimum tax	0
Tax credits	0
Total tax after credits	15,000
Tax as a percent of economic income	21.4%

Analysis

This real estate partnership, in its second year of operation, owns a building which cost $1,551,000 and land costing $170,000. Total assets of $1,662,000 are offset by $1,968,000 of liabilities. In the first year of operation, the partners deducted $56,000 more than their investments. In the current year, the partners were able to deduct losses of $201,000. The principal deductions were for construction and financing fees $121,000 and depreciation $104,000.

The investor in this tax shelter had wages and salaries of $62,000 and additional income of $8,000. He used the real estate partnership to shelter $14,000 of income. See any pertinent changes or modifications in the Tax Reform Act of 1976, Public Law 94-455.

SOURCE: *Tax Shelter Investments: Analysis of 37 Individual Income Tax Returns, 24 Partnership and 3 Small Business Corporation Returns*, Committee on Ways and Means, Sept. 3, 1975.

Q. *What is an acceptable format to follow in cases where a client is anticipating the purchase of an investment property and contemplates extensive rehabilitation and/or modernization?*

A. The following outline provides for: (I) recognition of net cash inflows derived from the property during the rehabilitation, (II) cash outflows in the form of capital improvements that represent the rehabilitation and/or modification of the property for its highest and best use, and (III) recognition of the value of the rehabilitated property at some future date, discounted to the present. Resolution of present values, i.e., net cash flows, capital improvements over time, and after rehabilitation capital value, suggests the "as is" present value, subject to the outlined future program of property utilization.

Central to this technique is the proper recognition of the time value of money and the provision for differential discount rates to reflect the relative risk(s) of the components of the investment model.

Investment property acquisition—Rehabilitation analysis

I. Cash Inflows				II. Cash Outflows			
Year	*(1)*	*(2)*	*(3)*	*Year*	*(1)*	*(2)*	*(3)*
Gross Income	____	____	____	Capital Improvements			
Expenses	____	____	____	XXXXX	____	____	____
NET CASH FLOW	____	____	____	YYYYY	____	____	____
Discount Factors	____	____	____	TOTALS:	____	____	____
PRESENT VALUES	____	____	____	Discount Factors	____	____	____
TOTAL (A):	____			PRESENT VALUES	____	____	____
				TOTAL (B):	____		

continued

Investment property acquisition—Rehabilitation analysis (cont.)

III. Capital Value Analysis

1. Capital Value After Rehabilitation: Net Cash Flow / Cap Rate Value in Year ____
   ________ / ________ = ____________(1)
2. PRESENT VALUE: Year______(Discount Rate ______);Factor______×______(1)=LL
   PRESENT VALUE (C):________________________________
3. MAXIMUM WARRANTED "AS IS" PRICE BASED ON IDENTIFIED AND PROGRAMMED HIGHEST AND BEST USE:
   PRESENT VALUE (C) + PRESENT VALUE (A) − PRESENT VALUE (B) = ________

Q. *What methods can be used to measure mortgage risk on real estate investment type properties from an investor's, consumer's, or interested third party's vantage point?*

A. The placing of a mortgage by a financial institution on an investment-type property is basically an investment decision—frequently a long-term proposition. The mortgagee looks to the property, by kind, location, environment, tenancy, rentals, operating expenses, present and future competition from similar facilities, and so forth. Three key variables in the mortgage investment equation are interest rate, payout term, and principal amount of money to be invested (usually a ratio to market value established by law and/or investment policies of a financial institution). These three factors, when resolved, represent the annual debt service that the property is expected to support. A variation of these factors is the mortgage constant, that is, the annual debt service divided by the original amount of the mortgage. The constant indicates the share to be claimed by the mortgage obligation of the total revenues generated by the property. Various mortgages and related constants are essentially perceptions and evaluations of mortgage risk on various kinds of properties; these are generated by financial institutions active in the mortgage investment market.

Suppose two similar investment properties have recently been financed, one (A) at 9 percent—10 years with a constant of 0.1521, and the other (B) at 9 percent, 20 years—with a constant of 0.1008. Taking the ratio of the constants (the smaller is always the numerator), 0.1008/0.1521 = 0.663, which, when deducted from 1.00 equals 0.337 or 33.7 percent higher rate (risk) of income allocation and claim. Implicitly, property A has a higher risk for many reasons—these could include, among other things, condition, design, trend of area, location, and so on. The tables in the Appendix (Rams' Mortgage Risk Tables), provide a series of risk factors, derived as noted, in ¼ percent increments, for a broad spectrum of constants. This can be used as a means for a quick evaluation of comparative mortgage risk. One simply selects that constant nearest the actual computed constant and obtains the related risk factor. For the illustrated case, in the RMR tables, one would choose 0.1000 (use top row of table for numerator of ratios used for analysis) and 0.1525 in the column; the table indicates a risk factor of 0.344, the error being 0.21 percent, because the nearest third and fourth place numbers are used from the precomputed tables.

Another case might involve X property with a recently placed mortgage for 9½ percent for 25 years (0.1049 constant) as compared to Y property at 10 percent for 15 years (0.1290 constant). Query: What is the implied risk on property Y in comparison to property X? From the RMR tables, the top row choice is 0.1050 and the column choice is 0.1300, with a risk factor of 0.192, or 19.2 percent, perceived and evaluated higher risk for property Y in comparison to property X. Several other adaptations and uses of the RMR tables are illustrated in Figure 1. Panel A involves similar properties over time. Deriving the slope of the line (via least squares) indicates the direction of risk over time. Panel B shows a comparative analysis of three areas/neighborhoods involving similar investment properties, and, as before, the slope (level, positive, or negative) of the lines suggests the direction of risk attendant to the properties under study. Panel C illustrates a further application on a within-neighborhood study involving older and newer competitive properties on a time-dimension basis.

Mortgage investments are economic transactions (events) that continue to occur over time and collectively shape and formulate investor attitudes and other real estate market participants—thus directly and indirectly contributing to a trend (see Cross–Impact Analysis regarding interaction of events and trends and so forth). This, in turn, becomes part of the fabric of the perceptions/expectations matrix of the thinking, actions, and reactions of the real estate investment community. While the outlined method does not represent any finality of measurement nor account for all global inputs concerning real estate investment risk, it does provide a means for some scale of measurement via readily available and accessible market measures of attitudes, perceptions, and related activities.

Another potential use of the RMR tables and related conceptual framework could include before and after analysis of flow of mortgage funds based on public sector inputs—neighborhood conservation, urban renewal, or the impact of some large-scale public-private developments (park, shopping center, water resource development, major roadway, bridge, subway, and so on). For it is axiomatic that the equity requirements/mortgage constant matrix is crucial to provide private sector involvement and participation. As a possible adjunct to a benefit/cost study, use of the mortgage risk factor methodology might provide some insight into measures of overall project risk in evaluating planned public sector activities and related investments. Used in conjunction with cross-impact analysis, it might serve as an important foundation via a series of scenarios on future growth and development of sectors of urbanized areas and central cities. Setting of threshold

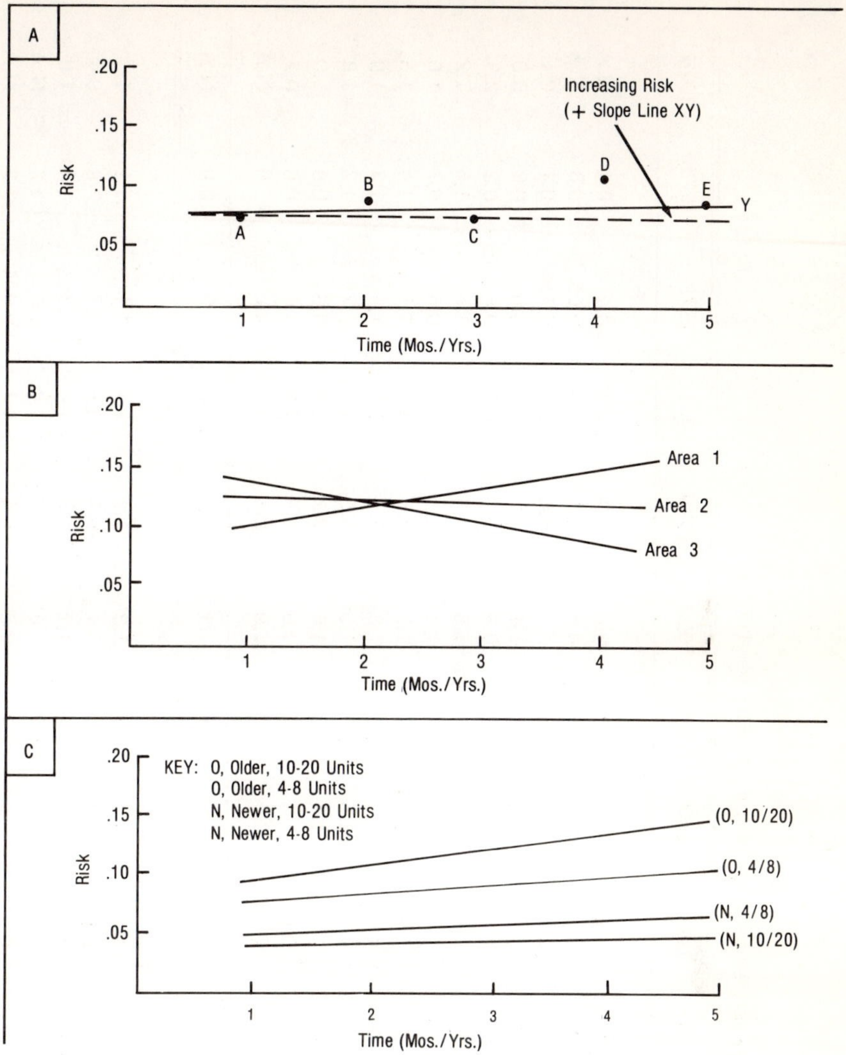

FIG. 1

levels of constants as a means to induce private participation may represent a beginning point of central city rebuilding.

Q. *When underwriting mortgage loans for food chain facilities, what information can be used to measure the competitive position of a company?*

A. A five- to ten-year study of profit margins can give a good indication of a food chain's competitive position. The following table outlines net profit as a percentage of volumes over a ten-year period for a number of food chains. Comparisons by size and specific geographical market penetration and concentration can provide insight into the relative competitive position of a given food chain.

Net profits after income taxes as percent of sales, 1965 to 1974

1973 sales size	*1965*	*1966*	*1967*	*1968*	*1969*	*1970*	*1971*	*1972*	*1973*	*1974*
$1 billion and over										
Allied Supermarkets	1.0	0.8	0.5	0.2	−0.5	−1.3	0.1	0.4	0.1	N.A.
American Stores	0.9	0.7	0.6	0.7	0.8	0.8	0.7	0.05	0.8	N.A.
Food Fair Stores	1.0	0.9	0.8	0.8	N.A.	0.6	0.6	−0.1	0.1	0.4
Grand Union	1.4	1.3	1.2	1.3	1.4	1.3	1.0	0.6	0.2	0.6
Great A & P	1.0	1.0	1.0	0.8	0.9	0.9	0.3	−0.8	0.2	−2.3
Jewel Companies	1.7	1.6	1.4	1.5	1.5	1.5	1.5	1.5	1.6	1.2
Kroger	1.2	1.1	0.9	1.1	1.1	1.1	0.9	0.5	0.7	1.0
Lucky	1.7	1.7	1.8	1.4	1.7	1.6	1.7	1.5	1.4	1.5
Safeway	1.6	1.8	1.5	1.5	1.3	1.4	1.5	1.5	1.3	1.0
Southland	1.4	1.3	1.5	1.5	1.5	1.5	1.6	1.7	1.7	1.8
Stop & Shop	0.9	1.1	1.4	1.0	1.0	0.7	0.4	0.6	0.8	1.0
Supermarkets General	1.4	0.9	1.2	1.4	1.0	1.0	1.0	0.4	0.6	0.2
Winn-Dixie	2.7	2.3	2.3	2.1	1.9	2.1	2.1	2.0	1.9	N.A.
Weighted Average	1.3	1.3	1.2	1.1	1.1	1.1	1.0	0.6	0.9	N.A.
$500 to $999 million										
Albertson's	1.9	1.4	1.2	1.1	1.2	1.1	1.1	1.1	1.1	1.1
Arden-Mayfair	1.1	0.8	0.1	0.5	0.4	−0.4	0.3	−0.2	−2.8	0.4
Colonial Stores	1.3	1.4	1.3	1.5	1.2	1.3	1.4	1.3	1.3	1.0
Dillon Cos.	1.8	1.6	1.7	1.8	1.8	1.7	1.8	1.8	1.7	N.A.
First National Stores	0.3	−0.1	−1.0	0.2	0.6	0.4	−0.1	0.004	−1.7	N.A.
Fisher Foods	−0.04	0.8	1.8	1.6	1.3	1.3	1.4	1.2	1.1	1.1
Giant Food	1.4	1.1	1.3	1.3	1.4	0.9	1.5	1.4	1.1	0.9
National Tea	1.0	0.9	0.9	0.6	0.7	0.5	0.6	−3.3	−1.6	−0.2
Pueblo International	4.2	4.3	2.8	1.7	1.6	1.0	1.4	−0.1	0.8	0.3
Weighted Average	1.1	0.9	0.7	0.9	1.0	0.7	0.9	0.1	0.1	N.A.

Under $500 million										
Alterman's	2.0	2.1	1.7	1.5	1.5	1.2	1.3	1.1	1.5	N.A.
Applebaum's	1.9	1.7	1.6	1.3	1.2	1.2	0.9	−0.1	−0.2	N.A.
Bayless Markets	1.3	1.3	0.8	1.4	1.8	2.0	1.9	1.8	1.6	1.4
Big Bear Stores	2.1	2.3	1.9	1.8	1.8	1.8	1.9	1.5	1.9	1.9
H.C. Bohack	−0.8	−0.1	0.1	0.4	0.4	0.5	−0.2	0.1	0.02	N.A.
Borman's	2.0	1.7	1.0	1.1	1.1	0.3	−1.2	0.3	−0.1	−0.8
Circle K	2.8	2.5	2.3	2.5	2.8	3.1	3.0	2.8	2.5	N.A.
Cullum Cos.	N.A.	N.A.	1.5	1.4	1.3	1.4	1.4	2.3	0.7	N.A.
Foodarama Supermarkets	1.7	1.7	1.7	1.5	1.1	0.8	0.5	−3.3	0.2	1.2
King Kullen	0.8	0.8	1.1	0.9	0.5	1.0	0.9	0.5	0.8	1.0
Loblaw	0.9	0.8	0.6	1.0	1.0	1.0	0.9	−0.2	−2.6	0.1
Marsh Supermarkets	1.0	1.0	1.1	1.1	1.1	0.5	0.8	0.6	0.8	N.A.
Munford's	5.2	2.5	3.1	2.6	1.7	1.5	1.9	2.0	1.8	1.7
Penn Fruit	0.3	0.4	0.6	0.8	1.3	0.5	0.6	−0.4	−1.0	−0.9
Purity Supreme	2.3	1.5	1.3	0.2	0.4	0.6	0.8	0.9	0.4	−0.5
Shop Rite Foods	1.5	1.4	1.3	1.2	1.1	0.8	0.6	0.7	0.4	0.7
Shopwell	0.5	0.5	0.5	0.7	1.1	1.3	1.3	0.6	0.05	−0.4
Star Supermarkets	1.4	0.7	0.8	1.6	0.7	1.0	0.8	0.6	0.8	0.7
Thorofare	0.8	0.7	0.5	0.8	0.9	0.8	0.9	0.3	−2.8	0.003
Thriftimart	1.4	1.4	1.1	1.2	0.7	0.01	−0.3	0.2	0.7	N.A.
Victory Markets	1.5	1.1	1.2	1.4	0.9	0.9	0.7	−1.8	0.2	0.6
Waldbaum's	0.7	1.0	1.0	1.1	1.0	0.7	0.9	0.5	0.8	0.6
Weingarten	1.0	1.1	1.5	1.4	1.2	0.7	0.8	0.7	0.1	N.A.
Weis Markets	4.2	4.5	4.6	4.1	4.0	4.4	4.5	4.1	3.8	4.2
Weighted Average	1.3	1.3	1.3	1.3	1.2	1.0	0.9	0.6	0.5	N.A.
Total Weighted average	1.3	1.2	1.1	1.1	1.1	1.0	1.0	0.6	0.7	N.A.

N.A.—Not available.

NOTE: For earlier years data for chains are available in Table 15-7, page 290, of *Organization and Competition in Food Retailing*, Technical Study No. 7, National Commission on Food Marketing.

SOURCE: Company Annual Reports, Moody's Industrial Manual, and other published sources. Federal Trade Commission Report No. R-6-15-23, 1975.

Q. *Some people feel that multiple regression analysis (MRA) is the "wave of the future" for assessment and fee appraisal work. What is the status and potential of this technique for real estate appraisal activities?*

A. Multiple regression analysis must at this time be rated as a mixed bag at best. The following are some examples of questionable applications of MRA derived from a casual survey of the literature.

a. In one case, multiple regression analysis indicated that the age of a house and mortgage interest charges for financing were not important price determinants. This does not seem to square with the real world—the study must have been a very unusual market area.

b. One study reported on a sample data base of sales ranging from $15,000 to over $60,000. This sampling ignores the basic reality of housing market segments, making no reference to such factors as consumer preferences in quality of housing.

c. Other MRA studies include one-story, 1½-story, and some two-story houses in one grand data base. This practice completely ignores differences in consumer preferences. Such factors as the preference for single-level houses by those in upper age groups are not taken into account.

d. Claims of "setback damage" on a condemnation taking are often made based on MRA alone, without specific considerations of highest and best use before and after the take. The assumption of a linear measure of damage, such as the 4-3-2-1 depth rule, seems very questionable.

Probably the most central deficiency of MRA is its failure to account for future market demand. The market transactions used as a data base are, by definition, historical evidence of value. The target of an appraisal, however, is market value—the present worth of *future benefits.* Comparable sales data are evidence of demand last year, two years ago, or even farther back. Markets change, however. Without an in-depth market supply-demand study and analysis MRA fails to bridge the gap between historical evidence and prospective utility-value.

Q. *In analyzing data, what method can be used to discern long-term trends that are frequently concealed by short-term variations?*

A. One simple method is the cumulative sums technique. It represents the cumulative sums (over time) of the difference between a specified mean $\overline{X}$ (but not necessarily the mean of the set) and a data point X at time (t). Figures 1 and 2 illustrate its potential.

For the period 1951 through 1970, *Staff Economic Studies,* 79 (1973) of the Board of Governors of the Federal Reserve System published both quarterly and weighted annual "percent constants" for mortgage investments of $100,000 and more made by fifteen life insurance companies on multifamily and nonresidential properties. The weighted annual percent constants for each year are shown in Fig. 1. A total of six turning points are noted. The same data is shown in the first column of Table A; column 2 shows the highest quarterly constant for each time period. The accumulated differences are plotted in Fig. 2. Three significant turning points are noted and the graph clearly shows the long-term trend of the weighed annual constants.

Figure 3 outlines the various configurations and long-term relationships that are possible between the specified mean ($\bar{X}$) and the cumulative sums of the differences (S plots). The selection of the specified mean ($\bar{X}$) is of primary importance in determining the shape of the resulting S curve. It is therefore possible to select an X that will result in the most informative shape of S curve.

TABLE A

Year	*Mean (Weighted) Constant*	*High Quarter*	*Difference*	*Cumulative*
1951	9.1	9.7	0.6	0.6
1952	9.2	9.6	0.4	1.0
1953	9.3	9.6	0.3	1.3
1954	9.2	9.3	0.3	1.6
1955	9.1	9.3	0.2	1.8
1956	9.4	9.6	0.2	2.0
1957	9.8	10.1	0.3	2.3
1958	9.4	9.7	0.3	2.6
1959	9.4	9.5	0.1	2.7
1960	9.5	9.6	0.1	2.8
1961	9.2	9.4	0.2	3.0
1962	9.0	9.1	0.1	3.1
1963	8.8	8.9	0.1	3.2
1964	8.7	8.7	0.0	3.2
1965	8.6	8.7	0.1	3.3
1966	9.0	9.2	0.2	3.5
1967	9.2	9.4	0.2	3.7
1968	9.5	9.6	0.3	4.0
1969	10.2	10.7	0.5	4.5
1970	11.1	11.2	0.1	4.6

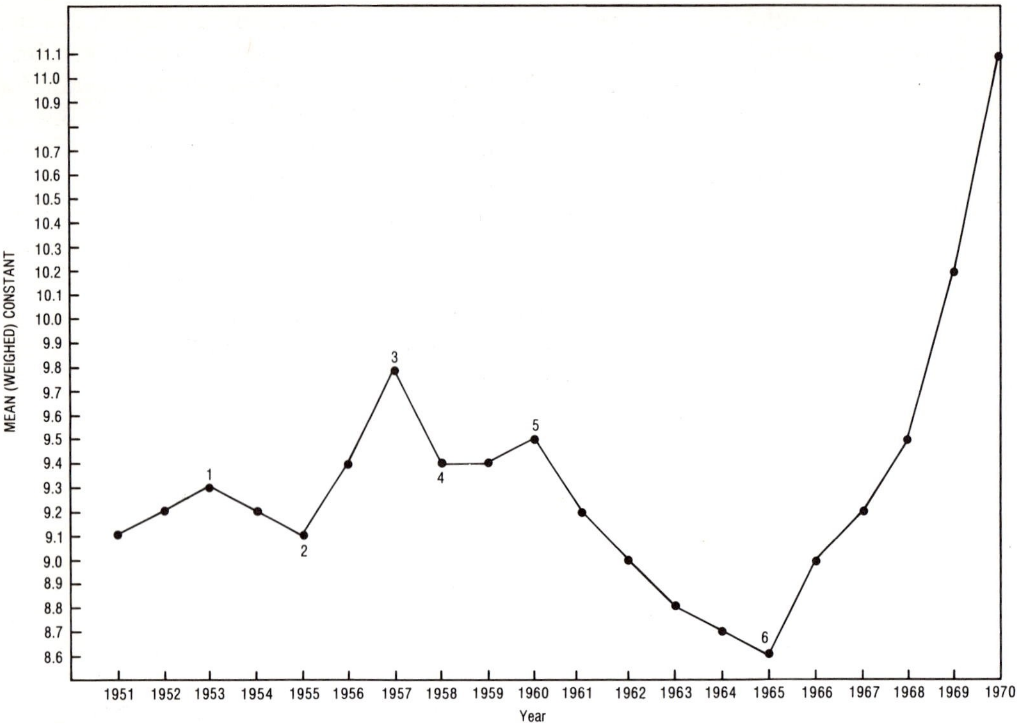
MEAN (WEIGHED) CONSTANT
11.1
11.0
10.9
10.7
10.6
10.5
10.4
10.3
10.2
10.1
10.0
9.9
9.8
9.7
9.6
9.5
9.4
9.3
9.2
9.1
9.0
8.9
8.8
8.7
8.6
1
2
3
4
5
6
1951 1952 1953 1954 1955 1956 1957 1958 1959 1960 1961 1962 1963 1964 1965 1966 1967 1968 1969 1970
Year

FIG. 1

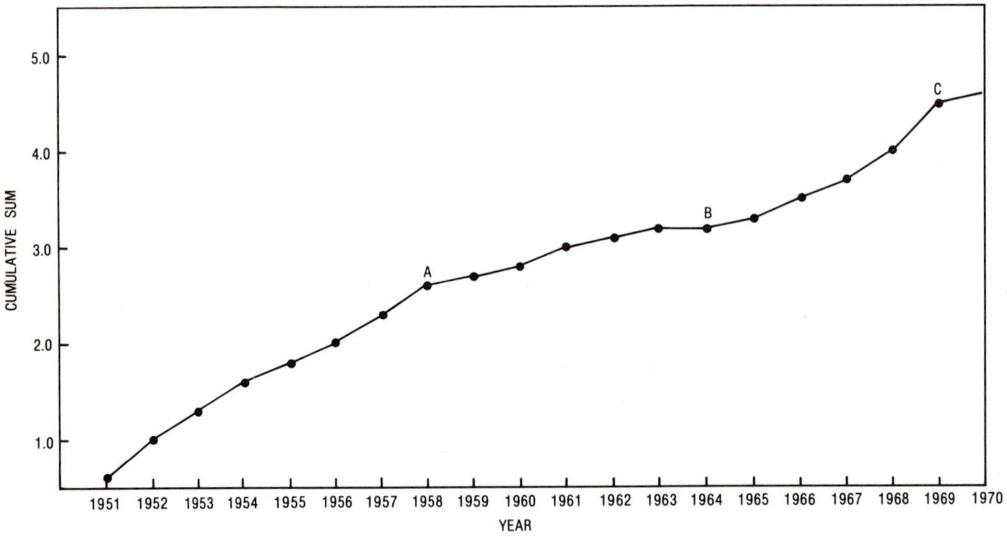
CUMULATIVE SUM
5.0
4.0
3.0
2.0
1.0
A
B
C
1951 1952 1953 1954 1955 1956 1957 1958 1959 1960 1961 1962 1963 1964 1965 1966 1967 1968 1969 1970
YEAR

FIG. 2

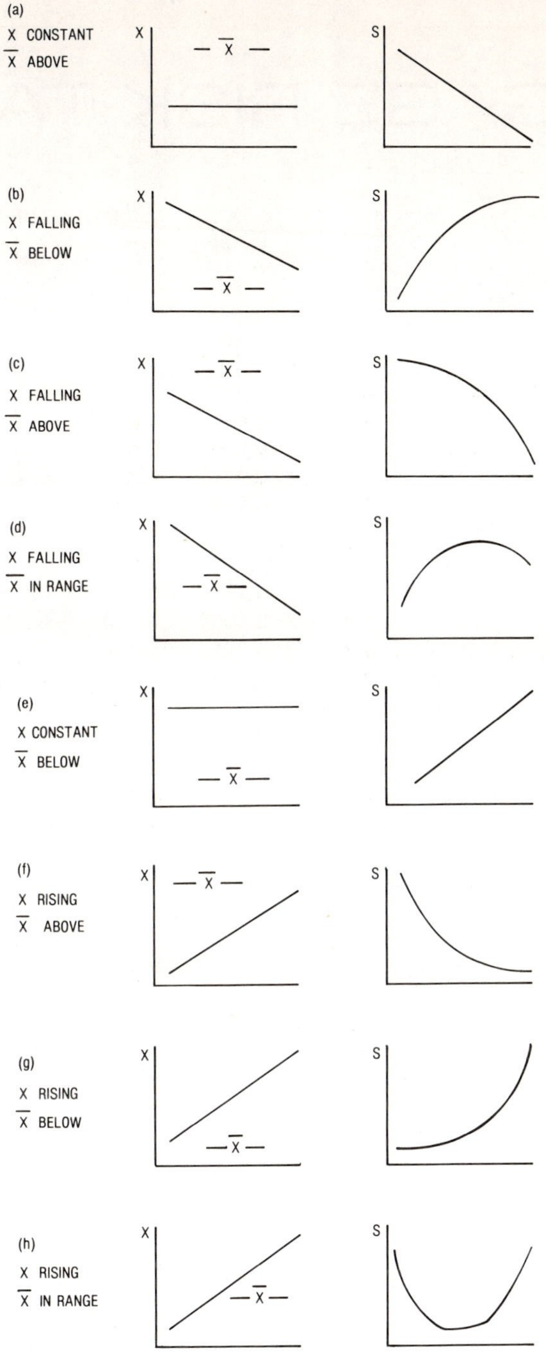

Source: Atomic Energy of Canada Ltd., Chalk River, Ontario, 1976.

FIG. 3 Basic shapes of X and corresponding S plots

MORTGAGE RISK TABLES

CONSTANT→ ↓	0.0700	0.0725	0.0750	0.0775	0.0800	0.0825	0.0850	0.0875
				Risk Factors				
0.0700								
0.0725	0.034							
0.0750	0.067	0.033						
0.0775	0.097	0.065	0.032					
0.0800	0.125	0.094	0.062	0.031				
0.0825	0.151	0.121	0.091	0.061	0.030			
0.0850	0.176	0.148	0.118	0.088	0.059	0.030		
0.0875	0.200	0.171	0.143	0.114	0.086	0.060	0.029	
0.0900	0.222	0.194	0.167	0.139	0.111	0.080	0.056	0.028
0.0925	0.243	0.216	0.189	0.162	0.135	0.110	0.081	0.054
0.0950	0.263	0.237	0.210	0.184	0.158	0.130	0.105	0.089
0.0975	0.282	0.256	0.231	0.205	0.179	0.150	0.128	0.103
0.1000	0.300	0.275	0.250	0.225	0.200	0.175	0.150	0.125
0.1025	0.317	0.293	0.268	0.244	0.220	0.195	0.171	0.146
0.1050	0.333	0.310	0.286	0.262	0.238	0.214	0.190	0.167
0.1075	0.349	0.326	0.302	0.279	0.256	0.233	0.209	0.186
0.1100	0.364	0.341	0.318	0.295	0.273	0.250	0.227	0.205
0.1125	0.378	0.356	0.333	0.311	0.289	0.267	0.244	0.222
0.1150	0.391	0.370	0.348	0.326	0.304	0.283	0.261	0.239
0.1175	0.404	0.383	0.362	0.340	0.319	0.298	0.277	0.255
0.1200	0.417	0.396	0.375	0.354	0.333	0.312	0.292	0.271
0.1225	0.429	0.408	0.388	0.367	0.347	0.327	0.306	0.286
0.1250	0.440	0.420	0.400	0.370	0.360	0.340	0.320	0.300
0.1275	0.451	0.431	0.412	0.392	0.373	0.353	0.333	0.314
0.1300	0.461	0.442	0.423	0.404	0.385	0.365	0.346	0.327
0.1325	0.472	0.453	0.434	0.415	0.396	0.377	0.358	0.340
0.1350	0.481	0.463	0.444	0.426	0.407	0.389	0.370	0.352
0.1375	0.491	0.473	0.455	0.436	0.418	0.400	0.382	0.364
0.1400	0.500	0.482	0.464	0.446	0.429	0.411	0.393	0.375
0.1425	0.509	0.491	0.474	0.456	0.439	0.421	0.404	0.386
0.1450	0.517	0.500	0.483	0.466	0.448	0.431	0.414	0.397
0.1475	0.525	0.508	0.492	0.475	0.458	0.441	0.424	0.407
0.1500	0.533	0.517	0.500	0.483	0.467	0.450	0.433	0.417
0.1525	0.541	0.525	0.508	0.492	0.475	0.459	0.443	0.426
0.1550	0.548	0.532	0.516	0.500	0.484	0.468	0.452	0.435
0.1575	0.556	0.540	0.524	0.508	0.492	0.476	0.460	0.444
0.1600	0.562	0.547	0.531	0.516	0.500	0.484	0.469	0.453

Risk Factors

CONSTANT→ ↓	*0.0900*	*0.0925*	*0.0950*	*0.0975*	*0.1000*	*0.1025*	*0.1050*	*0.1075*
0.0700								
0.0725								
0.0750								
0.0775								
0.0800								
0.0825								
0.0850								
0.0875								
0.0900								
0.0925	0.027							
0.0950	0.053	0.026						
0.0975	0.077	0.051	0.026					
0.1000	0.100	0.075	0.050	0.025				
0.1025	0.122	0.098	0.073	0.049	0.024			
0.1050	0.143	0.119	0.095	0.071	0.048	0.024		
0.1075	0.163	0.140	0.116	0.093	0.070	0.046	0.023	
0.1100	0.182	0.159	0.126	0.114	0.091	0.068	0.045	0.023
0.1125	0.200	0.178	0.156	0.133	0.111	0.089	0.067	0.044
0.1150	0.217	0.196	0.174	0.152	0.130	0.109	0.087	0.065
0.1175	0.234	0.213	0.191	0.170	0.149	0.128	0.106	0.075
0.1200	0.250	0.229	0.208	0.187	0.167	0.146	0.125	0.104
0.1225	0.265	0.245	0.224	0.204	0.184	0.163	0.143	0.122
0.1250	0.280	0.260	0.240	0.220	0.200	0.180	0.160	0.140
0.1275	0.294	0.275	0.255	0.235	0.216	0.196	0.176	0.157
0.1300	0.308	0.288	0.269	0.250	0.231	0.212	0.192	0.173
0.1325	0.321	0.302	0.283	0.264	0.245	0.226	0.207	0.189
0.1350	0.333	0.315	0.296	0.278	0.259	0.241	0.222	0.204
0.1375	0.345	0.327	0.309	0.291	0.273	0.254	0.236	0.218
0.1400	0.357	0.339	0.321	0.304	0.286	0.268	0.250	0.232
0.1425	0.368	0.351	0.333	0.316	0.298	0.281	0.263	0.246
0.1450	0.379	0.362	0.345	0.328	0.310	0.293	0.276	0.259
0.1475	0.390	0.373	0.356	0.339	0.322	0.305	0.288	0.271
0.1500	0.400	0.383	0.367	0.350	0.333	0.317	0.300	0.283
0.1525	0.410	0.393	0.377	0.361	0.344	0.328	0.311	0.295
0.1550	0.419	0.403	0.387	0.371	0.355	0.339	0.323	0.306
0.1575	0.429	0.413	0.397	0.381	0.365	0.349	0.333	0.317
0.1600	0.437	0.422	0.406	0.391	0.375	0.359	0.344	0.328

CONSTANT→ ↓	*0.1100*	*0.1125*	*0.1150*	*0.1175*	*0.1200*	*0.1225*	*0.1250*	*0.1275*
				Risk Factors				
0.0700								
0.0725								
0.0750								
0.0775								
0.0800								
0.0825								
0.0850								
0.0875								
0.0900								
0.0925								
0.0950								
0.0975								
0.1000								
0.1025								
0.1050								
0.1075								
0.1100								
0.1125	0.022							
0.1150	0.043	0.022						
0.1175	0.064	0.043	0.021					
0.1200	0.083	0.062	0.042	0.021				
0.1225	0.102	0.082	0.061	0.041	0.020			
0.1250	0.120	0.100	0.080	0.060	0.040	0.020		
0.1275	0.137	0.118	0.098	0.078	0.059	0.039	0.020	
0.1300	0.154	0.135	0.115	0.096	0.077	0.058	0.038	0.019
0.1325	0.170	0.151	0.122	0.113	0.094	0.075	0.057	0.038
0.1350	0.185	0.167	0.148	0.130	0.111	0.093	0.074	0.056
0.1375	0.200	0.182	0.164	0.145	0.127	0.109	0.091	0.073
0.1400	0.214	0.196	0.179	0.161	0.143	0.125	0.107	0.089
0.1425	0.228	0.211	0.193	0.175	0.158	0.140	0.123	0.105
0.1450	0.241	0.224	0.207	0.190	0.172	0.155	0.138	0.121
0.1475	0.254	0.237	0.220	0.203	0.186	0.169	0.153	0.136
0.1500	0.267	0.250	0.233	0.217	0.200	0.183	0.167	0.150
0.1525	0.279	0.262	0.246	0.230	0.213	0.197	0.180	0.164
0.1550	0.290	0.274	0.258	0.242	0.226	0.210	0.194	0.177
0.1575	0.302	0.286	0.270	0.254	0.238	0.222	0.206	0.190
0.1600	0.312	0.297	0.281	0.266	0.250	0.234	0.279	0.203

CONSTANT→ ↓	*0.1300*	*0.1325*	*0.1350*	*0.1375*	*0.1400*	*0.1425*	*0.1450*	*0.1475*
				Risk Factors				
0.0700								
0.0725								
0.0750								
0.0775								
0.0800								
0.0825								
0.0850								
0.0875								
0.0900								
0.0925								
0.0950								
0.0975								
0.1000								
0.1025								
0.1050								
0.1075								
0.1100								
0.1125								
0.1150								
0.1175								
0.1200								
0.1225								
0.1250								
0.1275								
0.1300								
0.1325	0.019							
0.1350	0.037	0.018						
0.1375	0.054	0.036	0.018					
0.1400	0.071	0.054	0.036	0.018				
0.1425	0.088	0.070	0.053	0.035	0.017			
0.1450	0.103	0.086	0.069	0.052	0.034	0.017		
0.1475	0.119	0.102	0.075	0.068	0.051	0.034	0.017	
0.1500	0.133	0.117	0.100	0.083	0.067	0.050	0.033	0.017
0.1525	0.147	0.131	0.115	0.098	0.082	0.066	0.049	0.033
0.1550	0.161	0.145	0.129	0.113	0.097	0.081	0.065	0.048
0.1575	0.175	0.159	0.143	0.127	0.111	0.095	0.089	0.063
0.1600	0.187	0.172	0.156	0.141	0.125	0.109	0.094	0.078

CONSTANT→ ↓	0.1500	0.1525	0.1550	0.1575	0.1600
				Risk Factors	
0.0700					
0.0725					
0.0750					
0.0775					
0.0800					
0.0825					
0.0850					
0.0875					
0.0900					
0.0925					
0.0950					
0.0975					
0.1000					
0.1025					
0.1050					
0.1075					
0.1100					
0.1125					
0.1150					
0.1175					
0.1200					
0.1225					
0.1250					
0.1275					
0.1300					
0.1325					
0.1350					
0.1375					
0.1400					
0.1425					
0.1450					
0.1475					
0.1500					
0.1525	0.016				
0.1550	0.032	0.016			
0.1575	0.048	0.032	0.016		
0.1600	0.062	0.047	0.031	0.016	

PRESENT VALUE OF ONE DOLLAR

Periods of Payment	2%	4%	6%	8%	10%	12%	14%	15%	16%	18%	20%	25%	30%	35%	40%	45%	50%
1	0.980	0.962	0.943	0.926	0.909	0.893	0.877	0.870	0.862	0.847	0.833	0.800	0.769	0.741	0.714	0.690	0.667
2	0.961	0.925	0.890	0.857	0.826	0.797	0.769	0.756	0.743	0.718	0.694	0.640	0.592	0.549	0.510	0.476	0.444
3	0.942	0.889	0.840	0.794	0.751	0.712	0.675	0.658	0.641	0.609	0.579	0.512	0.455	0.406	0.364	0.328	0.296
4	0.924	0.855	0.792	0.735	0.683	0.636	0.592	0.572	0.552	0.516	0.482	0.410	0.350	0.301	0.260	0.226	0.198
5	0.906	0.822	0.747	0.681	0.621	0.567	0.519	0.497	0.476	0.437	0.402	0.328	0.269	0.223	0.186	0.156	0.132
6	0.888	0.790	0.705	0.630	0.564	0.507	0.456	0.432	0.410	0.370	0.335	0.262	0.207	0.165	0.133	0.108	0.088
7	0.871	0.760	0.665	0.683	0.513	0.452	0.400	0.376	0.354	0.314	0.279	0.210	0.159	0.122	0.095	0.074	0.059
8	0.853	0.731	0.627	0.540	0.467	0.404	0.351	0.327	0.305	0.266	0.233	0.168	0.123	0.091	0.068	0.051	0.039
9	0.837	0.703	0.592	0.500	0.424	0.361	0.308	0.284	0.263	0.225	0.194	0.134	0.094	0.067	0.048	0.035	0.026
10	0.820	0.676	0.558	0.463	0.386	0.322	0.270	0.247	0.227	0.191	0.162	0.107	0.073	0.050	0.035	0.024	0.017
11	0.804	0.650	0.527	0.429	0.350	0.287	0.237	0.215	0.195	0.162	0.135	0.086	0.056	0.037	0.025	0.017	0.012
12	0.788	0.625	0.497	0.397	0.319	0.257	0.208	0.187	0.168	0.137	0.112	0.069	0.043	0.027	0.018	0.012	0.008
13	0.773	0.601	0.469	0.368	0.290	0.229	0.182	0.163	0.145	0.116	0.093	0.055	0.033	0.020	0.013	0.008	0.005
14	0.758	0.577	0.442	0.340	0.263	0.205	0.160	0.141	0.125	0.099	0.078	0.044	0.025	0.015	0.009	0.006	0.003
15	0.743	0.555	0.417	0.315	0.239	0.183	0.140	0.123	0.108	0.084	0.065	0.035	0.020	0.011	0.006	0.004	0.002
16	0.728	0.534	0.394	0.292	0.218	0.163	0.123	0.107	0.093	0.071	0.054	0.028	0.015	0.008	0.005	0.003	0.002
17	0.714	0.513	0.371	0.270	0.198	0.146	0.108	0.093	0.080	0.060	0.045	0.023	0.012	0.006	0.003	0.002	0.001
18	0.700	0.494	0.350	0.250	0.180	0.130	0.095	0.081	0.069	0.051	0.038	0.018	0.009	0.005	0.002	0.001	0.001
19	0.686	0.475	0.331	0.232	0.164	0.116	0.083	0.070	0.060	0.043	0.031	0.014	0.007	0.003	0.002	0.001	
20	0.673	0.456	0.312	0.215	0.149	0.104	0.073	0.061	0.051	0.037	0.026	0.012	0.005	0.002	0.001	0.001	
21	0.660	0.439	0.294	0.199	0.135	0.093	0.064	0.053	0.044	0.031	0.022	0.009	0.004	0.002	0.001		
22	0.647	0.422	0.278	0.184	0.123	0.083	0.056	0.046	0.038	0.026	0.018	0.007	0.003	0.001	0.001		
23	0.634	0.406	0.262	0.170	0.112	0.074	0.049	0.040	0.033	0.022	0.015	0.006	0.002	0.001			
24	0.622	0.390	0.247	0.158	0.102	0.066	0.043	0.035	0.028	0.019	0.013	0.005	0.002	0.001			
25	0.610	0.375	0.233	0.146	0.092	0.059	0.038	0.030	0.024	0.016	0.010	0.004	0.001	0.001			
30	0.552	0.308	0.174	0.099	0.057	0.033	0.020	0.015	0.012	0.007	0.004	0.001					
40	0.453	0.208	0.097	0.046	0.022	0.011	0.005	0.004	0.003	0.001	0.001						
50	0.372	0.141	0.054	0.021	0.009	0.003	0.001	0.001	0.001								

Note: Calculations are based on end-of-period compounding.

PRESENT VALUE OF ONE DOLLAR RECEIVED ANNUALLY

Duration of Payments	2%	4%	6%	8%	10%	12%	14%	15%	16%	18%	20%	25%	30%	35%	40%	45%	50%
1	0.980	0.962	0.943	0.926	0.909	0.893	0.877	0.870	0.862	0.847	0.833	0.800	0.769	0.741	0.714	0.690	0.667
2	1.942	1.886	1.833	1.783	1.736	1.690	1.647	1.626	1.605	1.566	1.528	1.440	1.361	1.289	1.224	1.165	1.111
3	2.884	2.775	2.673	2.577	2.487	2.402	2.322	2.283	2.246	2.174	2.106	1.952	1.816	1.696	1.589	1.493	1.407
4	3.808	3.630	3.465	3.312	3.170	3.037	2.914	2.855	2.798	2.690	2.589	2.362	2.166	1.997	1.849	1.720	1.605
5	4.713	4.452	4.212	3.993	3.791	3.605	3.433	3.352	3.274	3.127	2.991	2.689	2.436	2.220	2.035	1.876	1.737
6	5.601	5.242	4.917	4.623	4.355	4.111	3.889	3.784	3.685	3.498	3.326	2.951	2.643	2.385	2.168	1.983	1.824
7	6.472	6.002	5.582	5.206	4.868	4.564	4.288	4.160	4.039	3.812	3.605	3.161	2.802	2.508	2.263	2.057	1.883
8	7.325	6.733	6.210	5.747	5.335	4.968	4.639	4.487	4.344	4.078	3.837	3.329	2.925	2.598	2.331	2.108	1.922
9	8.162	7.435	6.802	6.247	5.759	5.328	4.946	4.772	4.607	4.303	4.031	3.463	3.019	2.665	2.379	2.144	1.948
10	8.983	8.111	7.360	6.710	6.145	5.650	5.216	5.019	4.833	4.494	4.192	3.571	3.092	2.715	2.414	2.168	1.965
11	9.787	8.760	7.887	7.139	6.495	5.937	5.453	5.234	5.029	4.656	4.327	3.656	3.147	2.752	2.438	2.185	1.977
12	10.575	9.385	8.384	7.536	6.814	6.194	5.660	5.421	5.197	4.793	4.439	3.725	3.190	2.779	2.456	2.196	1.985
13	11.343	9.986	8.853	7.904	7.103	6.424	5.842	5.583	5.342	4.910	4.533	3.780	3.223	2.799	2.468	2.204	1.990
14	12.106	10.563	9.295	8.244	7.367	6.628	5.002	5.724	5.468	5.008	4.611	3.824	3.249	2.814	2.477	2.210	1.993
15	12.849	11.118	9.712	8.559	7.606	6.811	6.142	5.847	5.575	5.092	4.675	3.859	3.268	2.825	2.484	2.214	1.995
16	13.578	11.652	10.106	8.851	7.824	6.974	6.265	5.954	5.669	5.162	4.730	3.887	3.283	2.834	2.489	2.216	1.197
17	14.292	12.166	10.477	9.122	8.022	7.120	6.373	6.047	5.749	5.222	4.775	3.910	3.295	2.840	2.492	2.218	1.998
18	14.992	12.659	10.828	9.372	8.201	7.250	6.647	6.128	5.818	5.273	4.812	3.928	3.304	2.844	2.494	2.219	1.999
19	15.678	13.134	11.158	9.604	8.365	7.366	6.550	6.198	5.877	5.316	4.844	3.942	3.311	2.848	2.496	2.220	1.999
20	16.351	13.590	11.470	9.818	8.514	7.469	6.623	6.259	5.929	5.353	4.870	3.954	3.316	2.850	2.497	2.221	1.999
21	17.011	14.029	11.764	10.017	8.649	7.562	6.687	6.312	5.973	5.384	4.891	3.963	3.320	2.852	2.498	2.221	2.000
22	17.658	14.451	12.042	10.201	8.772	7.645	6.743	6.359	6.011	5.410	4.909	3.970	3.323	2.853	2.498	2.222	2.000
23	18.292	14.857	12.303	10.371	8.883	7.718	6.792	6.399	6.044	5.432	4.925	3.976	3.325	2.854	2.499	2.222	2.000
24	18.914	15.247	12.550	10.529	8.985	7.784	6.835	6.434	6.073	5.451	4.937	3.981	3.327	2.855	2.499	2.222	2.000
25	19.523	15.622	12.783	10.675	9.077	7.843	6.873	4.464	6.097	5.467	4.948	3.985	3.329	2.856	2.499	2.222	2.000
30	22.396	17.292	13.765	11.258	9.427	8.055	7.003	6.566	6.177	5.517	4.979	3.995	3.332	2.857	2.500	2.222	2.000
40	27.355	19.793	15.046	11.925	9.779	8.244	7.105	6.642	6.234	5.548	4.997	3.999	3.333	2.857	2.500	2.222	2.000
50	31.424	21.482	15.762	12.234	9.915	8.304	7.133	6.661	6.246	5.554	4.999	4.000	3.333	2.857	2.500	2.222	2.000

Note: Calculations are based on end-of-period compounding.

CAPITAL RECOVERY FACTORS

Years to Recovery	2%	4%	6%	8%	10%	12%	14%	15%	16%	18%	20%	25%	30%	35%	40%	45%	50%
1	1.020	1.040	0.060	1.080	1.100	1.120	1.140	1.150	1.160	1.180	1.200	1.250	1.300	1.350	1.400	1.450	1.500
2	0.515	0.530	0.545	0.561	0.576	0.592	0.607	0.615	0.623	0.639	0.655	0.694	0.735	0.776	0.817	0.858	0.900
3	0.347	0.360	0.374	0.388	0.402	0.416	0.431	0.438	0.445	0.460	0.475	0.512	0.551	0.590	0.629	0.670	0.711
4	0.263	0.275	0.289	0.302	0.315	0.329	0.343	0.350	0.357	0.372	0.386	0.423	0.462	0.501	0.541	0.582	0.623
5	0.212	0.225	0.237	0.250	0.264	0.277	0.291	0.298	0.305	0.320	0.334	0.372	0.411	0.450	0.491	0.533	0.576
6	0.179	0.191	0.203	0.216	0.230	0.243	0.257	0.264	0.271	0.286	0.301	0.339	0.378	0.414	0.461	0.504	0.548
7	0.155	0.167	0.179	0.192	0.205	0.219	0.233	0.240	0.248	0.262	0.277	0.316	0.357	0.399	0.442	0.486	0.531
8	0.137	0.149	0.161	0.174	0.187	0.201	0.216	0.223	0.230	0.245	0.261	0.300	0.342	0.385	0.429	0.474	0.520
9	0.123	0.134	0.147	0.160	0.174	0.188	0.202	0.210	0.217	0.232	0.248	0.289	0.331	0.375	0.420	0.466	0.513
10	0.111	0.123	0.136	0.149	0.163	0.177	0.192	0.199	0.207	0.223	0.239	0.280	0.323	0.368	0.414	0.461	0.509
11	0.102	0.114	0.127	0.140	0.154	0.168	0.183	0.191	0.199	0.215	0.231	0.273	0.318	0.363	0.410	0.458	0.506
12	0.095	0.107	0.119	0.133	0.147	0.161	0.177	0.184	0.192	0.209	0.225	0.268	0.313	0.360	0.407	0.455	0.504
13	0.088	0.100	0.113	0.127	0.141	0.156	0.171	0.179	0.187	0.204	0.221	0.265	0.310	0.357	0.405	0.454	0.503
14	0.083	0.095	0.108	0.121	0.136	0.151	0.167	0.175	0.183	0.200	0.217	0.262	0.308	0.355	0.404	0.452	0.502
15	0.078	0.090	0.103	0.117	0.131	0.147	0.163	0.171	0.179	0.196	0.214	0.259	0.306	0.354	0.403	0.452	0.501
16	0.074	0.086	0.099	0.113	0.128	0.143	0.160	0.168	0.176	0.194	0.211	0.257	0.305	0.353	0.402	0.451	0.501
17	0.070	0.082	0.095	0.110	0.125	0.140	0.157	0.165	0.174	0.191	0.209	0.256	0.304	0.352	0.401	0.451	0.501
18	0.067	0.079	0.092	0.107	0.122	0.138	0.155	0.163	0.172	0.190	0.208	0.2555	0.303	0.352	0.401	0.451	0.500
19	0.064	0.076	0.090	0.104	0.120	0.136	0.153	0.161	0.170	0.188	0.206	0.254	0.302	0.351	0.401	0.450	0.500
20	0.061	0.074	0.087	0.102	0.117	0.134	0.151	0.160	0.169	0.187	0.205	0.253	0.302	0.351	0.400	0.450	0.500
21	0.059	0.071	0.085	0.100	0.116	0.132	0.150	0.158	0.167	0.186	0.204	0.252	0.301	0.351	0.400	0.450	0.500
22	0.057	0.069	0.083	0.098	0.114	0.131	0.148	0.157	0.166	0.185	0.204	0.252	0.301	0.350	0.400	0.450	0.500
23	0.055	0.067	0.081	0.096	0.113	0.130	0.147	0.156	0.165	0.184	0.203	0.251	0.301	0.350	0.400	0.450	0.500
25	0.051	0.064	0.078	0.094	0.110	0.127	0.145	0.155	0.164	0.183	0.202	0.251	0.300	0.350	0.400	0.450	0.500
30	0.045	0.058	0.073	0.089	0.106	0.124	0.143	0.152	0.162	0.181	0.201	0.250	0.300	0.350	0.400	0.450	0.500
40	0.037	0.051	0.066	0.084	0.102	0.121	0.141	0.151	0.160	0.180	0.200	0.250	0.300	0.350	0.400	0.450	0.500
50	0.032	0.047	0.063	0.082	0.101	0.120	0.140	0.150	0.160	0.180	0.200	0.250	0.300	0.350	0.400	0.450	0.500

Index to Functional Methods of Analysis

URBAN AND AREA DYNAMICS

PROBABILITY DYNAMICS

PROPERTY AND INVESTMENT DYNAMICS

Index